PHILOSOPHY AND SOCIOLOGY

PHILOSOPHY AND SOCIOLOGY

1960

Theodor W. Adorno

Edited by Dirk Braunstein

Translated by Nicholas Walker

polity

Originally published in German as *Nachgelassene Schriften. Abteilung IV, Band 6: Philosophie und Soziologie*. Herausgegeben von Dirk Braunstein © Suhrkamp Verlag Berlin 2011

This English edition © Polity Press, 2022

The translation of this work was supported by a grant from the Goethe-Institut.

Polity Press
65 Bridge Street
Cambridge CB2 1UR, UK

Polity Press
101 Station Landing
Suite 300
Medford, MA 02155, USA

All rights reserved. Except for the quotation of short passages for the purpose of criticism and review, no part of this publication may be reproduced, stored in a retrieval system or transmitted, in any form or by any means, electronic, mechanical, photocopying, recording or otherwise, without the prior permission of the publisher.

ISBN-13: 978-0-7456-7941-9 (hardback)
ISBN-13: 978-0-7456-7942-6 (paperback)

A catalogue record for this book is available from the British Library.

Library of Congress Control Number: 2021939028

Typeset in 10.5 on 12 pt Sabon
by Fakenham Prepress Solutions, Fakenham, Norfolk NR21 8NL
Printed and bound in Great Britain by TJ Books Ltd, Padstow, Cornwall

The publisher has used its best endeavours to ensure that the URLs for external websites referred to in this book are correct and active at the time of going to press. However, the publisher has no responsibility for the websites and can make no guarantee that a site will remain live or that the content is or will remain appropriate.

Every effort has been made to trace all copyright holders, but if any have been overlooked the publisher will be pleased to include any necessary credits in any subsequent reprint or edition.

For further information on Polity, visit our website:
politybooks.com

CONTENTS

Overview	vi
Lectures	1
Adorno's Notes for the Lectures	209
Editor's Afterword	253
Editor's Notes	257
Index	334

OVERVIEW

LECTURE 1 — 1

Are philosophy and sociology mutually incompatible? – Controversy with König and Schelsky (I) – Kant's influence on phenomenology and ontology – The origins of sociology in Saint-Simon – Psychology in Kant – Against 'purity'

LECTURE 2 — 13

Resistance to philosophy on the part of sociology – Comte's 'law of the three stages' (I) – The origins of sociology in France – Order and progress in Comte – The claim to priority on the part of sociology – Freedom of conscience and national sovereignty – Comte's conception of institutions – Driven towards dialectics – The concept of positivism – First nature and second nature – Political content of Comte's argument

LECTURE 3 — 25

Social Darwinism – Emphasis on subjectivity – Demand for systematic immanence in thought – The question of the utility of science – 'Sociological schizophrenia' – Priority of the social system (I) – Social compulsion – Sociology and philosophy as a dynamic unity

LECTURE 4 — 36

Comte's demotion of philosophy – The appeal of positivism – Comte's nominalism – 'The law of three stages' (II) – The pretensions of speculative thought – Controversy with König and Schelsky (II) – Against the demand for intelligibility – Ordinary language and logic

LECTURE 5 — 48

'Chosisme' (I) – Sociology addresses the constituted – Durkheim's critique of 'Ideas' in Comte – Durkheim's critique of Comte's concept of progress (I) – Durkheim's critique of Comte's 'law of the three stages' – 'Collective spirit' as explanation of social phenomena – 'Chosisme' (II) – Reification of society

LECTURE 6 — 58

Concepts and observation – Critical generosity – The category of 'meaning' – Priority of the social system (II) – 'Chosisme' (III) – The concept of 'understanding' – Theory of the unintelligible

LECTURE 7 — 69

Objective tendency – Mediation between social and individual domains – 'Chosisme' (IV) – Durkheim's critique of Comte's concept of progress (II) – The dialectic of progress – The violence of progress – The irrationality of rationality – Different modes of mediation in philosophy and sociology

LECTURE 8 — 81

A pause in the argument – Concepts of 'philosophy' and 'sociology' operating at different levels – 'Hyphen-sociologies' – Sociology as a recent discipline – Sociology and empirical social research – Max Weber's definition of sociology – Philosophy and facticity – The provincial situation of Germany

LECTURE 9 — 93

Transition to the theory of ideology – Space and time in Durkheim – On the mediation of mind and society – Concept of truth – The conceptual moment in exchange – The 'natural character' of the productive process is illusory – Concept of ideology presupposes an understanding of totality – Theory of ideology is philosophical rather than sociological

LECTURE 10 — 104

Truth not presentable in isolated theses – Historical development of the concept of ideology (I) – Forces of production and relations of production – Problems of constitution as social problems – Subjectivity in positivism (I) – Difference between Kant and Hume – Subjectivity in positivism (II) – Atomistic character of statistics – Relationship between truth and consciousness – Analysis of motivation

LECTURE 11 — 116

Theory of ideology behind the controversy between philosophy and sociology – Historical character of the mind – On the concept of total ideology – Against the all-encompassing suspicion of ideology – Danger of apologetic thought – Changing function of theories of ideologies (I)

LECTURE 12 — 128

Changing function of theories of ideology (II) – Slower transformation in the superstructure; 'cultural lag' – Apologetic tendencies of civil society – The truth moment of empirical sociology – Organized science and the independence of thought – The possibility of a theory of contemporary society (I) – The irrational character of capitalist society

LECTURE 13 — 140

The possibility of a theory of contemporary society (II) – Nominalism incompatible with theory formation – 'Political distribution' instead of market society – Social 'cement' – 'Diamat' – Dialectic not a method – Demand for intellectual freedom

LECTURE 14 — 151

Historical development of the concept of ideology (II) – Bacon's theory of idols – Critique of language – Theory of ideology not a psychology of 'interests' – The primal history of modernity – Making a fetish of history – More ideology or less

LECTURE 15   162

The dissolution of ideologies (I) – Technologies and mass media – Class consciousness – The 'sceptical generation' and technological illusion – Scepticism as an attitude (I)

LECTURE 16   173

Scepticism as an attitude (II) – Different kinds of ideology – Legitimating ideologies – Complementary ideologies – Meaninglessness as meaning – Controversy with Benjamin – Danger of oversimplifying the concept of ideology (I) – Danger of oversimplifying the concept of ideology (II)

LECTURE 17   185

Theoretical typologies in the social sciences – The ideology of concealment – Concepts created through their extremes – The dissolution of ideologies (II) – Priority of the genetic moment in the concept of ideology – Against the dichotomy of genesis and validity – On mediation – Truth as historical (I); the history in truth – Truth as historical (II); the genetic implications for meaning

LECTURE 18   197

Against Mannheim's account of genesis and validity – the genetic aspect of the mind as critical aspect – Against the idea that 'what has come to be' cannot be true – Example: logic in the development of music – Historical mediation of Plato and Aristotle

LECTURE 1
10 May 1960

Ladies and gentlemen,
This series of lectures was announced under the title of 'Philosophy and Sociology', and the title itself might give rise to misunderstandings for those of you who are just beginning your studies. I think it is my duty, therefore, to try and clear up such misunderstandings – such potential misunderstandings – here at the start. Since the person who is speaking to you right now occupies a position specifically designated as that of Professor of Philosophy and Sociology,[1] some of you might just expect that I should really try – like one of those clumsy and silly protagonists you hear about in fairy tales – to instruct you in philosophy and sociology with a single blow, so that you could somehow pick up both these fields in two hours of lectures a week throughout the semester. But such a thing, of course, is out of the question. It is not feasible in this series of lectures for me even to give you what would generally be called an introduction to philosophy or an introduction to sociology. What I would like to do, by contrast, and in accordance with my overall theoretical conception, is to offer you, with reference to a quite specific point, a kind of model for thinking. For what I should like to unfold for you here is something about the conflict, the problematic, that has historically prevailed in the relation between the two fields of philosophy and sociology, and which is becoming even stronger at the present time, and indeed from both of the sides involved. I should also like to try and explain, for those of you who happen to come from either one field or the other, something about the problem involved in the way these two

disciplines have come to be so personally united, as it were, in the case of both Herr Horkheimer[2] and myself, here at this university, even though, according to a very widely shared preconception on both sides, they are actually incompatible and have nothing to do with each other. Thus I would like, from a quite specific, critical, and decisive point of view, to shed some light on these two fields; and this, so I believe, will bring us right to a problem, a central one, that is of considerable relevance both philosophically and sociologically speaking, a problem that neither of these disciplines is able to evade. I am talking about the problem of the idea of truth, on the one hand, and the idea that knowledge is essentially determined by social factors, on the other. And I believe that, by starting from this single and central problem, it then becomes possible to shed some further light on the particular fields of philosophy and sociology; thus from this quite specific and expressly chosen perspective you may also – if it is not too presumptuous to expect this – gain a certain point of entry to both fields at once, and, above all, from each of these sides – I must really emphasize this – you may then be able to disabuse yourselves of the prejudice or preconception that, with philosophy and sociology, we are essentially dealing with two at least disparate, if not downright irreconcilable, spheres of thought.

The pressing need for such reflections lies in the fact, on the one hand, that we constantly come across philosophers who react rather naively to the kind of philosophy that seems interested predominantly in social problems by saying: 'Yes, but there must still be something like a philosophy which is right!' The idea of being 'right' that is at work here is generally taken over without further ado from a very specific and, I have to say right away, limited notion or conception of philosophy; what is understood specifically by philosophy here is the realm of that which immutably persists, of the purely intellectual or spiritual, of the truth that is detached from all human factors or conditions, even though we do not even bother to ask whether the philosophical tradition itself actually corresponds to this concept of philosophy, let alone to raise the more urgent and more radical question of whether, from the substantive point of view, philosophy should submit to this concept of the supposedly correct or 'right' philosophy, a philosophy that we could perhaps best define as one in which absolutely nothing happens that essentially concerns us. On the other hand, we find in the field of sociology that many people, and specifically very many young people, who take up this discipline effectively do so because – as we know from America – this is a promising, evolving, and increasingly popular field of study that also offers all sorts of potential applications across a range of professional contexts. In other words, people believe that they can thereby acquire a number of specific skills and forms of expertise, if I may put it that way, which may bring them academic distinction, or fame, or money, or perhaps just a secure professional position – all fine things in their way which, heaven knows, I certainly do not disdain, and which I would certainly not wish to discourage you from pursuing.[3] But, in thinking of sociology as a professionalized discipline in this way, many sociologists are tempted to regard philosophical reflection or investigation as some sort of disturbance or obstruction, like sand that has got into the machinery; so we start racking our brains about how it is possible to know social reality, or about the very concept of society, or about the relationship of static and dynamic factors in society,[4] or however we may choose to describe these problems, instead of just learning how to construct a questionnaire or how best to set up relevant 'interviews', etc., or whatever it happens to be that is required by the sociology of today, which in this sense could justly be described as an appendage of the economic system. Now I believe that in the context of the following lectures I shall be able to show you that sociology must actually call upon philosophy if it wishes to retain any genuinely scientific character for itself, if it really wishes to be anything more than a mere technique; and indeed I believe that those of you who do decide to study a subject like sociology at university level actually expect something more from such studies than mere technical expertise. Yet the resistance to philosophy that we encounter in sociology is not generally equivalent to the belief that we can evade the issue of scientific status simply by appealing to useful techniques of one kind or another; on the contrary, the resistance in question is given a rational justification and buttressed by claiming a greater scientific character for itself. Thus what is distinctive about this sort of critique of philosophy, if I can put it this way, is that it regards philosophy itself as not scientific at all, but as a field which only introduces something alien, arbitrary, and ultimately insusceptible of proof into the proper questions of social science – in other words, as a kind of ancient relic from the chest that we supposedly like to drag around, especially in Germany, but which actually only obstructs the task of elevating sociology to the level of a genuine science modelled on the procedures of the natural sciences. Now today I would simply like to say, by way of anticipation, that I believe this kind of exaggerated claim to scientific status, when it is specifically contrasted with the philosophical approach to things, is essentially reactive in character. In other words, this claim to scientific status, inasmuch as it refuses to go beyond the identifiably given,[5] and repudiates the idea of doing so as essentially 'unscientific', thereby reveals an inner tendency to regress to a pre-scientific level, and thus to retreat to what we could basically call the social practice of a reporter; and while there is of course nothing contemptible whatsoever about the task of gathering information and recording facts in the field of the social sciences, this process both presupposes certain theoretical elements and requires, if it is to enjoy any scientific dignity at all, further theoretical interpretation. And in this context, as you will see, the concept of philosophy actually signifies nothing other than precisely that. What I hope to do, in the second part of this series of lectures, later in the semester, is to address this complex, or indeed this conflict, between sociology and philosophy specifically as it presents itself from the side of sociology, and I intend to do so not in merely general or abstract terms but with reference to a current controversy of particular relevance to us here in Germany; it is a controversy that is partly connected with a contribution of my own entitled 'Sociology and Empirical Research',[6] to which Helmut Schelsky, my colleague from Hamburg, has responded in some detail in his essay 'The Current Position of German Sociology',[7] as indeed has René König in one of his recent essays.[8] I shall try and present something of this controversy to you in due course, including my response to the arguments advanced by my two colleagues, so that you will also get a good idea of what is involved in what one might call my defence of philosophy within sociology itself, with specific reference to an extremely concrete and developed sociological analysis.

But for the moment I would like to begin by introducing, in its most general form, the problem with which we shall be concerned throughout this semester, and indeed from every possible angle. We could perhaps put it this way: in Germany there is a philosophical tradition which – understandably or not so understandably – starts from Kant and which, remarkably enough, has continued specifically within those philosophical schools that originally found themselves in a certain opposition to capitalism, in other words within phenomenology and the existential ontology that developed out of it. This whole intellectual tradition – if I may just present it to you here in summary fashion, in an admittedly highly abbreviated and thus rather undifferentiated way that could give rise to all sorts of misunderstandings – ends up in the following situation. For the sake of clarity I concentrate on Kant here, although the same thing also holds for a great deal of modern philosophy, even if it is expressed there in very different terminology and with different points of emphasis. So, if we just stay with Kant for a moment, we can put the matter this way: the principal task of philosophy, according to Kant, is not to tell contexts. In other words, people believe that they can thereby acquire a number of specific skills and forms of expertise, if I may put it that way, which may bring them academic distinction, or fame, or money, or perhaps just a secure professional position – all fine things in their way which, heaven knows, I certainly do not disdain, and which I would certainly not wish to discourage you from pursuing.[3] But, in thinking of sociology as a professionalized discipline in this way, many sociologists are tempted to regard philosophical reflection or investigation as some sort of disturbance or obstruction, like sand that has got into the machinery; so we start racking our brains about how it is possible to know social reality, or about the very concept of society, or about the relationship of static and dynamic factors in society,[4] or however we may choose to describe these problems, instead of just learning how to construct a questionnaire or how best to set up relevant 'interviews', etc., or whatever it happens to be that is required by the sociology of today, which in this sense could justly be described as an appendage of the economic system. Now I believe that in the context of the following lectures I shall be able to show you that sociology must actually call upon philosophy if it wishes to retain any genuinely scientific character for itself, if it really wishes to be anything more than a mere technique; and indeed I believe that those of you who do decide to study a subject like sociology at university level actually expect something more from such studies than mere technical expertise. Yet the resistance to philosophy that we encounter in sociology is not generally equivalent to the belief that we can evade the issue of scientific status simply by appealing to useful techniques of one kind or another; on the contrary, the resistance in question is given a rational justification and buttressed by claiming a greater scientific character for itself. Thus what is distinctive about this sort of critique of philosophy, if I can put it this way, is that it regards philosophy itself as not scientific at all, but as a field which only introduces something alien, arbitrary, and ultimately insusceptible of proof into the proper questions of social science – in other words, as a kind of ancient relic from the chest that we supposedly like to drag around, especially in Germany, but which actually only obstructs the task of elevating sociology to the level of a genuine science modelled on the procedures of the natural sciences. Now today I would simply like to say, by way of anticipation, that I believe this kind of exaggerated claim to scientific status, when it is specifically contrasted with the philosophical approach to things, is essentially reactive in character. In other words, this claim to scientific status, inasmuch as it refuses to go beyond the identifiably given,[5] and repudiates the idea of doing so as essentially 'unscientific', thereby reveals an inner tendency to regress to a pre-scientific level, and thus to retreat to what we could basically call the social practice of a reporter; and while there is of course nothing contemptible whatsoever about the task of gathering information and recording facts in the field of the social sciences, this process both presupposes certain theoretical elements and requires, if it is to enjoy any scientific dignity at all, further theoretical interpretation. And in this context, as you will see, the concept of philosophy actually signifies nothing other than precisely that. What I hope to do, in the second part of this series of lectures, later in the semester, is to address this complex, or indeed this conflict, between sociology and philosophy specifically as it presents itself from the side of sociology, and I intend to do so not in merely general or abstract terms but with reference to a current controversy of particular relevance to us here in Germany; it is a controversy that is partly connected with a contribution of my own entitled 'Sociology and Empirical Research',[6] to which Helmut Schelsky, my colleague from Hamburg, has responded in some detail in his essay 'The Current Position of German Sociology',[7] as indeed has René König in one of his recent essays.[8] I shall try and present something of this controversy to you in due course, including my response to the arguments advanced by my two colleagues, so that you will also get a good idea of what is involved in what one might call my defence of philosophy within sociology itself, with specific reference to an extremely concrete and developed sociological analysis.

But for the moment I would like to begin by introducing, in its most general form, the problem with which we shall be concerned throughout this semester, and indeed from every possible angle. We could perhaps put it this way: in Germany there is a philosophical tradition which – understandably or not so understandably – starts from Kant and which, remarkably enough, has continued specifically within those philosophical schools that originally found themselves in a certain opposition to capitalism, in other words within phenomenology and the existential ontology that developed out of it. This whole intellectual tradition – if I may just present it to you here in summary fashion, in an admittedly highly abbreviated and thus rather undifferentiated way that could give rise to all sorts of misunderstandings – ends up in the following situation. For the sake of clarity I concentrate on Kant here, although the same thing also holds for a great deal of modern philosophy, even if it is expressed there in very different terminology and with different points of emphasis. So, if we just stay with Kant for a moment, we can put the matter this way: the principal task of philosophy, according to Kant, is not to tell us anything directly about the essence of things as such, but to exhibit the possibility of knowledge and to determine the limits of human knowledge. But if philosophy is to exhibit the possibility of knowledge, or, to put this in more precise and specifically Kantian terms, to exhibit the possibility of experience in general, then according to Kant's argument it cannot presuppose any kind of material content which, for its part, derives from experience but must remain 'pure', as Kant puts it.[9] 'Pure' in this sense effectively amounts to reflection on the cognitive function as such – in other words, on something purely intellectual that excludes any reference to real or material factors that might be reflected in this purely intellectual realm, or even form the presupposition of such a purely intellectual realm. In Kant's philosophy, specifically in the *Critique of Pure Reason*, this issue takes shape as the problem of what is called 'constitution'.[10] The *Critique of Pure Reason* is a work that investigates how knowledge is constituted or, in other words, if I can express this once again in a rather abbreviated form, tries to identify the factors or functions through which something like an objective world becomes possible in the first place, and thereby allows insight into the essential connections governing this objective world, whatever it may involve or contain. In the context of this method, however, the objective world itself is regarded as secondary or, in Kant's terms, as the constituted in relation to the constitutive,[11] as that which has been generated or produced over against the purely intellectual and productive principles which make something such as experience in general possible in the first place. And from here the argument then proceeds relatively simply and relatively plausibly: 'Well, something such as sociology, namely the scientific study of society, or even the sociology of knowledge itself, which investigates the social conditions of consciousness, all this is a kind of knowledge which already moves within the realm of the constituted, the realm of that which has itself been constituted. In other words, the objective world, here society, already belongs to the realm of experience, and the realm of experience itself must be regarded, in accordance with Kantian philosophy, as secondary; the task of investigating it cannot properly belong to philosophy but can only fall to the individual sciences which concern themselves with the relevant field.' On this line of argument, therefore, philosophy and sociology must appear incompatible with each other, unless we are to engage in a kind of *hysteron proteron* argument, where first principles are confused with last principles; in other words, knowledge itself would have to be derived from the object to be known, whereas for this whole tradition of thought all material or substantive determinations would already presuppose reflection upon the forms of our cognition or knowledge in general. Now it may perhaps surprise you when I claim that this theoretical outlook, which can generally be regarded as the core element of an idealist philosophical position, is still characteristic, to a very large degree, of so much contemporary philosophy which typically flatters itself for being anti-idealist in character, which constantly assures us, implicitly or explicitly, that it has moved beyond Kant, that it has overcome idealism. Yet I believe that it does not require that much acumen if we consider, for example, the most popular philosophy to have spread within the German universities, namely the so-called existential ontology of Heidegger, to rediscover such lines of thought still at work – albeit through recourse to a much older tradition – under the problematic name of the relationship between 'being' and particular 'beings', where the latter are supposed to be merely derivative in relation to the former. In the context of Heidegger's philosophy, 'being' is not, heaven forbid, supposed itself to be anything, is not at any cost supposed to be remotely tangible, to be connected with experience or with anything material whatsoever. On the contrary, it is supposed to be that which makes experience in a higher sense possible; or, as Heidegger's teacher Husserl put it, it is supposed to be available to categorial intuition[12] rather than to discursive or scientific concepts of any kind.[13] And over against this so-called knowledge of being, any substantive social knowledge, and especially any attempt at social self-reflection, can appear only as a kind of Fall, as a recourse to something secondary, whereas the task is precisely to return to what is first, namely to the concept of being. I may note in passing that I have just drawn your attention, with reference to one small specific model only, to a relationship between idealism and modern existential ontology which I nonetheless believe is of far greater relevance and significance than might initially appear. I believe that it is possible, and indeed even obligatory, to offer a detailed critique of contemporary existential ontology that will show how it is actually an idealism *malgré lui-même*, or, in other words, an unwittingly covert and thus, if I may put it in this way, miscarried form of idealism.[14] But I do not wish to elaborate on this today, as perhaps I shall have an opportunity in the next semester to look at these particular problems in more detail.[15] This opposition between philosophy and sociology also crops up in the context of the seemingly concrete theorems of contemporary existential ontology, as we can clearly see from certain remarks of Herr Heidegger from the pre-fascist era, when he once compared the sociologist to someone who just clambers up the façade of a building – the proud edifice of philosophy – and forces his way into the sacred precincts, only to make off with all of its splendid furnishings,[16] as Richard Wagner would put it.[17] This is basically the same kind of argument to be found in Kant as far as the relation to the empirical realm is concerned, except that Kant, with typically unerring and admirable honesty, proceeded far more gently in relation to psychology, which is something from which he similarly tried to distance himself in his own time, just as existential philosophy tried to distance itself from sociology in ours. When you read Kant, of course, you will find nothing regarding sociology in the sense in which we use the word. Incidentally, I would just like to point out here, if you want to get a good general idea of what is commonly understood by sociology, at least in Germany, that the Mohr publishing house has just issued a reprint of the short introduction to Max Weber's *Economy and Society*, which includes discussion of a range of basic sociological concepts.[18] I would strongly recommend all of you, if you can, to take a look at this little text. Although I myself do not share the specific conception of sociology that is defended here, I think the introduction to *Economy and Society* will provide an excellent starting point for those who would like to know – those of you who do not yet know – exactly what we mean when we talk about sociology.

Now I have just said that you will not find the term 'sociology' in Kant, a term which did not yet exist in his time and was first used by Auguste Comte,[19] about whom we shall have more to say shortly. However, the idea of sociology itself is actually earlier and derives from Comte's extremely insightful and important teacher, Count Saint-Simon.[20] But the principal writings in which Saint-Simon actually lays the foundations of sociology were only composed and began to exercise an influence when Kant was very advanced in years, or indeed only after his death, and he practically knew nothing about them. And the extraordinarily rich body of material on sociological issues that had emerged in the context of the French Enlightenment, especially in the writings of D'Holbach and Helvétius,[21] but also among the so-called Ideologists,[22] can hardly have been known to Kant either. The creation of sociology as a specific discipline is a relatively late phenomenon. We can say that this discipline comes to reflect upon itself as a kind of science only very late in the day, and there are very particular reasons why this is so – something that I shall also have more to say about in one of the coming lectures. But of course, in substantive terms, we are talking about something here which is already incomparably older, and I think it is actually a very good idea for you to dispose, once and for all, of the notion that sociology is a young science, even though we constantly encounter this claim, and one which is repeatedly defended by sociologists of all people. The precise point of time at which a science becomes independent, expressly reflects upon itself, or sticks a label on itself and the point at which such a science arises are two things which we can distinguish, though not in such a way as to conclude that a science really exists only once it has given itself its own name. And we can indeed say that, in this broader sense, sociology as a discipline is as old as philosophy, and that especially among the greatest representatives of ancient philosophy that separation between sociology and philosophy which will perhaps seem self-evident to many of you is not yet present at all.

When you read Kant you will constantly encounter a vigorous repudiation of psychology, and there is a specific reason for this. For Kant's philosophy is essentially an analysis of the faculty of knowledge – in other words, of the faculty of human consciousness itself. Now human consciousness, as it presents itself to Kant, is bound up with actual, living human beings, and in a certain sense is also itself a part of the empirical world. The empirical subjects or empirical human beings, as psychology deals with them, form just as much an object of our experience as, for example, are things in space or anything else. But Kant is seeking to identify the constitutive factors of experience in general, and in his analysis of consciousness he cannot properly therefore assume this consciousness insofar as it is itself an empirical fact to which I stand in relation. You have to remember that the British philosophy of his time, which represents one factor in the Kantian parallelogram of forces,[23] and particularly the philosophy of Locke and Hume, understood itself as a kind of psychology, as an investigation of the elements of consciousness.[24] And the fact that this British psychology, this British philosophy, was empiricist in character, and thus essentially denied the prevailing conceptions of valid knowledge as such, springs directly from the way this philosophy starts from our actually existing and transient empirical consciousness. But Kant wanted something very different; he specifically wanted to salvage eternal truth. But he wanted to salvage this precisely through an analysis of human consciousness. That, of course, is why he was particularly allergic to any conception of consciousness or the mind which would have turned this consciousness into something merely factual, simply into a piece of empirical reality; and that is why – in accordance with Freud's famous thesis concerning the pathos of the smallest differences[25] – he always strove with a quite particular passion to distinguish his own analyses of the mind, of consciousness, or of whatever else it might be, from psychology in the most emphatic possible way. With highly questionable success, it has to be said, for, in spite of Kant's express and constantly repeated claim (especially in the second account he provides of his theory of knowledge, namely the *Prolegomena*) that his analysis of consciousness has nothing to do with an analysis of the actually given empirical human mind or empirical human soul,[26] it is possible to show that he is nonetheless constantly forced to make use of particular expressions and particular considerations that are undeniably derived from the real actual life of particular individuals, from the psychological life of particular individuals. Thus the famous unity of consciousness, the synthetic unity of apperception, which is ultimately the most important concept in Kant's whole philosophy,[27] essentially derives simply from observing that what is called the 'I' is a unity only because it is aware of itself as something identical in the horizon of time – in other words, through the process of recollection, presentation and anticipation. Thus Kant's principle of identity itself is, if you like, actually drawn from psychology, which is why it also already involves the dimension of time; and, precisely because it is temporal in character, consciousness is determined in the first place as an empirical consciousness. Here I am merely drawing your attention to one side of the issues involved. For we are talking about an extraordinarily complex and many-sided question. Nor with these observations do I simply wish to tie Kant down to a merely psychological thesis. I have already mentioned that the psychological and the anti-psychological themes in Kant's thought work in some friction with each other, but here I just wanted to show you that the dividing line between pure Kantian philosophy and the realm of psychology is not nearly as clear, as sharp, or as unambiguous as Kant himself intended. And while the full force of the central element in Kant's critique of reason, namely the deduction of the pure forms of the understanding,[28] specifically and originally derives from the way that this deduction clings so closely to the experience of concrete and individual human consciousness, i.e. precisely through a certain proximity to psychology, it is surely remarkable to note that Kant, with his inimitable perceptiveness and his inimitable honesty and intellectual integrity, actually points out that he himself thereby runs the danger of making transcendental philosophy appear to depend upon the empirical; and in a sense one can understand the development of Kant's philosophy as an ever more emphatic turn against the perspective of psychology. Thus in the *Critique of Practical Reason* you will discover much more invective against any possible kind of psychological interpretation than you can in the first edition of the *Critique of Pure Reason*, where Kant was not yet quite so strict about these things – and this from a deep sense that any such static and absolute separation of the transcendental sphere of purely intellectual processes from the psychological sphere that involves the temporal embodiment of mind cannot actually be carried out. Now if Kant so strongly repudiated the real individual human subject in contrast to the pure 'I think' that accompanies all my representations,[29] i.e. in contrast to consciousness as a pure formal unity of experience,[30] then he would also clearly have to reject any reflection on society, namely sociology, as having any grounding or constitutive force as far as philosophy is concerned. For society, after all, is in fact something like a functional connection, a functional connection that obtains between individual empirical human beings, which would then indeed also appear as factors within a constituted field of knowledge. When Kant speaks in the *Prolegomena* of 'consciousness in general',[31] he does not actually mean – as the expression tends to suggest, and I believe for good reason – the consciousness which distinctively belongs to all human beings; that is to say, he does not mean something social, or a social consciousness, since for Kant the qualification 'in general' means consciousness as such, namely a consciousness without which something like an intrinsically coherent experience or an intrinsically valid case of knowledge could never be entertained at all. But in this famous formulation of 'consciousness in general' you may notice once again, and by way of anticipation, that it was not so easy for Kantian philosophy either to accomplish this separation from sociology, admittedly a discipline which did not specifically exist as sociology in his time. For what, in the final analysis, is this 'consciousness in general'? If you try and grasp what this 'in general' means, you will probably be able to think only of a consciousness that is not your consciousness, or my consciousness, or anyone else's consciousness but consciousness in general – in other words, a consciousness common to us all. The logical extension implied by the expression 'in general' already includes the 'we' in its very meaning, or, if you like, already implicitly includes society, although Kant would not be able to ascribe central philosophical significance to society precisely because it belongs to the realm of the constituted and enjoys a merely derived status. Now Kant certainly did recognize the significance of empirical psychology, and he would – I think it is safe to say – probably also have been able to recognize the significance of an empirical sociology. In the period when Kantian thought developed, which was still the period of Enlightenment and bourgeois culture in its ascendant phase, if I may be allowed to use such expressions, thinkers had certainly already sought to protect the traditional concept of philosophy from being confused, contaminated or conflated with the merely empirical; however, they did not yet display that exaggerated fear of the empirical that has become widespread today and serves in a way to complement that blind enthusiasm for 'the facts' and everything empirical which is equally widespread these days. This yawning gulf between extreme fear of the factical, on the one hand, and an intoxication or orgiastic obsession with the facts, on the other, can sometimes make it look as though we of the older generation are the reckless ones, while the younger generation seems to display the sobriety that we sought in vain to acquire.[32] But things were not yet like that in Kant's time. On the contrary, in the context of his critique of reason there is still plenty of room for psychology – and, I might plausibly add, for sociology too – as long as we make the following qualification: 'All this belongs to the realm of the constituted; none of this may provide your starting point of departure, if you are trying to justify the fundamental principles of philosophy itself.'

In the climate that prevails today around the problem of philosophy and sociology, there has been a quite decisive change precisely in this regard; when I said right at the beginning of this lecture that, in a sense, the Kantian problematic is still directly relevant for us in this connection, I must now correct that claim somewhat or present it in a more nuanced manner. In other words, what we find today is that philosophy is now hardly inclined to allow sociology any room at all, and that both fields have parted from each other in mutual acrimony. They now display a mortal fear of coming into contact with each other and thus I might even say of infecting each other – something it would almost need a Freud to explain. The idea that the sciences must be legitimated as purely and autonomously as possible without borrowing anything from elsewhere is an inheritance from the nineteenth century which has played a very important role in connection with the problematic notion of presuppositionless enquiry,[33] a notion that continues to draw on that inherited idea; while philosophy is increasingly thrown back upon its own resources as the sphere of its authority is progressively cut back by the advances of the so-called positive sciences (and it is of the essence of scientific progress that poor old philosophy, which once also embraced geography, medicine and who knows what else, increasingly finds itself robbed of any connection with such fields). The result is that philosophy guards even more jealously the position that it has now at least managed to establish for itself as just one branch among other branches of enquiry, which is why it not only refuses to tolerate any invasions of its own territory on the part of sociology or psychology but even attempts wherever possible to attack these disciplines even in areas where they perhaps seem to be most appropriate. Thus in the Kantian tradition today, insofar as this still survives in Germany, we no longer find that Kantian tolerance towards psychology as a kind of positive science in contrast to philosophy. There is no question of this, and what we find instead is that psychology and especially sociology appear from the start as a threat to the philosophical peace; and where modern existential ontology does pay any attention to psychology or sociology, it specifically tries to do so in a way that gets rid of the empirical salt, of the empirical thorn, and seeks to grasp the psychological realm by means of extremely formal categories that have been purged of any actual concrete meaning. In this connection you might think of the fashion for so-called *Daseinsanalyse* or 'existential analysis',[34] a trend which is very pronounced today, in contrast to the psychoanalysis that explores psychical life as a field of concrete experience. Thus we can say that modern philosophers in general, if they are philosophers in an emphatic sense and not simply methodologists like the logical positivists for example, are anti-sociological in outlook – with the exception, I would add, of a very few individuals, some of whom you will find here in Frankfurt. Thus the anti-empirical tendency of philosophy is now extended to fields that have been removed from the realm of philosophy. Where there is still something such as philosophy to be found, it tends to treat sociology negatively and refuses to let it be even in its native territory, so to speak. And in the next lecture you will hear how the reverse is also true as far as the kind of naive sociology which does not reflect upon itself is concerned.

LECTURE 2

12 May 1960

Ladies and gentlemen,
    In the last lecture I took Kant as a starting point and model for exploring the traditional resistance and antagonism which some disciplines have displayed towards sociology and all forms of truth or knowledge that appeal to the factual domain. In terms of the central problem I have already indicated, I should now like to do the opposite and introduce you to the kind of resistance to philosophy that one typically encounters in the field of sociology. And here you may be surprised by two things in particular. The first is that such resistance has by no means always characterized our two disciplines – for we shall soon be exploring certain theoretical positions for which the distinction between philosophy and sociology did not yet exist at all. But secondly you will also see that the rejection of philosophy on the part of sociology goes back a very long way, and that ever since 'sociology' has expressly existed as such – since it became aware of itself as a specific discipline and adopted this elegant name cobbled together out of Latin and Greek – the anti-philosophical impulse has remained alive in the field of sociology. I shall shortly illustrate this with reference to Auguste Comte. But I shall also show you that the reasons for this resistance of sociology to philosophy are very different from those you may generally imagine when you try and understand the problematic relationship between these two fields – and this all recalls Benjamin's observation that the quotations in his writings are like robbers that assault the reader on the open road and make off with his convictions.[1] What I mean is that sociology has

not simply proved to be the more progressive or more enlightened discipline in comparison with the less enlightened or reactionary discipline of traditional philosophy; on the contrary, we shall see that sociology, at least in its specific Comtean sense, arose in a polemical reaction to philosophy which was seen as a destructive expression of Enlightenment. In other words, the sociologists of the Comtean period actually reproached philosophy for the same kind of things that our rustic and forest philosophers tend to reproach sociology with today. This may already give you some insight into something which I regard as of the utmost importance, and which I would like you to think about right here: there is no theoretical position, of whatever kind, whose function within society is entirely independent of the social and historical situation at the time. There is no truth that cannot be abused and turned into ideology, no theoretical position that cannot be brought to serve the opposite of what it undertakes to claim. And this alone should already suffice to make you sceptical in the face of the all too hasty identification of theory and praxis that is popular today.

But, to return to Comte and his struggle against philosophy, I should just like to remind you in brief that the concept of 'progress', which along with that of 'order' is one of the highest concepts in Comte's sociology, found exemplary expression in his famous theory of stages.[2] He assumes three stages in human historical development: firstly, the theological-dogmatic stage; secondly, the metaphysical stage; and, thirdly, the stage which he calls the positive or scientific stage, the stage which in Comte's eyes culminates in sociology. The really noticeable thing here, and this already reveals one of the remarkable analogies between the arch-positivist Comte and the arch-idealist Hegel, is that the real polemical thrust of this conception – and one never knows with Comte whether we should speak of a philosophy or a sociology here – is directed more against metaphysics, in other words against philosophy, than it is against theology, and this is precisely because in his own time Comte was concerned principally with speculative philosophy as a specifically critical force. You have to realize – and this is the only really essential difference between Comte's theory and that of Saint-Simon, which Comte basically just devoured and simply expressed in different terms – that, while Saint-Simon still expressed the entire pathos of revolutionary eighteenth-century bourgeois culture, Comte already betrays anxiety in the face of the disintegrating tendencies of the bourgeois revolution. Throughout Comte we detect the fear that philosophical concepts, especially those of freedom, equality and fraternity – in other words, the Enlightenment ideas that in a certain sense lay behind the French Revolution – threaten to undermine every kind of social order and thus lead to anarchy. It is this position which motivates Comte's general attack on philosophy, and this is very similar to a passage in Hegel – although one can also of course find many other passages in his work that would rather contradict this – where he says that speculative philosophy actually finds itself allied with religious faith in opposition to a merely rationalistic or merely reflective form of thinking.[3] I might add here, since it is also part of my task to alert you to certain possible research projects in this field, that it would be extremely instructive, especially for those of you who are specifically interested in the relationship between philosophy and sociology, to consider undertaking a comparative analysis of Comte and Hegel, for, despite the flagrant differences that are undeniably evident here, you will also find some extraordinary similarities in both thinkers.[4] In my own lectures, where the history of philosophy is concerned, I constantly have to point out that the divergences between officially quite opposed schools of thought, such as those of empiricism and rationalism, are actually much less striking, when we look at the specific content of the theories in question, than we might otherwise suppose. And this is one of the reasons why we always warn beginners in philosophy against over-emphasizing or immediately exaggerating the conflict between Locke and Leibniz, or Kant and Hume, for example, or between early empiricism and the early seventeenth-century rationalists, between Descartes and Hobbes. Or at least we must warn against taking these oppositions as if they were absolute, and indeed I think we shall have good opportunity in due course to see why these mutually antagonistic schools do not actually constitute such absolute oppositions as we might easily believe. What Comte calls the metaphysical stage, the second stage of human development, is characterized by the way in which it supposedly objectifies or ascribes independent existence to various intellectual essences or entities, as Comte puts it,[5] over against the facts which are subsumed by means of them. This argument is simply that of a rigorous nominalism that rejects the objectification of any concept as mere dogma, and Comte regards such objectification of concepts over against the facts as nothing but a kind of semi-secularized theology. He tells us again and again that metaphysical concepts are actually nothing but theological notions that have been half-heartedly filtered through reason.

Let us just look at a couple of revealing passages to see how Comte uses sociology to argue against philosophy. I shall be quoting mainly from the little selection from the *Cours de philosophie positive*, which was published by Kröner in 1933 and edited by Friedrich

Blaschke.[6] It is of course no longer that easy to lay your hands on this edition today, but it is probably still easier to find than the huge Dorn-Waentigsche translation that was published by Gustav Fischer in Jena in 1923, which is incredibly unwieldy.[7] If you want to familiarize yourselves seriously with Comte, as I certainly recommend that you do, I would just advise you, for humanitarian reasons as it were, to try and get hold of the little selection of texts that I have mentioned and take a good look at it. For the three-volume edition is truly monstrous and indescribably dogged, garrulous and repetitious; no human being could reasonably be expected to read it from beginning to end. In any case I am completely opposed to the mendacious academic practice that insists that one must have closely studied great tomes of this kind, even though we all know we will never read them from start to finish the moment we pick them up. And in Comte's case this is simply impossible. On the other hand, you will certainly come across some extremely interesting and thought-provoking things in his work, and Blaschke's edition, to the extent that I have perused it, is very useful in this regard. To read the material in French rather than in German translation would naturally be rather time-consuming here. Nonetheless, I would like to take this opportunity, since we are about to look more closely at a few things from Comte and then some things from Durkheim, just to say that I believe a good knowledge of French is quite indispensable for the study of sociology – and I say this specifically for the sociologists among you, and especially for those who are only just beginning your studies in this area. Sociology emerged in France, and it is only when you are capable of reading in the original certain French sociological texts which are either untranslated or have sometimes been translated very poorly indeed, and here I am thinking especially of things like the *Années Sociologiques*, the journal founded by Durkheim,[8] that you will really be able to understand the origins of sociology, and thereby acquire a richer concept of sociology than you will if you do not enjoy immediate access to the French texts themselves. And, quite apart from that, I believe it is an extraordinarily serious matter that fewer and fewer people are familiar with French today and imagine that they should rush to study English instead, since France is no longer a great power. I would say that, for anyone who seriously claims to share in the heritage of Western culture, if I may put it this way, it is just as important to be able to read and speak French as it is to read and speak English. And if that has been denied to many of you by our rather rigid educational system, I can only honestly advise you in the strongest terms to try and remedy this situation however you can. For I believe this is an element of culture and education that you really cannot do without. The university itself cannot directly provide this for you, for if you wish to study the romance languages at university level a sufficient knowledge of the language in question is effectively already presupposed. But all this just in passing.

Let me come directly to some of the passages in Comte where he specifically criticizes philosophy, and here I would particularly like to draw your attention to the fact that the objections originally raised against philosophy by sociology were expressed in a distinctly authoritarian spirit, namely in the spirit of the existing order, rather than in the revolutionary spirit that one typically and naively expects to find here. In this connection you must remember that the entire Comtean system is based on the idea of an equilibrium between the two principles of order and progress, where Comte defends the principle of progress precisely insofar as he speaks for the bourgeois society that has become emancipated from the structures of feudal and absolutist authority but also on behalf of order, insofar as, just like Hegel, he not only sees the horrors of the French Revolution but also sees that the ruthless realization of bourgeois equality, i.e. of the exchange principle as the sole criterion of society, tends to deform and unhinge the structure of society itself; in other words, he sees that this naked exchange relation is ultimately all that remains, and that this deformation of society threatens to expose it to what might typically be described today as 'atomization' or 'massification' – to use popular expressions which in Comte's time were just as superficial and inadequate for capturing the real historical dynamics involved as they are today.

So I shall now read you a passage which will reveal this connection between the philosophy that is criticized by Comte, namely metaphysics, and the politically restorationist tendencies of his own thought. And here I simply want to bring out one Comtean thought which will show you precisely how the bourgeois principles of progress and rationality are combined with the principle of order in Comte. For here you will discover a very ancient Platonic theme, although the good Comte himself would doubtless be turning in his grave if he could hear me, over a hundred years after his death, ultimately describing him as a Platonist. And this is the thought that the task of ruling society essentially falls to a kind of science, indeed specifically to sociology.[9] For Comte envisages sociology as a scientific discipline, as a neutral and entirely objective authority that stands above the play of social forces and is capable both of directing human progress – where this is understood in Saint-Simon's sense as the progressive unfolding of the technical forces of production[10] – and also of somehow containing and neutralizing the disorganizing, destructive and anarchic forces that arise and develop within society itself, and this idea, once again, strongly recalls the role of the state in Hegel.[11] On this Comtean conception, therefore, sociology represents a kind of classless authority hovering above the play of social forces. And this anticipates a notion that we also encounter in the history of sociology in more recent times – in other words, something like the idea of the 'free-floating intelligentsia' in the work of my former colleague Mannheim.[12] This idea is already present in Comte's doctrine, and ultimately in Saint-Simon's doctrine as well.

What Comte says is basically as follows. He criticizes the principle regarding the freedom of conscience – namely the principle expressed with particular force by Fichte[13] but already affirmed by Kant – which claims that every single human being is responsible only to his own conscience, a principle which, as Comte quite rightly sees, embodies one of the most fundamental impulses of the bourgeois metaphysics of freedom. And it is typical of the way Comte already links philosophical concepts to specific social developments when you find him coupling this concept of the freedom of conscience with the concept of national sovereignty. Thus he goes on to say, in a passage you can find on page 49 of Blaschke's edition: 'It is also quite easy to estimate the value of the principle of the sovereignty of the people. It is the second conclusion drawn from the principle of the freedom of conscience, one which has been transferred from the intellectual domain to the political domain. This new stage of metaphysical politics' – in other words, a politics which is supposed to spring from pure principles rather than merely conforming to the given facts: the kind of politics espoused by Fichte in a rather extreme way[14] – 'was required in order to proclaim the downfall of the old regime and prepare the way for a new constitution.' As you can see, you already have a kind of sociology of knowledge here. Comte continues: 'The peoples had to award themselves the right to change the already existing arrangements at will; otherwise all restrictions could only proceed from the old regime itself, the existing authorities would have to be maintained, and the social revolution' – in other words, the French Revolution – 'would have failed. It was the dogmatic canonization of the sovereignty of the people alone that made new political experiments possible.' And then you can see the trajectory of Comte's thought when he immediately goes on to say:

> Under any other procedure the political transformation, the element of utopian participation, would have required the very powers that it was supposed to destroy. Yet, despite the temporary assistance provided by this dogma, we cannot fail to recognize the tendency to anarchy

it involves; for it generally opposes any kind of institution, condemns those higher up to a dependence on the mass of people below, and transfers the much censored divine right of kings to the peoples themselves. This metaphysical spirit finally manifests itself in a similar way as far as the relations between peoples are concerned.

And so on and so forth. He then goes on to speak, rather perceptively, about the anarchy which increasingly afflicts the relations between peoples and countries with the emergence of the modern nation state. This anarchy only encourages the possibility of utterly devastating wars, and that to greater extent than was the case under the Ancien Régime, where in the eighteenth century monarchs could sometimes wage war with one another for decades without these wars necessarily impinging that much on their respective populations, apart from the people involved in the armies themselves or connected with the regions immediately affected by such conflicts.

You can see that Comte here accuses philosophy, critical thinking itself, because it would tend, through its abstract reasoning as Hegel would say,[15] to dissolve actually existing institutions. And from this he concludes without further ado, without providing any real justification for this view, that this critical effect would be synonymous with anarchy – in other words, that it would prove entirely destructive and ultimately undermine the self-preservation of society itself. The notion that a society of self-responsible individuals enjoying civic equality might lead to a more meaningful arrangement of things by virtue of its own internal dynamics and its own objective character, namely because all individuals share an interest in their own self-preservation – as Kant could still suggest in his *Idea for a Universal History with Cosmopolitan Intent*[16] – this notion is something that has really already fallen away in Comte; instead we find him bestowing a right to exist on institutions as such, an idea that can be traced back to the older tradition of the French Enlightenment, and particularly to Montesquieu.[17] The process of critique and the resulting dissolution of institutions is basically identified with anarchy. The deeper reason for this, of course, is that in the time of Comte and Hegel independent civil society had reached a critical point – in other words, a point where it had already begun to produce pauperization from within itself, where it was no longer possible to see how society could be preserved within civil society and the formal equality that came with it. The idea of the self-preservation of society in spite of these antagonisms or through these increasingly evident antagonisms was first really developed by the early socialists in opposition to the great bourgeois philosophers of the same period whose thought already betrayed a certain apologetic character; and insofar as Comte came to speak for a bourgeois class that already felt threatened by the emerging power of 'third estate', we find in his work that the concept of social institutions retrospectively assumes the very lustre that it had forfeited in the French Revolution. This lustre is no longer guaranteed simply by tradition, however, but now has to be renovated, or, to put it more exactly, has to be restored precisely by means of the science of sociology whose mission this is. I would like to supplement the passage I just read out to you with another one which you will not find in the little edition but only in the very large one I mentioned earlier. The passage runs as follows:

> There is certainly no need for us to examine all the other central dogmas of revolutionary metaphysics in the same detail, which the attentive reader can now easily subject to an analogous assessment through a similar procedure; for in all other cases, as I have already shown with regard to the most important principle, the reader will soon easily recognize the following: the unconditional affirmation of a temporary manifestation of modern society, by appeal to a formula that is extraordinarily fruitful and indeed indispensable when applied in its proper historical context to the mere destruction of the old political system, ends up, when applied and transferred at an inappropriate time to the conception of a new social order, only by fundamentally obstructing the latter precisely because it leads to the unlimited repudiation of every genuine government.[18]

Now in these passages, however obvious their limited and reactionary character may be to you, you can actually detect a dialectical element which is certainly quite alien to Comte the arch-nominalist, and it is this: the same rational principles which once represented truth, insofar as they hastened the dissolution of an old social order that had become an unacceptable fetter on human development, may drive society towards destruction when we cling to them in a completely unreflective way, at the point, in other words, when society has become nothing but an unfettered exchange society.

I lay such importance on pointing out all this here because it helps you to see how some of the conceptions that are commonly ascribed only to speculative philosophy – such as the dialectical idea that the same things, here the same theoretical approaches, can assume entirely different and mutually contradictory functions – can sometimes be detected in a position which, in terms of its own self-understanding or its own apparent intentions, is utterly opposed to all dialectical speculation. I point this out precisely so you can see what I am trying to do here. I want to show you, in a whole variety of contexts, that the sources of dialectical thought do not lie in the speculative inclinations of the individual thinker, or in any merely intellectual processes as such; I want to show you how thinkers such as dear old Comte, who would never be suspected of harbouring such inclinations, nonetheless find themselves driven to dialectical conceptions simply by the force of the subject matter they engage with. Thus we find that Comte – and this is really a point where this positivist philosophy crucially differs from philosophy in the emphatic sense – sets social organization in dogmatic opposition to the idea of freedom of conscience on account of a hidden premise that is not really examined at all. This is the premise that it is better that something such as organized society should exist than that it should not exist. But this effectively ignores the fundamental question which preoccupied many schools of thought in the ancient Greek Enlightenment, such as the Cynics, that wondered whether organized society was not deeply problematic, and hardly something to be endorsed, in comparison with the state of nature. This philosophical question has already been decided in Comte, and the profound hostility to philosophy in this kind of sociology is ultimately sustained by the way in which a whole series of premises, which philosophy would reflect upon and specifically examine, are here simply assumed as something positive.

Now the term 'positivism' is actually ambiguous in a very deep sense, as you can see in an exemplary way if you study the work of Auguste Comte. Thus, on the one hand, the epithet 'positive' implies that the scientist, for example, should stick to the facts, to what is positively given, to what is really there, rather than getting lost in useless fictions or illusions. But at the same time 'positive' also always implies a certain theory of value, one that claims we should ascribe higher value to what is the case, to what one clutches as it were, than to what is merely possible rather than actual. Thus positivism always harbours the idea – rather like a moral maxim – that the bird in the hand is worth two in the bush. These two concepts of positivity play into each other. If Comte believed – although at first this appears highly paradoxical and barely credible in view of his 'scientific' self-understanding – that he might ultimately be able to found a positivistic religion,[19] this is intimately connected with the way he literally makes a cult of the facts; looked at more closely, this essentially involves the idea that those who administer the facts as facts, namely the representatives of organized science, also claim to be able to direct and control social reality completely. To put this another way: the decisive turn which this sociology adopts in contrast to the concept of critical philosophy, a concept which Comte expressly opposes, is that his own thought is one that moves in advance within the parameters of the rules, of the facts of society as it actually exists. Thus the laws and principles in accordance with which civil society is organized, such as the principle of exchange, are not themselves grasped as things that have a history, that have come to be, that are problematic in any way; on the contrary, all this is taken positively in the sense that we must hold to what is actually there – or, as I prefer to put it, that we must proceed in a purely system-immanent fashion. Instead of critically exploring the contradictions and internal problems of the system in which we move and find ourselves, instead of ultimately grasping the system itself as something historical and conditioned, as something that possibly may not be simply binding for all time. The decisive theoretical flaw we find here is that, since the exercise of self-possessed and autonomous thought is incapable of corroding institutions or undermining society, we must really call a halt to such thinking. Thus we demand that thought should not only orient itself to facts and respect facts in the general scientific sense, but that it should essentially accommodate itself to the facts – in other words, basically content itself with what can positively be observed here and now; it may be able to improve on this in some sense, but it should still accept or receive it as a datum rather than attempting to show how it has come to be something problematic, and possibly something riven by internal antagonism. You might say, if you like, that in Comte we may already make out that element which later became decisive for the positivist conception of social science, namely the doctrine of accommodation for which the task of social thought and its scientifically based claims is to encourage human beings to adapt to given social realities, and thus tacitly dispense with the question whether the given social realities are truly adapted to them, i.e. whether these social realities could really survive the judgement of a truly independent and self-possessed reason. Now there is another passage where this aspect, which I have just emphasized, is expressed even more clearly. You can find it on page 79 of the little Kröner edition, and perhaps I can read some of it out for you here. Once again Comte is basically trying to identify metaphysical ideas with theology, with the ultimate intention of eliminating both at a single stroke. He says: 'Whether the processes in question are traced back to supernatural intervention, or are explained by the recourse to the existence of the corresponding essences' – and this of course is the criticism he makes of philosophy, and especially the older medieval realist tradition of philosophy, although he throws early modern metaphysics in here too – 'is certainly a distinction within approaches that are ultimately identical. It does not prevent the one from repeating the features of the other.' In other words, theology and speculative metaphysics are essentially the same. They both spring from an excess of imagination over observation, and their content derives from a desire to discover absolute concepts.

> For social science this simply permits arbitrary and indeterminate judgements with regard to these processes, since the latter are not regarded as something that is subject to natural laws. The spirit of all theological and metaphysical speculation is ultimately delusory, and, while it sees itself as unconditioned, its application to experience is arbitrary; and the entirety of social science today is basically the same. The distinctive method of positive philosophy, by contrast, consists in the subordination of imagination to observation.

And this is what he is after: the subjection of fantasy to observation. 'The method provides a broad and fertile field for the imagination, but the latter' – and this 'but' is the very dogma of positivist social science in our own day[20] – 'is restricted here to discovering and perfecting the collation of observed facts, or to its role in facilitating new investigations in a fruitful manner. It is this approach, which subordinates our understanding to the facts, that must be introduced into social science.'

Nobody can fail to recognize the legitimate aspect of this critique of a purely speculative form of thought which has simply run wild or has evaded any serious engagement with the facts, but when you examine these Comtean formulations more closely they actually imply that the conceptual elements employed in the social sciences must be exempted from any kind of independent scrutiny if they are to represent truth, or, in other words, that the relevant concepts must accommodate themselves to the realm of empirical observations in advance. We ought to think just as the reality that we observe before us requires us to think. As for the element that Comte here calls fantasy, the features of spontaneity and independence – in other words, the element that allows us to envisage something that ought to be, something beyond the mere enactment of what already is – we find that this whole sphere of possible conceptualization must be relegated, in the best case, to the realm of auxiliary hypotheses formation.[21] But Comte's ideal is precisely this: as long as science functions in an orderly fashion, as long as we have a sufficient number of observations, there is no longer any need whatsoever for fantasy. This is a typical example of the rather patronizing attitude that later came to prevail in the social sciences, the attitude that says: 'Well, of course, we can't do without theories altogether, we've got to have some idea of what we're talking about.' First of all, that's usually nothing but lip-service, for we clearly don't take the theoretical issue seriously anyway, and just have the feeling: 'Well, you know, once we have collected enough facts, the theories can simply disappear; the reality is, the task of the social sciences is to adapt to their material.' In other words, we should proceed as we do in the natural sciences, even if this means ignoring the difference that human society is indeed a society of human beings, of free and rational subjects who do not relate to their society as to some alien nature that confronts them, for what essentially concerns them involves this nature. It is they who shape this nature and who must therefore try and ensure that it genuinely corresponds to their own practice of knowledge and freedom. In this context we might say that Comtean philosophy reflects back the 'second nature'[22] which our society has become once existing relations have come to prevail over actual individual subjects, reflects it back as if it were 'first nature', as if the same principles for knowing and the same modes of behaviour that are appropriate in the face of real and actual nature were just as appropriate in relation to society itself.

Since we do not have enough time today to go on and examine a further question in connection with Comte, let me just mention here that the arguments in the passages that I have been reading out actually derive from a period of specific political struggles,[23] and that the element of speculation, or, rather, anti-speculation, that you find here clearly sprang from the politics of the time. Napoleon had once issued certain edicts against the school of the Ideologists,[24] a philosophical school of the late Enlightenment that attempted to provide a kind of sociology of the 'facts of consciousness' and thus trace these facts back to their real functions. Now the kind of authoritarian argumentation which Napoleon mobilizes against unfettered or free-floating reason is precisely what you find in Comte here. We already glimpse here that the same social consciousness which once unfolded under the sign of the liberation of the subject would now once more restrict the freedom of the subject, and in essentially arbitrary ways, through the power of institutions – a tendency which eventually culminated and found its most consistent realization in the heteronomous politics of Fascism, in the total state.

LECTURE 3
17 May 1960

Ladies and gentlemen,

I would like to continue our discussion of certain passages from Comte's *Cours de philosophie positive* that we began in the last session. And I would just remind you that we talked about the way in which the concept of observation and therefore of what is factual gets played off in Comte against the realm of the imagination. I would also remind you that Comte believes that the neglect of the facts is encouraged by the untamed exercise of the imagination, a neglect that he identifies with a failed or inadequate adaptation to the actual given circumstances of society. In Comte, therefore, you already find, in rudimentary form, something like the theory of adaptation that later played such an important role in Spencer, and indeed has continued to dominate the field in American sociology to this day. I would add, in passing, that all this is not without interest in historical terms, for many of you will know that the theory of adaptation in the context of sociology is what has appropriately enough been dubbed 'social Darwinism'; in other words, Darwin's theory of adaptation, of the 'survival of the fittest', of the specimens that are best adapted to the actual conditions of life, is essentially transferred to sociology. But you find such theories, or at least this general idea, in Comte even before the development of Darwin's theory of adaptation, which surely shows that the spirit of positivism in sociology unfolded in an immanent way and certainly has no need to be traced back to influences from biology. The fact that the concept of adaptation first makes its appearance in the context of sociology – although it now certainly enjoys a more secure scientific status in biology than it does in sociology – seems only to strengthen the possibility that the Darwinian conception itself was influenced by social ideas that actually derived from the competitive mechanisms of modern society, from the question of survival or otherwise in the specific context of economic struggle. (This possibility has already been suggested in various ways, and, in connection with our own concern with the relationship of philosophy and sociology, it clarifies the relationship between sociology and other concrete particular disciplines.) Thus I suggest that these ideas can ultimately be traced back to sociology and found their way into biology only later on,[1] and that this account is more plausible than the tired old story about Spencer that you get from the standard histories of science.[2]

Now the downgrading of imagination in comparison with observation – a direct consequence of the theoretical approach we have been considering – gives a distinctive twist to the concept of the subject, and this is actually what defines the relationship of philosophy and sociology. If you just recall for a moment, including those of you who have not specifically studied philosophy, what you know about the great idealist systems of the post-Kantian period, especially those of Fichte, Hegel and Schelling, you will certainly be aware that a remarkably elevated and emphatic concept of subjectivity stands at the heart of all these philosophical doctrines. It is quite true that Hegel's philosophy of objective idealism restricts the unrestricted validity of the concept of the subject as an utterly creative and spontaneous agency, a view that is particularly characteristic of Fichte; but in Hegel too the entire world can ultimately be regarded as the product of subjectivity, and the exemplary demand which this lays upon knowledge, upon philosophy as science, is precisely this: thought must exert itself to move beyond the mere facts, to penetrate the facts in a really thoughtful way, and, to express this task in traditional philosophical language, to bring out the very essence of the matter. Of course we cannot just talk about this tendency in a purely general and unqualified way. I need to say this because I feel obliged to present these things to you in a properly differentiated fashion. For there is a real danger that such general characterizations threaten to obscure or obliterate significant distinctions. And I believe that it is the duty of a lecture course such as this not to pass on any misleading ideas merely for the sake of offering you a straightforward orientation at the start. Now the concept of the subject, as you find it in philosophy, is itself ambiguous in many ways. Thus in Fichte, and to a certain sense already in Kant, the 'subject' is distinguished from the individual.[3] The subject can be seen either as a social subject or as a purely intellectual entity, i.e. as an abstraction from the actually existing empirical subjects, or again as the ideal subject of scientific cognition, we might say, as the spirit of science as distinct from the individual human subjects who may embody it. Now this emphatic concept of the subject, which you can trace back to Kantian philosophy, of course also already implied for the German idealists some restriction of the meaning of actual empirical subjects. Thus even the most extreme speculative idealism would not have claimed that any individual, if I may put this rather crudely, could just think away wildly in their own way and simply construe a world of their own making. Rather, each thinking individual serves as a representative of this higher, universal, transcendental or objective subject, must try and live up to the full and undiminished significance of what can be found and observed, and thereby correct the limited and arbitrary aspects of a merely individual subjectivity. Hegel's philosophy already follows this through to the very end when he calls, with a seemingly paradoxical expression, for freedom towards the object.[4] This refers to the capacity on the part of the subject to abandon oneself to the object, to immerse oneself as thinking subject in the matter itself, instead of simply spinning this out of oneself, turning it into a mere product of oneself, as it were. Nonetheless, the thought of the thinking subject as a spontaneous and productive subject is crucial for German Idealism, and indeed for the entire philosophical tradition. It is no accident if, in contrast to the passage I have already cited, where Comte speaks of the excess of imagination over observation, we find something very different even in Kant, a thinker who was notoriously cautious and reserved in his attitude to speculative thought. For Kant accords a central place to the concept of the imagination, and specifically to the original and productive power of the imagination which gives unity to the things of experience. In other words, what you find in sociology, to put this rather crudely here, is a kind of anti-subjective tendency: on this view the subject is not supposed to inform or shape reality in any way through its own intellectual processes or through its own activity, but simply keep to what reality provides. And in the course of time this has produced a requirement that anyone who is engaged with empirical sociology today can readily experience for themselves;[5] and this, if I may exaggerate somewhat just so you understand what I am talking about here, is the requirement for the self-liquidation of the thinking subject. I believe that what distinguishes the positivistic spirit from the spirit of philosophy is this notion that the subject must effectively eliminate itself in order to attain the truth, whereas philosophy holds that the object only reveals itself at all through its exposure to the power and freedom of the subject. This is one of the most crucial distinctions here. Thus when the sociologists among you are learning how to prepare interviews these days, you will be told that it is imperative in all cases to suppress any thoughts of your own, that you ignore your own views when drawing any conclusions about the people before you, that you keep entirely to the relevant data; in short, if this suppression of your imagination, this restriction of your own freedom, appears to you here as the natural requirement of scientific research, this is ultimately connected with the attitude that early sociology already adopted in relation to the spirit of philosophy. I just want to present you with this idea here, and simply help you to see that these demands, which you will of course encounter not only in sociology but in every field of scientific research and investigation, are not nearly as self-evident as they may initially seem to be, for such demands actually already imply a very specific conception of scientific or objective knowledge, and one that is anti-philosophical in character. And it will be our task here to reflect expressly upon the question whether this ascetic approach which science constantly expects of us actually represents a freedom towards the object, whether it gives us more of the object, or whether under certain circumstances it even gives us less of the object, or whether perhaps this question can ultimately be decided simply in these terms.

In any case, this Comtean demand at the expense of the free subject has a certain implication for sociological thought which I would like to draw to your attention even at this preliminary stage, and that is the way this demand essentially directs the process of thinking. By encouraging you to avoid speculation and orient yourselves to the given, you find your thought is already referred to the categorial forms and the givens that you happen to encounter as they are. This tacitly presupposes the existing order, the particular arrangement of things that you find before you, although this presupposition is never actually made explicit, and the existing order is not only turned into the criterion of truth but is thereby elevated to the norm that is supposed to govern thinking as such. And this specific concept of adaptation has had these two sides to it right from the start: in the first place, we must unreservedly register the facts as faithfully as possible, while taking care to deduct all costs incurred by the process of subjectivity, so that the remainder, what you are finally left with, is the truth; in the second place, there is already something normative or prescriptive about this adaptation or accommodation on the part of knowledge to what is currently the case; thus knowledge itself is supposed to take its measure from the existing order of things as they are, though it may perhaps improve things in a gradual way. In other words, the conception of sociology which we have started with already contained the demand for the kind of immanently systematized thought that has been proclaimed as an explicit programme in a recently published book by René König, a work to which we shall return in due course.[6] It is the kind of thinking that requires a guarantee of its own utility, that sets itself up as its own criterion by asking: 'What am I good for? How can you best use me in the world as it is?'

Here, ladies and gentlemen, I am touching on a problem that I realize is extremely important to many of you, and it may be best to say a few words about it towards the beginning of the lecture course. For the question you come up against here – the idea that thought must be licensed by its utility – is a very serious one. It is not something that can just summarily be decided with an expression of academic arrogance: 'For God's sake, all we are talking about is applied knowledge, and that has nothing to do with truly autonomous and binding knowledge.' What we have here is a genuine contradiction, and I think it is best for you to recognize this contradiction precisely as a theoretical and philosophical contradiction. If you really do recognize it and comprehend its necessity, this may help you to avoid the idea that this contradiction can simply be removed or abolished by science itself. If you are seriously committed to your studies, I believe you will see that the idea that the specific discipline with which you are engaged is capable of eliminating for you the contradictions which actually give it life and spirit is an illusion or daydream that you must be prepared to renounce; as is the idea that the realm of science or research could offer you any existence, or even any consciousness, that would be free of contradiction. For that would in fact assume that the world can be captured without remainder in terms of consciousness itself or any features of consciousness. It would be to ignore or forget something essential – that our consciousness is ultimately only a rather inadequate and tentative way of dealing with reality itself and that nothing simply guarantees or assures us that reality is not itself contradictory. What I am trying to say is this: you yourselves as knowing subjects, all of us as knowing subjects, always already oriented in some way towards the whole, the absolute, the truth – in other words, every thought,[7] however unassuming it may be, simply by presenting itself as a claim, even an unassuming claim, to be right already harbours a kind of internal dynamic, already bears something like a concept of objective truth or objective rightness within itself. And thought feels itself somehow stalled or cheated if its claim is not honoured – in other words, if it is not actually given what it believes it may rightly expect from reality. On the other hand, the way the world is arranged means that we actually risk ruin if we fail to adapt sufficiently to it. Hence the pertinent saying: 'Primum vivere, deinde philsophari'.[8] In other words, we must first earn a living for ourselves before we can start thinking at all, and the idea of free, disinterested and emphatic truth already presupposes the kind of life we can secure only through a certain kind of accommodation to realistic ends and interests. Thus we can actually live and then perhaps think in an emphatic sense only if we perform what is often described as 'socially productive labour'. All intellectual labour, and thus all academic and scientific labour, is also part of this socially productive labour.

As individuals engaged in scientific or scholarly disciplines, and specifically as sociologists who have to deal with a particularly sensitive and contested field, we are compelled to do certain things that allow us to earn a living, in other words, to function within the existing order; and this remains the case even if we do not restrict our thinking to the immanent demands of the system in which we find ourselves but reflect critically upon that system as philosophy enjoins us to do. On the other hand, we thereby find that our soul is deprived of 'its God-given right', as Hölderlin puts it,[9] that the innermost dynamic of thought is somehow stifled or cut off. Now it often happens that students, and perhaps many of you here, especially if you have been thinking long and hard about these things, feel like coming up and reproaching us, your academic teachers, as follows: 'Well, what on earth are we supposed to do then? On the one hand, as sociologists, we must try and find some role or function to perform within the whole existing set-up; at the same time we must not only entertain a distinctively critical attitude to this set-up but also know that these roles and functions we are meant to take up actually run counter to a range of insights that we have specifically acquired by understanding the mechanisms of society – and it is you pernicious sociologists who are responsible for this! – look what the Lorelei has done with her singing.[10] You have tempted us with the prospect of some kind of free and undiminished truth; and now we find we cannot actually live with this truth, and when we go out and earn a living, we cannot fail to have a bad conscience about it, although in the world as it is in today you can hardly expect us to go hungry!' Now this objection does indeed capture the predicament in which social thought inevitably finds itself today, although I think it is rather unjust to reproach sociology itself with this, or even to claim, as I have occasionally heard it said, that you have merely been drawn into a kind of sociological schizophrenia. It is unjust because the contradiction that I pointed out for you is not one that is produced by thinking, by the discipline of sociology, but is actually the contradiction inherent in society – a society whose understanding of reason, of *ratio*, has been shaped by the concept of a binding and comprehensive idea of truth, but one where reason is also always tied and limited in a particularistic way to merely instrumental rationality. When you find yourselves in this situation, the gravity of which I certainly do not underestimate, and then complain to us, your teachers, who must pursue knowledge, you are acting as if someone who tries to diagnose a difficult situation must actually be held responsible for the fact that the situation in question exists – and this is a kind of psychological mechanism that is indeed extraordinarily common. In this connection I like to cite the remark of Helvétius that the truth never hurt anyone except the one who told it.[11] I would advise you, therefore, to respond in a different way before you throw in the towel – in other words, before you just say: 'Ah well, what's the point of all this sociological reflection? I'll just learn the required skills and techniques and get a decent job at the end of it. This damn sociological theory can only lead me astray – to the devil with it!' So before you go down this road you would be better off, I believe, if you at least try and understand this contradiction, under which you and I can assure you all of us suffer, as an objectively grounded contradiction, and reflect upon it as such. My own view, if I may introduce this here, is that you will actually get further in your knowledge of facts, of the relations and connections involved in society, if you take on board these uncomfortable theoretical reflections than you will by just focusing relentlessly on the functional connections of society. For it is a rather remarkable paradox that when we simply try and perform our functional roles within society, when we reduce our own knowledge to this merely functional level, we generally find we actually no longer know or understand anything at all, or that our knowledge is extraordinarily impoverished as a result. In other words, to put this in logical terms, if you completely reduce the practice of thought to the mechanisms of social adaptation, if you allow thought no other possibility beyond that of unreserved accommodation, then thought ends up as nothing but tautology. It ends up with what empirical research likes to call 'the preparation of the facts', where you basically have no more than what you have already. Any judgements you come up with are all really nothing more than 'analytical judgements', mere repetitions or classifications of what is already there anyway. Yet I would suggest that the spirit of science, if we are still using the word 'science' in all seriousness and are not merely referring to various techniques and procedures, surely consists precisely in bringing us further, in giving us more, allowing us to see or understand more, than the orderly and efficient repetition of what we already hold in our hands.

Now the objection against imagination in favour of observation, which I talked about earlier, naturally has a certain plausibility. There is no doubt that the notion that mysterious forces are at work in society, things beyond the world of observable fact, can easily lead to all kinds of wild speculations and mythological explanations. If you consider Plato's doctrine of the state from this perspective today, for example, and try and picture the essential character of a human society that is supposed to follow from assuming the reality of pure forms or essences or supposing that the soul essentially consists of a rational, a spirited and a desirous element,[12] what you will find is an extremely arbitrary and highly stylized expression of the actual society of the time. On the other hand, it has to be said that it is only the imagination, only the element in sociology which goes beyond the recording and collation of connections, that is able to bring such facts into any meaningful connection with one another – and this is a central problem which I hope these lectures will specifically encourage you to think about. Comte's line of argument – and here Comte can really stand in for the positivist position in its entirety – supposes and essentially starts from the idea that all connections between social facts are fictive in character, or, as we might put this today in slightly more polite, friendly and elegant terms, are simply scientific models, while the only thing that is true, by comparison, are the facts themselves. The problem that I am trying to draw to your attention here is this: this assumption, in which you are unreflectively raised as sociologists, already downplays the possibility that social relations and connections precede and pre-form the individual data. I am talking about the kind of approach that says: 'But something like a system of society doesn't really exist at all, it's just something that exists in the heads of philosophers!' – and here that means: in the heads of certain backward sociologists who are not scientifically respectable in the first place. The objector might continue: 'Something like a social system is not actually present, and it is highly questionable whether we can even speak of social systems at all; the only real thing here are the facts which can be observed and collected on the basis of our questionnaires and controlled experiments, the facts which can be captured in our protocol sentences, the facts we can take home with us.' Here is the reason, to state it very simply, why I believe we should hold on to a philosophical concept of society in the context of modern sociology – a discipline which is now even proud to be a 'sociology without society', as René König puts it.[13] To state the matter simply once again: it is surely impossible to avoid recognizing that we actually live in an all-encompassing social system, that the facts we find and the things we encounter within this system are already significantly pre-formed through this system. All the individual social acts that we perform as social beings are interrelated, and not in some merely arbitrary way but in accordance with certain rules within a quite specifically organized context. Even in our immediate experience we find that we encounter individual social facts within the context of a system that cannot be pinned down as readily as facts themselves may be, and this is the justification for continuing to hold on to the idea of society, of critical reflection, of an interconnected whole, of a predetermining structure, of a system, in short, for continuing to hold on to the social categories which sociology originally took over from philosophy. Here, of course, we encounter an objection which is frequently raised by the philosophy of science and by contemporary empirical sociology – the objection which Helmut Schelsky specifically raised against me quite recently, something about which I shall have a lot more to say later on in these lectures[14] – runs like this: 'You all talk about a social system that somehow goes beyond the individual facts; you say there is an exchange society in which equivalent elements are exchanged for one another, in which we encounter real things that at the same time are not real things;[15] you make all kinds of clever remarks in this connection, but where, after all, is the system you talk about, the system that allegedly stands behind the facts, if you don't also have the facts themselves? Are you just relying on some special intuition? That would surely be a very curious or indeed laughable situation for someone who appeals to self-conscious reason as emphatically as you do. Or are you just trying to play off your own so-called simple pre-scientific or pre-reflective experience against the demands of science? You certainly won't get far with that, for if you want to be rigorously scientific in your approach this kind of pre-scientific experience can only be regarded as basically dogmatic, as something that is not ultimately binding at all! You have to start by bracketing out such experience and subjecting it to the scrutiny and control of science if it is to serve as a reliable source of truth!' Now I do not wish to go into this question fully at this point. But it strikes me like this: the idea that the system which we ourselves experience as an extreme form of compulsion itself requires theoretical justification in terms of individual facts already implies a kind of reversal of the order of knowing, of the process of experience, a reversal that is already framed in terms of the basic rules of the established sciences.[16]

But I think I may venture to say, even at this point in today's lecture, that we experience the social pre-formation in question whenever in our own social behaviour we try to act in a way other than that which the pre-existing social system essentially requires of us. This is a fact which was accorded an undeniably central place even by empirical sociology in relatively recent times – and I would say ...;[17] I am referring to Durkheim, whom we shall soon have more to say about in a different context, and to his concept of '*contrainte sociale*' or social compulsion.[18] Durkheim effectively put it like this: 'If you want to know what society is, just ask where it hurts; it's where you come up against something that is so much stronger than your own action and your own behaviour that you cannot really do anything about it or even resist it without provoking the most tangible and specific consequences.' I think you have only to perform the thought experiment of imagining what would happen to any one of you if you no longer consistently observed the rules of exchange, if you no longer subjected your labour to the law of equivalent exchange, if you no longer arranged your private life in such a way that you also get something back for what you give, if you were no longer prepared to put your life on anything unless you expected to receive the equivalent in return. You cannot just discover this ubiquitous principle of exchange, this omnipresent principle, as another fact precisely because it expresses a structural totality which is never simply or exhaustively given in any finite or particular case. But this fundamental aspect of social compulsion – in other words, the way you have to conform to the regular norms of the organized already existing whole – is something you can directly experience for yourselves from the resistance you meet as soon as you try to act otherwise. This force of the social, which finds its most powerful expression in the so-called folkways,[19] in the established mores and practices of a specific culture, had such a tremendous impact on Durkheim's sociology that he even employed the concept of '*chose*', or thing, to capture it.[20] He not only made this '*contrainte sociale*', this alien compulsion that is opaque to us and to every individual, into the social as such but also regarded it as the ultimate fact: the fact that appears largely independent of ourselves precisely because we do not experience it as our own. Instead we experience it as something alien and opposed to us, almost like a brick wall we must bang our head against. With a positivistically inclined sociologist such as Emile Durkheim – and perhaps he is the last sociologist of whom this may be said – you find that a central question of philosophy – the conceptual entwinement of social facts through the system that goes beyond these individual social facts – is transformed into the ultimate social given. This immediately leads to a considerable problem, since Durkheim, who was particularly hostile to any tendency to hypostasize concepts, here goes down the same road precisely by hypostasizing something that is itself mediated and conceptual in character and turning it into an ultimate criterion. This is not something purely immediate in character: it is a nexus of facts rather some particular fact in the sense in which we use the word in the context of experimental observation, for example. I just wanted to point this out here to show you how the simple exercise of reason, even in what you might call a pre-philosophical sense, already reveals how we can go beyond the concept of particular observable facts without thereby falling into fanciful speculation.

Let me just close for today by saying that philosophical concepts, if they are worth anything at all, are not concepts that dwell in some other separate world, in ill-famed higher spheres that lie far beyond the particular sciences or disciplines. On the contrary, philosophy is ultimately nothing but rigorous self-conscious reflection upon the actual world, upon what you encounter in the experience of your own field of research or investigation. This should already suggest that, while we have indeed begun by exploring the difference between the spheres of philosophy and sociology, these disciplines are not merely antithetical but also constitute a functional or dynamic unity.

LECTURE 4
19 May 1960

Ladies and gentlemen,
I would now like to look at another passage from Comte, and this will allow me to say something more about the original motivation behind the highly critical view of philosophy which sociology has tended to adopt. There is one particularly relevant passage, which I shall now read out for you, although it is not entirely clear in all its details. I shall not try and interpret those parts of the text which are very difficult to clarify in unambiguous terms, a situation that is hardly rare in Comte's work. The passage starts as follows: 'Metaphysical philosophy' – namely the kind of philosophy which Comte contrasts with 'positive' philosophy – 'with regard to its method and doctrine resembles theological philosophy; in every case it can only amount to a simple transformation of the latter.'[1] Here in a thinker such as Comte, who defended a historical and developmental approach to things, you may recognize, for the first time, a thought that would later play a major role in sociology and in the theory of science in general, and possessed a great significance for Nietzsche in particular.[2] This is the thought that the so-called metaphysical ideas were really secularizations of theological concepts, concepts which reappear here in a much paler or more diluted form, but which allegedly share the same theological nature and origin as those concepts – as we can see from their essentially dogmatic character, which is impervious to any confirmation in terms of experience. Yet this thought, which was already formulated in the radical phase of the Enlightenment, assumes a very distinctive form

in Comte. For he then says: 'This metaphysical philosophy possesses very little intellectual force, and thus much weaker social power'[3] – that is, to spell it out, a much weaker social power than theology. Now in one sense this observation is quite right. For, as it turns out, the sublimated propositions of metaphysics and speculative philosophy, propositions which no longer actually seem to apply to solid reality, are infinitely less suited to the task of shaping or integrating the masses, and thus perform a much weaker function in reality, than the old theological dogmas. And here we have to say that not a lot has changed since Comte's time. But the interesting thing about this passage, and the reason I am drawing it to your attention, is that it identifies precisely why sociology reproaches philosophy in the first place – and once again this captures the overall intention of sociological positivism at its inception. We might say that, for Comte, philosophy comes off worse than theology, in spite of his own theory of progress, in spite of the fact that he thinks philosophy involves a more rational approach than any theology, precisely because it does not retain as much integrating social power as the latter. Now this represents a tremendous turning point, one which has become famous in American philosophy and sociology in particular under the name of pragmatism, the roots of which you can ultimately trace back to this earliest form of sociology. It involves the idea that the truth of a theory can be defined in terms of how it holds up or finds itself confirmed in reality. In later forms of pragmatism, especially in the work of John Dewey,[4] this doctrine has been developed in a very subtle and sophisticated way. Here in Comte it is expressed in a rather crude and primitive form, and this very crudeness allows us to look behind the scenes at what we could perhaps call the primal history of pragmatism. The underlying thought here is just the notion that a philosophy or theoretical position is to be measured in terms of its power to promote society or to encourage the 'social community', as we recently used to say. We should thus ascribe positive value to those theories which have the power to maintain society and enhance social cohesion and a negative value to those which lack this power. When people talk about the destructive character of intellectual reflection and philosophy, the cheapest and most pathetic charge that we may regularly expect to hear in the intellectually enfeebled climate of today, you will recognize this attitude in its ultimate consequences and its basest shape – I say basest, because the question of truth is neglected here in favour of the question of effect, of the effect on society, because the factor which maintains or promotes the social order – something which in itself is quite alien and external to the truth claim of what purports to be genuine knowledge – is unwittingly taken to be the criterion of the proper truth claim in question. This is already implicit in Comte here, and you should recognize this as a motif that we shall encounter later on in our discussion of sociology, where it is even presented as a kind of philosophy. For you will find that the sociology which is so proud of its own allegedly more rigorous or scientific character in contrast to philosophy unwittingly ends up somewhere else: it smuggles in a certain element – allows this element to 'creep in' unawares, as Kant would say[5] – that cannot be reconciled with this supposedly scientific character at all. To put it quite bluntly, because it takes society and the process of socialization as its specific object, sociology concludes that whatever helps to strengthen this process, to promote the cohesion of society, is itself also something positive – like society as the true object of sociology – and that whatever weakens this cohesion is thereby something negative. Yet the really fundamental question as to whether this process of strengthening the existing network of social relations must be something unconditionally positive is not raised at all. You will find the effects of this approach everywhere – for I do not want you to imagine that, because we started with the venerable Comte, I am really just shooting fish in a barrel here, and that all this is no longer relevant to the much more exact and rigorous social science that we do today. For you can see the effects of this Comtean attitude in what is probably the most influential and comprehensive sociological system today, at least where our Western world is concerned – I am talking about the theory developed by Talcott Parsons.[6] He specifically distinguishes between the concepts of a 'functional' and 'dysfunctional' social system, where functioning social systems, those which are basically capable of maintaining or preserving themselves, come off better than those which do not function successfully. A higher value is automatically accorded to the former, although the extraordinarily far-reaching philosophical question that undoubtedly arises here does not come into view at all. It is surely enough to point out to you that we can easily conceive of societies that may function at an extraordinarily high level and effectively perpetuate themselves – thus we might think of the society which existed in central America at the time when Cortés conquered Mexico[7] or of the Egyptian society which survived for thousands of years in a rather ossified state. In this connection we might argue that this functioning meant that, in a sense, there was no such thing as the human individual, that the functioning of such societies was achieved at the expense of what such a society might be thought to function for – namely the existence, the development, the productivity of the particular elements out of which that society is composed. You can see, therefore, why it is worth staying for a moment with Comte's formulation of the issues – with the passages I have read to you, and which one might easily be tempted to pass over without further thought because they just sound like a very stale expression of common sense. But if we examine them a little more closely, they may let us glimpse certain implications that one would otherwise never have suspected. This is the secret here – we can discover something if we tarry with such passages and give some serious and sustained attention to the seemingly incidental remarks which frequently crop up in Comte's massive tomes, even if Comte himself did not ultimately accord that much significance to them in their original context.

The passage continues: 'These characteristic features [the diminished intellectual force and weaker power of metaphysics as compared with theology] are well suited to the temporary task which it [i.e. philosophy] possesses as far as individual and social human development as a whole is concerned, which is why it offers less resistance to the positive spirit.'[8] In other words, Comte celebrates the fact that philosophy, precisely because it does not function so well as a form of social cement, can easily be outplayed by the spirit of positivism in this regard, which makes the latter much more attractive as a result. And this is actually quite right. For a form of thinking which is concerned merely with registering the facts and refuses the labour of interpretation, which is labour in an emphatic sense, already obeys the principle of following the line of least resistance, and such an approach is indeed simpler and more tempting for those who naively fail to think through the kind of connections which I am trying to bring out for you here. And in fact, historically speaking, Comte has proved right. In by far the larger parts of the world the positivistic conception of sociology has proved to be incomparably more attractive than theoretical thought in the proper sense. Here in Germany there is still a strong intellectual tradition that is capable of challenging this approach, and there are also specific social reasons why the intimate connection between positivism and the bourgeois order has never proved as powerful here as it is elsewhere; but that is precisely why we in Germany are still inclined to underestimate the enormous attraction that is exercised by positivistic sociology. With the critical analyses that I am presenting here, I believe that I may be somewhat ahead of the intellectual consensus in Germany, or at least ahead of the public German view of things in general. But I am convinced that, in this regard as in many others, we shall find that we have actually become very like America, and that is why we should already be reflecting and thinking critically on these matters, something that only really happened in America itself at a relatively late stage of the process we are discussing.

This is all I wanted to say about the passage that I read out to you today. Now there is also another particular formulation of Comte's which I would like to draw to your attention. And here, in what we can only call an insight grounded in hatred, Comte has clearly recognized a problem that has arisen from the transformation of theological ideas such as that of God the Creator into the idea of causality,[9] or that of the existing created world into a world of things. This is what he says: 'On the one hand' – and I shall talk only about this 'on the one hand' because his 'on the other hand' is somewhat obscure[10] – 'the increasing sophistication of its concepts' – i.e. those of philosophy – 'increasingly allows the entities in question to become nothing but abstract names of the relevant processes, so that such explanations' – i.e. those provided by philosophy – 'are absurd, whereas this could not happen as easily with theological concepts ....'[11] Here you find that Comte, in a similar way to Hegel, allies himself with theology in opposition to what Hegel describes as the critical, reflective and rationalizing thinking of philosophy.[12] In this connection it is particularly interesting to note, especially for those of you who are studying philosophy, that Comte has stumbled here upon a thought, and a very subtle one, that Hegel had developed in his *Science of Logic* and which one would surely never have expected to find in Comte. I shall explain what I mean. Comte basically says that the principle of causality, or the question concerning the genuine ground of things, in the end no longer requires us to seek further back to find the source of things in a creative God; on the contrary, the principle simply traces efficient causes, becomes paler and paler, and finally turns into nothing but a general name for the particular phenomena which it subsumes – so that such a universal concept ends up losing its meaning. We might almost say that Comte maliciously blames metaphysics for the fate that he himself brings down on it through his own kind of thinking. Comte effectively says: if you no longer have anything solid, no real entities to show us, if these entities have finally turned into nothing but general concepts, nothing but abstractions, then they no longer possess any explanatory force – they are just abbreviated expressions for the particular facts they subsume, mere tautologies that no longer say anything new about what they describe. They can no longer withstand the critique that positivism raises against them and must therefore be cast aside. Comte doesn't quite express the issue as precisely as I have put it here, but when he says that philosophical concepts have simply become names for the processes they refer to, this can only mean that they really just become abstractions from what they want to grasp. As nothing but abstractions that are drawn from the latter, they cannot serve in turn to explain it. Hence Comte concludes, to use his words, that they are absurd. Now you can find the very same line of argument in a very interesting passage from the second part of Hegel's *Science of Logic*, in the section of the text that specifically discusses the problem of 'ground'.[13] There is something else that I would just like to emphasize here so that you are not tempted to pass over these things too quickly: Comte owes so much to the general trend that we can describe philosophically as the spirit of nominalism that he is actually able to lay his finger, in an extraordinarily consistent and perceptive manner, on one of the most vulnerable points of so much philosophy, which naturally operates with general concepts in order to explain what these concepts intend yet no longer actually reflects upon the relationship between the concept and what it is supposed to grasp.

Now I would just like to read you one more passage from Comte – this is the last one – in order to clarify the original conflict between philosophy and sociology, this time from the side of philosophy. Comte writes as follows: 'The theological stage ...' – but if you are to follow all this I must just remind you that he distinguishes three basic stages of development. This is Comte's famous law of three stages, which is supposed to govern the progress of reality, society and the human mind.[14] The first stage is the theological-dogmatic stage, the second is the metaphysical stage – where concepts take the place of dogmatically posited essential beings or agencies – and the third is the positive stage. This is the stage where our thought turns directly to society, operates by means of observation and classification, and basically models itself on the natural sciences – an approach which is now widely accepted as a matter of course in empirical sociology today. Thus the idea that the natural sciences should provide the model for empirical social thought, and that society itself represents a kind of nature, is something you already find here in Comte. I believe that I pointed out to you earlier how this reflects the way that society in this phase has already assumed such power and predominance over human beings that it has become something like a 'second nature', as Hegel specifically calls it.[15] We then come to believe that this 'second nature' can be observed and investigated as an objective reality, that is, as a reality that is independent of us human beings. But in a rather remarkable way the thought that this second nature is distinguished from that other nature, from first nature, precisely because it consists of us human beings, is forgotten or repressed. In other words, as subjects we are not just confronted with a radically different and separate object, for the object of the social sciences already involves the subject – human beings who seek truth – as a necessary and decisive element. You must keep all of this in mind if you really want to understand all Comte's talk about the theological, the metaphysical and the positive stages of thought. You will always find this characteristic slant in his work: that in spite of his confessedly scientific mentality he is always ready to flirt a little with the theological approach – in the name of the purely positive – basically in order to execrate speculative philosophy. Indeed it borders on the grotesque to see how in his later period Comte actually tries to develop a sort of positivist theology.[16] In other words, he derives from society certain static forms that are supposed to represent absolute concrete essential structures, although the thought never strikes him that this ultimately amounts to a gigantic tautology: in reality here society effectively just venerates itself, as indeed Durkheim later consistently argued in relation to all kinds of primitive societies, showing in detail how their religious ideas are really projections of their own collective spirit, or, in other words, precisely how society venerates itself in this way.[17] But it is a remarkable fact that, for a very long period of time, sociology has wavered over whether it should expressly recognize and criticize this process by which society venerates itself in and through its own ideas, or whether instead it should make its own positive contribution to this procedure, as I have briefly attempted to show you today that Comte tried to do.[18]

Now the last passage I am going to read for you today is this:

> The theological and metaphysical regimes, since they turned the human mind into the supposed source of universal explanations, gave speculative tendencies a presumptuous and overweening character that served only to remove them from the humble procedures of ordinary wisdom [i.e. from ordinary reason as we might say today]. Whereas everyday reason contented itself with observing events and thereby discovering certain relations that allow it to make predictions of a practical character, the pride of philosophy scorned such successes and expected the revelation of impenetrable mysteries from some kind of supernatural illumination. Sound philosophy on the other hand [i.e. Comte's own] replaces essential causes with real laws and connects its own speculations with easily understandable concepts.[19]

There are two things worth noting here. One is the charge of vanity, which positive thinking always likes to level against speculative thinking. Thus it is said that, if we take our own concepts, something that we have created, as the warrant or essence of truth, instead of humbly keeping to what reality offers us, we simply puff ourselves up immeasurably and take an illusory pleasure in what Nietzsche expressed positively when he claimed at the beginning of Zarathustra that he enjoyed his own spirit.[20] A human being who is truly free, who is not fettered in a positivistic sense, does take joy in thinking, can experience happiness whenever something is revealed that cannot just be read off from the facts that are presented to us. But here this is all reduced to a vain and selfish pleasure on the part of an individual who deems himself superior to every demand for solid and reliable insight. Now I will not deny that philosophical speculation involves the possibility of such self-glorification or self-aggrandisement, although the philosophers who are most often suspected of this are also the keenest to insist – perhaps because of this very danger – that the concept of the creative subject that is ultimately identical with the truth (and Kierkegaard once directly said that the subject is truth)[21] must also be distinguished from the feeling, contingent and merely empirical subject that every single individual is. But when you read Fichte, or also Hegel, or his arch-enemy Kierkegaard, you will probably also discover this undertone, and you will certainly encounter it in Nietzsche, and the positivist spirit has actually performed an enormous service by emphatically bringing out the element of vanity in the untrammelled philosophical spirit that has apparently cast off any relation to actual things. But this issue really has two sides to it. For the denunciation of the supposed vanity of philosophical thought can also become an ideology, an excuse for glorifying that which renounces thought and even presents its own obtuseness and intellectual inadequacy as the ultimate expression of the highest sense of responsibility where genuine knowledge is concerned. And since it remains easier not to learn anything in the world rather than to come to learn something in the world, this latter danger seems in the general intellectual condition of the age, in this present moment, to be more pressing than the danger of vanity or hubris which thinkers such as Comte have emphasized. But there is something very curious about vanity anyway. In the course of my life I have repeatedly observed that people who repress their vanity or their narcissism, and are so keen to adopt an emphatically objective attitude far removed from any suggestion of vanity, are actually even more haunted by the spectre of their own status and reputation than those who to some extent admit and reflect on their own vanity, if that is what it is, instead of denying it, and in this way reduce its hold. This is just a psychological point in passing rather than something I would like to pursue in more detail here.

Perhaps I could now just read you something of my own – hopefully without thereby incurring the charge of vanity myself; it is a passage which touches specifically on the problem that emerges in Comte at this point, and it comes from a piece about the relationship between sociology and empirical research which I contributed to the Festschrift for Helmuth Plessner;[22] I might just add that this piece, at least in part, provoked that controversy with König and Schelsky which encouraged me to give today's lecture in the particular form I have.[23] I quote: 'A researcher needs 10 per cent inspiration and 90 per cent perspiration' – this is what people always say, and it certainly captures the spirit of Comte and of positivism; but this saying,

> which is so eagerly quoted, is also small-minded and designed to prohibit thought. For a long time now the self-renouncing labour of the scholar has usually been to relinquish thoughts that he did not have anyway in return for poor remuneration. Today, when the better paid office chief has replaced the scholar, the lack of spirit is not only celebrated as a virtue of the team player devoid of vanity but already institutionalized through research strategies which can only regard any expression of individual spontaneity as an unwelcome source of interference. But the antithesis between sublime inspiration and painstaking research is itself absurd. Thoughts do not just descend on us but have to crystallize, even when they do emerge suddenly, through persistent and subterranean processes.[24]

And at this point I attempted to reveal – in an approach quite different from that we adopted today – through a fragmentary analysis of the process of intellectual production the questionable nature of this antithesis between bursts of inspiration, either glorified or despised as required, and the labour of detailed research, either glorified as a solid contribution to science or despised as mere pedantry, again as required. I tried to show how difficult it really is – when we seriously examine how insight and knowledge come about – to maintain this whole opposition in this rigid and congealed form. For we must recognize how these two aspects or moments mutually presuppose and condition each other, and how they both degenerate into a parody of themselves as soon as they are entirely separated from each other and each one is posited as absolute in its own right.

The second thing which I would like to draw to your attention is the use of terms such as 'sound' or 'healthy' or 'easily understandable' – the expressions that we just encountered in Comte and that already sound rather like Babbitt.[25] Thus the latter demands that all intellectual labour must be socially useful, must exclude all useless eccentric ideas, must be truly solid – solid also in the sense of proving serviceable within an existing social 'set-up' – and is certainly not supposed to satisfy any vain expectations in its own right. Terms such as 'sound' or 'healthy' effectively imply that the normative consciousness that governs such intellectual labour is a suitably adapted and non-deviating 'normal' consciousness, since such philosophy and sociology can naturally produce no other criterion of what is 'sound', 'healthy' or 'sick' than that provided by the statistical average. Our own accommodation to this statistical average has already been smuggled in here as the criterion of truth or as the criterion of the quality of scientific research. When we are told that our thinking must always be 'easily understandable', you will find that consciousness as it is, as currently encountered in society, has been made the criterion. This has obvious implications for our intellectual and cultural life: since some idiotic film or other is easily understandable, whereas a serious theoretical claim or a significant work of art is not, a higher value is then accorded to 'the easily understandable'; and today, when the culture industry has successfully coalesced with sociological research, the consequences of this demand for whatever proves easily understandable have been driven to extremes. In saying this to you now I am not offering up some sentimental and culturally conservative lament or some kind of Jeremiad with regard to these things. I would not even be tempted to do so, since it is quite clear to me that such a lament would be entirely powerless in the face of the power of these social tendencies. Thus I am certainly not appealing to your vanity here, or to any sense that we, as an elite, are somehow beyond this demand for what is easily understandable. On the contrary, I would like you to recognize that the notion of the elite itself also belongs to the same store of ideas, the same conceptual world, that is reflected in such expressions as 'sound' or 'healthy' thought and 'easily understandable' ideas. And I realize that the institutional bodies that see the discovery and communication of results as their central task also ascribe a particular importance to the sound and healthy minds of those that they co-opt for their activities. But I simply point this out in passing. What I am really trying to bring out here is something else: in the kind of thinking where the claim to scientific status and the pathos associated with it is so powerful – as it clearly is in this founding document or positivist manifesto of Auguste Comte – we should notice how an essentially normative concept such as that of 'the easily understandable' is surreptitiously introduced at a particularly important point of the argument, even while sociology here conspicuously fails to do what one must surely expect from this discipline. In other words, we would expect sociology to investigate consciousness itself, to consider the social conditions of the consciousness that it takes to be normative, namely the social conditions of the sound or universal human understanding in question. And I believe that this is the strongest kind of argument in principle – for I am simply offering you a model here – which can be fielded against positivistic thought in general, namely that in a sense it is not positivistic enough. In other words, it contents itself with a very particular set of categories – those it requires to provide a stable foundation for itself – without analysing these categories themselves in social terms. Thus you find that, when they say that something must be easily understandable or generally intelligible, people are appealing to a general consciousness which is not some inborn or natural human faculty of reason, not some pure logos supposedly independent of all particular conditions – and Comte himself, of course, would certainly be the last person to claim such a thing. On the contrary, they are appealing to a consciousness that for its part is socially produced. What is introduced here as a criterion for science and thereby for society is itself something that has arisen within society, something the social defects and origins of which can be analysed. This is the reason, if I may point this out here, why I undertook to develop a 'theory of half-culture' in a contribution that was presented last year at the Berlin conference of the German Society for Sociology and that has been published in the *Proceedings* of the society.[26] In this piece I specifically attempted to examine categories such as 'the healthy' or 'the easily understandable', categories which are treated as normative for social science, and to explain them in social terms. In other words, I tried to show that the 'normal consciousness' presupposed here is not really normal at all but is actually a product of social debilitation and oppression.

Now I would hate you to suspect here – to say this once again – that I am just digging up things which are merely arbitrary or incidental, merely *lapsus linguae* on Comte's part, things which are of no great significance for the general attitude or consciousness that is at issue here. I shall entirely disregard the fact that all these themes which I have just extracted from Comte will surely be quite familiar to you in your everyday experience of intellectual life and that, in a sense, you will have seen and heard all this before. But I would like to draw your attention to this point in particular: the intellectual approach which Comte effectively inaugurated now claims to have found exemplary scientific formulation in the contemporary theory of logical positivism which has presented these things, from the mathematical point of view, in the most advanced and sophisticated way. And precisely here, in this logical positivism, we find that one of the criteria for meaningful propositions is that they can be presented in terms of everyday language[27] – so that his theory too comes very close to the category of the easily understandable or the readily intelligible. Here we see how a category such as 'everyday language', fraught as it is with innumerable social presuppositions, unwittingly appears as if it were somehow before or beyond society, namely in terms of logical constructions. Yet it is exactly here that a positive science, and specifically sociology, would have every reason to be sceptical and would certainly wish to subject this category to further critical examination. With this I would like to conclude, for now, what I wanted to say about the structure of sociological thought in terms of its opposition to philosophical thought. And here I have claimed the right to reflect upon these things, as I believe we should have to reflect upon them from the perspective of philosophy. But do not imagine for a moment that I intend to stop and rest up at this point. For I shall soon go on, in a very similar fashion, to reflect upon the anti-sociologism that is so characteristic of philosophy. And I hope to be able to show you that this antithesis is wholly unfruitful and thereby offer a possible way for you to get beyond these rigid conceptions and oppositions. To begin with, however, I shall continue this structural analysis of some fundamental problems of social positivism in the next lecture by looking very briefly at Emile Durkheim's specific criticisms of Comte. This will also give me an opportunity to bring out certain fundamental problems of positivism in general, and particularly its paradoxical attempt to produce a kind of thinking which effectively lacks concepts.

LECTURE 5
24 May 1960

Ladies and gentlemen,[1]
[...][2] [T]his is what 'facts' mean here – I shall come back to this later on when I have occasion to present this concept in more detail. We are talking about facts which, above all, reveal a certain character of resistance and impenetrability with respect to the subject. Where the understanding of the subject is concerned, and also – even more decisively for Durkheim – where the behaviour of the subject is concerned, we are talking about '*des choses*', about 'things' in the sense that, for Durkheim, '*des faits sociales sont les choses*'.[3] In these facts and things the individual human being encounters resistance, comes up against a solid mass, which he can do nothing about and which is stronger than the will or understanding of the individual subject. Thus, for Durkheim, as you should clearly bear in mind right from the start, the criterion for what he calls the social as such is precisely this distinctive character of impenetrability, of something set over against us: it is this which manifests what we should really regard as the object of sociology, as distinct from the field of psychology in particular.

Durkheim continues as follows: 'Comte, we have to admit, certainly declared that social phenomena are natural facts, facts which are subject to natural laws' – by which Durkheim means the causal-mechanical laws of nature. For this reason, so Durkheim claims, Comte 'implicitly recognizes the character of these phenomena as a thing [*chose*].'[4] It should be pointed out in passing that this is not entirely accurate, since, as you may remember, Comte's concept of social facts also, and above all, includes laws such as the dynamic law of progress or the static law of order, and you cannot of course really regard a law that always holds for the thing-like elements that are covered by it as itself a 'thing'. In this context, Durkheim is clearly interpreting his intellectual ancestor Comte rather freely. Durkheim goes on: 'For in nature there is nothing but things [*choses*].'[5] Now for the philosophers among you I should point out that the standpoint rather dogmatically presupposed by Durkheim here – and from this you can easily see how closely the philosophical and the sociological problematics are really entwined – is the standpoint of naive realism. The idea that actually there is nothing in nature but things blithely ignores the Kantian problematic, or indeed the epistemological problematic in general, with a mere flick of the pen, or rather violently suppresses it altogether. In other words, the conflict between sociology and philosophy that we are interested in – and it is probably a good idea to note this specifically here – arises partly because the sphere in which sociology moves as a particular science is already a constituted one from the epistemological or philosophical point of view. Thus the epistemological problems that prevail within this sphere are very different from those that arise for epistemologies or theories of knowledge in the narrower sense. So you do not find that sociologists say something such as: 'We are not worried about the general epistemological problems regarding the constitution of our domain and we shall simply keep to what is already constituted here.' On the contrary, they extrapolate from the specific character of the particular science without further self-reflection, as if the epistemological problematic were thereby effectively eliminated or simply suspended. You might say therefore that this just reflects the division of labour between the individual science that is positively concerned with the facts, on the one side, and the self-reflective examination of the epistemological problem of constitution, on the other. It reflects it in the distorted sense that the individual science, relieved of the epistemological problem of constitution, now believes that it has somehow dealt with the epistemological problematic through its empirical investigation of the facts and has thereby decided the whole issue. I think that it is really important for you to reflect on this relatively simple circumstance, which simply results from the division of labour involved in different disciplines, since part of the constant baying between philosophy and sociology can basically be traced back to this misunderstanding, if I may put it in this rather innocuous way.

Durkheim then continues: 'But when Comte attempts, on the basis of these philosophical generalities, to apply his principle and to construct the science that is supposed to be implied by it, he ends up taking ideas as the object of his investigation.'[6] I shall come back to this story about 'ideas' later, but I should like to draw your attention right here to a problem that is already involved in this formulation. Now in general I would rather try and develop the so-called big problems of philosophy and sociology micrologically by reference to particular passages than by offering you gigantic overviews of the whole scene, an approach in which the essential and specific differences usually only disappear from sight. The equivocation we are concerned with here lies in the word 'idea'. It is of course true that Comte, like any thinker or writer, deals with concepts – in other words, operates with concepts. This is just as true for the good Durkheim, as I shall soon show you, as it is for Comte himself. But the word 'idea' is ambiguous here, for on the one hand it serves to designate concepts, unities involved in facts, conceptual forms and structures – in short, the conceptuality we cannot help deploying when we make use of language at all. On the other hand, it can look as if Comte's sociology is also concerned with 'ideas' in the way, for example, that intellectual and cultural history are. Thus when we write a history of the idea of progress, or the idea of freedom, or the idea of humanity, or the idea of the nation, or whatever it may be, we are naturally talking about ideas in a quite different sense. Given this equivocation, Durkheim treats Comte as if he were really a kind of cultural and intellectual historian, as if he were specifically concerned with the history of ideas, such as the idea of progress, whereas this kind of interest – which was certainly characteristic of Dilthey[7] – was really quite foreign to Comte. For when Comte spoke of progress he was following in the footsteps of his teacher Saint-Simon and thinking primarily in very concrete and tangible terms about the progress of the technological forces of production and thus of the growing quantity of goods and commodities that have become available to human beings in the process.

Durkheim continues: 'The principal object of Comtean sociology is in truth the progress of humanity in time.'[8] Here again I must say that this is expressed a little bit demagogically, insofar as the concept of 'progress' – and those of you who have any knowledge about the history of dogma will already know this – is only one aspect in Comte's general theory and is balanced in turn by the complementary concept of 'order'. And I believe it would hardly be going too far to say that the real pathos of Comte's thought, the ultimate interest behind it, derives more from his concern with social order than from the idea of progress. Indeed, the latter already appears here in something of the problematic and ambiguous light that has accompanied the concept of progress from the later nineteenth century and right up to our own time. I would also like to say, in all fairness to him, that at this point Comte is more complex and differentiated in approach than he appears to be from Durkheim's account. The latter says: 'Il part de cette idée.' I think Durkheim means that 'he starts from this idea', where the 'il' refers to Comte himself. Thus he says: 'He starts from this idea that there is a continuous and uninterrupted development of the human species, one which consists in the ever more complete realization of human nature' – he uses the word '*réalisation*': today we would probably speak of *Selbstverwirklichung* or 'self-realization', if I may be permitted to use a German word that is as unattractive as the French here – 'and the problem that he addresses is that of discovering the order' – i.e. the law-like character – 'governing this evolution, this development.'[9] Now the sentence that follows is really very interesting, and I would like you to pay particularly close attention to it, since we shall have to discuss it in more detail as we proceed. Durkheim says: 'To suppose' – to stipulate, or we might even say to make the fundamental assumption – 'that this evolution' – i.e. this continuous self-realization of humanity – 'exists just means that its reality can be established' – i.e. can properly be verified – 'only once science has been established, once scientific investigation has been carried out.'[10] And from this Durkheim now concludes somewhat boldly, I have to say, in a way that hardly seems logically compelling: 'Thus' – and the 'thus' is key here – 'we cannot even make this progress into an object of investigation unless we take it as a mental conception [*conception de l'esprit*] rather than as a thing.'[11] Now Durkheim's conclusion is clearly not compelling, since no one can possibly object to our constructing social progress as an 'ideal type' – if I may invoke the conceptual apparatus of Max Weber here – to determining specific criteria for this ideal type, and then comparing empirical reality with the latter to see if that reality corresponds to it. If we are to shun any form of concept that is not already saturated in facts and observations, as Durkheim does in this passage, this effectively and literally amounts to sabotaging insight and knowledge itself, for without such conceptual anticipation then anything such as the empirical domain, anything such as empirical research, is not conceivable at all. Thus, for example, if you do not have any concept of the family, of what the family is, of the crisis in which it finds itself – according to whether one holds that it will inevitably succumb to this crisis or will actually display its resilience and overcome the crisis in question (and both claims, as we know, have been defended with substantial arguments in our own time)[12] – I repeat, if you do not have some such conceptual construction at your disposal, it is quite impossible to undertake any empirical investigation regarding the family at all. In other words, you can observe something here that is very characteristic of the sphere of positivism as a whole, but especially so of the positivism defended by practitioners of the natural sciences. What I mean is this: as soon as they begin to philosophize, they always prove more Catholic than the pope; they prove more hostile to philosophy and much more hostile to the world of concepts than they ever can be at the moment when they are actually pursuing their investigations. The natural scientists and the sociologists who carry out their factual investigations, given the structure of the sciences and disciplines in which they are respectively involved, are quite unable to maintain the kind of ascetic posture they preach with regard to all thinking and cannot remain true to the cult of observation alone, a cult which is itself the product of a certain abstraction.

Durkheim now goes on: 'In reality what we are talking about here' – i.e. the idea of progress – 'is a completely subjective notion, for this progress of humanity does not exist at all in reality. That which exists, and that alone which is given to observation' – the concept of the given, *le donné*, plays an absolutely enormous role here – 'are just individual societies.' Here you can already see something like Spengler's form of cultural pluralism[13] *in statu* pupillari,[14] as it appears in a text that is seemingly formulated in very rigorous scientific terms. For Durkheim is referring here to 'individual societies that are born, develop, and die quite independently of one another.'[15] Now of course one could also instantly object that this is actually a thesis that neglects the facts.[16] We might argue, for example, that the origin of Christian civilization in the West and the decline of classical civilization are not completely independent processes which have nothing to do with each other, that on the contrary these civilizations are intertwined in all kinds of ways and that the one is entirely inconceivable without the other. At this point, therefore, we could already object to Durkheim that the pluralism he stipulates in principle here is itself somewhat unresponsive to the facts and is insufficiently self-reflective in character. On the basis of this theory, Durkheim later goes on to attack Comte's law of three stages, which we discussed in the course of the last two lectures.[17] What Durkheim says is this:

> Quelque grands services que Comte ait rendus à la philosophie sociale, les termes dans lesquels il pose le problème sociologique ne diffèrent pas des précédents. Aussi, sa fameuse loi des trois états n'a-t-elle rien d'un rapport de causalité; fût-elle exacte, elle n'est et ne peut être qu'empirique. C'est un coup d'oeil sommaire sur l'histoire écoulée du

genre humanin. C'est tout à fait arbitrairement que Comte considère le troisième état comme l'état définitif de l'humanité. Qui nous dit qu'il n'en surgira pas un autre dans l'avenir? Enfin, la loi qui domine la sociologie de M. Spencer ne paraît pas être d'une autre nature.[18]

Now we don't need to spend any time at this point on the critique of Spencer,[19] and I shall just offer a quick translation of the passage for you now: 'Although Comte performed a great service for social philosophy or sociological theory, the concepts' – we should probably translate this specifically as 'categories' – 'in terms of which he poses the problem of sociology do not really differ from those of his' – more or less metaphysical – 'predecessors. Nor does his famous law of three stages have any relation to causality. If it were exact, it could be nothing but an empirical law' – as indeed Comte would certainly have claimed – 'but with a summary glance at history' – or with a grandiose overview of history, as we would probably say – 'this concept is just imposed on the human species. Moreover, Comte quite arbitrarily regards the third stage as the definitive one for humanity, although nobody can say that a further stage could not arise out of it in the future.'

If you just think about what is being said here, you will find that Durkheim's entire objection to Comte essentially amounts to the claim that he employs concepts that cannot be verified in detail and in every case by reference to empirical facts. But I believe that what we should draw from this, and what I have already tried to show you here in a rudimentary way through the translation I have just provided, is of course that no linguistic expression whatsoever, let alone a scientific discipline that involves processes of classification and progressive generalization, is conceivable if it dispenses with concepts altogether. And even the observation of the '*donnés*', or the givens, that we are supposed to be dealing with is completely inconceivable without reference to the conceptual dimension. Comte reproached idealist philosophy – and you may remember that in the last lecture I said there was something right about this – with a tendency to hypostasize its concepts, i.e. to treat these concepts as if they somehow enjoyed an existence independently of the objects or the material to which they are applied. But we can see that the uninhibited positivism endorsed by Durkheim also tends to hypostasize the concept of the *donnés*, or the facts; in other words, it treats the facts as if they were something we could identify and interpret without any conceptual mediation whatsoever. But just as there are no concepts, or no concepts that can be described as true, unless they are fulfilled, unless they can be corroborated in relation to some material content and refreshed or regenerated with reference to such content, so too there are no facts that we can simply gather and interpret independently of the relevant concepts. For I should like to point out to you here, if I may be allowed a brief excursion into intellectual history, that this whole and, in a sense, very extreme theoretical position of Durkheim's contradicts his own practice – which ultimately led to a large-scale theory involving the explanation of social phenomena in terms of collective spirit. You can probably understand the emergence of this theory and the enormous influence that it exercised only if you appreciate the relevant cultural and intellectual context. You have to remember the decisive controversy that preoccupied the French intellectual world around 1890 or 1900, let us say specifically around 1900, namely the contrasting positions adopted by Bergson and Durkheim.[20] Thus Bergson employed a metaphysical concept of intuition in order to criticize that concept of fixed and rigid fact which is presupposed by the natural sciences, and therefore he also insisted on a quite different aspect of human knowledge. Durkheim, on the other hand, brought the whole weight of the tradition of the natural sciences in particular to bear against Bergson himself – a fact, incidentally, that is not without a certain irony, since it was actually Bergson who came out of this very tradition and in reality enjoyed a closer relationship to the natural sciences than Durkheim himself. But we might say that in Bergson the sphere of the mind – and indeed of the mind conceived as independent of the entire causal-mechanical structure based upon the classification of facts – is itself hypostasized in a way that is very similar to the manner in which the facts are hypostasized in Durkheim. And we can probably only understand the one-sidedness, let us call it, or a certain narrowness, that characterizes the two great theoretical minds in France around this time, and that both exhibit in their own way, if we see each thinker as a corrective to the other. Although I should also say here that we cannot restore a truth or a philosophical concept that has broken apart into separate halves merely by adding together or recombining the fractured elements. For we would surely find ourselves in a very sorry predicament if we tried to produce the truth about society by appealing to some kind of synthesis of these elements.

The view that I have talking to you about here, the really crucial issue and central argument of the passage from Durkheim I just read out for you, is thus the idea of *chosisme*, namely the idea that science is essentially concerned with things.[21] Let me just say *en passant* that, in comparison to the epistemological positivism that prevailed at the time, namely the so-called empirio-criticism that was defended by Ernst Mach, Avenarius and their followers,[22] this doctrine of *chosisme* is a remarkably heterodox or heretical one. For they would certainly have claimed that the 'things' in question here are not 'given' to us at all, whereas it was precisely the givenness of things that Lenin, as is well known, so strongly emphasized in his famous polemic against the empirio-critical school.[23] In this respect, we might say, he was actually Durkheimian, although he would certainly be turning in his grave to hear himself described in this way. And it was the real empiricists, by contrast, who always said that what is given to us, what is immediately given to us, is nothing but the facts of consciousness, and that we only really know anything about things once we synthesize these facts of consciousness and thereby come to form regular and law-like connections which then possess a certain stability. I mentioned earlier that, from an epistemological perspective, there is a specifically dogmatic or, if you will, a pre-critical or naive-realist element that has found its way into this theory of Durkheim's which takes itself to be so scientific. But, as we usually find in such cases, in thinkers to whom we must concede considerable intellectual powers, and who, like Durkheim, possessed an astonishing wealth of material knowledge, the genuine problems are actually hidden in conceptual errors and false inferences of various kinds. That is why I would like to take this opportunity to say something about this problem of *chosisme*. I pointed out that the criterion for what constitutes *'un fait social comme chose'*, a social fact considered as a thing, which is precisely what sociology is supposed to address for Durkheim, is a certain impenetrability to the understanding, is the resistance which the social domain exerts with respect to human activity. Thus once a certain custom or practice is established and we act against it in some way or other, then we immediately get to feel the consequences in the sharpest and most disagreeable way, even if what we have done in this case is not especially reprehensible or has actually caused no serious harm to anyone. You could just try the following social experiment: if you find yourself in the company of people who basically share and conform to the prevailing social ideas and attitudes, and you venture to express a view that seriously differs from the established one, you will instantly encounter the kind of resistance I am talking about, as well as a kind of ostracism and defamation which corresponds precisely to the state of affairs that Durkheim was thematizing here. And indeed this was something that was also discovered as the real object of sociology quite independently of Durkheim, and roughly at the same time, in the context of American sociology with Sumner's book *Folkways*.[24] This is certainly also connected in part with the entire movement of *Jugendstil*, with the world of Ibsen for example, where the self-emancipating individual distances himself from what Ibsen called the compact majority[25] and thus in one way or another directly challenges the existing mores of society, the *'faits sociaux comme de choses'*. We might also point out, and it has indeed been pointed out before, that Durkheim, who came of age in France after the 1870s in a somewhat unfavourable situation as a French Jew, really came to experience society in the way that we can also essentially experience it today, namely as something that hurts us. Society is there where we feel the friction, where we come up against an obstacle, where our own impulses are subjected to controls that are stronger than we are. It is something to which we ourselves certainly belong, something that reaches into the innermost depths of ourselves, but with which we still cannot identify, and which we still cannot regard as our own. I believe that Durkheim performed a very great service, and one that is certainly not sufficiently appreciated today, when he laid such extraordinary emphasis upon this dimension of social existence, something which completely escaped the attention of positivism, and essentially made it into the criterion of sociology itself – although this also immediately led him into some of the same confusions and complications as Comte before him. From the perspective of the kind of empirically minded sociology that developed after Durkheim, this fundamental experience of the social dimension itself as resistance, as basically repressive, came to look like a prejudice, and the attempt was made to cleanse sociology completely of what had actually defined the *'faits sociaux comme de choses'* for Durkheim and to get along without this conception altogether.

I have already pointed out that, in a sense, this construction of *'chosisme'* was developed on the basis of an analogy with physical nature. Thus the attributes which Durkheim confers on the *'choses'* are ultimately the same attributes which in earlier times, before the theory of electrons and so on, had been ascribed to *res extensa*[26] or to the primary qualities of things, as in Locke for example.[27] Now if you think about this, you can already see the model for this *'chosisme'*: it is the impenetrability of nature, that which cannot be understood or constructed in terms of concepts, which is being transferred to society here. The considerable theoretical significance of this is that society is registered as nature in Durkheim. In other words, he not only wishes to apply the conceptual apparatus of the natural sciences, the processes of observation and classification, to the field of society – something which had already been done long before by others, as I pointed out before – but finds something like the impenetrable character of nature in the very concept of society. In this light, society itself now seems just as hardened, just as thing-like, as first or primary nature is. In other words, to point this out for you here as the theme for our next session, society in its hardened and reified state is, on Durkheim's theory, really the only proper object that sociology possesses, even if Durkheim himself fails to reflect upon the mechanisms of reification. There is something quite right about this, for society is indeed reified; but there is also something wrong about it, for Durkheim not only absolutizes this reification but even allows it to furnish the criteria for the procedures of sociology as a science. To this extent, therefore, what is demanded of science is not to disclose reality but – to take up our earlier remarks – simply to adapt to it.

LECTURE 6
31 May 1960

Ladies and gentlemen,
Despite the rather long break since our last session,[1] you may recall how I said on that occasion that the principal objection raised by Durkheim, from the perspective of the intermediate phase of positivism he represents, against Comte and the older form of positivism associated with him can be expressed as follows. He complained that the concepts employed by Comte were not strictly derived from the field of observation but were developed rather freely as conceptual anticipations that cannot really be justified in scientific terms. Now there are two things you can learn in this connection, and this is basically why I am focusing on these two contrasting positivist authors in terms of their relation to philosophy in the context of these lectures. In the first place, you can learn that the trial to which sociology submits philosophy, one which in a certain sense we may simply extrapolate to cover the entire process of the European Enlightenment, actually has no beginning and no end. In other words, you can learn, from the perspective of this kind of positivism, that there is no form of thinking whatsoever that cannot somehow be accused of indulging in metaphysics, and that there must surely be something not quite right about this form of argumentation which finds itself intrinsically afflicted by a sort of 'bad infinite' in this way. Now I have already drawn your attention to what is not quite right here, and in a sense it is something extremely simple. It is just the point that thinking without concepts, and thus also that thinking without anticipations, a thinking that does not move

beyond experience, beyond the merely observed, beyond the domain of 'protocol sentences', cannot in principle be avoided. Without concepts there cannot even be order in a positivist sense, although no concept is ever wholly fulfilled by that which it subsumes. And that difference between conceptual theses and the claim which concepts possess within a positivist intellectual framework, one which has characterized sociology for the last hundred and fifty years, will give rise again and again to the process we have indicated, where one thinker will berate the preceding thinker as a theologian in disguise. This can easily make the whole process itself appear extremely confusing, indeed almost maddening, although we should try and think it through very carefully rather than just swallowing such a narrative. I say that we should not simply be confused by it, and thus just reject it out of hand, for it cannot be denied that the sort of criticism which Durkheim directs at Comte is also based on something true. In other words, the kind of grandiose structure, the imposing Veronese-style fresco, that the good Comte has designed *contre cœur* is actually incompatible with the concept of positivism that he himself defends. And it is also true that the force of that aspect of the Enlightenment through which it constantly consumes its own predecessors has something irresistible about it. Even at the opposite pole of such thinking, namely in Hegel, we find that the irresistibility of the process of the Enlightenment, and thus also of positivism, is illuminated by philosophy itself, when for example Hegel speaks in this connection of 'the fury of disappearing',[2] of the irresistible power which consigns every fixed content, every objectively binding content, to a kind of destruction as soon as it is rigorously confronted with experience.

But, having said all this, I would also like to warn you against a mistaken approach which I may inadvertently have encouraged by the way in which I treated Durkheim's ideas earlier. We should take care in principle not to make things too easy for ourselves, especially when we are dealing with thinkers or texts in an explicitly critical way. In other words, the process of criticism also involves a certain degree of generosity. Thus when we hold Durkheim firmly to account, as I have done up till now for the sake of precision, because he thunders against '*les concepts*' that are deployed by Comte even though he too makes very emphatic use of concepts, such as the concept of a social or collective mind which plays a central role in Durkheim's mature theory of society, and in the thought of his circle this may sound rather obvious, or like bringing owls to Athens, as they say. It looks a bit like the kind of criticisms that, God help us, we all too often come across in the context of official examinations.

We must always give some breathing space, as it were, to the things that we are dealing with in a critical way, and I say this particularly for the sake of your own critical work. Otherwise we risk falling into a very inferior sort of over-literal criticism and an overly familiar approach with regard to the object. What I am saying is that this aspect of the issue that I pointed out to you, namely that Durkheim himself also operates with concepts, can hardly be something that somehow escaped such a perceptive and epistemologically aware sociologist as he was. In such cases this is not really a question of 'fairness', which is surely not a genuine category where intellectual matters are concerned, but more a question of what I would almost like to call intellectual economy. Thus, in cases where we seem to come across egregious blunders in the context of otherwise highly significant intellectual achievements, we should never simply rest content by triumphantly exposing such things but, rather, should try and get behind what was meant by these particular formulations, even when they seem as limited and rudimentary as the ones which I presented to you in our last session. Thus I would suggest to you that what really motivated Durkheim's criticisms of Comte, what he really meant to say in this connection, is that he finds that, after all, Comte has ascribed a kind of overall meaning to history, and therefore if not exactly a Hegelian – for Comte actually had precious little interest in Hegel – he was still somehow in thrall to the old metaphysical tradition. For this tradition proceeded on the basis of the reality or substantive nature of concepts and interpreted individual existing things in terms of these concepts. In this sense it was always inclined to ascribe the content implied by those concepts to the phenomena themselves as their inner meaning. Thus what is basically at issue here is the controversy between the idea that history has a kind of meaning and the idea that it does not, and Durkheim can quite rightly and plausibly object to Comte that, as a positivist, he is obligated to reject the notion of history having a meaning, even though he does bestow a kind of meaning on history and society precisely by maintaining that history exhibits a coherent and persisting structure and even demonstrates the concept of progress.

I believe that this really takes us to the heart of the controversy between sociology and philosophy, and I would like to bring you to the point where you do not feel that you have to plump for one side or the other in this controversy but can actually recognize the serious issue that underlies this entire question. Thus on the one side we have a view that would on no account be cheated of the idea of an ultimate meaning, since the idea that human existence itself is utterly meaningless is almost impossible to bear. Now this is hardly a convincing argument, for we cannot validly conclude from the usefulness or agreeability of a certain idea or thing to its genuine reality, as Nietzsche especially has shown in a particularly powerful way.[3] On the other hand, the idea also finds support insofar as we are aware that, in examining reality, we find certain universal and persisting structures in relation to which particular things really appear as specific details in which the universal in question is reflected. And to start with we are simply terrified – and I would say legitimately terrified – by the crassness, the obtuseness, the sheer stupidity of the idea that we can only simply register the facts as they present themselves without even attempting to disclose what actually stands behind them. That is one side of the question, but there are also extremely weighty and serious considerations that speak for the opposite side of the question, and this is why the argument between philosophy and sociology that we are concerned with here is a serious one. This is not some merely apparent or superficial conflict that we could banish from the world by projecting a supposedly higher and superior intellectual sphere for one of the terms involved. For here we are talking about a quite genuine and legitimate antithesis which thought cannot simply avoid or instantly resolve. The pathos, if I may call it this, which attends the other side of the question is the pathos of the position which will not allow itself to be duped or taken in. I would almost like to say, if I am even going to employ the category of meaning, which is a secularized theological category, that this pathos suggests that we do greater honour to the idea of such meaning when we do not actually seek it in the world of hopeless, ephemeral and broken existence, when we hold it back from that world, than we do when we still attempt to bestow a meaning on what currently exists – something which can always degenerate into an exercise in apologetics. Here we face an aporia, for, if we possess no idea of such meaning, we cannot even name that lack of meaning which the positivist approach requires in the cause of truth. On the other hand, however, every attempt to transform such meaning into something factual or actual, i.e. to ascribe meaning to existence as it is, is itself ideological and inevitably condemned to failure. I believe that you must recognize this basic question at issue between philosophy and sociology – and what I am really trying to do in these lectures is to address one single question rather than two different fields – and think it through in the most resolute way possible. Otherwise one runs the danger of either clinging remorselessly to the pedantic accumulation of mere material or to the pathetic delusion of digging for meaning, to borrow an expression of Max Weber's.[4] And this means that you must be quite clear that the two schools of thought involved here actually do exercise a very serious criticism of each other. In other words, sociology is quite right to challenge any metaphysical construction and ask what right it possibly has to ascribe such meaning to history with all its sufferings and its meaninglessness. On the other hand, philosophy can of course equally challenge sociology and point out that, if it lacks the relevant concepts, if it lacks the thought of a possibility against which existing reality needs to be measured, then it is also incapable of grasping the real world itself. In this case sociology does not comprehend a thing but sits motionless before this reality like a surly counter clerk who simply registers all the details.

For now I just want to present this problem to you as I have done. But already here today I would like at least to help you get a little beyond this extremely crass alternative. Thus I would like you to notice that the concept of meaning I have employed here, and which may also suffice to characterize the nub of the opposition between Comte and Durkheim, is still too undifferentiated in itself. In other words, the concept of meaning is beset with equivocations, for it involves many different senses which we must take care to distinguish if we are to have any thought of dealing with this aporia, this seemingly irresolvable contradiction, which I have presented to you today. Thus, on the one side, the notion of 'meaning' may suggest, for example, the search for something hidden, something positive, some kind of justification that is to be found within individual existing things, that shines through them as it were, and by virtue of which all that exists, and especially the realm of society, reveals itself as essentially meaningful. I should say in passing that it is surely one of the paradoxes of Comte's philosophy that, while he certainly denies the idea of such meaning in the sense of some preordained or superordinate structure, he nonetheless intends to justify reality as it now is. When earlier on I presented you with a kind of metaphysical ideal type for positivist thought, I may perhaps have proceeded a little too faithfully, for precisely that consciousness of a pure negativity, of the evacuated meaning of mere facts, which I regarded as the justification of positivist thought itself, is generally quite lacking in the positivists of today. For they tend to be utterly content with themselves and to feel completely at home in their world bereft of meaning, and even to rejoice over the elimination of every meaningful aspect or feature as if this elimination were meaning itself. What a true and legitimate critique would have to hold against positivist thought as a whole is probably not so much that it fails for its part to envisage anything positively meaningful, but that it does not reflect upon what Kierkegaard called the condition of objective despair[5] that finds expression in its own intellectual outlook on things. In other words, positivism has no metaphysical insight into its lack of metaphysics. This lack of self-consciousness, of critical self-reflection, is in our view of the matter a much more telling objection to positivism than that raised by the idealistic thinkers who would typically reproach the latter for lacking any sense for higher things, or for eternal values, or whatever else they like to invoke. Now the contrary or second sense of 'meaning', which you must clearly distinguish from the first, is the one which really comes off badly in narrow and unreflective positivism. This is the sense of a comprehensive context or interconnection as this is reflected in the individual and the particular. I have already given some idea of how this is to be understood. Thus we can say, for example, that the meaning of some particular forms of social behaviour lies in the exchange relation that objectively underlies them, without the individuals in question being or needing to be specifically conscious of this, and without their deliberately or expressly engaging in this exchange relation. In a certain sense they are only acting under the compulsion of this relation; it determines what they do and, to that extent, is objectively implied in everything they do, even if they would not for their part think of their action in these terms. I believe that this second sense of meaning, from the sociological point of view, is simply connected in the first place with the way that as social beings we live within a social system that precedes us and largely determines us in a variety of ways. And it is this second concept of meaning that basically escapes positivism in its eagerness to repudiate the first concept of meaning. This is why positivism ends up literally not seeing the wood for the trees, in other words, not seeing society for the social facts. And this, in turn, tends to prove extremely detrimental as far as the character of society as currently constituted is concerned. That is all I wanted to say for the moment about the situation regarding the problem of philosophy and sociology, as we have perhaps managed to elucidate it somewhat up to this point.

But now I would like to look more closely at Durkheim's concept of *chosisme*, which he specifically mobilized against Comte in the passage that I interpreted for you earlier. Here again I would warn you not to dismiss this problem all too easily, for those of you who are studying the human and social sciences may readily be tempted to say: 'Well, this is obviously a crude reapplication of concepts derived from the natural sciences and simply transfers the idea of solid and impenetrable matter that once belonged to those sciences to the field of the human and social sciences. But we have long since ceased to believe in this kind of thing even in the context of the natural sciences, and anyway the theory of knowledge has long since shown that this crude, unreflective and unmediated conception of matter has peculiar problems of its own.' Nonetheless, I would ask you to join me and think rather more closely about this concept of *chosisme*. I have already mentioned the name of Max Weber on several occasions. As far as modern or, rather, pre-modern sociology is concerned, namely the sociology of our parents' generation, it is precisely here that the crucial difference between Max Weber and Durkheim is to be located – and in this connection I take the view that anyone who studies sociology today must certainly know something about the great controversies of that period. Weber claimed that the specific task of sociology itself was to 'understand' social processes, to make these processes intelligible to systematic investigation as something that is meaningful in its own right.[6] Durkheim, on the other hand, seemingly in complete agreement with the tradition of the natural sciences in the West, challenged this sort of approach. What motivated him in this regard was simply the problem of projection: wherever we believe that we understand something, we achieve this understanding by translating what is to be understood in terms of our own categories and our own experiences; in other words, we turn the object we encounter into ourselves, into the subject. Thus we are always in danger of putting our own image of ourselves, whether this is a wish-fulfilling image or whatever image it may be, in the place of that object which it is our task as scientific investigators precisely to cognize purely as such. But in addition Durkheim also has another very good reason for his approach, as I have already suggested to you, namely that distinctively opaque, compulsive and oppressive character of the *faits sociaux*, of society itself, which makes itself felt whenever we run up against it, and which does not really permit this kind of identification with ourselves, this kind of translation into 'the native land' of our own truth. To this extent, therefore, Durkheim's thought stands in emphatic contradiction to the entire German tradition as this is represented, apart from Max Weber, by the name of Dilthey, who did not regard himself as a sociologist at all, and by the name of Ernst Troeltsch.[7] And I believe that, generally for us here in Germany, despite the American-style scientific trends that have made themselves felt more recently, the suggestive power of that older German tradition of the human and social sciences is still extraordinarily strong. So strong, indeed, that it is very salutary for you to recognize the full seriousness of the objection to 'understandability' that finds clear expression in Durkheim's '*chosisme*'.

Now the model for the concept of 'understanding' itself was drawn from the field of individual psychology, as will soon become very clear to you and as has indeed already been suggested by what I said earlier. It is not just in the context of Dilthey's theory that the notions of 'understanding' (*Verstehen*) and 'empathy' (*Einfühlung*) are connected, for they are also remarkably closely related to each other in reality more generally. And we find a kind of empathetic understanding wherever I believe, as an individual psychological subject, that I am genuinely capable of comprehending the actions of other human beings – and in the case of sociology we are talking about social action, either the action of groups or the socially determined action of individuals. Now it is interesting to observe here that Max Weber was not entirely comfortable at this very point – in spite of the contrast between the German and the Durkheimian approach to these issues. That is why he tried so hard to formulate his theoretical concepts in a way that freed his own concept of 'understanding' from this psychological component, this psychological element of motivation.[8] When you really get up close and look more carefully at the differences between two competing theoretical approaches, you will very often discover that, in a sense, the same thing, the same issue, finds due expression in both of them, although refracted in a very different way – but in such a way that one can hardly avoid the impression that an identical experiential core also ultimately lies behind these mutually conflicting views, and that the essential task of any truly objective form of knowledge is, or would be, precisely to discover and expose this identical core. You know – or the sociologists among you know – that the concept of purposive rationality plays a decisive role in the thought of Max Weber, and that he was actually far more interested from a social perspective in the idea of rational action than he was in social reality as such. Thus in the context of the controversy we are talking about right here you may now be able to grasp the real significance of this concept of rationality in Weber. For on the one hand rationality is something we are able to understand: something I can find in myself, something we can all find in each one of us, insofar as we are all members of bourgeois society, because rationality itself is nothing but that unity of bourgeois reason which is more or less effectively embodied in every single bourgeois individual. At the same time, however, rationality is calibrated in advance to the demands of reality and has already been purified of the merely psychological determining features of the individual precisely in order to facilitate the self-preservation of the individual, so that rationality has become that indwelling authority within us which is furthest away and most objectively detached from the contingent aspect of the singular individual. Thus you find that Max Weber's attempt to relate understanding to forms of rationality as far as possible also reveals a moment that is not so dissimilar in a way to the Durkheimian moment – namely Weber's attempt to uncover an authoritative form of social action that transcends the mere individual, albeit a form of authority that we are supposedly able to 'understand'. Now one might say that, at this point, Durkheim went further and proved more radical than Weber in the sense that he could not rest content with such a concept of rationality as this. For in order to discover the relevant determining social factors Durkheim appealed to less understandable elements with which it is much less easy to identify ourselves. That is why observations regarding primitive peoples, observations of an essentially ethnological kind, play such an extraordinarily important role in Durkheim's school. If you have time to look at *L'Année Sociologique* above all, as well as the studies by Hubert[9] and Mauss[10] in particular, you will be confronted with an almost overwhelming abundance of such ethnological material which, in the sense of *chosisme*, i.e. the identification of social facts, cannot be reduced to individual occasions for acts of 'understanding'. In this regard we only have to consider, for example, 'la dot', namely the dowry, and its significance in primitive societies. This approach has also had enormously important consequences for modern sociology. For this is the source of what in contemporary sociology is now called social anthropology,[11] which in a sense reapplies this method – that makes what cannot be understood into the very object of sociology – and translates it back into the context of our own cultures. Its proponents thus attempt, as Mead[12] and Geoffrey Gorer[13] have done, to grasp contemporary American society and its rituals in terms of categories derived, for example, from the society of New Guinea. I am simply drawing your attention to these conceptual and historical connections with the most recent developments in social science so that, when we really look more carefully at Durkheim's thought, you can see that this is not just some peculiar concern of '*les terres allemandes*'.

This Durkheimian thesis of unintelligibility, as we might call it, arises from the experience that society is really to be found precisely there where I do not understand it, where it hurts, where I encounter it as compulsion. I believe that there is a profoundly true moment to Durkheim's theory at this particular point, and I believe that you would be depriving yourselves of a crucial aspect of social knowledge if you failed to recognize for yourselves the significance of this moment in Durkheim's theory. For, in the first place, considered from the perspective of social phenomena with which as real human beings, and even as researchers and investigators, we all have to deal, society does indeed exhibit a truly reified and congealed character.

Society is not something that can be understood immediately or in every respect, and it repeatedly confronts us as this enigmatic reality, this reality we cannot understand, of which Durkheim speaks with such enormous pathos. Or perhaps I can put it better this way: the methodological exclusion of understanding itself actually reflects something eminently real, namely the experience of the unintelligibility, of the very unreason, of the world insofar as we repeatedly come up against the unreason of society, insofar as we are repeatedly driven to discover that our ever so rationally organized world cannot even order its affairs in such a way that we are not imminently threatened by that world. For it seems that the whole thing – and I am not using this word in the sense of *chosisme* here – could blow up at any moment. In a way this experience is rightly and legitimately reflected in Durkheim's conception of society. And in this regard the concept of rationality in Max Weber seems rather naive about it insofar as it fails to recognize the problematic character of this rationality even in a supposedly rational form of exchange society. In other words, if I may appeal to an old and famous formulation, in the world that we inhabit, with its prevailing structure of exchange, the relations between human beings are reflected back to us as if these relations were really properties of things, and the objective reason why the world appears to us in a thing-like way lies precisely in the reified character of our own experience.[14] Thus Durkheim's *chosisme* expresses a correct consciousness of the reification of the world; it precisely and adequately reproduces the ossified character of the world we encounter, and of positivism as a whole, insofar as it makes use of intrinsically reified methods, is tailor-made to suit the world as it is. This means that the world has no good reason to moan about the way human beings are constantly subjected to tests and questionnaires, by appealing instead to the idea of human dignity for example, even while human beings themselves, in terms of their entire consciousness and the way in which they react to things, come more and more to resemble just what is expected of them in such tests and questionnaires. Now while this aspect or moment is registered by Durkheim, it is also elevated into a scientific norm. There is something rather remarkable that is implicit in the normative character of science here. On the one hand, the scientific approach is completely justified, for when science wants to understand reality – and I use the word 'understand' very laxly in this context – it must take over the categories in which the actual world stands before it and make these categories its own. Thus in the face of a reified world it must not act as if the world were immediately present or accessible to us, for then sociology would really fall back into the kind of cosy and romantic notions of 'the land and its people' that you find expressed, for example, in the writings of Wilhelm Heinrich Riehl, who was much influenced by Lorenz von Stein.[15] And even today you can find people who endorse this kind of thing, remarkably enough, in the field of industrial sociology.[16] Now however this may be, sociology cannot afford to ignore this reified character of experience unless it wishes to propagate an image of the world that is quite insufficient to express the actual state of things. Yet the ideal of science, as described above, in a sense also deprives science of its own ability to think. It is thereby forbidden to do precisely what it really needs do here – namely to explain the reified character of experience, the *chosisme* itself, as something that has come to be, as something that has been produced, rather than – as in Durkheim's case – hypostasizing it as an ultimate given and thus conferring a kind of absolute status upon it. Since Durkheim refuses to clarify and look more closely into '*les faits sociaux*', i.e. into society as a collective entity that supposedly cannot be understood, it is not so surprising that he also ends up by glorifying this collective entity in its positivity in an ultimately unquestioning way, and by singing the praises of a society expressly based upon the division of labour on account of the solidarity it generates.[17] In this regard he failed to see that the difference between the compulsive solidarity of a society based on the division of labour and the kind of solidarity that might obtain between free human beings is nothing less than the difference between hell and heaven. In other words, what Durkheim describes as '*faits sociaux*' and what qualifies as 'things' is something reified or thing-like which has arisen or come to be what it is, and the task of a sociology that really answers to its objects would be to comprehend the production of that reified character, the genesis and the emergence of those ossified relationships which literally appear to Durkheim as if they are a second nature that is simply there. Thus finally – and here I suggest a way in which we might rescue something from the concept of 'understanding' – if we refuse to look away from this ossification of the social world, if we refuse to translate this world back into something supposedly immediate, but attempt instead to derive this ossification itself from social processes, then perhaps we can after all understand these *faits sociaux*, these apparent *choses*. Thus what has arisen, what has come into being, itself becomes a sign, as it were, for the processes from which it has emerged and in which it is has been sedimented. In this sense it might then prove possible to move beyond this stubborn *chosisme* with which we began.

LECTURE 7
2 June 1960

Ladies and gentlemen,

To begin with, I would just like say a few more words about the problem of '*chosisme*' and the apparent unintelligibility of social facts, for in this connection Durkheim is motivated by something to which we have perhaps not yet paid sufficient attention. I have already pointed out to you that all of these sociologists from the period we have been discussing here shared a certain interest in securing the independence of sociology vis-à-vis other neighbouring disciplines. This was connected with the specific situation in which sociology, as a young science, found itself competing with the old and long-established world of the *universitas litterarum*. These considerations may easily seem rather pedantic, and it has become common especially today, when the call to integrate the sciences which have been torn apart from one another through the division of labour can be heard on every street corner, to sneer rather cheaply in this connection. But I believe that this outlook still expresses a genuine and essential point, as I showed you only recently by reference to the model of the unintelligibility and impenetrability of social facts as these features were so forcefully registered in Durkheim's theory of scientific sociology. In other words, remarkably enough, anti-philosophical sociology also involves something upon which philosophy itself lays particular emphasis, namely the kind of objective tendency which contrasts with merely subjective individual acts and with individual cases of consciousness.[1] Even Max Weber, who does still insist on the criterion of intelligibility, exhibits this aspect very strongly. Thus one might almost say that we are dealing here with an attempt to translate Hegel's doctrine of objective spirit or Marx's theory of the objective tendency of history[2] into the terms of a particular science, with an attempt to do justice to those forms of experience which are so central for the thinkers who begin from the perspective of totality, but does so in terms of a radically nominalist form of thought which actually knows nothing about the totality, a form of thought which nonetheless repeatedly comes up against individual facts that clearly cannot be understood simply in terms of themselves as merely individual phenomena – and here that means facts which cannot be causally derived in the crudest sense from what preceded them either. Now the curious thing is that such an eminently synthetic and nominalistic sociologist as Durkheim actually inherits this tendency from the realm of philosophy and the great speculative theories of society and, I would say, intensifies it almost to the point of parody. In other words, he specifically defends the doctrine that the social dimension is not really commensurate with the idea of individual action at all. You will know that in his most famous investigation – namely the classical investigation *On Suicide*,[3] which dates from his early period and which basically established his entire sociological approach – he makes abundant use of statistical methods of research. But the use of statistics in Durkheim has an entirely different meaning than it does in the sort of social enquiries in which statistics had already played a significant role throughout the nineteenth century, at least from around the early 1820s.[4] Durkheim trusted in statistics, since he believed that his model of suicide, which takes the figures for suicide as a whole to be constant at least within specific more or less historically self-contained periods, allowed him to conclude that a certain regularity of the social order found expression there, a regularity moreover which had nothing at all to do with the specific psychological motivations of the particular individuals involved. For the statistical element takes no account whatsoever of the psychology behind the individual suicides but, if it is concerned with anything, is directed towards those aspects which again largely transcend the specifically psychological or quite particular situation of individual human beings; in other words, the statistical element is essentially directed, in accordance with Durkheim's theory, towards the way in which people belong to specific religious groups and towards the stronger or weaker integrating power that is exercised by such groups. It is thus directed to capturing that characteristic form of human life which Durkheim ascribes to the religious groups in question. And, as far as the scale of such integrating power is concerned, Durkheim assigns the highest place to Catholicism.[5] You may remember that this idea regarding the integrating power of religion already plays a central role in Comte's sociology, where it is expressly contrasted with the more destructive and non-integrating characteristics of philosophical and metaphysical thought, as I specifically pointed out to you earlier on. But we also have to add that Durkheim's thought, at this point, is really revealed as an example of typically reifying thought precisely because it shows no interest whatsoever in the way in which these objective motivations are in turn also subjective – in other words, are mediated in and through the particular individuals involved. For the suicides which are grasped by means of these statistics, and rather absurdly classified in terms of the three types of egoistic, altruistic and anomic suicide,[6] are nonetheless all of them individuals; and an act such as suicide, which in general clearly violated and still violates a clearly established social norm, at least in Western civilization, is certainly not something that just transpires over and beyond the conscious awareness of individuals, as if people simply destroy themselves in the way in which drones are more or less quite ready to do when they allow themselves to be stung to death after they have performed what was required of them. On the contrary, all these human suicides, the quantitative constancy of which Durkheim triumphantly proclaims as he classifies them under the aforementioned rubrics, are still also motivated in each case through the actual situation, psychology, and suffering of particular human beings. Thus simply to say that this fact of suicide is a social fact does not really get close enough to the facts, for if this social fact is to emerge in the first place it is also necessary for certain motivations to make themselves felt within the particular individuals, motivations to which no attention is accorded in this account. And the real problem which completely eludes such an approach is precisely how these individual chains of human motivation are nonetheless organized in such a way that they satisfy the statistical law of the greatest number. For it is indeed a very remarkable fact, and one that, as far as I can see, the social scientists and theorists of knowledge have still not thought properly about, that the statistical law of the greatest number has not, at least until now, been applied solely to blind and non-self-directed objects and processes – matters which lend themselves to calculation in terms of probability – but also to individuated self-conscious beings; to beings, in other words, which, in contrast to such blind determination through the order of the universe, also involve another aspect which would surely lead us to expect that something more was at work in such beings beyond or contrary to that statistical law. Yet this is by no means the case. I would certainly not venture to decide this question here, but I would like at least to suggest one way in which we might attempt to provide some kind of answer to it. For this problem may itself be connected with the fact that society, to this day, has unfolded in a blind and nature-like fashion. In other words, we find that human beings, under the compulsion to which they are submitted within society, do not actually behave so differently from those atoms which, according to a statistical analysis, react in terms of the relevant laws of probability rather than in terms of genuinely understandable causal processes that relate specifically to the individual.

Thus in Durkheim this problem is simply left open. In accordance with his whole approach, the 'collective mind' is already basically hypostasized at this point. And in the later writings of Durkheim's school, which lavish particular attention upon the religious conceptions of primitive peoples, which are themselves seen as simply reflecting such a collective mind, this tendency to hypostasization is taken to an extreme. Thus with this kind of sociological approach you find yourself confronted with a somewhat paradoxical fact. For while this sociology seems entirely nominalist in character, always seems to start from the individual case and from the individual observation, to foreground individual observation rather than general laws and concepts, it then proceeds in such a way that the dialectic (and I do not mean the dialectic in a specifically technical sense here), the polarity, the tension – in other words, the interaction between the individual and society – essentially disappears from view, and it simply subsumes the individual without further ado under purely social concepts. One might say that a social science which has forfeited its own concept, and thus consists in nothing beyond the registration and classification of facts, is typically in danger of splitting apart into two unconnected domains, neither of which can properly claim truth for itself. Thus, on the one hand, you get a sociology in the narrow sense which now actually believes that it can justifiably downgrade the individual into a function of society, which is what happens in the sociological school we have just been discussing;[7] on the other hand, you get a kind of psychology which has long since also found its way into sociology under the name of social psychology and in countless other theoretical forms; and this approach, in contrast to the former, believes it can infer the social realm directly from norms and regularities revealed in the behaviour of individuals, as the great psychologist Freud himself believed, rather naively from a theoretical-scientific point of view it has to be said, when he said that on his view sociology is really just applied psychology.[8] Thus both of these very one-sided approaches, if we may put it that way, derive from a reified opposition between the domain of society and that of the individual, between the 'domain of the many' and the 'domain of the individual', as it has occasionally been described.[9] These approaches fail to realize that both these so-called domains need to be recognized as internally bound up with each other if the analysis of either is to yield any rigorous meaning. Not the least of the tasks that fall to a philosophical reflection on sociology, it seems to me, is precisely to think through the relationship between these domains in a new and much more fundamental manner than has hitherto been the case. In the past people have tried either to explain the whole simply on the basis of one or the other of these two domains, or to present both domains as entirely independent of one another. But in the latter case they failed to see that, if we are dealing with the same facts explained from the perspective of two quite different spheres, there must ultimately be some sort of mediation which actually lends unity to both of these different forms of explanation. You can see from this just how quite tangible questions of sociology, akin to those regarding the explanation of *'faits sociaux'* such as the underlying regularity of suicide, spontaneously suggest philosophical, i.e. epistemological, reflections and raise questions about human motivation in terms of social or psychological factors. And I would like to say here that even the realm of statistics, which is surely the favourite mother if not exactly the favourite child of sociology, is ultimately built up through a process of abstraction from the individual facts, just as the individual facts for their part are only possible as aspects or moments in that universality that finds expression in statistics. And a deployment of statistics which has forgotten the process of abstraction inevitably involved really runs the danger of becoming a fetish and leading to the sort of assertions which crop up all too often in empirical social research under the name of 'spurious correlations',[10] i.e. statistical correlations, which in reality are quite devoid of meaning.

This basically concludes our examination of *'chosisme'* and Durkheim's theoretical approach to these matters. To sum up, finally, I would say that what we can learn from Durkheim, at least in contrast to Max Weber, is that our understanding of society cannot be reduced to the meaningful and purposive-rational action of individual subjects, as Weber puts it.[11] On the other hand, these emphatically social facts – such as social solidarity, the phenomenon of suicide, the essence of primitive religion – are not simply to be accepted as an unchangeable given but should be derived from the regular objective processes of a specific society. Thus the thing-like character which Durkheim talks about does indeed accurately reflect the fact that the regular processes to which we are subjected as social beings actually unfold over and beyond our own consciousness, and the fact that these processes are incommensurable with our own inner life and to that extent are not something we can actually understand. Nonetheless, they are potentially understandable if we are capable of revealing the principle which governs the society in question.

But you will recall that I told you that Durkheim's theory also has a specific substantive side to it. I am talking about his critique of Comte where he rejects the notion of progress, as I pointed out earlier with reference to one particular passage.[12] And I believe that I really ought to say a little more here about this question of progress, simply because, if you are attending a series of lectures about the problem concerning the relationship between philosophy and sociology, you would surely expect to hear at least something about the concept of progress. For on the one hand this is really a concept that has sprung from philosophy, and it goes back to the thought that humanity is in some sense moving towards the Kingdom of God, an idea which is clearly outlined in Augustine's work *De civitate Dei*.[13] And through various stages of secularization, the most important phase of which is represented by Bossuet,[14] the great French theologian of the baroque era, this idea eventually came to expression in the later Enlightenment. Thus Condorcet, in his *Esquisse*, was the first to present the idea of 'progress' as the fundamental principle of history.[15] And then, finally, in Hegel's doctrine of history as 'the progress of the consciousness of freedom', the idea of progress becomes the very content of philosophy itself.[16] Thus we are dealing here with an unquestionably philosophical theme, albeit one that, as you will remember, also plays an enormous role in the sociology of Comte, as indeed Durkheim specifically complained. The notion of progress is a model that has emerged again and again throughout the field of social thought, and I believe you have a right at least to ask what we have to say about this problem of progress in the light of the considerations we have just been pursuing. The first thing to say is that it would be far too quick simply to list all of Durkheim's shortcomings for him, in the way they like to do just across the border: 'Well, of course, he is living in the middle of the Age of Imperialism, and therefore no longer possesses the great faith in progress that once characterized bourgeois culture in its ascendant phase, and that is why he rejects the notion of progress and therefore represents nothing but pure decadence.' Now, of course, one cannot think about these things in this way, unless we are really willing to ignore the experience that lies at the heart of such theoretical conceptions. In the first place, Durkheim already saw quite clearly that we could no longer talk about the kind of direct and ongoing progress in which people had still believed in the late eighteenth and the early nineteenth century. He saw that history is susceptible to terrible regressions, and you will perhaps remember from the passage that I read out for you that his outlook was actually not that far removed from Spengler's conception of the plant-like emergence and disappearance of cultures as self-enclosed social wholes.[17] This observation is connected with the fact – as Spencer in particular recognized[18] – that the so-called primitive cultures have here gradually been drawn into a far closer relation to contemporary social thought than they were in Comte's philosophy. In this regard, Comte can still be regarded as a late representative of Enlightenment thought insofar as he actually somewhat naively hypostasizes the image of Western civilization. There is no doubt that Durkheim recognized all of this. He is one of the first sociologists to be extremely cautious about deploying the concept of progress, and who realized that in relation to many social structures, especially the static social structures of exotic peoples, as in the case of Chinese culture over thousands of years, the attempt to evaluate them in terms of the concept of progress is to introduce an external perspective that is entirely alien these cultures themselves. On the other hand, this can hardly be the whole truth either. I would just like to add this comment here: even in Comte the question of progress is not that simple, for insofar as Comte also describes progress as a principle that dissolves the inherited traditional structures of society, and introduces the opposed or complementary principle of order to counteract this, we can already potentially recognize the thought that society through its development exceeds its own limits, or, in other words, that progress does not unfold in a straightforward or unambiguous manner, and that, on the contrary, society also regresses to more primitive stages. Now this possibility is not only recognized in Durkheim, as I pointed out to you before, but is actually already implicit in the fears that originally motivated Comte's sociology. Nonetheless, I believe it would be precipitate if, before the threat of regressions that we can observe in our society today, we gladly repudiated the concept of progress in the name of science and exclaimed instead: 'Well, of course, there's no such thing, and we just have to stick to the facts!' But it would be equally naive to hypostasize the concept of progress and strike up a kind of sociological sermon to the effect that things are somehow always getting better and better. Neither of these approaches is the truth, and perhaps I have already said enough to encourage you to reject such rigid alternatives without simply resigning yourselves to a sceptical shrug, so that you may be able instead to recognize the truth moment of such a concept, as well as its moment of untruth.

On the one hand, therefore, there is unquestionably progress in the sense that human beings are increasingly capable of subjecting nature to themselves – that is, both the external nature with which they must come to terms and, to an ever greater degree, the inner nature which they shape through social and psychological means. They are therefore capable, if I may put like this, of bringing more and more of the world of objects under their control, and this brings about a whole range of things which can really be described in terms of progress. Thus in periods which cannot immediately be identified as times of catastrophe it has been possible to alleviate need and distress for groups of people who in earlier times were exposed to periodic starvation, to massive levels of child mortality, and to various other things of this kind. I think that to deny this aspect of progress would be just as obtuse as the way in which the hollow and superficially declaimed[19] optimism all around us today also deceives us about the dark and threatening character of the world in which we live. Thus rationality has certainly increased in the sense of our domination of nature; the means which human beings have at their disposal in their constant interchange with nature have been refined and developed to an ever greater degree, and, however partial or restricted this process may have been, it still also harbours the potential of progress for the world as a whole. In other words, it is perfectly feasible today to envisage a social condition of humanity in which the natural catastrophes of society – famine, wars, dictatorships and such-like things – no longer exist, whereas it was not even possible to think of such potential in earlier phases of society, just as the conception of a humane and rationally organized society that would be worthy of human beings was never actually framed as such in earlier historical stages of society. The fact that this conception really only belongs to such a late phase of human history surely suggests that the potential in question has itself grown over time. On the other hand, we also have to concede that this progress has unfolded only in a blind kind of way, that it has unfolded, as I would like to say, at every step by reacting to problems that humanity has constantly had to confront in the realm of technology, or in the attempt to master acute and recurrent crises. Thus the example of progress that, rightly or wrongly, probably strikes us today as the most obvious is the way that the danger of systemic crisis in capitalist society has been averted, or at least significantly reduced or postponed. Yet this has only come about because the enormous economic crisis that began with the catastrophic collapse of Wall Street in 1929 posed a fundamental threat to the further development of the whole economic system itself. Thus we were simply forced to think about the kind of policies that would enable us to control the movement of the economy as a whole, policies which have at least been maintained over the last thirty years or so, along with the horrific interlude of the last war, and have found their most significant expression in the macro-economic doctrines of John Maynard Keynes and his school.[20] This too was an example of blind progress insofar as it sprang simply from the desire to preserve the existing social order without really grasping one essential thing, namely the question of how to establish a form of society itself in which the possibility of such catastrophes would be excluded – and such a conception of humanity, one which would be capable of averting such catastrophes, one which could really be described as progressive in the most fundamental sense, has not existed to this day.[21] This is not because there have never been human beings who were capable of thinking the thoughts which I am expressing to you here, thoughts which are so simple that, God knows, you certainly don't need me to express them for you. But they are thoughts which the whole course of your earlier education and the current state of the world itself have almost driven out of you, so perhaps I have to say them explicitly to remind you of something which in reality you all know as well as I do or any one of us does. But the only reason such thoughts have not been developed, or at least why they have not given rise to genuine progress, why they have remained powerless in social terms, is because the society in which we live, in spite of all its tendencies towards integration, has continued to be a society of mutually hostile and conflicting interests. There is really no actual and effective site, no third position, as it were, over and above this society which would be capable of thinking through these contradictory interests. In other words, the blind way in which progress has unfolded up until now is itself nothing but the consequence of the fact that we continue to live in a fundamentally divided society, that, in spite of an ever-advancing rationality in specific parts of society, in spite of this particularistic rationality, the whole has remained irrational to this day.

Now this has certain quite decisive consequences for the structure of progress itself. The most striking consequence – to go straight to what is essential here – is that the element of violence which is required to dominate nature if human beings are to meet their needs and master the chaotic conditions of social existence has only been maintained and perpetuated within human beings themselves and the social arrangements in which they live. Thus society and the forms in which it is organized continue to exert a certain almost unbearable pressure on individuals, a pressure which, in turn, provokes a kind of resistance, since there is no substantial correspondence between the interests of human beings and the prevailing social order without which these human beings cannot actually survive. In other words, to put this in psychological terms, society encourages those destructive tendencies which Freud explored and identified in his important late text on *Civilization and its Discontents*.[22] These tendencies are always liable to explode and to destroy the whole social order, as we can perhaps see from the apparent readiness of the masses in all countries, and I really mean all countries, to compete with one another and prepare for utterly devastating wars in the name of 'the nation' and actually to fall upon one another in the most savage way. In the present age I hardly need to spell out the consequences in this regard. This element of violence in progress qua domination of nature generates a kind of context of guilt, is continually reproduced in the relations between human beings, and itself gives rise to the forces which turn against progress. The greater the productive forces involved in this advancing process have become, the greater and more terrifying too are the forces which are ready to inhibit this progress. We are no longer simply talking here about some mere relation between humanity and a stage which has in reality already been superseded, or a situation in which humanity is merely holding on to such a superseded stage of development. In other words, we are not just talking about the phenomenon of historical stagnation, as this is described, for example, in the sociology of Simmel.[23] What we are actually taking about here is a regression to barbarism.

We must also point out that this rationality, this constantly advancing rationality, is embedded in an irrational whole, that it remains caught up in something irrational, and that the function of rationality is thereby actually intensified in this irrationality. Thus today, for example, the rationality that is invested in technological progress remains embedded in the continuing irrational division of the world into two completely irreconcilable and mutually threatening power blocs, with the result that every specific advance in the application of rationality assumes a double face. We might say that, within the prevailing irrationality of the whole, every advance, every example of progress, in any concrete particular case, also immediately takes on a threatening or terrifying character. We might say that every particular expression of rationality that does not correspond to any rationality on the part of the whole thus actually emphasizes the aspect, and only that aspect, which threatens to destroy anything worthy of human beings that still remains in the world. In other words, the price of progress becomes higher and higher, without our ever actually being able to reap what this progress really promises. You will all have recognized something like this from the simple fact that, although the process of automation and mechanization, the progressive rationalization of the labour process, reduces the amount of work time that is required, we do not actually appear to be any better off as a result. For we see that all human beings, and I mean all human beings without distinction, find themselves even more thoroughly caught up in the social system, even less capable of autonomy and self-determination, than they have probably been in any other phase of history. The merely particular rationality which is not reflected in terms of the ultimate concern of humanity as a whole now really leads towards the kind of devastated life which the irrationalists of every school have observed, and in this they can for their part lay claim to a particular truth. In other words, the world is indeed increasingly disfigured through a rationality that essentially consists in a constant increase in industrial output and the productive forces of society, where there is no higher perspective from which we might legitimately recognize the interests of nature itself, and where the latter is regarded solely in terms of domination. And what you can all observe for yourselves along every major motorway, where the surrounding landscape is ruined by advertising billboards on every side, is simply a telling allegory for what is unfolding at the heart of human things themselves. Thus you must also be able to acknowledge the significance of the irrationalist critique of progress without simply rejecting it through some over-romanticized attachment to the idea of progress. Instead you should understand that critique itself as an aspect or moment of this progress; you must understand, in other words, that it is because the world is actually not yet rational enough, not yet properly transparent to itself, not yet genuinely self-determined, that it does indeed repeatedly manifest the horrific features which are then lamented from certain romantic perspectives that have been given an essentially reactionary and retrospective twist. Here we might adapt Feuerbach's remark and say that it is not enough to be opposed to romanticism, for we must somehow stand above it.[24] In other words, we must be able to acknowledge the truth moments in that critique of the rationalized and technologized world and take them up into the way we attempt to construe progress and rationality. In particular, we shall have to reflect upon the core of irrationality within the rational itself as it exists today, namely upon the fetishization of instrumental means in a society of universal exchange, a society which forgets that these means are simply means rather than ends in themselves. In other words, we must reflect upon the fetishization of production and the productive apparatus at the expense of living subjects themselves. What this means today is that the quantity of goods and commodities is fetishized at the expense of any genuine self-determination on the part of human beings.

I believe that I have at least provided you here with the outlines of an answer to the question concerning progress or the absence of progress. I cannot pursue the matter any further at the moment, but I hope I may be able to say something more fundamental in this regard in one of our later sessions and to offer you a more fully developed theoretical account of two basic sociological-philosophical categories (the static and the dynamic) which will make these things rather clearer for you.[25] But first, before we move on to such matters, I would just like to respond to a specific suggestion from some of you and say some very sweeping things about the difference or distinction between philosophy and sociology. For we can properly understand the question concerning the mediation between philosophy and sociology only once we have elucidated the distinctions which really are involved here. A mediated unity is a unity-in-difference, not merely some fusion or conflation of things which are actually different from one another.

LECTURE 8
14 June 1960

Ladies and gentlemen,

I should like to use today's lecture in a sense to interrupt the course of our previous considerations and pause for a moment of self-reflection. To tell you the truth, this springs directly from self-reflection on my part, as I have realized a couple of rather remarkable things. In the first place, up until this point I have essentially been talking about the mediation between sociology and philosophy, about the basic problem involved in their sometimes very complex relations to each other – and especially about the way this was expressed in the critique of philosophy or of conceptual-metaphysical thinking that was mounted by two thinkers who belong, methodologically speaking, among the most important figures from the field of sociology. I am talking about the thought of Comte and specifically about Emile Durkheim's *Règles de la méthode sociologique*. But then I said to myself: 'In these lectures you surely have to make sure, if people are not just going to miss the wood for the trees, that you actually say quite firmly what sociology and philosophy are, and at least indicate what the difference between them is, before you can broach the difficult and complex questions of mediation that are involved here!' For, methodologically speaking, we must surely accept the proposition that any insight into a manifold unity of phenomena which are not just immediately one with each other can only properly be acquired when we also begin by distinguishing the phenomena in question, and hold fast to this distinction, if we are really to avoid the famous night in which all cats are black, or perhaps grey, depending on the region where this saying is found.

But in trying to say something quite firm about the difference between our two categories – about whose rather complicated relations we have been talking all this time – I discovered something a little surprising, which certainly surprised me too. And this is that it is by no means easy to indicate this difference, since in the first place the two disciplines are so different that the idea they might have something in common actually emerges rather late in the day and is derived from elsewhere. In other words, the definitions of both these concepts, of 'sociology' and 'philosophy', belong in the first instance to two quite different levels. Yet it is only really possible – and this too is a logical-methodological insight – to indicate the difference between two concepts, and especially the difference between substantive fields, in terms of something they have in common. But the fact that sociology and philosophy are both of them fields of intellectual activity is naturally so thin and abstract that the relative differences could hardly be determined on this basis. And even if we wanted to estimate the difference between them by reference to the concept of science, that would be wholly insufficient, for philosophy cannot just be counted as merely one of the sciences since one of its tasks is to constitute and to criticize science, to explicate the possibility of science itself. It is not appropriate to identify the concept of philosophy in advance with that of any particular kind of science. And that is the difficulty raised by all these preliminary conceptual clarifications which I am about to introduce in order to hold apart what must then be mediated. This raises the famous old logical problem of the difference between the 'concrete' and the 'concave'.[1] And the comparison of 'concrete' and 'concave' is actually not so strange in this case, for if you take the concept of the 'concrete' in its primitive and pre-scientific sense, namely as the realm of facts, this more or less captures what sociology now is. So I don't want to offer you definitions of the concepts of 'sociology' and 'philosophy'. It is not possible in the context of these lectures to embark on a critical discussion of the concept of 'definition' itself, and I have talked about this at length in other lecture courses, especially those which specifically address dialectical and epistemological questions.[2] Moreover, if you consult the indices that have been put together for the texts of Kant, Hegel or Nietzsche, you will find so many insightful critical reflections on the concept of 'definition' that I don't really need to say anything more on this issue here.[3] Instead I would rather start by discussing what in fact is traditionally thought to be involved in the concepts of 'sociology' and 'philosophy' respectively. However, I shall also take this opportunity – with specific reference to sociology – to speak briefly about one definition. This will perhaps also make it clear how difficult the problem of definition turns out to be more generally, and not only in relation to this particular discipline. First, it must be acknowledged that sociology is an individual science which takes a quite specific field as its object and addresses this field in a direct or immediate way, i.e. addresses this field with *intentione recta*, to use the terminology of philosophy, rather than primarily in the context of self-reflection. In other words, it tries to apprehend and grasp the objects with which it is concerned in a direct or immediate way, in much the same way that you expect any other so-called positive science to proceed. Sociology is a positive science and, indeed – if I deliberately put this as comprehensively and as cautiously as I can in order to reduce at least a little the possibilities for misunderstanding – is the individual science of the social realm. Thus sociology is concerned both with social facts and the social relations within society, and equally with the concept of society itself. In other words, just to make this element of complicity clear to you from the start, it is capable both of presenting society and its facts precisely as they are, of clearly identifying particular groups of relations or groups of facts within this given and existing society, and, on the other hand, of taking the interconnections of society itself, or the social totality, or whatever you wish to call it, as its specific object. This is 'the social' in the broadest possible sense, something that can range – we might say – all the way from the structure of an exchange society or the structure of socialization itself to such highly specific phenomena, let us say, as the relations internal to some particular business or enterprise. In the first instance sociology simply confronts the social as its object, without necessarily raising the question about how this object itself is constituted. At least this is how it proceeds to begin with, although in the further course of its investigations it finds itself forced to ask the question 'How does something like the society we live in come about in the first place, or how is all this constituted?' And from here it is led, for example, to categories such as the exchange relation between human beings, or those of domination and exploitation, or of the reproduction of social life. And, going further still, it is led to ask how its own concepts are constituted, whether these concepts can claim unconditional validity, or what determines the selection of these concepts, and so forth. But in the first instance the way in which the social is posited or presupposed as its object can roughly be compared with the way that nature is presupposed as the object of the natural sciences. Here too we move from the most general categorial determinations of theoretical physics right through to highly specialized fields concerned with the technological applications of science, or to special areas such as colloid chemistry and other such things, which bring us into remarkably close proximity to highly concrete and particular phenomena.

Here you have to recognize that this narrowed sociological focus on particular relations within society, or in other words on highly concrete relations, has gone extraordinarily far these days. Already in Germany you can see examples of this development everywhere in connection with what in this country we have come to call 'hyphen-sociologies': industrial sociology, the sociology of town and country, the sociology of religion, or of whatever the particular area happens to be; and in America this narrowed focus[4] has developed to a quite tremendous extent – the task is to provide the most scientifically precise and narrowly focused analysis as possible of particular social domains, such as the phenomenon of urbanism, namely the idea of the city as a social group, for example. Now at first this all sounds very simple and straightforward. Nonetheless, I believe that most of you, to the extent that you are specifically concerned with sociology, will soon encounter a certain difficulty here. For you will find that sociology – and I have to admit that it is remarkably similar to philosophy in this regard – cannot simply be studied in the way that one studies the natural sciences, or even, in my view, in the way one studies a discipline such as geography or history. For here you never quite clearly know how you should begin, never really know what the first step is, or how to proceed to the next; in other words, you are not provided with any reliable hierarchy of objects, and thus with any conception of scientific experience or *didachē*[5] with regard to these objects. Most of you will probably already be familiar with this feeling, and I would suggest that the reasons which have expressly led sociology towards a constant symbiosis with philosophy, or, to put this more modestly, which still lead us to look towards philosophy to save us, as if it were really able to offer assistance here, are connected in part with the fact that, with sociology, there is no firmly prescribed order in the object, and thus no firmly prescribed order for how to study it either.

For sociology was never something that could be identified, in a process lasting over a thousand years, as a distinctive discipline of its own which had a clear place in the *kosmos noetikos* or could be discovered on the map showing all of the scientific disciplines. It is quite true that there have always been sociological observations of one kind or another; from the perspective of today, for example, we may look back at the analysis of the division of labour, or the attempt to bring the division of labour into a meaningful relationship with the idea of justice, which we find in Plato's Republic,[6] or we may recall the critique of humanly created practices and institutions in contrast to the basic nature of the human being which can already be found among the earliest of the Sophists – all of these intellectual elements can of course be described as 'sociological' from the contemporary standpoint of the discipline concerned with society as we have now come to know it. Yet sociology is absent from the ancient catalogue of scientific knowledge. It is true, of course, that Faust, alas!, has studied philosophy, theology, medicine, and law[7] – but definitely not sociology. And I think that, if sociology were to crop up in the famous catalogue at the beginning of Faust's opening monologue, we'd all have to smile – if only because we would then imagine that, from the very start, he would perhaps have reflected far more carefully about his problematic relationship to Gretchen than this otherwise extremely learned man was actually capable of doing. Now, however that may be, sociology certainly does not yet occupy an established place in the system of the sciences. And there is a real social reason for this. For a society which is truly and completely interconnected, a society which – to put this more formally – constitutes a totality where every process is a function of all the other processes or is a function of the whole, is something which did not previously exist.[8] In earlier times the overall situation was much more like that we still find today in purely agrarian areas which have not yet been wholly caught up within the capitalist network, and where in certain circumstances the links between one village and another are rather loose or tenuous. The history of philosophy shows us that thought has recognized phenomena which are secondary in a categorial sense, i.e. which are not specifically phenomena *about* society, or *about* socialization – such as the phenomenon of the city, or more precisely that of the city state – and has done so long before it turned directly to the concept of the social or of society itself, even though the latter is the general concept under which these particular phenomena or manifestations essentially fall.

Now this curious character which attaches to the structure of the concept of sociology is responsible for the fact – and this indicates another difficulty involved in this concept – that all sorts of things have actually come together to produce the concept of sociology. These things cannot really be brought under a common denominator precisely because this concept of the social, which I spoke to you about at the beginning of today's lecture, is too thin to provide the required unity in this respect. What actually fed into this sociology was an older element which was still quite unacquainted with the concept of 'sociology' or that of 'society', and which might perhaps better be described as political philosophy or 'philosophy of the state'. It was only later that specific theoretical reflection upon society, upon the nature of socialization, finally found expression in sociology. Other specific forms of speculation and specific disciplines relating to specific aspects of the social order also fed into sociology – such as the entire body of thought which was dedicated to law as a social reality and was never merely confined to the institutionally defined context of jurisprudence. In this sense, therefore, we might say that the problems addressed in Hegel's *Philosophy of Right* also belong, in large measure, to those sociological problems which are specifically addressed today in the kind of sociology of law which is probably most familiar to us through the researches of Georges Gurvitch in France.[9] Sociology has also absorbed the theory of institutions and social arrangements generally, which play such an important role in Durkheim's thought but also in what is described in America as 'institutional analysis'.[10] In addition, sociology has incorporated the analysis of individual political forms and structures insofar as these can also be understood in terms of the general life process of society, and it has finally also absorbed the whole field of what we now describe as 'empirical social research' – although the concept of such research is also usually grasped too narrowly and interpreted exclusively in terms of market and opinion research.[11] It is quite true that such empirical social research, at least in its streamlined contemporary form, sprang essentially from the needs of market research, but originally there was also quite another side to it. The questionnaire technique itself ultimately derived from a desire to bring about specific improvements in the social conditions and opportunities of various groups, and thus from the need to acquire precise and reliable data in this connection.[12] Given the enormous significance which the methods of empirical social research have now assumed, and particularly in Germany over the last decade, I suspect that many of you mistakenly imagine – and I believe we should be quite open about this – that sociology and empirical social research are really the same thing. It may even have occurred to some of you that sociology and social statistics are identical with each other. What happens here is what we often find in the sciences generally; in other words, those who understand least about the disciplines in question are also those who are most tempted to idolize these disciplines or make a fetish of them. Whereas those who have some serious understanding of empirical social research, those who have also actually been closely involved in the development of such research techniques (such as my colleague Paul Lazarsfeld at Columbia University, for example),[13] have always emphatically maintained that what we call 'empirical social research' is really an auxiliary discipline that merely furnishes data which it proceeds to classify and elaborate. But the data themselves, if they are to speak, if they are to become something really meaningful, must first be brought into another context.[14] And my colleague Gunzert,[15] here in the university, will certainly have told you something very similar about the significance of social statistics if you are also attending his lectures. What I want to say to you here is actually quite simple, and it is this. If you are studying sociology, then of course it is absolutely necessary for you to know about these empirical methods if you are going to get your teeth into some actual material and do something rational with it. And it is absolutely imperative for this corrective approach to be taken really seriously after the nonsense encouraged by certain kinds of theory developed in Germany during the Third Reich, where several of the resulting categories were converted into truly insane systems of thought. On the other hand, God forbid you should imagine that you have learned what sociology is simply by mastering these techniques. For all of these things, taken on their own, are basically pre-scientific in character and, if you want to reach any level of scientific insight at all, you will have to embed them within some meaningful theoretical context of one sort or another. It is only then that you can discover their specific significance. Moreover, I would even venture to suggest that those empirical investigations which are so commonly identified with sociology these days can only prove genuinely fruitful when they are already conceptualized within certain meaningful theoretical contexts – in other words, when the questions which underlie the empirical investigations are framed in such a way that something essential for our insight into society or for the continued existence of society actually depends on them. In this regard I would like to recall, for example, our good old study *The Authoritarian Personality*, which once caused something of a stir in the world,[16] precisely because this study – and I am well aware of its methodological defects with respect to the representativeness of the sample and the general theoretical framework – nonetheless allowed us to answer certain specific theoretical questions. It showed, for example, that the so-called mass basis of totalitarian movements does not directly depend, as was initially believed, upon the economic position of those who were attracted by such movements.[17] Thus it broke with the prejudice that fascism is nothing more than a petit bourgeois movement and conclusively demonstrated instead that the presuppositions behind commitment to these totalitarian movements are much more plausibly to be found in specific social-psychological factors than in any direct relation to membership of some such social group. But once again it must be said, if you are to avoid misunderstanding here, that these social-psychological data, in other words the factors involved in the character in thrall to authority, are themselves socially mediated, although they do not depend simply upon the fact that individuals belong to specific groups, or upon the immediate interests of these individuals. For the phenomenon of the authoritarian personality is determined by the structure of society as a whole, which is why we require a theory of society in order to relate this personality structure to society to start with.

This is all I wanted to say about the concept of sociology at this point. The difficulty of arriving at a satisfactory concept of sociology is something that I may now be able to show you in a rather drastic way after what we have already tried to explain in the lectures so far. So I would now like to read you the definition that Max Weber placed right at the start of his late work *Economy and Society*, in other words at the beginning of his most important work. This is what we read in the opening paragraph of the brief text on 'The Fundamental Concepts of Sociology', which has just been reissued by Siebeck, and which I hope I have already recommended all of you to take a look at:[18]

> Sociology (in the sense in which this highly ambiguous word is used here) is a science which attempts to interpret the understanding of social action in order thereby to arrive at a causal explanation of its course and effects. In 'action' is included all human behaviour when and in so far as the acting individual attaches a subjective meaning to it. Action in this sense may be either overt or purely inward or subjective; it may consist of positive intervention in a situation, or of deliberately refraining from such intervention or passively acquiescing in the situation. Action is social in so far as, by virtue of the subjective meaning attached to it by the acting individual (or individuals), it takes account of the behaviour of *others* and is thereby oriented in its course.[19]

Now there is no doubt that Max Weber had reflected very carefully on this definition. Nonetheless, I imagine that, to put this very modestly, you can already see that in terms of our discussion of the method and character of sociology there is no way this definition can be regarded as universally compelling. All you have to do is recall what I have already shown you in some detail. For the concept of 'understanding' which is central here has been expressly contested by a thinker as important and influential for the history of sociology as Emile Durkheim. According to him, the genuinely social domain, the genuine object of sociology, actually begins, we might paradoxically say, precisely where understanding fails or is lacking. You will remember that in one of our last sessions I attempted to grasp this unintelligibility, this form of social life which is resistant and inaccessible to any process of identification, and to make this very unintelligibility intelligible to you in specifically social terms,[20] namely in terms of the category of alienation and reification.[21] Yet this intelligibility at a second level, as it were, is of course something quite different from the intelligible character of society, namely its openness to human 'understanding', as Weber conceived this. And also, I might specifically add here, Max Weber's definition involves an extraordinarily difficult problem which, on the surface, it rather seems to skate over. For the concept of 'understanding' at work here is one that is developed, in the first instance, by reference to the singular individual. I am able to understand something that is similar to me, something with which I can empathize or identify. But this immediate capacity for identification, of course, is also possible only in terms of individual action and individual forms of behaviour. Yet the object of sociology is precisely not the behaviour of individuals as such – that is basically the domain of psychology – because the forms of behaviour with which sociology is concerned are essentially social forms of behaviour. Thus if Max Weber's definition is to be upheld at all, the behaviour of groups or what is genuinely social behaviour must be trimmed and treated in advance as if it were identical with the behaviour of singular individuals regarded as unities which can be understood in their own right within these groups and broader wholes. This is surely right, but only in a quite particular case, namely in the case of rationally constituted societies, whereas there are certainly other social forms which cannot possibly be derived from this idea of the intelligibility of individual action, social forms which would then completely elude this conception of 'understanding'. I have only mentioned all this as an example to show you that it is not a matter of laxness or lack of responsibility on my part if I have tried to develop the concept of sociology for you in terms of various different fields and a broad conception of 'the social'. For sociology is a discipline which in a way has been rather thrown together, like those abbeys or monasteries that only came together over centuries as they absorbed the entire complex of earlier structures and outhouses and hardly represent a single unified whole. And this is why sociology does not lend itself to ready definition. Thus instead of really worrying about this and more or less pedantically searching for some such definition, you would be much better advised to acknowledge, and then go on to explain, the complex nature of sociology, namely the distinctive complex – in the architectural sense of the word – or coalescence of sociology out of relatively heterogeneous elements and components.

In comparison, I would now just like to say a few words about the concept of philosophy. Philosophy is certainly not concerned with the factical in the same way as sociology or the other special sciences are. This was once expressed in a way that may seem naive in terms of our conceptual outlook today, but it is certainly quite sufficient for an initial approach to the problem. Thus it used to be said that philosophy was concerned not with the phenomena but with the essence, not with the facts but with the essence. In this traditional concept of philosophy, from which we need at least to begin, the extremely difficult question regarding the precise relationship between the so-called essence and the so-called facts or data is one that can remain open for the moment. But at least it is clear that philosophy does not concern itself directly or immediately with the facts, and that society does not principally provide the object of philosophy. Now even when a naive or ordinary person, if there is such a thing, approaches philosophy, he or she will certainly not expect philosophy to furnish any information about social things but will expect it to say something on a range of different questions, such as those which are central to Aristotle's *Metaphysics* or Kant's *Critique of Pure Reason*; in other words, questions about the nature of being or what is truly real, about the relation between being and beings, between matter and form, between possibility and actuality, or about the relationship between the Good, the True, and the Beautiful; or again about concepts such as God, freedom and immortality, or finally about the possibility of knowledge, of binding and objectively valid forms of knowledge as such, and all that this implies. These, at any rate, are the traditional themes of philosophy, and the attention of philosophy is drawn to specifically social aspects and elements only when we thoroughly try and work through these themes, only when we develop a critical consciousness of this philosophical thematic, only when we realize that these themes cannot be addressed or resolved directly at a single stroke. And this thematic also changes in the course of the history of philosophy itself. There are a whole range of philosophical concepts which once enjoyed the highest dignity, such as the concept of virtue in ethics or that of natural beauty in aesthetics, but which, for good or ill, have slowly but effectively died out. But the intention of philosophy, at least since the beginning of the early modern age, and to some extent implicitly in antiquity, must be described as *intentio obliqua* rather than as *intentio recta*.[22] In other words, in this context we do not just enquire directly into these things, these essences or these concepts. For when philosophy enquires into these matters, it thereby also enquires into the possibility of the question itself and into the constitution of these objects, since essences and concepts themselves are not facts and cannot therefore simply appear before our eyes with the kind of immediacy which, according to sociology, the '*faits sociaux*' are actually or allegedly supposed to possess. It is therefore an essential feature of every philosophy – and something you can already find in Plato as well as in later philosophy from Descartes onwards – that it never simply makes immediate claims or assertions about things. For it always expressly reflects upon these claims and assertions themselves. The famous Socratic question – 'How do you really know that?' – and thus the awareness that he brought about regarding the 'eidenai tou mē eidenai' (εἰδέναι τοῦ μὴ εἰδέναι)[23] – our knowing that we do not know – is surely the earliest and most authentic expression of this moment or element of reflection which belongs intrinsically to the essence of philosophy. This is part of the reason why philosophy has no immediate object as such, and why it does not immediately know or refer to society either. It is only through this element of reflection that philosophy acquires a relationship to society, whether it believes that it is able in its own right to prescribe norms to society, or whether it mounts a critique of society which measures the latter against its own claims and standards, or whether it recognizes itself and its own subject as a social subject, and thus reflects upon itself as something essentially social in character. In short, the relationship between sociology and philosophy is not something that can be laid down right at the start. On the contrary, it is something that is really produced only through self-reflection on the part of both disciplines as they are unfolded and developed. And science too is not something that is simply given or self-evident in the eyes of philosophy, for philosophy expressly reflects on the truth of science, on the question of whether scientific thought is present at all. Now insofar as philosophy is nothing but the theory of science, which is effectively what the proponents of analytic philosophy have tried to turn it into these days, there is also a sense in which it can actually be called pre-scientific – that is, pre-philosophical. For it accepts a certain concept or intellectual form, namely that of science, which it is essentially the task of philosophy to criticize and to grasp in terms of its inner possibility and basic problematic.[24]

Now I would also just like to add that this structure which I have outlined for you is also connected in a certain way with the fact that the functional roles which philosophy and sociology discharge within society are subject to constant variation, and that they can sometimes even exchange places in this regard. In the opening lectures I already pointed out to you that in Comte's time sociology actually undertook to defend some very traditional values against the critical efforts of philosophy which tended to weaken or dissolve these values. And in terms of its origins, and in terms of the rather narrow sense in which it is now largely understood, we have to say that to this day sociology has remained an apologetic science, whereas philosophy has basically been a critical one. Nonetheless, in our own rather narrow and provincial German situation, as I would describe it, we also encounter the opposite situation. For in Germany philosophy did not emancipate itself from theology as thoroughly as it did in other Western countries, and has remained markedly apologetic in character. Thus to a considerable extent it has continued to defend the notion of absolute values, of unconditioned validity, of the independent character of the mind and its objective expressions, whereas the distinctive achievement of the Enlightenment – namely the recognition that whatever claimed intrinsic being or independent existence in itself had actually emerged and come to be what it is over the course of time – was appropriated by sociology. In Germany therefore one generally needs to proceed in the opposite direction to good old Comte. The issue for us now is not so much to defend the truth of sociological science against the corrosive effects of philosophy as to defend the elevated truths of philosophy against the corrosive effects of sociology. In one of our upcoming lectures I hope to be able to say more about the implications of these apologetic tendencies. For now, I should just like to close by reminding you, in relation to the social function of these two basic issues, as I laid this out for you today, not to divorce them from each other in a somewhat primitive way, as Schiller, for example, attempted to do.[25] In other words, the social function of both philosophy and sociology is something that changes along with the structure and the needs, and especially the apologetic needs, of the society within which these disciplines exist. For I believe that we must never forget that philosophy and sociology are both forms of intellectual life which have their specific place and value in society, and that they can properly be grasped only in the context of the social totality, rather than being treated as if they were something detached and utterly independent.

LECTURE 9
28 June 1960

Ladies and gentlemen,
In the last session Professor Horkheimer offered you a brief introduction to the theory of ideology[1] and laid particular emphasis upon the element of necessary social illusion that is involved here. For at the end of the session, if I am correctly informed, he explained to you that the exchange relation, as far as labour is concerned, inevitably appears to both sides, to both the employer and the worker, in a quite different way. In other words, the employer has the feeling – and inevitably has the feeling – that the worker has received full recompense for his labour, while the worker has the feeling of being somehow short-changed in the process.[2] Now the reason why both of us in the context of this lecture course have now moved straight on to discuss the theory of ideology – which is generally regarded as a special field within sociology, as a specific branch of sociology that has received the rather problematic title of the sociology of knowledge – the reason we have moved on in this way to say something to you about the theory of ideology in this context is really very simple. You will perhaps recall that in my last lecture I attempted, in a somewhat drastic fashion, to clarify the difference between sociology and philosophy. At the same time I also tried to develop for you certain themes and motifs that might help you to understand that both of these disciplines, for all the genuine differences between them, are nonetheless intrinsically dependent upon each other. And, if we now try to say at least something about the concept of ideology, the reason for this is quite simply that the theory of ideology or the sociology

of knowledge is the area where, to put this very straightforwardly, these two disciplines, in spite of the separation imposed by the division of intellectual labour, clearly intersect with each other. This is an area where philosophy and sociology are both equally involved, since sociology here clearly finds itself confronted with philosophical questions, while at the same time it makes certain demands on the understanding and sometimes even the explanation of philosophical questions. And this problematic relationship between the two disciplines has also basically been evident, I would say, for at least the last fifty or sixty years or so, which is why in Germany for about forty years now the field known as the sociology of knowledge has aroused such intensive interest. In Germany this goes all the way back to the work of Mannheim and Scheler,[3] and indeed to Lukács's book *History and Class Consciousness*,[4] where the author attempted to show in a fairly rigorous way how the form assumed by some of the most important modern philosophies, and especially those of Kant and Hegel, could be derived from and explained in terms of social factors, and specifically in terms of the economic relations of production that prevailed at the time. On the one hand, sociology, qua sociology of knowledge, turns its attention directly to the intellectual products and expressions of mind or 'spirit'. Here, once again, it is probably Durkheim who provides the most drastic and perhaps the most radical example of this kind of thinking. For in the later phase of his thought he made an extraordinarily radical attempt to take even such fundamental forms of consciousness as space and time and our most basic categories or logical concepts – which Kant had regarded as constitutive for knowledge as such – and derive them specifically from social relations. Thus he tried to derive space from the necessary articulation or spatial dimension involved in land ownership, to derive time from the order of successive generations and their relations to property, and to derive the categories and especially the processes of classificatory thought from the needs of a feudal-hierarchical community which had modelled its thought-forms in accordance with its own form of social existence.[5]

Now it is easy to criticize this attempt of Durkheim's – which is why I shall not spend much time on this question here – by pointing out that these derivations are compromised by a serious methodological error on his part. For the definitions and determinations which Durkheim provides already presuppose those same basic forms and concepts that are supposed to have been derived from something else. In other words, if you try to derive the conception of space from the necessity for demarcating neighbouring domains of property – and you can try this out for yourselves as a thought experiment

– you will find that all the expressions you can employ to accomplish such demarcation are already unavoidably spatial in character. You cannot accomplish the derivation without already presupposing the representation of space itself, and to that extent the derivation which Emile Durkheim offers is not really stringent in this form. This is so obvious that there is no need to dwell on it any further. On the other hand, I believe it is also important to say something more at this point, if only to counter something of the hubris or overconfidence that is characteristic of sociology in its pioneering phase. For sociology is tempted to believe that it is capable, on its own, of explaining anything and everything without really reflecting upon its own epistemological conditions. So you can already see from this that, precisely where sociology makes an extremely radical claim to provide the quintessential conditions of knowledge itself, it is inexorably led back to fundamental epistemological questions, so that sociology here ends up passing over into philosophy. But quite apart from this – and I imagine that this must all be fairly clear to you by now – I believe that we should also approach this whole complex of issues with some care, and certainly not content ourselves with some comfortable either/or. We shouldn't just be content to say, 'There you are, Durkheim has made a conceptual error here, and is clearly shown to have done so. Case closed!' Now it may well be that these categories, insofar as they possess objective validity, are necessarily presupposed if we wish to make any valid judgements or distinct assertions about spatial, temporal, logical-classificatory relations. Nonetheless, it is quite possible that these conceptions have indeed been formed and developed within just such social constellations, just such levels and types of social life, as those described by Durkheim. And the problem which must remain open here, which cannot simply be prejudged in this context, is the problem of genesis and validity. In other words, we have to ask whether we would ever have recognized this objective character of the validity of space, time and the categories if the genetic processes we are talking about here were not already at work. Perhaps I may just add that Kant's famous arguments about space and time – which basically claim that we cannot represent anything spatial or temporal to ourselves if we did not already possess the universal, all-encompassing and infinite representation of space and time as such – that this Kantian doctrine is nonetheless incomplete in one respect. Kant is certainly right to say that we could never come to experience anything spatial in particular unless we already represent space itself as that which encompasses all particular parts of space.[6] And in the same way he says that we could never speak of any particular time if there were no consciousness of time as such. But it seems to me that Kant has actually told only half the story here. For while we cannot represent anything spatial or temporal to ourselves without that single space and time within which this particular spatial and temporal thing or element would be a part or specification at some determinate point, it is equally true that we cannot represent any space to ourselves without reference to something spatially or temporally determinate that would fall within this space. And if you now make the attempt to represent time as such to yourself without reference to something temporal that would transpire within this time – and analogously in the case of spatial things – you will immediately find that this attempt to represent utterly empty space or utterly empty time to yourselves is just as impossible as the contrary attempt to represent something determinate and empirical in space and time without reference to the form of space and the form of time. This is quite simple: if you try and represent time to yourselves without reference to 'something' through which you can become aware of the flow of time and of change over time, you stumble on a void or vacuum – not in the sense that such time has no particular content, but in the much more critical and tragic sense that your mind is no longer even capable of grasping this void or vacuum itself. It would no longer really be time as such, but simply nothing at all. This brief epistemological reflection is so simple that it would never really make it into or receive any serious attention from the existing theories of knowledge, but if you actually go and apply it to the problematic which I have just been discussing, you will immediately find that this problematic, closely connected with Durkheim's thesis as it is, is by no means as simple as it first appears to be in the light of the criticism that I mentioned to you at the beginning. Let us just consider these concepts of 'space' and 'time' – and please forgive the rather lax talk of concepts here, for I realize perfectly well that space and time themselves are not concepts, and I am using these expressions only to emphasize the universality of space and time at their highest level in contrast to any determinate instances of space or any determinate instances of time. Now if, in order to be able form the concepts of space and time in the first place, you concede that space and time as such cannot be conceived without reference to something that is itself spatial or temporal, then Durkheim's thesis that space and time are derived from particular, factual, social givens with some specific spatio-temporal location surely no longer appears so absurd. It is not that we should conclude from this that space and time must now simply be derived from what is specifically spatial and temporal. It is not as simple as that. But if space and time on the one side and what is specifically spatial and temporal on the other are reciprocally dependent on one another if they are to be conceived or represented at all, then this intrinsically necessary relationship of space and time to some spatio-temporal social reality is certainly not as absurd as it looks at first sight. I just wanted to say this here to show you that, even at the highest level of abstraction, the problem that is raised by the sociology of knowledge – the problem regarding the possibility that forms of consciousness are determined by society – is not such a simple matter as it may initially seem from the perspective of narrow-minded philosophical apologetics.

When we say that sociology deals with the mind or things of the mind as a specific field of its own, and that the question concerning the social dimension of the mind is one of the principal themes of sociology, I believe that it is imperative to move beyond these somewhat general epistemological considerations in order to formulate what we want to say here in rather more concrete social terms. Yet because we are talking about such general categorial structures and states of affairs here, it is an extremely difficult matter to translate these directly in terms of actual, tangible or concrete social phenomena. So even if we do speak about specific social phenomena in this connection we must still remain on a relatively high level of abstraction, quite simply because the concepts in question are also located on an equally high level of abstraction. Now I believe that the basic motif which sociology seeks to exploit in favour of its overall approach here has considerable plausibility. And this is the idea that what we call mind or spirit – the whole field of human consciousness, both the general consciousness of the species, or universal social consciousness, and the consciousness of particular individuals – is not an isolated or self-subsisting realm of its own. On the contrary, mind or spirit itself is an aspect or moment which is bound up in all kinds of ways with the overall life-process of humanity. On the one hand, I think it is quite evident that the process of social labour, and ultimately the preservation of the human species itself, is utterly inconceivable without this aspect or moment that we describe in terms of mind or spirit; on the other hand, it is also clear that mind or spirit itself springs from the need for the self-preservation of the species and also from the specific social forms or institutions that are bound up with this – and the most essential of these developments, it seems to me, is the historical process in which physical labour, by means of which human life is directly secured and sustained, became separated or divorced from mental or spiritual labour. This came about in such a way that the process of physical labour was essentially prompted or initiated by that of mental labour[7] – something which seems entirely plausible in the context of conceiving and then executing a specific end or plan. Indeed we might say – and this will allow you to appreciate the extremely dialectical complication and difficulty of these things – that, if this separation between physical and mental labour had not come about, and if so-called mental labour had not already involved the planning or organization of social production and thus also control over the labour of others, then society, at least in its earlier stages, would probably not have been able to reproduce itself in the first place. This separation of mental from physical labour is itself something that has to be explained in terms of the life-process of society, and it is only at a much later stage that it eventually took on the character of a now simply irrational form of domination – in other words, came to assume its ideological and illusory character. Now if what I have said here is right, then it follows that the absolute independence of mind or spirit is itself a socially necessary illusion, for, in fact, mental labour has come to be separated from physical labour only over the course of history, and only now finds itself subject to a distinctive law of its own. In order to express the problem in a rather extreme form: no mathematical proposition could be conceived, could even be learned or repeated, without the existence of those social processes in which the life of those who elect to pursue mathematics is itself sustained and reproduced. On the other hand, of course, to put this in a rather facetious and exaggerated way, the validity of the simplest mathematical propositions is quite independent of whether one has eaten one's lunch or not. In other words, the world of the mind is dependent in the sense that it can only exist in the context of the material process of life which it presupposes and effectively relies upon; at the same time, its claim to be independent, to produce something internally coherent and consistent, is also legitimate rather than simply illegitimate. The element of untruth here begins to appear only when this independence on the part of the mind is itself made into an absolute, when it forgets the moment of its own dependency or its own relation to the real process of society – in other words, when mind or spirit comes to fetishize or worship itself, as we might put it in a rather emphatic way that goes far beyond the particular context of our present discussion. Now this idea of the independence of the mind is ideological in the quite specific sense that the class character of society itself is here ignored or repressed, so that the actually existing relations of domination are legitimated through the intrinsic and unconditional right of the mind to control or subjugate all that is. Thus among the arguments offered in defence of the existing relations of production you will constantly encounter the idea that it just happens there are clever people and stupid people, and the supposedly clever people, namely the ones with better minds, have justifiably higher claims and expectations than the others. These arguments, and others like them, are the last remaining dregs, as it were, from this momentous historical process in which the mind has asserted its complete independence of physical labour. And since these dregs are all that remain, the thesis in question looks like an extremely suspect and problematic one which has been well and truly contaminated in the process. Now this is where the theories diverge – over the question whether the sphere of the mind functions as a distinct social sphere or whether it is absolutely conditioned by, or is absolutely dependent upon, social factors. And this is also where the various theories of ideology diverge, and diverge, if I may anticipate, in a rather paradoxical fashion. You will easily see how the sociological theory of ideology, specifically with regard to this question – namely whether the sphere of the mind is entirely conditioned or not – inevitably comes up against fundamental philosophical questions. In fact this problem is already formulated in Hegel,[8] and if Hegel is generally seen as a metaphysician of the spirit[9] – and God knows, Marx is hardly blameless in this regard – and thereby also as the principal ideologist of the Prussian state, this actually does him a tremendous injustice. I would just like to point out that in this connection Hegel is infinitely more perceptive and more consistent than his idealist successors and their more limited conception of idealism, as indeed Marx and the Marxists otherwise recognized very well.[10] For already in Hegel we see that the process of spirit, of objective spirit – which is more than the subjective content of individual human consciousness – in other words, the substrate of philosophy, is identified with the historical process, with the real life process of society. What you find in Hegel, therefore, is not so much an attempt to derive the social realm from 'spirit' as an attempt to decipher society itself[11] – precisely by identifying and bringing out the spirit of society, in other words, the constitutive social forms of a specific epoch. And the so-called spirit of a historical epoch is not something that can possibly be detached from the forms in which society produces itself. In fact Hegel never conceived of the life of spirit as something that is somehow independent of the life of the social forms through which it finds expression. On the contrary, the life of spirit for Hegel is nothing other than the self-unfolding of the productive forces of society itself.

Now if it is true that you find an emphatically materialist motif, if I can put it that way, in Hegel's mature philosophy, at the height of his powers – in the *Phenomenology*, which I cannot really regard as one of the philosopher's early writings – you will also discover that Marx endorses a concept which eludes any simple sociological reduction to social relations and is actually the necessary condition of his version of the theory of ideology. I am simply talking about the concept of truth in Marx. Now I do not believe that anyone has ever really undertaken a thorough investigation of Marx's concept of truth. This would certainly be an extraordinarily important and fruitful project to pursue, and maybe one of you here today might consider this as a possible subject for a doctoral thesis. For between the Marx-dogmatism of the East and the Marx-phobia of the West these problems have actually been shamefully neglected for the most part. If you take the concept of socially necessary illusion as seriously as I have indicated you should, and in the form in which I have presupposed it up until now, it is evident that we can properly speak of illusion only if there is also something true or non-illusory in contrast to such illusion. And this concept of truth, for its part, naturally presupposes that, in analysing the illusory itself, we encounter something other than illusion, and that we don't just dogmatically say in a purely gestural way: 'Well of course, the base equals truth, the superstructure equals ideology.'[12] For this very distinction, as a distinction of true and false, already presupposes a concept of truth which is not exhausted in this distinction. You can say that the base is true, the superstructure is false, only if you possess a concept of truth here, or, better, if you develop a concept of truth here, which enables you to distinguish what is indeed true and what is indeed false. The socially necessary illusion needs to be derived from the exchange relation, namely the exchange relation as you have now come to understand it. Marxian theory analyses the way that exchange, which is actually a relation between human beings, necessarily appears to us as a quality of things, as their value, and derives this from the fact that the comparable element between the goods which are exchanged, namely their value, is something abstract, i.e. the socially necessary labour time. It claims that this abstract equivalent of exchange can no longer easily be recognized in terms of its actual relationship to living human beings and living labour. Thus once it has been abstracted and become independent in this way, it ceases to appear as a direct relation between human beings and therefore becomes reified.

I would just like to point out in passing how you can clearly see here that Marxian theory already involves a decisive element that cannot be captured by a vulgar or primitive concept of materialism. And that is the insight, where the decisive issue of exchange as the principle of reproduction of life is concerned, that social reality itself already contains a conceptual moment, namely this moment of abstraction.[13] We have to distinguish between the illusion produced by this abstraction and that which lies behind it – the actual living labour that is made up of human labour power and the contribution of material nature, two aspects that need to be distinguished but can never wholly be divorced from each other.[14] In mounting this critical analysis of illusion, of the fetishized exchange relation, of the abstraction that marks our concepts and ultimately the mind itself, you already discover something that represents the truth moment in contrast to the ideology in question. I should just remind you once again that the exchange relation makes it seem as though we were dealing quite rightly with things here. Herr Horkheimer pointed out to you that matters inevitably appear one way to the employer and a different way to the worker.[15] Now the claim that we are dealing quite rightly with things here already suggests a specific concept of truth, one which implies that an equivalent exchange has actually been accomplished. But it is only critical reflection that can reveal that this relation of equivalent exchange cannot possibly be equivalent, can show in other words that the labour time the worker provides is greater than the labour time that is required for the reproduction of his own life. Thus the worker necessarily gives more than he or she receives, and the entire gigantic process of capitalism, of the accumulation of capital, actually rests on this 'more' which has thus specifically been defined as surplus value.

Now it is probably important for you to take a moment here and be very clear that the employer's deception here, if I may put it this way, lies in the fact that what he provides already involves congealed labour as well as control over the relevant natural resources – in other words, factors that cannot actually be derived from the process of exchange itself, although they inevitably appear to him as natural givens. I say 'inevitably' because these categories – the congealed labour which already enters into the productive process and is always more than the immediate expenditure of the worker's labour, together with the so-called natural resources – involve more than merely individual achievements. For these are categories which actually spring from the whole process of society, from the totality of the productive process. And this totality of the productive process thus appears to the particular individual employer as if it were naturally given, as something over which he has no power, so that he cannot genuinely and in all honesty imagine that he gives less than he receives in this transaction. But the illusion lies precisely in the way that this natural given is a socially mediated given; in other words, what the employer offers the worker and what the latter claims as renumeration already expresses the underlying class relationship and the entire developed form of exchange society or developed market society.

I want to really emphasize this point because it is here – and I believe this is decisive for understanding the relationship between philosophy and sociology – that you discover a central social reality which cannot be grasped at all in the usual common and garden sociologies. And this is that the social totality, in other words, the interconnection of all the subjects that engage in exchange here, is prior to the economic behaviour of the individual subject. The forms of behaviour of the individual employer and the individual worker can really be derived only from this totality, yet the usual positivistic form of sociology attempts to reach some more or less objective social insights only by abstracting from the forms of behaviour of individual human beings, whether this be individual employers, individual workers or some third party. But then the question of ideology – and this is a quite decisive point – becomes a question of theory. So it is not enough simply to say, 'That is ideology', based on nothing more than a general suspicion, or something of the kind.[16] It's not like someone telling a lie that we can immediately see is clearly to their own advantage, and we say: 'That's just a load of ideology', or 'There you go, rationalizing again.' If we want to use the term 'ideology' seriously, if it is to be more than a mere *façon de parler*, then it needs a specific theory of the totality of society behind it, and only when it has such a developed theory to back it up can we legitimately speak of 'ideology'. Where this is not the case, the concept of ideology is just so much blather. And it is no accident that it has become blather, for the concept is thereby robbed of its force, is converted into something that can be used for any purpose and thus can no longer meaningfully be used at all. Nor can it be decided in some immediate and isolated fashion whether something is ideology or not ideology – and let me add right away that there can never be any such immediate or isolated decision regarding truth, or at least regarding truth in the emphatic sense of a comprehensively interconnected whole. We may well be able to come to a true judgement – immediately and with precious little theory – about whether the ventilation system in this room is functioning properly or not, but as soon as you try to determine, for example, whether something such as public opinion is constituted through the consciousness of singular individuals, or is a pure reflection of social institutions themselves, you discover that no such simple decision about truth is possible. For what is required in this regard is a fully articulated theory that is intrinsically bound up with concrete, critical and corrective individual investigations.[17]

Here you see how a motif which Hegel introduced into philosophy also reappears in the theory of ideology, namely the claim that truth does not amount to a declaration,[18] that truth is not something which is merely particular or restricted in character. For the truth is the whole[19] – and here the whole must mean critical insight into the construction of society as a whole, critical insight into the totality of society and into the relationship between this totality and its individual aspects or moments. But such a critique may well result in the recognition that the whole in question does not live up to its own concept, namely the concept of a justly organized and meaningfully self-reproducing whole, and thus conclude that it has itself become 'dysfunctional', as this is so felicitously put today. In other words, the social whole no longer accomplishes precisely what it was supposed to accomplish, for the human beings who are exposed and subjected to this interconnected whole are also mortally and fatefully threatened by the very society to which they owe their life. Now this category of the totality – namely the interconnected character of society as a whole through the fundamental structures within which social action transpires – cannot be derived from the facts in a simply immediate way. The category of totality is not itself a pure fact and cannot be established purely by inference from the facts. And to that extent we might say, if you will forgive me the paradox, that the very doctrine which people love to reproach for being opposed to philosophy, indeed for being alien or downright hostile to philosophy – namely the theory of ideology in its most rigorous form, when it goes beyond the merely factual, grants conceptual thought a moment of independence and resists its dissolution into facticity – must itself inevitably be recognized as a philosophical theory rather than as a merely sociological one. Next time, precisely in order to make this clear, I shall talk to you about the difference between the notion of objectivity which is implied in this theory and the problem of subjectivity as it treated by what I describe as a kind of rustic sociology.

LECTURE 10

30 June 1960

Ladies and gentlemen,

In our last session we considered a range of issues regarding the concept of ideology and the basic problem surrounding the theory of ideology as such. And I might just remind you that the most essential thing which emerged here is that the theory of ideology in its classical form – if I may use that expression for once – does not imply the adoption of some kind of universal relativism or general scepticism with regard to the idea of truth itself. For the concept of ideology in its telling form actually presupposes a very emphatic concept of truth. But this concept implies that truth cannot be presented as a single isolated thesis, for it is formed and articulated by reference to the whole. Sociologically speaking, this means that both the origin and the function of ideologies, along with their truth content or lack of truth content, can be revealed only in terms of their relation to the social totality rather than, for example, by reducing them to certain isolated social factors, or by fishing out certain singular claims or theses as identifiably ideological. This brings me to a distinction which may perhaps have become rather blurred in philosophy today, but which is nonetheless of considerable significance with regard both to the relationship between philosophy and sociology and to the theory of ideology. This is the distinction between the objectivity of truth and mere subjectivity.

To start with, we might say that any and every concept of ideology effectively presupposes the distinction between an objectively valid truth and a merely subjectively distorted truth, rather as Plato expressed this in classic form with his distinction between *alētheia* (ἀλήθεια) and *doxa* (δόξα).[1] But then we must also point out that the theory of ideology itself has undergone that peculiar transformation which derived ideologies, or what were originally described as 'idols', simply from subjective factors or from aspects of human beings themselves. This approach eventually reached a point, especially in the French Enlightenment with the work of Helvétius and D'Holbach,[2] where it became possible to identify the objective social conditions of ideologies. The objectivity of ideologies, that is to say, the objective necessity and the objective untruth of ideologies, was then further developed in the context of the classic Marxian theory of ideology. However, after this culmination of an objective theory of ideology, we might say that, from a certain point onwards in the later phase of bourgeois society, the entire theory of ideology fell back once again to the very early bourgeois stage of a merely subjective approach. Perhaps we shall have an opportunity to say something more precise about this particular issue in due course. But, if we don't in fact have time to do so properly, I would just like to draw your attention to Hans Barth's book on ideology,[3] where the history of this concept and the various transformations it has undergone are presented in an exemplary and extremely penetrating way. I think it is probably more important for you to get a clear idea of the historical development of the concept of ideology from Barth's book than by troubling yourselves to study in any detail certain products of what is currently called the sociology of knowledge.

Now when I talk about the objectivity involved in the concept of ideology I am trying to bring out the following: that the strict or classical form of the theory of ideology derives consciousness and its forms from objective social processes and, indeed, wherever possible from the sphere of production, and in this sphere of production from the relationship between the forces of production and the relations of production. I need to explain these particular terms to you, for otherwise you will find it really difficult to understand what is truly at issue in this strict version of the theory of ideology. By the 'forces of production' you are to understand all those forces through which human beings essentially engage with nature, and especially to the extent that this engagement with nature takes the form of social labour rather than the more or less contingent practices of gathering or hunting or other such archaic activities. To put it rather crudely, to understand the concept of the force of production here you should simply think of human labour power, along with the available technical forces of production, namely the entirety of those technological means which allow human beings to engage with nature. By 'relations of production', on the other hand, you should understand the entirety of social relations, but especially those relations which involve control over the means of production and prevail up to some particular time within some specific form of production as a whole. Now the balance or equilibrium between these two categories – the forces of production on the one side and the relations of production on the other – is only ever temporary in character, and they generally tend to diverge from one another. Thus the relations of production, to the extent that they continue to represent relations of exploitation and domination to this day, have a tendency to perpetuate themselves, to become independent, to carry on existing in an irrational manner. In this way they tend to act as a fetter on the rational forces of society, namely the forces of production, or, in extreme cases, in the catastrophes that repeatedly afflict society in times of crisis and war, even in large part to destroy those forces. When we consider the serious threat of destruction that hangs over the productive forces, in other words, over all human beings, precisely through the prevailing relations of production – through the divergences between the two great dominant social systems in the world today – then I hardly need to say anything more here. In any case, the strict version of the theory of ideology insists that ideologies come into being when the relations of production into which human beings are born and within which they act become a kind of second nature to them, and one which pre-forms all the categories through which they have now come to think.

You have all heard talk about the way the heritage of the great tradition of philosophy is preserved in the critical theory of society.[4] I believe that this is a particularly good place to see what this, and thus our central claim about the relationship between philosophy and sociology, really means and grasp it more deeply than has perhaps been possible in the context of our earlier discussion. You should remember – and this will also be vaguely familiar to those of you who have not specifically studied philosophy – that the problems of knowledge that preoccupied Kant are all what are known as problems of constitution. In other words, Kant is not really concerned with the correctness or otherwise of particular judgements about particular objects, and the Kantian theory of knowledge does not therefore deal with instances of knowledge in the context of certain already established relations of subject and object. Rather, it addresses the question as to how something like a knowledge of objects, how something like organized, internally coherent, and meaningful experience, is actually possible at all. The Kantian theory of knowledge is not a theory which relates specifically to the truth or otherwise of particular cognitive acts in the context of an already established world of objects. Rather, it investigates how this world of objects, and how our own thinking relationship to this world, comes about in the first place. When we say the heritage of classical modern philosophy, namely of the great tradition of Kantian and idealist philosophy, is preserved in the context of the theory of society, what this means, I believe, is essentially this: that the aforementioned problems of constitution have become problems internal to society. In other words, the theory of ideology is not interested in showing how particular interests lead us to misrepresent certain situations or circumstances which unfold in the context of some already existing relation between people and things. Thus the old Enlightenment theory of religion as a deception perpetrated by priests is an approach that is quite alien to the theory of ideology in its strict form, for it is actually a purely subjectivist conception which assumes a *dolus magnus* or mendacious stratagem in the context of an otherwise simply given reality or some given or explicit existing consciousness. Now the theory of ideology in its strict form is not concerned with this sort approach. On the contrary, the essential thing here, and the thing you really need to understand if you are to grasp the concept of ideology in its full import and thereby avoid a merely subjectivistic interpretation of ideology, is that the categories of cognition themselves are intrinsically pre-formed by society as a whole, and also in particular by the relations of social production which are actualized at the expense of truth. According to this theory, truth is to be found in the social forces of production, there where human life actually produces and reproduces itself, whereas this realm of social production is obscured or concealed by the forms within which it takes place. But these forms effectively precede all individual consciousness, all individual intention, all subjectivity in such a way that ideology inevitably arises by virtue of the social totality. In other words, every actual ideology in the strong sense inevitably emerges because in a sense we are unable to think outside the context of this a priori framework – and I deliberately use this expression from the great modern tradition of philosophy – outside the context of the a priori categories of bourgeois society. And it is only because these a priori categories lead to internal contradictions – which is where Hegel comes in – such as the contradiction I presented to you earlier regarding the positions of the worker and the employer in the process of production; it is only by recognizing these contradictions that it is possible for us to break through this universal context of delusion which surrounds us. It is precisely because we are talking about something total here, about a universal context of delusion, that the claim behind the theory of ideology is an extraordinarily profound and radical claim. I would venture to describe it as a philosophically constitutive claim insofar as it goes beyond pointing out the questionable character of false or problematic judgements with regard to certain individual facts or phenomena. In contrast to this, contemporary sociology of knowledge in the positivist sense – which is typical of contemporary science generally and of the science of forms of consciousness in particular – is essentially subjectivistic in character.

And here I would like to draw your attention to a general point which holds for every kind of positivism, and which in the lectures so far I have perhaps not yet indicated as strongly or brought out as emphatically as is required if you are really to understand the current controversy between positivism and the dialectical theory that we are defending here. For I would argue that positivism as a whole is subjectivistic in orientation. Here I am using the expression 'subjectivistic' in the sense in which Hegel speaks about the mere 'philosophy of reflection'.[5] I do not actually want to get into the fundamental problem that Hegel addresses in this context since in this course of lectures, which is essentially concerned with the internal relationship between the disciplines of philosophy and sociology, I cannot explore the development of the Hegelian philosophy as such. But I certainly would like to go into more detail here about this thesis regarding the subjectivism of positivist thought. For those of you who have been following our reflections rather straightforwardly so far this thesis will probably sound like a provocative paradox. For the positivist will typically say something like this: 'It is you speculative thinkers, you who like to talk about a totality that you never really have a firm handle on, that basically think in a purely subjective fashion; it is you who simply see the world in your own terms. It is we, on the other hand, who concern ourselves with the facts as they are given, the facts that can be observed and verified in accordance with the method of the natural sciences.' In other words, the positivist will try and turn the tables here and claim: 'You are the true subjectivists, namely those who have no rigorous notion of truth at all.' Now this conception on the part of positivism seems to me quite false. The older tradition of positivism, both in its classical version in Hume and in its later elegant development in terms of the natural sciences during the nineteenth century in thinkers such as Mach and Avenarius, had actually admitted its subjectivistic character quite openly insofar as all of the facts that were supposed to furnish a firm and reliable foundation for positivism are identified precisely as facts of consciousness. Thus it was repeatedly said of Hume, with a certain if not entirely compelling justification, that his theory of knowledge, and the entire philosophy that it supported, is essentially a psychologistic theory.[6] And this implies that he was basically interested in reducing all cognitive acts to certain subjective conditions, and that the criterion of truth is ultimately the adequate relation of judgements to the connected subjective givens of consciousness or to the subjective data of consciousness.

Here I would just like to add something else that touches on the history of philosophy, which is that the real difference between Kant and Hume should be located at this very point. For Kant the sphere of the transcendental, which is also a subjective sphere, is essentially the object of philosophical analysis, although the direction of his interest is an expressly objective one. In other words, Kant takes the objectivity of knowledge as his starting point and then seeks to ground this objectivity by showing how the claim to objectively valid knowledge and the subjective constitution of experience are reciprocally dependent on each other. The fundamental intention of Kantian philosophy, in contrast to positivist philosophy, was an objective one, and there are formulations in the *Critique of Pure Reason* which make this unambiguously clear.[7] I think you should be very careful here not to treat the subjectively oriented method of the *Critique of Pure Reason* as an analysis of consciousness on something like the Humean model and thereby misunderstand what the Kantian philosophy is really trying to do. Kant's insight here, his fundamental point, is that objectivity is supposed to be confirmed or explicated through subjective analysis in his sense, whereas in Hume, by contrast, the concept of objectivity itself is criticized through subjectivity and thereby deliberately eliminated. I just wanted to point this out in passing here for, if you bear this clearly in mind from the start, it may well help you to understand the *Critique of Pure Reason* later. Hegel went on to take this very moment of objectivity as mediated through subjectivity as the cornerstone of his entire philosophy, and it seems to me that in this particular regard – as in so many others – Hegel proved to be a truly consistent Kantian and the genuine heir of Kantian philosophy.[8] But of course I can suggest this only in a merely summary fashion here and must leave you to explore the relevant texts to substantiate these claims.

Although it is not possible to develop the problem of positivism as a whole here, we can say that positivism in its recent form differs from its older version in one respect. For in one way or another it has rumbled this subjectivism and has realized that this reduction to the merely subjectively given cannot be reconciled with that claim to objectivity on the part of science which positivism also defends. And we could probably interpret the entire reformulation of positivism in recent times, by Russell and Whitehead on the one hand[9] and by the so-called Vienna Circle on the other,[10] precisely as an attempt to obviate or overcome this arbitrary appeal to merely subjective givenness, to something which cannot possibly account for the objectivity of knowledge. This was accomplished by replacing the concept of the immediately given and its various relations – my sensations and impressions in Hume, or the given as a whole and its complex connections in the later positivist theories of knowledge – and making protocol sentences into the ultimate given. For it had become clear that something like the basis of knowledge is quite inconceivable without the mediation of linguistic expressions. Here I shall ignore the fact that the introduction of language through the protocol sentence already brings a particular aspect into play which escapes the demand for verification or falsification insofar as every linguistic expression through its own objectivity inevitably points beyond the particular observations that are supposed to be captured by it. I just wanted to say that, of course, even where we stay with this formulation of the protocol sentence as the ultimate datum, the content of these protocol sentences is interpreted as a merely subjective givenness. Thus the question regarding the constitution of subjectivity itself, the question regarding the objective context within which this subjectivity stands, remains just as unanswered as the question regarding the objectivity of the linguistic expression and its objective origin, even though the latter, especially on this theory insofar as it is itself a semantic theory, is made into a sort of criterion of truth. I would say, therefore, that even with these recent forms of positivism we are still talking about a rather shameless subjectivism, and that one could show that these ultimate criteria are criteria of mere subjectivity where the further question regarding the objective connections in which such criteria stand is basically avoided. These subjective givens are retained in their immediacy and treated as an ultimate fixed datum rather than really being seen as moments within the totality of the life process and the process of cognition. I like to express this by saying that positivism as a whole, in concentrating on such fixed immediacies in this way, is in reality a reified or thing-like form of thinking, in spite of Hume's critique of the concept of thing.

Now if we accept here that the entire objectivity that is claimed by positivism, which believes it has avoided all subjective projections, is a mere illusion, one can certainly say that the positivist conception of the social world – in the domain of that which is already constituted, namely in the domain of knowledge about society – must also be described in certain essential aspects as merely subjectivistic in comparison with the theory of ideology in its classic form. I would like to bring out two specific moments for you in a really trenchant way. Firstly, the positivistic approach to the facts of consciousness and the forms of consciousness, to the prevailing ideologies insofar as they can be identified, to the behaviour, the attitudes, and on occasion even the practical motivations of human beings, is essentially focused on individual subjects, while at the same time it neglects the relationship of these individual subjects to one another and the factors which govern this relationship. This is especially true where statistics are concerned. I believe it is often overlooked that the statistical approach is atomistic, if I can put it as boldly as that, in the sense that it takes the individual consciousness as its point of departure, for the underlying elements of any statistical assertion are just singular individuals which are then brought under some common denominator, in terms of their shared characteristics, of what is numerically identical – or at least almost identical – or non-identical with respect to them all. But the resulting universal propositions or regularities are abstracted from the individual subjects without its being acknowledged whether or to what extent these individual subjects are already pre-formed by the overall context or relationship in which they stand to one another; in other words, if I may use this expression once again, to what extent they are pre-formed by the relations of social production.

In addition, we must recognize that the positivist sociology of knowledge and therefore all the empirical-sociological claims that we make about culture are based to a considerable extent upon the individual consciousness of the subjects in question. But this runs the tremendous danger of hypostasizing the consciousness that individuals currently have with regard to themselves and then, as so often happens in America, of expressly elevating this consciousness into the norm. You must not forget that there is an extraordinarily intimate connection between market research, the interest in discovering potential customers, and the empirical methods that are available at the time. There is thus a real tendency towards simply identifying the *'volonté de tous'*,[11] or the prevailing majority opinion, with the truth in the spirit of a purely subjective nominalism: 'Twenty million Americans cannot be wrong.'[12] Thus if you go out and buy some entirely dubious cosmetic product, then this – since no criterion of truth other than the agreement of the greatest number is permitted – is precisely the measure of truth. And it requires a considerable critical effort to get beyond this mentality. For we are soon bound to encounter the fatal objection: 'Well, you'd better tell us which product is the good one by identifying some objective features or characteristics independent of the subjects in question', or again: 'Just tell us which plays or which pieces of music are the good ones as distinct from those which constantly pour out of our television sets or our loudspeakers.' But any attempt to offer some such abstract objective hierarchy of values entirely detached from the experience of these subjects would itself be just as false and inadequate as the mere subjectivism we have rejected, for truth is constituted in the relationship of both moments to each other. It does not lie in contrasting statistical generalizations about the consumers of radio programmes, hygiene products, or things of this kind, on one side, with a hierarchical conception of the True, the Good and the Beautiful grounded in metaphysical values, on the other. For this consciousness which has split the world into these two complementary moments is precisely that reified consciousness which I was talking to you about before – and is also, I might point out, the very consciousness that shrinks from the Hegelian effort and labour of the concept. Now Hegel, whom I mentioned earlier, had a particularly acute and perceptive awareness of these things, as we can see from his famous reflections on the question of 'public opinion' in the *Philosophy of Right*, when he claimed that it was worthy of respect and contempt at the same time.[13] For an aspect of sound common sense is also involved here – and all these statistical generalizations also involve aspects or moments that reflect true human needs, and to that extent are worthy of our attention, if I can put this rather crudely, but also of our contempt to the extent that public opinion, we would surely say today, has become ideology to an extraordinarily high degree. In other words, it has become a form of thought that expresses the currently prevailing objective relations of production, which are merely reflected in such thinking. Thus public opinion as such, which to a considerable extent is nothing more than a reflex of the existing relations of power, does not have much directly to say about truth. Since the forms of social power have now so explicitly and effectively taken over what today is charmingly called 'the means of mass communication', since this development has taken place, the functional dependence of so-called public opinion on the realities of social power has naturally become incomparably more difficult to overlook. Thus I would say at this point that, if we consider the interest of philosophy, which grasps the concept of truth in terms of objectivity, and indeed as an objectivity mediated by human subjects, and the interest of sociology, which shows how the subjective contents of consciousness and the forms of consciousness are already essentially mediated by forms of socialization, we can see that, contrary to the vulgar notion that people will often encourage you to believe, there is actually no opposition or divergence between philosophy and sociology here, for at this point these two criteria in truth converge on each other. And even as I have tried to point out for you the differences between these disciplines, the whole point of what I am attempting to accomplish in these lectures is to show you that precisely what differs in each case here is nonetheless essentially interconnected. Thus from the social perspective one might say that the subjective consciousness is not something irreducible that we have to accept or reproduce simply because it looks like the first reliable thing we can lay hands on in our surveys or questionnaires. For this consciousness is itself largely derivative in character. On the other hand, we must also add – which brings me back to Hegel's point that public opinion must be respected too – that the subjective consciousness of human beings also contains a certain truth content. Thus a theory which simply ignores or overrides the consciousness that human beings have with regard to themselves is just as deluded as the opposite approach is obtuse – the approach which simply takes human beings à la lettre, just as they rate or assess themselves, as people like to put it. Whether we prefer the deluded approach or the obtuse one here is a matter of taste. I would say that this essentially depends on what we are confronted with in the particular case. It might be that today, for example, certain investigations regarding the consciousness of workers would show that the workers in question do not actually feel themselves to be workers.[14] Now such a view of the matter is not itself decisive insofar as, objectively speaking, in terms of the position of these individuals within the productive process, the difference between the owners and the workers, and everything else involved here, is certainly much the same as it was a hundred years ago. On the other hand, we would have to add – and this is a problem belonging to the critical insight into truth within sociology, in other words to the relationship between sociology and philosophy – that, even if no worker in the world regards himself any longer as a worker, this implies that, at the very least, certain internal changes in the concept of the worker have taken place (to express myself very cautiously here). These changes mean that we can no longer apply the image and concept of the worker in the same direct or immediate way in which they were formerly applied. The most brilliant theory of surplus value no longer has any use at the point where the workers literally no longer know that that is what they are.[15] If we neglect this, we are blinding ourselves to the fact that the subjective moments of people's own consciousness are also moments of objective social reality.

For those of you who are specifically interested in sociology, I would also just like to mention that this is perhaps a good place to appreciate the quite particular significance that attaches to one specific field of sociological research. I am talking about the field of so-called motivational analysis. This is a field which does not simply content itself with registering individual subjective views, opinions, forms of reaction, types of behaviour as irreducible givens which simply need to be translated into Hollerith cards,[16] to be subsumed and interpreted, as they say – and 'interpreted' here is just a fancier word for 'cashed out'. For motivational analysis specifically attempts to take these realities, which positivism sees as irreducible, these so-called givens, these findings which you directly come upon, in order to grasp them in their broader context and see how they are determined. That is why I believe that the development of motivational analysis, and above all its progressive refinement far beyond what has been accomplished so far, would prove extraordinarily significant for empirical social research in particular. At the same time, however, I would not wish to oversimplify or paint an over-rosy picture of that unity of sociology and philosophy which I have tried to present for you today in terms of these intellectual models. It is enormously tempting to imagine that we can move beyond mere subjectivism, that we can discover the social objectivity, the objective character of the social process we are seeking, if only we pursue the positivist analysis as far as possible – that is to say, if we no longer simply stick with the immediately given but try to extend it through further processes of empirical verification. Unfortunately this is not the case. Now this is not just on account of the inadequacies of our current scientific practices – which God knows I have no desire to denigrate – but rather for quite categorical reasons, namely because the motivations for the specific socially observable perspectives, rigid views, ideologies, modes of behaviour, etc., cannot simply be traced back causally to individual effects and individual motives, to what one has heard in the parental home, in the school, in the beer hall on the train, or wherever else one could mention. Yet unless we try and anchor motivations in this way, it seems we can't get to them at all, and everything just threatens to dissolve in generalities. And anyone who is involved in empirical social research will rightly tell you that questions that cannot be related to quite specific effects, and if possible from just last week, are not rigorous or precise. This is all very well from the methodological point of view, yet method and the claim to method are not identical with the claim to truth. Thus the ideological effect that is exercised by cinema, to take a concrete example of a characteristic ideology, probably cannot be measured by claiming that someone who sees a film called *Yet Spring Will Come Again*[17] is bound to come out with a lower intelligence quota than he had when he went in. But since the whole system of film production, and this also – and perhaps indeed especially – holds for the supposedly higher quality films, in principle shares the form of *Yet Spring Will Come Again*, we should say it is the totality of films which ultimately effects or encourages that state of consciousness which one would be wrong to ascribe specifically to one sentimental film about an ordinary woman, for it is simply a function of the producers which make it into that sort of film in the first place. Now I am speaking here of the totality of films, but what a slight thing that is, surely the weakest thing imaginable, in comparison with the totality of all those social mechanisms that affect us as a second nature. In other words, if ideology, as I have argued, is actually mediated through the totality of society rather than through so-called individual effects, individual causal processes, individual dependencies, then we cannot just break through what I call the context of delusion simply by identifying these individual effects and processes. For it will be possible to break through it only by achieving theoretical insight into the specific character of the very totality that produces ideology itself.

LECTURE 11[1]
5 July 1960

Ladies and gentlemen,

In the last session we discussed certain aspects of the theory of ideology. But it is now time to tell you, or rather explicitly underline for you – for this has of course been implicit in all of these lectures so far – that the theory of ideology constitutes the real stumbling block where the controversy between philosophy and sociology is concerned. The fundamental argument is that the claim to the objectivity of truth, as this is upheld by philosophy, is essentially undermined by sociology, since the latter, instead of actually addressing questions of truth, already subjects every idea of objective truth to doubt by suspecting it of ideology. Sociology allegedly tries to replace insight into any kind of binding truth or validity by exposing the source of the thesis in question. Now you will all be more or less aware that, during the 'Third Reich', the discipline of sociology fell victim to such objections as this, or, as I would prefer to say, to such pretended objections as this. Yet the intellectual attitude which finds expression in this particular schema or prejudice has certainly not been banished entirely even now. I recently encountered something of this kind in relation to a book of mine in which certain social aspects of music played a specific role. One of the most highly regarded German critics – and one incidentally who was by no means entirely unsympathetic to my own writings – responded to the way in which I indicated certain social relationships at work here with the apodictic claim that it was well known that he himself rejected the idea of such a relationship between music and society, and that this was really just a matter of personal opinion.² Now I believe that this attempt to convert such questions into an issue of personal belief – one person sees cultural and intellectual things in the context of society, another person will have nothing to do with this approach; it just depends on the sort of person you are – really belongs in a pre-scientific sphere of thought. In other words, it shirks the necessity of knowledge, where such social connections could really be established, or at least tries at some point to call a halt to the process of knowing, and turns instead to the field of subjective preferences.

But if someone cannot feel the connection between Beethoven's music and the ideas of humanity which were still very much alive in Germany in the period following the French Revolution, if someone cannot feel in Richard Wagner the connection with imperialism and the pessimism of a class that no longer has a future, if someone cannot feel in Richard Strauss anything of the tremendous entrepreneurial élan that his music captures, I would have to say that their actual experience of the object itself is to some extent impoverished, and that they simply perceive less in terms of the object in question.³ If the intellectual and cultural things in our experience assume any life at all for us, this life actually consists in their relation to the social world. But this relationship to the social is beyond mere conjecture, since the mediations that are involved can be established well beyond any merely biographical or merely genetic connections. Thus when we say, for example, that the history of painting or the history of music in a sense arises on the historical basis of bourgeois society itself, we can identify the relevant mediating factors here, albeit in a rather abstract and general way. For the advancing power of technology – namely the advancing control over the material of nature which goes hand in hand with the development of bourgeois rationality itself – this progress in technology and in the rational domination of natural material is precisely what furnishes the principle in accordance with which – in the fields of art I have chosen to mention here – the productive forces have unfolded and the history of these arts has developed. In saying this, however, I have no intention of denying the internal or immanent character to be found in the history of cultural and intellectual products. Thus I do not wish to deny that there is such a thing as the history of mind or spirit, although I would harbour reservations about treating this history in too self-contained a way and hypostasizing it as a kind of pure cultural or intellectual history. I do believe, however, that the forces which constitute this history of spirit – and in a way that to this day has admittedly never been fully analysed in really concrete terms – must be described in large measure as social forces, even though one is hardly aware of them as such. In other words, the productive forces which unfold in the cultural and intellectual sphere are actually none other than those which unfold in the process of society as a whole. And the task of revealing the mediations which are involved here in a genuinely concrete manner is one that has barely been addressed as yet. The social examination of cultural and intellectual matters is something that has fallen into discredit only through the wretched habit of simply coordinating the expressions and creations of culture with certain social trends or even social groups, and doing so in a way that is decreed from above. No real attempt is made to disclose the cultural objects themselves in terms of their own immanent character or their own intrinsic meaning. And there is no doubt that the Marxian theory of ideology – from a relatively early point onwards, and certainly already with Mehring[4] – bears considerable responsibility for this simplification and vulgarization of the concept of ideology, a process which has effectively triumphed in the East today.

But I don't really want to get into all this in detail here – we shall have more to say about it in due course, since this is a crucial question where the relationship between society and culture, between sociology and philosophy, is concerned. Here I would just like to consider this complex of issues in the light of the ideas we have tried to explore in the last few sessions, and which I hope may now start to prove fruitful. What I mean is that the theory of ideology in its strict form – as I presented it earlier and as Herr Horkheimer explained it to you as a necessary form of false consciousness – is precisely not one that relativizes the concept of truth. On the contrary, as I pointed out in the last few lectures, it actually holds fast to an objective concept of truth. It is a remarkable fact that those versions of the theory of ideology, or, perhaps I should say, those formulations of the sociology of knowledge which do represent forms of sceptical relativism and thus express a weakened conception of knowledge, are approaches which specifically fail to employ the concept of ideology in its really strict formulation. These are all later and somewhat etiolated expressions of the theory of ideology. In other words, I am talking here of what we might call the totalized concept of ideology, an approach which seems to intensify the concept of ideology to the greatest possible degree and extend it way beyond its merely particular classical formulation, although it actually ends up by fundamentally weakening and eventually destroying the concept of ideology. Now everything is ideology, which is just what we find in the radically relativist and sceptical-positivist doctrine of Vilfredo Pareto.[5] In other words, everything is equally true and equally untrue, so that the only direct conclusion to be drawn here is actually that power alone decides the matter – a theoretical transition that was openly and, I would say, almost innocently endorsed in the early period of Italian fascism before it was specifically recommended in propagandistic terms in Germany under the auspices of Herr Goebbels. In the early writings of Mussolini, who expressly regarded himself as a disciple and advocate of Pareto, you will easily recognize this obvious transition from universal philosophical relativism to the doctrine of power that was espoused by fascism, as I have already indicated to you.[6]

Now, ladies and gentlemen, I have to say that, if you really want to achieve anything fruitful with the concept of ideology, if you wish to avoid the kind of clichéd thinking that says: 'Ah, so that's where it comes from! It can't be worth anything after all.' This is the kind of thinking which disposes of the expressions of mind and culture on account of their ancestry, just as it has occasionally disposed of whole groups of people on exactly the same grounds. In response to such thinking I believe you cannot do better than take the expressions of mind and culture seriously in themselves and try to explore their truth and their untruth, their inner coherence or their incoherence. The path which offers insight with regard to ideology is not that of abstract classification but the path of determinate critique. The spirit of supposedly total suspicion with regard to ideology, the kind of defeatism which imagines it is already entitled to ignore intellectual and cultural experience itself because it can point out the origins from which the expressions of mind or spirit have arisen, this sort of approach, rather than preserving any genuine critical power, should actually and more appropriately be compared with the sceptical mentality of an old hand who has seen far too much in his life and now basically regards everything as equally true and equally untrue. Yet everything that belongs to mind or spirit implicitly makes a claim to truth. And even when, subjectively speaking, this is not the case, when the film producer who actually makes rubbish is perfectly ready to admit at the party after his third whisky that this is all that it is, we find that his creations involve a number of features that indirectly recall moments which belong to the traditional work of art, moments which bear on the claim to truth content. That is why such creations still have something about them which both evokes and contrasts with the question concerning truth. The only appropriate approach to the things of mind or spirit is one that tries to explore their immanent truth content, their immanent substance. The question concerning ideology in a sense loses its meaning where really significant works are concerned, for if ideology is actually nothing but false consciousness we could also say that ideological expressions of culture are really just bad expressions of culture. In order to decide what a good or a bad expression of culture is, we cannot appeal to topological considerations about where a given expression of culture is to be correctly located. The only thing which helps here is to enter into the heart of the matter itself, for every other approach remains abstract in the pejorative sense, i.e. imagines that it can spare itself any serious engagement with mind or spirit and its substantial expression simply by recourse to the entirely generalized idea that mind or spirit is essentially dependent on society. Such an approach already fails to recognize what is decisive here, namely the difference between genuine and false consciousness, for that is something that can be determined only immanently rather than externally through some abstract process of coordination or through exercising the famous 'suspicion of ideology'. This sort of suspicion – the wholly general recognition that everything connected with mind or spirit has something or other to do with society – initially says absolutely nothing about the matter in question, above all because the fact that something or other has arisen within the context of something else says nothing as yet about the truth of what has arisen or not arisen as the case may be. You are only really tempted to believe that it does since we are all more or less victims of the mythological idea that what is true and exists intrinsically as something eternal and immutable cannot have arisen or come to be. This is the idea that there must be something absolutely first in the order of being, as *prima philosophia* has always claimed to show, and that something is already disqualified if it comes from somewhere. On the one hand, of course, everything comes from somewhere, but this completely abstract way of relating something valid to its genesis is by no means equivalent to making an appropriate judgement with regard to the matter in question, for it actually tends in general to avoid such judgements. Now it is characteristic of the whole period of the theory of ideology in its declining phase, as I would describe it – since it essentially dissolved the Marxian conception of ideology precisely by extending it too far – that it does not really get beyond this abstract theory of dependence, or at best simply produces certain correlations between ideology and society without actually being able to establish any relation to what is 'true' or 'false' in the matter in question. In this regard the late bourgeois theory of ideology that we find in Pareto or Mannheim cannot really be distinguished from the alternative extreme that is currently endorsed in the Eastern bloc, namely that mechanical application of the theory of ideology which equally avoids engaging with the experience of the inner logic or otherwise of the expressions of mind or culture that it chooses to consider. In short, it is not actually the critique of ideology that is relativistic; rather, it is the kind of absolutism that is so popular these days, namely the belief in those celebrated absolutely binding values that we try so hard to maintain because we think that we cannot possibly manage without them. It does not occur to us that the very rigidity of these values which we want to endorse is itself simply a reflection of the rigid and reified consciousness that searches for such values without even reflecting that this need itself, this need for a supposedly firm foundation, as yet says nothing about what is really at stake. At this point we must not fail to recognize Nietzsche's insight that the need for some substantial spiritual reality hardly suffices to prove that such a thing exists. If I fear that I shall die and be lost for all eternity, and thus infer my immortality from this fear of death, then this itself is more a proof of mortality, as Nietzsche says somewhere, than it is a proof of immortality.[7] And I would say that there is actually precious little difference between the painful need for so-called eternal values, which we see around us today and is so anxious to defame any critical reflection on things, and the general attitude which I have been describing for you.

Perhaps you will allow me at this point, in these otherwise quite objectively oriented lectures, to address a few words directly to you regarding your own personal attitude and fundamental orientation. For I would specifically like to warn you about the danger of apologetic thinking. In other words, I would like to warn you against regarding thought as a means or instrument that is meant to provide you with something or other, that you can firmly hold on to, that will basically reconfirm for you something that is already in force, something which has already been confirmed by the tradition. For it is an essential and distinctive character of thought that it remains open. And to think in accordance with premises which already effectively sanction the result of thought – in the sense of some particular and established positivity – even before it has abandoned itself to its own movement, to think in this way is to engage in pseudo-activity, to indulge in a spurious kind of thinking altogether. If you look upon your studies as anything more than the acquisition of technical knowledge or expertise for the purpose of proving your academic credentials, then I would say that there is a crucial moral problem that every one of you will basically have to confront at some point or another. In other words, you must summon the intellectual courage to avoid letting your thought simply be dictated to or regulated in advance by everything one is already supposed to endorse or believe, whether it be as a Marxist, as a Christian, as a liberal, or whatever it may be. Thus in all of the judgements you make you should beware of this ominous 'as' which invariably belongs to the sphere of heteronomy – the heteronomy which you have effectively relinquished as soon as you seriously undertake to study something, in other words, as soon as you seriously attempt to understand something on the basis of your own reason and your own knowledge, although we are constantly in danger of falling back into such heteronomy under the overwhelming pressure of the world in which we live. That the power of thinking may destroy something, whatever it may be, is no argument against this thinking if such destruction appears compelling – that is, if the thing itself calls for destruction. For destruction of this kind, if we are talking about genuine thinking here rather than a merely sophistical exercise of ingenuity, is not an unmotivated play of thought that is simply intent on tearing something down, as people like to say. Rather, it is motivated by the thing itself, which is all that justifies such thinking. And if a thing is bad, it also deserves to be recognized in thought as the bad and inadequate thing that it is. When we try and avoid this, when we fail to confront it, and even regard such avoidance as a higher kind of ethos, we are acting more pharisaically rather than more ethically. And if you learn anything at all in these lectures, it should be a fundamental self-criticism with regard to this attitude which threatens to reassert itself on all sides today to a quite disturbing degree. The concept of 'the positive' which people love to employ in this connection has itself already assumed a rigid, ossified and reified form. Thus as soon as we start looking round for so-called values, we see that things which once enjoyed a substantial living presence within a culture have already become alienated from us, have already ceased to be binding on us, and are now abstractly fixed and retained as 'values'. I would almost say that, as soon as we explicitly start asking about values, we find that the values in question for that very reason no longer actually exist, that such things are only falsified when they are grasped in terms of the category of value, one which specifically derives from the sphere of political economy and, not by accident, reflects the mere relation of exchange. That we should have something solid to hold on to, that we want to bind ourselves to something reliable, cannot possibly be a criterion for anything. For science in the emphatic sense – namely the kind of knowledge which is not limited simply to the acquisition of expertise or information – really begins only when we move out into the open space of thought, when we completely relinquish the illusory notion that thought must yield or produce something wholly determinate – like the profit we secure through haggling. Anyone who would measure thinking by this yardstick soon falls back into dogmatism, and I would just remind you that, with very good reason, Kant actually treated dogmatism and scepticism as equivalent to each other.[8] The reason for this is simply that what I happen to accept dogmatically – when I take or believe something to be true without being involved in this truth myself, or without spontaneously recognizing this truth on my own part – can just as easily be replaced, according to the pragmatic considerations of the moment, by something else that is accepted in an equally blind and heteronomous way. Thus objectively speaking – once reason has abdicated its task of distinguishing between truth and untruth – we see how the dogmatic approach and the sceptical approach immediately pass over into each other. A thinker who halts the process of thinking in order to preserve something or other – and today this has already shrunk to something as thin and meagre as being as such – has thereby merely abandoned thought to arbitrariness. The thinker thus works against just what he had hoped to hold on to precisely by undermining its claim to truth. Thus he no longer even raises a claim to truth, but rather, for the sake of that reified possession of something he could not contemplate losing, he now just posits and manipulates it. What is truly relativistic, ladies and gentlemen, is not the exercise of trenchant critical insight but the blind acceptance of a truth that could be just as easily exchanged for another one. Such a need actually reflects what I would describe as a reified consciousness, that is, a consciousness which no longer really achieves a living experience of objects. This consciousness is at once both rigid and changeable; in other words, it operates with hard and fast categories yet is also intrinsically capable of arbitrarily exchanging certain aspects or moments for a whole range of different ones. At some point in the not too distant future I hope to offer you a developed theory of reified consciousness,[9] as I have already done with regard to the phenomenon of 'half-education'.[10] Just let me say here that the reified consciousness takes the object in advance as something rigid and alien to the subject, and typically as something conventional or externally approved; while, on the side of the subject, the reified consciousness actually comes to resemble a thing – in other words, increasingly adapts to the prevailing world of things, to the preponderant power of the existing order. In accommodating itself to what is as it now is, without any apparent alternative, such consciousness imagines that it can actually secure and acquire, in an external way, those normative features which have already been lost to it precisely because it cannot distinguish between true and false, because it no longer has access to living experience. What I just want to say, ladies and gentlemen, if you will forgive me this outburst of pedagogic eros, is that you must take care, and take care above everything else, to recognize the dangers of this reified consciousness, one which nowadays has developed an entire vocabulary for itself – and I will not even try to qualify this claim[11] – that will allow you to identify the typical thought-forms of just such reified consciousness. I would say it is probably more important than anything else that I might say to you in particular about the relationship between sociology and philosophy if I encourage you in your own intellectual life to do everything you possibly can to resist this reification of consciousness, which has probably infected all of us in one form or another. One has only to think, for example, of the division or separation of knowledge into a sphere of facts, which belong in sociology, and one of ideas, which belong in philosophy, or, again, of the separation between the question of genesis, which belongs in sociology, and the question of validity, which belongs in philosophy, or whatever other rigid dichotomies you care to mention. These habitual modes of thinking, which fundamentally underlie the controversy between sociology and philosophy, are themselves actually nothing other than an expression of such reified consciousness. And the most important task for the theory of knowledge today, with regard to human cultural and intellectual life generally, is surely to show that these rigid pairs of concepts which are effectively presented to us as if they had nothing to do with each other, in truth only represent the rupture between consciousness and objectivity. They merely mirror or reflect that state of alienation which the need for values, for being, for rootedness, for a sustaining centre, or whatever it may be, hopes to escape. This I believe is the central thought which should enable you to address the fundamental problem of philosophy and sociology with which you will surely continue to be confronted. I am perfectly aware, of course, that whatever I can say to you on this subject is really nothing but a formal indication that you will have to realize and develop in terms of your own thought and experience, although I certainly cannot presume to articulate this thought for you here with any genuine rigour. This reified consciousness – this consciousness which seeks something it can rely on externally and hardens itself in the process, is simply the correlate of the administered world. Thus what is relativistic here, if I may repeat the point, is certainly not the realm of living experience that resists such consciousness. On the contrary, we find that there is actually a profound affinity between the blindness of a reified consciousness which simply accepts things without immanently engaging with them and a relativistic habit of thinking for which any truth can arbitrarily be replaced by another one. And this holds for our attitude or position in relation to any theory. Today any theory can be snapped up and abused by reified consciousness. There are no theories which enjoy any special privilege in this regard or are intrinsically protected against this mechanism. Even a theory such as the Marxian one, in which the concept of reification plays such a significant role,[12] is by no means immune to reified consciousness simply because it specifically reflects on this concept. The apologetic need that I have described as the real enemy of living consciousness is actually the expression of a weakened consciousness, an expression of anxiety, which nonetheless points back to an entire social order which we still have every conceivable reason to fear, just as we had before. It might initially be possible to repress this anxiety by looking for the sort of value system we mentioned and trying to take our bearings from that system. But such repression works no better than any other kind, as psychology teaches us: the sense of security that we gain by finding something we can rely on, as we say, is paid for by an even greater sense of insecurity and anxiety when we realize that we do not really believe in what we are clinging to and have merely produced it because we need it. What is intellectually demanded of us, therefore, before we can even engage with the concept of ideology, is to open ourselves to the living experience of the thing itself instead of prejudging the matter by imposing external correlations upon it.

Now, ladies and gentlemen, if I may leave these reflections for the moment, you may also have learned something else from the considerations we have pursued so far. And this is that the correlations between theoretical forms and social forces which you are probably used to regarding as more or less self-evident or straightforward cannot really be described as such. Consider, for example, the culturally conservative or traditionalist theory of ideology which over thirty years ago now was particularly associated with the name of Max Scheler, a colleague of mine from the early Frankfurt days and a figure of considerable intellectual stature.[13] He produced a kind of catalogue which sought to establish a correlation between intellectual thought-forms and some specific social outlook, or certain social tendencies, and even, if possible, particular social groups. Thus Scheler claimed that revolutionary thought was essentially a form of nominalistic thought,[14] whereas conservative thought was essentially Platonic-realist in orientation, and he offered other correlations of this kind. Now I think I have already said enough in the last few sessions, although we didn't go into this in detail – and I would ask you to think back on our earlier discussion here – to show the inadequacies of such an approach. Let us just consider nominalism, the view that sees individual things alone – or, in the idiom of modern positivism, individual facts alone – as *ousia* (οὐσία), as that which truly exists; by contrast, it regards all concepts, and in the last analysis all theory, simply as the abbreviated expression of the facts which they subsume, and it refuses to grant any genuine significance to theory itself.[15] Now according to Scheler's theory – and I would say this holds for ordinary consciousness as well – it appears that nominalism is intrinsically critical and revolutionary, that it dissolves established ideas in a sceptical spirit, whereas Platonism, by contrast, is conservative, static, preservative and, indeed, noble in comparison with that common or plebeian element that, so we have all been told, is essential to nominalism. I think that the considerations we have already pursued will have shown you that this is not actually the case. From the late medieval period onwards the emerging bourgeois culture struggled against a feudalism oriented towards a philosophy of conceptual realism, and did so in increasingly nominalist terms. Right up to the threshold of the modern period, the age which is marked by names such as Saint-Simon and Comte, philosophical nominalism has actually been connected in a specific way with the interests of the revolutionary class of the time, namely the bourgeois class. And the great bourgeois theorists who criticized feudalism, such as Locke in his *First Treatise*,[16] were also nominalists without exception. But then we notice that a peculiar functional change also starts to take place. When a theoretical understanding of society, and thus the claim to grasp something about the essence of society by passing beyond mere appearances, had effectively entered philosophy by way of Hegel, and when in terms of real social conflicts the bourgeois order was obliged to defend itself against newly emerging social forces, was obliged, in other words, to assume an increasingly apologetic posture, it did not turn back to the theory of conceptual realism, to Platonism, or anything of the sort. That was something that occurred only at a much later phase, with Scheler for example, and even then only in a more or less desultory fashion. Rather, what actually happened, and this is perhaps characteristic for the life of ideologies in relation to society generally, is that the nominalist theory was retained qua nominalism, though now employed to serve in a way that was completely opposed to its original function. For early nominalism was fundamentally critical towards the idea of the objective existence of essences, etc., and you will all know that the tremendous development of the modern natural sciences was effectively made possible by renouncing the whole construction of essences and the idea of objectively existing substantial forces. But from a certain point onwards we see how the same nominalism simply becomes a means of refusing any conception of the social whole that attempts to go beyond the façade of the immediately given, a means of defaming any such approach as arbitrary, as nothing but an airy and ungrounded construction. Nominalism thus becomes a way of denigrating theory qua theory – as we would say today – or making us suspicious of theoretical thought right from the start for the sake of a world which cannot intrinsically be justified in the light of the concept or any theoretical reflection. In this sense the whole positivist movement is to a large extent intrinsically ideological because it effectively prevents reflection on the hypokeimenon (ὑποκείμενον),[17] the underlying substance or hidden essence of society, and promotes the cult of strictly observable facts instead. In other words, a theory which assumed a critical or revolutionary significance in the context of one social phase – and can actually still exercise it in another social phase – may then also come to serve apologetic purposes without changing that much in its purely theoretical form. Where theoretical form is concerned, it is not particularly easy to discern any great differences between Hume, on the one hand, and Ernst Mach and Avenarius, and ultimately recent logical positivism, on the other, yet the social function of these theories has almost been reversed. Here again you can see how important it is to avoid the kind of reified consciousness that would attempt in a purely static way to identify some theory or other as the ideology of a particular class or a particular constellation of interests. What determines the functional significance of a theory in the context of society is the specific social juncture we are talking about, the relevant social totality, rather than the ephemeral doctrinal content, or, as perhaps I should say, the doctrinal content taken merely on its own, of the particular theories in question. We shall pick up the discussion from here[18] on Thursday next.[19]

LECTURE 12[1]

7 July 1960

Ladies and gentlemen,
Let us recall what I was saying to you at the end of the last session in connection with our reflections on the theory of ideology as a typical area of conflict between philosophy and sociology. I pointed out that, although individual ideologies originally emerged in specific social contexts, and thus also received their original significance from these same contexts, this does not mean that these ideologies, in terms of their material content or their truth content, are simply exhausted by the function they assumed in those contexts, or that they constantly exercise the same function over time. I also attempted to show that a specific intellectual approach, namely that of nominalist scepticism, from the beginning constituted one element of the bourgeois ideology which represented a critique of older feudal-ontological, hierarchical and objectivistic ideas, but that this approach changed its function after the French Revolution and from the point when the bourgeois order finds itself threatened by a new class. In this context the nominalist approach assumes a different and indeed quite contrary function, namely a specifically apologetic one. In other words, an approach which was originally developed in order to dissolve rigid and dogmatic notions which lie beyond the reach of experience now serves as an attempt to defame and disqualify any comprehensive theory in favour of the mere empirical confirmation of the facts, while, formally speaking, the nominalist approach has remained the same.

Now what this means, ladies and gentlemen, is that bourgeois society does not change its ideology along with the changed position of the bourgeois class in the context of class conflicts. Rather, if I may put this in a very compressed and simplified way, it employs the same ideology but for a purpose quite contrary to that which it formerly served. This has also been expressed in terms of a sociological law which is all the more remarkable for being one of very few principles which is actually shared by Marxist and so-called bourgeois sociologists alike. This is the law, which I would like at least to mention here, that in its Marxist form asserts that the 'superstructure' of society changes more slowly than the 'base'.[2] In the context of American non-Marxist sociology this notion was first expressed I believe by Ogburn[3] – although I may actually be mistaken about this – when he introduced the concept of 'cultural lag' to indicate that consciousness and the existing forms of culture, as they put it in the anglophone world, are not seamlessly or immediately congruent with the base and the conditions of material production, and not even with the relations of production. For the ideologies and the superstructure exhibit a certain life of their own, a certain tenacity or tardiness as it were, in relation to the base. Now this idea has become very widely accepted and no one is really surprised by it any more. Yet one of the tasks which fall to philosophy or to sociological reflection is surely to expend some very serious thought on things which we initially regard as quite natural. Now if you just conduct a thought experiment, ladies and gentlemen, and imagine that the superstructure changes more rapidly than the base, we could in principle make that appear just as plausible as the opposite, for the changes and transformations of the base are directly connected with far greater conflicts and catastrophes for the life of human beings than those changes at the level of world views which are certainly not registered so immediately in one's own experience. But then we also tend to ascribe much greater mobility to the realm of mind and culture – and the sphere of ideology coincides with this realm – than we do to the level of material relations. It is the intellectual categories we have at our disposal – as sociology has repeatedly shown – that allow us in the first place to stand back from the particular rigid and confining relations which surround us and to envisage other contrasting possibilities which may well appear to us in the context of reflection, even though they do not immediately appear that way in the context of reality. And the sociologists, especially Karl Mannheim, but also others, such as Spengler, have tried to establish a direct connection between mobile relations at the level of society and the sphere of mind and culture.[4] Spengler himself formulated the famous thesis of an inner connection between the realm of the mind and the realm of money[5] – and there is indeed an extraordinarily significant structural relationship[6] between money as the universal medium of equivalence and the coining of concepts that can be employed to stand in anywhere for anything.[7] Thus it is actually a rather remarkable fact that the realm of mind should change more slowly than the material basis of society. If you really want to understand this, I believe you should realize something very important that is generally the case with these categories of formal sociology, with all these rather formal considerations, such as the one I have just mentioned, and it is this: we must always pay close attention to the specific content and the specific social functions in play if we wish to provide a convincing account of these things. Thus we have to recognize that the social movements and developments that unfold in connection with class conflicts, for as long as society itself remains essentially arbitrary and irrational, will continue to render certain social groups superfluous, to weaken or disempower them, to destroy them in a literal or metaphorical sense, while under this prevailing irrationality the explicit progress of ratio, which develops in the grip of this irrationality, is incapable of bringing happiness or fulfilment to anyone. We could almost say that it is becoming easier to make out and identify the victims of the twists and turns of social progress than it is to say who is really advantaged by it. As far as progress or advantage is concerned, this is distributed in a very indirect and complicated fashion in terms of the standard of living of society as a whole, rather than being something we can grasp in a straightforward way at all. The most obvious example of this is familiar to you all from the situation of the present and the recent past: over very long periods of time the standard of living of the proletariat in the so-called socialist countries has actually declined rather than improved. Now if we ignore for a moment these countries and the specific conditions prevailing there in terms of the relation between ideology and the social base, we might say that in general the very groups which have been socially dominant, and whose interests the dominant ideologies have served in the past, no longer see a positive future for themselves. On the contrary, since the idea of a truly and comprehensively just organization of society is closed off to these groups, they find themselves more or less compelled to look back and yearn for a past that was better for them. Thus there are many substantial groups of the population – such as the entire agricultural sector, which has found itself in a permanent crisis for at least the last hundred years or so, or the petty bourgeois class with its memories of a supposedly golden age of free entrepreneurs – which are threatened by decline and further loss of status and freedom. That is why, I would say, all of these sectors become *laudatores temporis acti*. They are socially motivated to yearn for their past precisely because the idea of a future in which their own interests and those of society as a whole might coincide has been denied to them. But this means that these groups which have been ground down by the processes of history are almost compelled for apologetic reasons to cling to the ideology of the past, especially since this enables them to preserve subjectively something of that social status or prestige which had already been eroded objectively through the process of history. In this way it is actually in their own interest, if I may put it this way, that the superstructure does not change as quickly as the underlying social base, not only because this preserves their hope of re-creating the conditions of the past but also because the mere possession or retention of this ideology – of that hierarchy of intrinsic values which often goes hand in hand with elitist notions of one kind or another in Germany – gives them something of that '*status complémentaire*' that they are actually losing in reality. Here, ladies and gentlemen, we are certainly moving in the realm of subjectivity, of subjective facts of consciousness, although we still have to understand them, or attempt to understand them, precisely as functions of objective social processes. Yet this tendency which I have just described for you is strengthened even more by the fact that psychology is drawn in the same direction, namely backwards, in a process which I have just tried to explain socially and objectively in terms of the situation of those who continue to cling to ideologies that have objectively been superseded. It is certainly one of the most significant insights that we owe to modern psychology – and by modern psychology here I am thinking simply and exclusively of psychoanalysis in its strict Freudian form – that the unconscious is timeless, as Freud himself put it in a rather extreme and sweeping way,[8] or possesses a certain kind of rigidity. Thus although the libidinous energies of the unconscious, as he puts it, are plastic in character,[9] i.e. can assume different forms under different circumstances, the unconscious nonetheless constantly reveals a tendency to fall back to the archaic form that once belonged to it. I cannot provide you with any detailed justification for this here, and nor at this point can I explore the question as to whether we are really talking here about a tendency which belongs intrinsically to the unconscious itself or one which is psychologically produced under particular conditions – in other words, whether this archaic character of the unconscious is not ultimately a kind of regressive formation produced under the compulsion of social pressure.[10] For my part, as I may as well confess to you, I incline to the second hypothesis. Psychoanalysts of the strictest sort would probably condemn me for this and would say that our consciousness and its dynamic character is really only a very narrow instinctual offshoot of the unconscious, one which expressly allows us when required to deal with reality, to adapt to reality, or to test reality, as they say in psychology. But whenever there are acute disturbances in the relationship between the personality and reality, they would say, there is also always an immediate tendency for the overwhelming mass of primitive, undifferentiated and archaic elements to reassert their power over us. Now whatever conclusion we come to about this controversy, these regressive and backward-looking forces of the unconscious and human psychology tend to produce a certain affective structure which binds human beings to what are really superseded forms of consciousness, even when in conscious terms they should be quite capable of recognizing these connections between the social process and the objective obsolescence of ideology which I have tried to point out for you. I believe that it is really only in this context that the fact of 'cultural lag' or the slower transformation of the superstructure in relation to the social base can properly be understood.

Let me at least try, in a few words, to explain the remarkable fact that the same theory which once exerted a critical and even revolutionary effect in the context of bourgeois society has itself turned into an apologetic theory. The interest of society itself became apologetic from a certain, almost dateable, historical point of time which roughly coincides with the period of Napoleon's political dominance. We might say that society, or, in other words, the class which controls the process of production, here turns against the idea of fundamental critique precisely because it has become aware that the dynamic which this very form of society released is now tending in a direction that leads beyond it. It is very interesting to note that the first great bourgeois thinkers in the period when the bourgeois class established its dominance for the first time, namely Hegel in Germany and Comte in France, already recognized what we are talking about: the fact that society reveals a tendency to drive beyond itself or in a sense even to destroy itself. And in the shock of this initial experience they expressed this recognition quite openly without ideological trappings, if I can put it this way. For it is really only at a much later stage that bourgeois society now shamefully refuses, as it were, to acknowledge this tendency – an eminently objective one – but tries, rather, to deny it. Yet in Hegel it is quite clearly and unambiguously expressed that society also produces poverty precisely with its wealth.[11] At about the same time Comte talks around the question in an admittedly rather unclear and prolix fashion, but he has precisely the same thing in view when he repeatedly refers to the tendencies that threaten to dissolve society and implies that the latter has to be held together by a kind of reliable order that is to be provided by science, that is, by science understood in a nominalistic-empirical manner. Now this apologetic tendency on the part of modern bourgeois or civil society springs from the fact that it is already felt deep down, at the heart of this society, that something is not actually in order, that this society, in its own innermost principle, harbours something that tends to drive it apart and dissolve it. Thus the most suitable apologetic means of neutralizing any fundamental critical reflection on society is to argue or insist that fundamental critical thought of this kind, this inheritance of the great tradition of bourgeois rationalism – which confronts society with its own claim to rationality – is something essentially unscientific in character, something windy and speculative that no one can possibly rely on any more. And here the other wing of bourgeois consciousness comes into play – a consciousness that was divided from the first into a rationalist wing and an empiricist wing – namely the empiricist tradition which implies from the start that there can be no such thing as an objectively valid theory of the whole and no such thing as social objectivity. It also contests the idea that society is built up according to certain principles and specific structural relations, that society is really a system, and insists instead that scientific knowledge merely consists in the identification of individual facts. In a seemingly radical expression of critical consciousness it ends up sabotaging the critical truth that early bourgeois thought had once set in motion. This is how it comes about that the same nominalistic theory, when maintained in a rigid and undialectical manner, accomplishes the very opposite of what was intended when the theory was initially conceived. The simple fact, which always immediately diverges from the totality, since the totality is never completely captured in any individual fact, thus sabotages the concept of totality, which is then easily charged with being something unverifiable, i.e. something that cannot be possessed wholly in terms of any individual fact or even any intermediate field of observable facts. This is what we need to say about the peculiar transformation in the function of nominalism which has occurred in critical empiricism and which also lies at the heart of the controversy between philosophy and sociology as this presents itself today – a controversy which in Germany has recently achieved a certain topicality, if I may put it this way, through a dispute between my colleague Schelsky and myself which touches specifically on these questions.[12]

Now, ladies and gentlemen, here once again I really do not want to make the issue too easy either for me or for you. Thus I would certainly not like you to go away from a lecture like this with the idea that I am simply defending the cause of philosophy against the claims of empirical knowledge, and doing so in a simply undialectical and culturally arrogant way that you might well suspect is ultimately elitist in character. But we are not just talking here about a standpoint that is being defended by one professor against that of some other professor, or by the majority of other professors, simply because he wants to uphold the dignity of his own discipline, namely the discipline of theoretical philosophy, which is essentially oriented to the concept of the universal. For if that were really the case, then I believe the fundamental problem we are talking about here would be utterly trivialized. And it is my task not to trivialize problems for you but to encourage you, in a more than merely academic sense, to think for yourselves about the things we are discussing here, so that you will appreciate that they are indeed hard and challenging things, things which exert a considerable power over us, inescapable things which take their own course and go their own way. Any other approach would never really get beyond the hackneyed realm of contending world views, and I would certainly not want to be responsible for wasting your time on such discussions about who defends one kind of theory and who another. I have the feeling that this kind of discussion belongs to a rather carefree past, and the times are far too serious for us to indulge in such things. In other words, I think my task is also to say something about the truth moment which is involved in the very strong empiricist attitude now adopted in sociology, as well as in philosophy, at least in countries outside Germany. I believe it is all the more necessary to insist on this point because of the particular cultural and intellectual situation in Germany and the rather provincial character of this situation in the face of current conflicts in the world at large. For in Germany, generally speaking, one is still not really aware of the overwhelming power which these empirical tendencies are now exerting not merely in sociology but in philosophy as well. And I believe that if you are somehow to rise above this controversy, as they would have put it in the era of German Idealism, then you really need to recognize the full force of what motivates this development and not allow yourselves to be fobbed off by all too slick and superficial forms of argument.

In contemporary sociology – and this is perhaps the decisive distinction in contrast to philosophy – we are no longer dealing with genuine theory at all. We might say that even the great sociologists of the previous generation, such as Max Weber, no longer actually had a theory of society. What they had on the one side was a relatively subtle and developed methodology and epistemology which they could basically draw from the philosophy of their time – in Weber's case from the South-Western German school of Windelband and Rickert[13] – while on the other side they were confronted with a collection of facts and the question of how to organize them. It has rightly been said, and formulated as an argument against him, that Max Weber, the most important German sociologist in the entire period after Marx, did not possess a theory of society at all.[14] We might say that the implicit polemic against Marx's work, which to such a large extent underlies Weber's own work, consists not in replacing Marx's theory with another different theory about the essential character of the superstructure in relation to the base but in contesting the very possibility of any such comprehensive theory of society in the first place. Thus those enormous collections and organizations of material information which we owe to the industry of Max Weber always serve the great *thema probandum* or central argument that something like a conception of society as a totality is actually impossible. Thus a form of a-theory, or anti-theory, has here become theory. This motif, already present in Max Weber, may also be traced in Durkheim. For in his work you can see that completely divergent strands from Kantianism are combined in an almost grotesque way to produce a positivism modelled essentially on the natural sciences. This remarkable hostility to theory which we encounter even in works that are widely regarded as the most significant contributions to sociology has finally degenerated from being one of the tired old cultural values of the upper classes into the sort of threadbare research programme where some young man in some college or other expects to get his Master's degree and become a proper social scientist just by comparing the housing conditions of a hundred black students in Michigan with a hundred black students in St Louis; whereas he imagines, of course, that history has already shown that he is far superior to those merely 'armchair thinkers' who have continued to engage with the questions that preoccupied Marx or Durkheim. Now I certainly do not wish to deny that there are certain circumstances in which such investigations – if they do really serve to improve the housing conditions of the black population in some particular city – actually prove to possess greater pragmatic value than the entire *Division du travail* or all of Durkheim's works on the origin of religion[15] have been able to show. But we cannot simply take this pragmatic advantage as the criterion for the cognitive content of such a theory itself. Now, ladies and gentlemen, this lack of theory and this hostility to theory – which has now almost assumed the character of a 'world view' in the field of sociology and often tends to taboo on any thought that is not immediately substantiated by 'facts and figures' – is not something that you should regard as simply or wholly ideological. It is clear that there is a certain ideological function at work here, since in the thicket of all these empirical investigations it is no longer really possible to learn anything about society itself. And this conclusion has occasionally been defended as such – as I believe René König once did, although in conversation with me he has also distanced himself from the idea.[16] And when, finally, it is even claimed that sociology should free itself from the concept of society, since it can now rely simply on the compelling results of all these particular investigations, this is just the royal road, as it were, for dispensing with critical theory altogether. For if there is no such thing as society, then there is naturally no such thing as a critique of society, and this certainly smooths the way for a sociology that will actually perform what today is called 'socially useful labour'.[17] This ideological dimension can hardly be denied, and I do not think I have to say much more about this here. But it is clear that this is all an expression of a weakened and merely adaptive consciousness, whether this is because human beings no longer have the power or even the will to rouse themselves to develop an understanding of society as a system, or whether this is because – and I regard this second point as the more decisive one – under the pressure of currently organized forms of science and knowledge, human beings constantly have to ask permission for every thought they express and are constantly required to show how far the thought in question is verifiable and acceptable within our system of culture and education – and indeed in the world as a whole. And this effectively undermines their readiness and capacity for exercising any really independent thought. I should just say in passing that we are not simply talking about a phenomenon which is characteristic of positivist sociology here. For we can readily identify analogous phenomena in every field of the so-called human sciences which have been marked by positivist thought. Thus it would be quite unjust simply to lay into sociology in this respect, while ignoring the tendency in certain forms of philology to resist cultural and intellectual insight by insisting on purely demonstrable factual material. I just wanted to mention this here as a kind of plea for sociology, albeit a rather modest one.

But the tendency I am talking to you about here goes beyond this ideological function, beyond this weakening of subjective consciousness in relation to theory, for we must also seriously ask ourselves another question – and I would at least like to broach this question now without being able to resolve it for you directly here, as I am indeed generally reluctant to offer you definitive solutions for these difficult issues. In other words, we must really ask ourselves about how things stand with regard to the possibility of theory today, and especially the possibility of a theory of contemporary society, when we complain that no such theory currently exists.[18] For there is no good reason to assume that people are any less gifted or perceptive now than they were sixty or a hundred years ago – and indeed the productive forces have surely been infinitely intensified over this period of time. The problem of the lack of any truly adequate theory of contemporary society is not some great secret or mystery jealously guarded by a few initiates, for the birds are all clearly singing it from the rooftops. And anyone who is concerned with the relationship between social theory and philosophy will immediately sense this lack in a particularly drastic fashion, although no one would take the risk of presenting a developed theory of contemporary society in anything but a fragmentary manner. Yet if we tried to explain this in exclusively psychological terms, then I believe we would be failing to grasp the full gravity of the situation at issue.

At various points in the course of these lectures I have claimed that society is antagonistic in the sense that, while *ratio* is constantly at work here as a means for controlling inner and outer nature, nothing has really changed in terms of the irrationality of society itself insofar as there is still no really transparent general social consciousness that would be capable of directing the social processes themselves. And, if I remember rightly, I also made a further claim which may well seem plausible to you even without much further elaboration. It is this: the more the rationality of the means, the more the particularistic rationality in society, as I would call it, continues to grow while society as a whole remains basically irrational, then the greater the contradictions become, and the greater the danger that this particularistic rationality will only produce more suffering for human beings and will eventually even destroy the whole interconnected system. One might also express this by saying that the particularistic forms of rationality within the prevailing irrationality of the whole mean that this irrationality becomes stronger rather than weaker. The situation today, when we can ourselves annihilate millions of human beings at a stroke, is more irrational than that of the past when some plague was also certainly capable of wreaking enormous destruction. This is because the contradiction between our potential for limiting or resisting death and the reality in which we could actually produce and organize it in countless ways has become more flagrant than ever. So we might say – to repeat the point – that, while the appearance of rationality constantly increases in our society through the particular way in which it functions, this society actually becomes ever more irrational at the same time through the growing contradiction between what is actual and what is possible.

We could perhaps express this in economic terms and say that, the more our society passes over from one based on exchange relations towards one that is based on the direct control over production, and thus over consumption on one side and blindly persisting market relations on the other, the less this society can be measured in terms of a concept of rationality that was effectively modelled upon the notion of equivalence, of like for like, of fair exchange. There is actually ever less exchange in society. The market as it survives today is what economists call a pseudo-market,[19] and rationality has become a merely technical rationality for calculating or predicting the processes of this essentially controlled market. We are no longer talking about the rationality of 'the invisible hand'[20] through which the social whole was said to reproduce itself of its own accord, albeit in a somewhat painful and laborious way.[21] But if society itself today, in its objective form, can no longer really be measured or assessed in terms of its classical bourgeois concept of rationality, namely in terms of the rational calculation of exchange, then society to an increasing degree also eludes a real theory of society, for theory is the question concerning the immanent rationality of this society. You must not forget that the system, the negative system, of capitalism which Marx outlined is a system in the dialectical sense that it derived the concept of rationality from civil society itself, precisely as this concept was presented in the classical doctrines of political economy and the associated theories of surplus value. Marx then proceeded to ask how far the society in question corresponds to the rationality to which it lays claim in accordance with its own ideology or theory with regard to itself. Now you will know that bourgeois capitalist society in the age of Keynesian theory actually no longer lays any claim to such economic rationality. But it is almost impossible for a theory of society to express this society in rational terms if the society no longer has any such rationality about it. Thus in a certain sense we might say that contemporary society eludes theory because that which effectively provides the substrate of theory – namely the relationship between the rational theoretical claim of the whole and its actual reality – no longer exists in the same way as before. Theory is the question concerning immanent rationality, and where this rationality has essentially been reduced to issues of immediate economic management on the one hand and a very complicated and opaque system of social security[22] on the other, then this rational substrate is no longer present at all. We could also put this a different way by saying that positivism is not merely a lie and not just ideology, and thus does not simply express some human weakness in relation to realm of theory. For positivism is also a necessary expression of consciousness insofar as the decline of our society itself is reflected in the pluralism, in the indifferent and disintegrating multiplicity, that characterizes particular insights that can no longer be unified in any convincing way. But that is something which we shall have to take up in the next session.

LECTURE 13

12 July 1960

Ladies and gentlemen,

In the last session I engaged in a certain thought experiment with you, or, to put this more simply, I tried in a somewhat experimental way to suggest a thought that bears on the very possibility of social theory today. As you will remember, we were wondering how an originally progressive bourgeois social theory – namely the nominalist critique of dogmatically given universal concepts – was eventually transformed into an apologetic social theory, although the nominalism itself remained basically unchanged. And you may also remember that I insisted upon this observation in emphatic contrast to the rather crude and unsophisticated thesis that was endorsed by Max Scheler in his sociology of knowledge. For he attempts to establish a fundamental equivalence between nominalism and progressive social tendencies on the one hand, and between realism – in the sense of Platonism and conceptual realism – and apologetic social tendencies on the other. Now I think I should point out to you in this context that, as with all these things, the crisis of theory formation we find today is only the culmination or intensification of a process which has a very long prehistory behind it – and this is an insight that we owe to Hegel, along with many other important insights. We might put this by saying that theory in the emphatic sense is not really possible at all under expressly nominalist conditions, i.e. when concepts are deprived of all substantiality and regarded simply as *flatus vocis*, as so much 'sound and smoke', and are interpreted at best as abbreviated expressions of what they subsume. Thus the question concerning the possibility of theory itself in the modern age after Descartes has always gone hand in hand with attempts to transcend the position of nominalism which has effectively been mandated by the course of history and which cannot indeed simply be abolished by force. These were attempts to transcend the nominalist position by pursuing its own implications, to get beyond this approach precisely by thinking the nominalist problems through to the end, which is in a way what Kant does and in particular what Hegel does.

Let me now just try and show you, at least in summary terms, in what way nominalism is actually incompatible with the development of theory. Now one of the essential aspects of nominalism – and this is the aspect which really facilitated the rapid growth of the modern mathematical natural sciences – is the claim that we cannot know the inner being or so-called essence of things, whether this is because, as in the most extreme form of nominalism, the very idea of the essence of things is repudiated – and the independent character of the concept is just the thesis that something like an intrinsic essence or substantial concept belongs to things – or whether because, in a more mediated form of nominalism such as that represented by the Kantian philosophy, it is claimed that, while things may indeed have an inner essence, any real insight or knowledge concerning the latter is closed off to us on account of the laws which govern the limits of human experience. Here I shall ignore the rather paradoxical character of the claim that we have no insight into the essence of things, something which is itself presented as an essential insight and thus appears to presuppose what it denies, namely that anything such as an essential insight is even possible. This argument was in fact subsequently mobilized against nominalism in a particularly emphatic fashion by Hegel. But if it is not actually possible for knowledge to grasp the essence of things, if a properly mature conception of knowledge that has relinquished all illusory pretensions merely requires that we stick to the given facts, that we simply order and classify these facts and finally attempt to bring them into some kind of rational connection, then theory is not really possible because the theoretical concepts we employ are not just duplications of that classificatory principle which has been imposed on things in order to bring order into this chaotic multiplicity. And this order merely serves a practical cognitive purpose by helping us to manage or manipulate the data, as we would say today, and makes no claim to any theoretical insight that might reveal anything about the essence of the matter. In other words, once the conceptual aspect is eliminated, even as a merely relative independent moment in intellectual experience taken as a whole, then the concept of theory basically loses its meaning, which is why consistent and rigorous nominalism theory is no longer really at all possible. So it is merely a matter of 'cultural lag', if you want to put it that way, or a function of the delayed adaptation of cultural and intellectual life to the conditions now imposed upon it, if the nominalist philosophers at the beginning did nonetheless attempt to develop something like a genuine theory. And when we read one of the most important of these nominalist theorists of knowledge, such as David Hume, we can never entirely suppress a certain feeling of paradox to see how a sort of thinking that tends to challenge the very possibility of any meaningful and internally coherent form of knowledge nonetheless also presents itself as a kind of theory of knowledge. I have already drawn your attention to certain social tendencies of our own time and thereby raised the question as to how far an adequate form of theory is now at all possible; and I finally suggested to you that the positivism that prevails today does represent an adequate consciousness of our situation insofar as the decline into embracing mere facticity on the one hand and vacuous formalism on the other actually corresponds to the incipient decline of bourgeois society itself. Yet this is not just something that you should see as externally conditioned by social changes, for I think I have also shown you in the context of these brief reflections that it is something equally grounded in the logic of the concept itself. But I would also specifically ask you, in the light of certain reactions to what was said in our last session, not just to take these reflections of mine home with you like so much ready change, or treat them like a finished result: 'There you have it, Adorno has told us that the world as it is today just has no room for theory.' For I should warn you, above all, precisely not to go and draw the reassuring and comforting conclusion – or, rather, discomforting conclusion – from all this that we no longer need the labour or exertions of the concept, that we should just leave well alone and content ourselves with the role of a mere epistemological technician. I believe that I hardly have to spell out that disturbing sense which comes over us when we realize that the kind of knowledge we are offered no longer lives up to its own concept, no longer satisfies the very concept of knowledge. I should like to think, if you have been prepared to follow my reflections thus far, that this will have become quite evident by now. Thus we might formulate the experimental thought with which we closed last time – if I may summarize the point once again – in the following way: where the thing itself, namely society, has been abandoned by *ratio*, i.e. where the unreason in the relation between the social forms of production and the actual level of the productive forces has become manifest, we find that theory has also forfeited its rights with regard to society – and this is because theory always really means confronting a thing with the rationality which is internal to it or, rather, confronting something with its own claim to embody rationality. A theory of bourgeois society in the emphatic sense was possible precisely because this society itself, from the time of its most important apologists onwards, already laid claim to rationality in terms of its own real form, namely the rationally mediated conceptual form of equivalence. The critical theory of society found itself in a quite different situation as far as liberal-bourgeois society is concerned, if I may put it this way, insofar as it only had to question this society directly, to ask how far it lived up to its own claim to rationality, in order to reveal the untruth of this society by confronting it with its own concept. In other words, the critical theory of bourgeois society was nothing but the ideology of that very society expressly contrasted with the reality.

But this aspect or moment which I have talked about must nonetheless be described only as one particular aspect or moment. And I am quite serious when I say this, and it is not to be interpreted on the schema of one huge leap forward in the last session and one huge leap back again here, if I now also tell you that, in a sense, contemporary society in particular is indeed accessible to theoretical insight to an especially high degree. This is because all of the complicated processes of mediation which prevailed in liberal society in its heyday have now fallen away. Society has become all the more transparent as a result, just as the process of distribution in relation to any social product has become directly transparent to us, namely the movement of the product from the producers through to the various points of distribution, where the latter now play the role once performed by independent agents in the circulation of the market. The theory of society was basically what was then called political economy, and this political economy essentially involved the insight that, for all its structural regularity at the level of the whole, this society also always displayed an irrational aspect or moment at the level of the social and economic vicissitudes affecting individuals. Adam Smith's famous remarks concerning 'the invisible hand'[1] that governs the fate of society also has its negative side. For this 'hand' cannot actually be perceived at the level of the particular or in the fate of the individual economically productive and socialized subject. It can be perceived only in relation to the totality of such individuals. Otherwise, the hand would be described not as 'invisible' in the first place but, rather, as a 'visible' one, just as some social or economic plan is said to be 'visible' these days when you can go and look it up or actually see it in black and white. In other words, this idea of the objectivity and the rationality of an overarching process that is realized over the heads of individuals was expressly bound up, in this classical version of the theory of society, with the irrationality of social actions on the part of individuals, and this moment of irrationality thus continued to be evident. Now, in place of this notion of political economy, which intimately connects the rational and irrational moments with one another in such a remarkable way, what confronts us in large part today could be described more accurately as a mechanism of political distribution than as a genuinely economic process. Formally speaking, the old market processes do continue to exist, but contemporary economists – at least those who are still interested in investigating crucial social processes and are not simply content to pursue mathematical calculations of various possibilities and eventualities – are quite capable of showing that these market processes are actually an illusion; that what lies behind them are simply principles of distribution that are determined by the exercise of economic power and can thus more properly be described as political mechanisms of distribution. And to a certain extent this displaces that specific irrationality which once constituted the problem for major theoretical reflection in the past, namely the question of how something rational – the reproduction and indeed the expanded reproduction of social life itself – can possibly emerge from all those countless individual actions which are often deeply entangled with one another and the ultimate effect of which cannot be precisely calculated. This means that, in a certain way, the social whole has now actually become much more transparent than before. One might almost say that the irrationality in society has shifted to the extremes. Thus, on the one hand, the irrationality has moved in a direction where the highest agencies which carry out these economic plans can hardly be said to plan the whole outcome in a fully conscious way, for they do not get beyond their own particular interests and take only general interests into consideration in an indirect fashion – only when this is required if they themselves are to keep going, or if they wish to avoid being caught up in the catastrophe that, deep within society, still threatens to emerge at any moment. On the other hand, the irrationality is still present in the sense that it is possible in totalitarian states for particular groups of the population to be expressly singled out at any moment as people who should be excluded or destroyed – precisely because, under the existing conditions of production, this society is no longer capable of reproducing itself in an unimpeded way.

When I said to you last time that it is questionable how far it is possible to develop something like a social theory for a society which has in essence become as irrational as ours, this thesis should be supplemented by the opposite and complementary one: the issue of what today still constitutes the veil that conceals all this. In a world where in fact any child can see the absurdity of the current order of things, how is it possible that this arrangement is preserved and maintained not simply by means of sheer force, or by the power of bayonets, or rather of missiles, to put this in a more contemporary way, but also through the consciousness of the human beings which it has produced and which are themselves constantly threatened by it?[2] And a theory of society would then inevitably be driven in a subjective direction. For once the secret has been exposed, as it really has been by an almost completely planned society that at identifiable points it is nonetheless completely unplanned, such a theory would only have to explain the set-up on the subjective side of things, the set-up that holds the whole thing together so that it continues to exist, for good or ill, in the forms that have been historically provided for it. Thus the impossibility of developing a theory, which I demonstrated to you last time when I demonstrated the loss of rationality on the part of society itself, and the superfluous character of theory once the essence of society has become manifest can now be recognized as two dialectical sides of the same state of affairs.

If I spoke to you earlier about the changing function of nominalism in society – and about the way in which the bourgeois class, the reflective class par excellence, which was once so concerned with theory, later turned its back on theory – I would not wish you to misunderstand me at this point. For it is not as if I were now defending the view that things are any better when nominalism is no longer deployed apologetically and we instead simply cling to the idea of a critical theory of society. If the nominalistic theory which I described for you in detail with reference to figures such as Comte and Durkheim has eventually turned into a prohibition on thinking in the so-called free world – a prohibition which effectively substitutes the socio-technical registration of facts for the supposedly mythological attempt to comprehend society – then things have not fared any better for the version of theory that is endorsed in the realm beyond the Iron Curtain,[3] where it appears, at least, to have been maintained in its orthodox critical form. And I believe that nothing could be more fateful than the misunderstanding that might tempt you to regard what passes for theory there as in any way superior to what we can find over here in the Western zone. I may be guilty of a seemingly impermissible but ultimately quite correct generalization if I tell you that anything by way of social or philosophical theory which flourishes in the Eastern zone really belongs in the category of third-rate literature. It consists simply in adopting a range of concepts which have seen better days, divesting them entirely of their authentic content and, indeed, largely transforming them into their opposites, and then simply using them to legitimate the powerful interests of whatever cliques happen to be in charge and in a position to exercise an irrational control over everyone else. We find ourselves in a very difficult situation in this regard, since the complete vulgarization of dialectical theory that we find over there no longer really allows us to explore it or take it seriously as theory. And there really is a certain mentality or intellectual level which lies so far beyond the possibility of any immanent critical engagement[4] that even people as little disposed to violent confrontation as I am myself, for example, cannot do anything but emphasize the utterly impoverished character of such theory. In a very similar way, there would have been something absurd about any attempt to refute the theory of National Socialism as a theory, when in reality it never took itself seriously as a theory at all, even if objectively speaking it actually represented one. For it was, firstly, a way of trying out what people might be brought to do and, secondly, a way of developing specific techniques through which human beings could be rendered compliant and obedient – and it is just the same with the so-called theory of 'diamat'.[5] I only need to remind you that a dialectical theory, which is essentially nothing but the movement of its own concept, cannot be fixed or tied down, cannot be statically reduced to some immutable doctrine about society, one which is constituted precisely as it is once and for all. And as soon as such a theory is simply enthroned as a state religion it does not merely succumb to the usual phenomena of ossification, something to which, according to Georg Simmel,[6] every intellectual and cultural product in the world is eventually exposed. What happens is that the theory thereby enters into direct contradiction with its own intellectual content. Here I would just like to draw your attention, as is surely legitimate in a lecture course concerned with philosophy and society, to a thesis which has repeatedly been endorsed in a quite foolish and uncritical way since Mach, namely the thesis that theory is a 'reflection' of society.[7] This idea, which we also have to say is not one of Marx's most illustrious contributions,[8] is completely untenable because no judgement is a copy or reflection of the situation or state of affairs about which the judgement is made. For inasmuch as a theory intends, aims at, or refers to a state of affairs, the latter is also thereby inevitably first constituted in some way. In other words, independently of this judgement, there is no state of affairs which is just given and merely mirrored or reflected in the judgement in question. It is quite impossible to criticize the concept of reification, the concept of reified consciousness, the concept of the rigid separation and opposition of subject and object – and such critique is unconditionally implied in the essence of a dialectical theory – while simultaneously endorsing an utterly reified conception of the relationship between knowledge and thing, between subject and object, a conception which turns subjective consciousness into a mere copy or reflection of the object and thus already effaces that dialectical relation between subject and object which it is the vital and essential task of dialectical theory to grasp. I will not try and decide here whether this fatal fall into the very reification which was supposed to be overcome is already implied in the formulation of a materialist dialectic that intrinsically downplays the moment of mind and independent reflection and thus ends up ascribing the dialectical movement to matter itself in an ultimately fanciful and mythological way. The basic difficulty probably arises from the fact that the formulations of Marx, which have congealed over time and are now presented to us in this rather enfeebled dogmatic form, in their original context were not really intended as philosophical theorems at all, and certainly not as an expression of ontological or metaphysical materialism. They once possessed an entirely different value and significance which certainly cannot be captured by the concept of some total 'world view', as people like to call it. But I do not really wish to go into these matters any further here. Perhaps we shall have an opportunity to learn more about this when we have actually concluded our observations about the concept of ideology in the contemporary world. In the Eastern bloc today we see an extremely revealing terminological transformation whereby the concept of ideology is now actively embraced in a positive sense, even though it was originally understood as a critical concept that was meant to identify and expose the necessary appearance of false consciousness. In these circumstances it is quite legitimate for us to explore this problematic term 'ideology' in order to show what is really happening over there with that reification of dialectic into a heteronomous 'world view' that is simply imposed on everyone. And this theory – which in contrast to the subjectivism I talked about before has actually retained the objective moment that was emphasized by the great philosophers, as I tried to explain to you in the last session – has also been expressly decreed as such an ideology, or, in other words, as a world view, and then adopted in a heteronomous fashion, without anyone being able to consent to it for their own part in a responsible or autonomous way. As a result, people there have effectively fallen back into the very subjectivism which, as I said before, is the latent essential principle of a nominalism that nonetheless likes to present itself as eminently objective. In other words, the merely subjective declarations of those in power are deceptively elevated to the status of intrinsic and independent truth.

But since I am specifically attempting in these lectures to develop something akin to the elements of a dialectical theory for you, I should like to take this opportunity to say more about what is actually meant by the term 'dialectic' here. For I believe it would be a complete misunderstanding of the concept of dialectic if you tried to think of it as a kind of method, as something which you just need to apply to reality in the same rigid and reified way that is usually encountered in the Eastern bloc, and which will then serve as a nutcracker with which you can now disclose the meaning of all phenomena. Now when I speak to you of dialectic I do not pretend to offer you some kind of universal cognitive instrument which will enable you to deal with whatever on earth comes your way. Indeed, I would almost say that the meaning of dialectic as I am trying to present it to you here is the exact opposite. The point is, rather, to immerse yourselves in the phenomena themselves with all the experience and intellectual energy that you are able to draw upon, and to approach these phenomena by making full use of all that you know and have theoretically reflected upon; thus you must allow yourselves just as much to be guided by the phenomena as you must also measure the phenomena in terms of the theoretical material that is already available to you. And both these aspects or moments, that of your own experience and that of theoretical reflection, must be able to modify each other and interact with each other in an open and flexible way so that neither moment is simply reified or rendered independent in relation to the other. In this sense, therefore, dialectic is not a method waiting to be applied in order to crack open the truth of everything, and it is certainly not a world view. As far as philosophizing simply in terms of so-called world views is concerned, everything has in fact already been said by representatives of the great philosophical tradition – especially by Kant and Hegel – when they repudiated the mere arbitrariness and consequent untruth that results from such an approach.[9] I shall not attempt to offer you a definition of dialectic, which would only violate the very principle – if it can be called a principle – which I have already introduced to you on innumerable occasions in other lectures and seminars. Thus I have pointed out that dialectic is not a claim or proclamation,[10] not some fixed reproducible thing to which everything can be subjected. But I should perhaps at least attempt to characterize for you, at least indirectly, what is at stake here. This is the attempt to expose ourselves to our experience, and to articulate the contours of this experience r – without rigidity, without appeal to anything fixed and immutable, to any self-identical framework, as Herr Heidegger so eloquently likes to put it[11] – but without simply falling into relativism as a result. For the task is to hold on to a concept of binding and objective truth precisely in the constant movement of the concept and the constant relativization of partial or individual insights. If I were to express this negatively – and I cannot provide you with a recipe for how this is to be achieved in substantive terms, although this is exactly what I am trying to get across to you in as differentiated a manner as possible – I would say the central task is this: to renounce all forms of reified and ossified consciousness and think in a way that nonetheless upholds the concept of objectively binding truth and objectively binding insight. The latter cannot simply be measured in terms of particular individual facts, since it is only really grounded in the texture of the whole which theory presents for you in an external form. If one tried to express this approach in terms drawn from the history of philosophy – to return to something we said earlier on – we could describe it as an attempt to develop a kind of critical self-consciousness with respect to nominalism. This would take us beyond the nominalism that has become obligatory for everyone after the loss of an objectively binding social and intellectual order of things, and help us to discover in the analysis of what is accessible to our own individual experience an objective content of its own as long as we actually address, hold fast to, and essentially orient ourselves to this experience.

This programme is simply meant to suggest the general direction of travel or orient you to what we basically have in mind here and, God knows, is certainly not intended to provide you with a ready definition of dialectic or of dialectic as we teach it. But it does involve a demand which in the age of reified consciousness people find it enormously difficult to fulfil, and this is the demand for intellectual freedom. This requires that you give yourselves over to the phenomena in a sovereign, independent and flexible kind of way. One aspect or moment of such cognition is fidelity to the facts, a readiness to immerse yourselves in the particulars of real existence, a mistrust of abstract and questionable concepts that are simply foisted on things in advance. At the same time, we also have to acknowledge the equal necessity for the complementary movement provided by our own intellectual powers. In other words, it is not enough to point your finger at appearances, as it were, and simply keep saying: 'Here, this is just how it is, and that's that; this is just what to think, and that's that!' For you must also have the capacity to move from one system of relations, from one 'frame of reference', to another. You must have the capacity – like the shifting camera angle in a film – to look at things not only in really close proximity but from a considerable distance as well. In short, you must try and cultivate what Hegel refers to as freedom towards the object, but to an extent that goes far beyond what he was describing in these terms. And it actually seems to me that what can perhaps be called the objectivity of cognition – when something truly essential is revealed to you which is certainly not a matter of some rigid and conceptually static 'essence' – is closely bound up with that capacity for flexibility on the part of the subject, that ability to immerse oneself in the object and to step back from it, to engage with the object in an experimental spirit. Yet all of these categories have specifically been ruled out for us today, above all by the demand for a supposedly clean and efficient method – one that can in principle be arbitrarily exchanged at any time for any other – in the ossified business of contemporary science. The ability to distance yourselves from the business of science as it is currently practised, and thus to maintain an inner freedom in the face of the well-worn categories that it continues to employ, is probably the most essential thing here if you are really to comprehend – at least in a way that goes beyond the mere acquisition of information – what I have attempted to describe for you as the basic intention of dialectic. If now, in conclusion, and this is permissible only at the end rather than at the beginning of a lecture, I may offer you a formula, along with an urgent request not to misunderstand it as a formula, it is just this: dialectic would in fact be a consciousness that resists both reification and relativism. Here I simply note in passing that the so-called triadic schema, of which you have doubtless heard so much, plays no role or merely an entirely subordinate role in such thinking.[12]

I would like to say this: since this semester is rather short, and under no circumstances would I wish you to see you go away empty-handed after we have had to drop more sessions than I would really have liked,[13] I have decided to give another lecture on Thursday 28th,[14] and I would be very grateful to you, given that the lectures are conceived as a whole, if you could all arrange to attend that one as well.[15]

LECTURE 14
14 July 1960

Ladies and gentlemen,
I think we can now return to our reflections on the concept of ideology and, if we are lucky, bring this discussion to a close today. First of all I would just like to say a few words about the history of the concept of ideology. At least with regard to some of the principal stages of this history, the story has been very well told and vividly presented by Hans Barth in his book *Truth and Ideology*, which was published in Zurich in 1945. And I would certainly take this opportunity to recommend it to you if you wish to orient yourselves with respect to this whole complex of issues.[1] Now of course there has always been talk of something like false consciousness, and indeed of supposedly widespread false consciousness. One only has to think of Heraclitus and his talk of the foolish and deluded 'many'.[2] This was a common enough topos in ancient thought, and it might be rather grandiose to interpret this simply as a justificatory or defensive ideology on the part of an old aristocratic order which found itself threatened by emergent democratic movements in Greece during the sixth and seventh centuries BC. For it seems to me more likely that the claim to authority, or perhaps also to the market value, which the more or less unattached or wandering philosophers of the time cultivated was naturally bound up with the fact that they presented themselves as initiates in possession of true insight, whereas others were in thrall to mere 'opinion'. And of course this notion is reproduced in Plato's fundamental distinction between truth and appearance, where appearance is generally identified with

immediate sense perception, while truth is identified with reason. Now whatever we may think about the disparagement of the sensible element in knowledge which is implied here, this thought already involves something which has been decisive for the entire history of the modern concept of ideology – namely that the essential task, in contrast to all ideology, is precisely to break through immediate appearances, through some semblance or façade, and penetrate to some more or less concealed core. Here again you can see that the problem regarding the historical significance of nominalism and conceptual realism, which we have repeatedly touched on in the course of these lectures, is not really that simple. And in today's lecture I should like to encourage you, with specific reference to this intellectual model, to maintain a free and open mind with respect to such hackneyed and well-worn notions. For it is of course the case that nominalist movements take sensuous knowledge, the immediately given, i.e. that which is mere semblance or appearance for the other philosophical approach, to be the only real source of knowledge, while what is concealed by appearances, truth in the sense of alētheia (ἀλήθεια),[3] is scorned as a purely metaphysical construction by Enlightenment thought in the broadest sense. Yet this very distinction between essence and appearance, between the underlying structural laws and the outer façade, expresses precisely what is central where the recognition of ideology is concerned. For the task is to see through the phenomena of the façade – the surface phenomena which serve to conceal what effectively holds the whole process together – and thus allows us to recognize the essential laws or principles which are at work. And to that extent the theory of ideology in its classical form is also the heir to philosophy insofar as it opposes a concept of essence or structure to the merely ephemeral and deceptive phenomena of the façade.

Now this tendency towards objectivity, which I have specifically emphasized here, has generally not been as uncontested in the history of the theory of ideology and has certainly not proved as dominant as this might originally appear. I shall try and explain why. In the early bourgeois phase of social development in Elizabethan England, Bacon was the first person who seriously attempted to identify those more or less constant intrusions or disturbing factors which made scientific knowledge, or knowledge properly based upon experience, effectively impossible.[4] Yet he proceeded in an intrinsically subjectivistic way, as is indeed already suggested by the long-established talk of 'the many', *hoi polloi* (οἱ πολλοί),[5] whose eyes are covered by a veil which only an esoterically initiated few are able to remove. The four 'idols' which he identified are all essentially subjectivistic in the sense that they are ascribed either to human nature as such or simply to particular structures of consciousness, without raising the issue of essence at all. Thus the problem as to how far these forms of consciousness are themselves determined by society does not even arise – not to mention the really profound and in this field utterly decisive question about the necessity of such deceptive appearance, and ultimately about the truth content which this kind of appearance itself also involves. In other words, Bacon's doctrine of idols, if I may say a few words about this here, offers us a partly anthropological and partly psychological doctrine of the illusions or disturbances to which our consciousness is exposed merely from the side of the subject, as it were, in its relation to objects, which are taken as things that are just there in themselves in the sense of naive realism. On this conception, therefore, the task of knowledge is simply to experience these objects in the most adequate and least distorted way, but thereby also in an essentially passive way. Many of these 'idols' are unreservedly idealist in character, such as the so-called *Idola specus*, or the Idols of the Mirror,[6] which refer to the idea that the individual – in other words, psychological – nature of particular human beings impedes their knowledge of the truth because it leads them to introduce certain factors which diverge from universal reason.[7] This is basically the first appearance of a theme which subsequently proved hugely influential for the psychological relativism of a later time under the name of the 'personal equation'.[8] On the other hand, with the idols that are described as 'Idola Theatri',[9] we find something that returns in the Enlightenment motif of simple class betrayal. Here the idols – or, if you like, the ideologies – the false images of reality, become nothing but a matter of attitude, of deliberate betrayal, of cunning persuasion. What is criticized now are those late manifestations of the rhetorical tradition that emerged out of a decaying feudalism, a tradition that, within the older scholastic discipline that had itself built on classical school of rhetoric, had certainly once seen better days. These 'Idola Theatri' are really no different from the types of ideology that we could describe today as political propaganda in the narrow sense, the manipulated tricks which are simply designed to sway people as required. By far the most interesting of these idols from the perspective of the theory of ideology are unquestionably the 'Idola Fori',[10] for these idols are actually rooted in the realm of language, are conceived in terms of a critique of language, and spring from the claim that language, as a universal means of communication, intrinsically produces certain forms that end up functioning independently and thus cannot actually express adequately what they are supposed to mean.

It is worth noting that, in the later phase of bourgeois thought, this particular motif – namely an examination of ideology that amounts to little more than a critique of language and a concern with the objective assumed by subjective communication – turns out to be one of the essential forms in which contemporary positivism undertakes to absorb and at the same time to neutralize the theory of ideology under the banner of semantics, an approach which is particularly popular in many places today under the name of 'analytical philosophy'.[11] Now I certainly do not deny the value of such investigations, which require the close analysis and critical examination of language itself and the ways it is used. For I believe that such investigations can prove immensely productive and that one may learn an enormous amount from the examination of language about the social whole and the actual character of the world in which it is used and spoken. And as many of you will already know, I have frequently undertaken enquiries of this sort myself.[12] But the problematic aspect of a theory of ideology which is oriented solely to the critical examination of language, so it seems to me, lies in the fact that such an examination, pursued in isolation from other things, can easily become a kind of fetishism. In other words, this approach comes to believe that the confusions and deceptive tendencies which we can observe in language can all be traced back simply to the supposedly equivocal, impure, non-logical and emotionally coloured employment of words – whereas what we have to recognize is the constant interaction between words, to see them as a kind of force-field between what they are in language and what they have come to mean, and thus what real society is. And to the extent that the former approach treats language, qua means of communication, as an absolute, what you have here is another attempt to offer a subjective theory of ideology, albeit one that is couched in a seemingly more objective form.

Now the history of the concept of ideology, which I shall not try and present for you in any real detail here, starts with the insight that, behind the idols we mentioned earlier, there lie certain interests of one kind or another, such as those already suggested by old Bacon with his 'Idola Theatri', but it eventually leads to a developed insight into ideology as a socially necessary illusion that is nonetheless grounded in objectivity. I believe that we can hardly insist too strongly that the concept of ideology can only be employed in a serious way as long as it is not interpreted in terms of a mere psychology of interests. Yet the concept of ideology eventually met with a remarkable fate, for after Marx had formulated his great insight that the task was to criticize ideologies while simultaneously deriving them, and in a sense thereby also redeeming them, in terms of their objectivity, this concept of ideology was effectively lost, and the idea of ideology reverted to a kind of subjectivism which was extraordinarily similar to that which we find in the early phase of bourgeois society, in the pre-Enlightenment period of Bacon and in the later Enlightenment period of the eighteenth century. Thus it is quite possible to show that the theory of ideology which has found conclusive expression in Pareto[13] is really nothing more than an attempt to understand all contents of consciousness purely in terms of psychological interests without reference to the objectivity of society. I have already said something about the origin of this retrogressive development and the reasons behind it, and also about how it erases the distinction between truth and lie – or untruth – which is contained in the concept of ideology itself. Here I would just like to point out that the objectivity that attaches to the concept of ideology also contains an aspect or moment of its own truth, and indeed in a manifold sense. Firstly, in the sense that, if some form of consciousness is produced through a necessary process, then something of this necessity itself will also find expression in this consciousness. The consciousness in question, therefore, is never utterly and completely forsaken by truth. So we see that Marx criticized the theory of free and fair exchange as presented in liberalism. Yet in doing so he also acknowledged and held on to something that was implied in this ideology, namely the fact that such exchange is realized under the formal conditions of freedom and that, in contrast to the feudal phase that had gone before, concepts such as freedom and equality are in fact also involved and advanced here. In other words, once we emphatically speak of 'ideology', then that which is characterized as 'ideology' is no longer simply being characterized as a 'lie'. On the contrary, it is already characterized as something which is necessary in order to legitimate the social reality which the ideology captures, and also as an aspect or moment that expresses something of the essence of the society which produces this ideology. For although it is true that the process of exchange is neither free nor fair in bourgeois society, and although it is false to say that the employer and the worker encounter each other on nothing but the basis of their own labour in the act of exchange, it is still true that exchange involves some kind of equivalence, and that a more searching investigation – namely the analysis of labour value and the commodity form – is required in order to show that something more is involved in the exchange relation. Moreover, we must also recognize that ideologies in their classical form almost always involve an aspect or moment that points beyond the real social conditions to which they are applied. Thus bourgeois society basically claims: 'Here we are dealing all the time with actual things, we are a society made up of free and equal partners who exchange their labour time in a reciprocal manner, a society in which' – let me put it this way – 'each person gets his due.' Now, of course, as critics of ideology, you can easily show that this is not the case. But, once such an ideology is formulated, the claim to such a society is already formulated too – the claim for there to be a society of free and equal members, a society where everyone would indeed receive their due. So, when we criticize a society based on exchange, it does not imply simply that exchange is to be abolished: it also implies that what exchange promises – that we are not cheated or deceived in the process – is actually to be achieved and fulfilled. In this sense, therefore, you can also apply the concept of dialectic to the theory of ideology. The very concept of dialectic means that exposing the difference between ideology and reality already serves and intrinsically implies the possibility that the criticized ideology not only fall away, but also that it be realized. The critique of ideology harbours the possibility that ideology shall become reality, and it is precisely this which essentially distinguishes a genuinely penetrating critique of ideology from the purely negative or purely subjectivistic critique of ideology which believes it is merely dealing with the more or less contingent and subjective sources of a mistaken or deluded consciousness, sources which can be eliminated or removed at will. If I said that ideology also expresses something true, I must come back in this connection to classical ideology, in other words, to the ideology of liberalism. For I want to say something to you about precisely why in this case we are really talking about ideology par excellence, the very model for the concept of ideology generally. Here you must also remember that this theory – as formulated in the context of classical political economy which basically claims that the whole is held together precisely insofar as all its constituent moments pursue their own interests independently – also expresses truth because society does indeed reproduce itself, and reproduce itself in a continually expanding way, through this mechanism of competition or, to put it more accurately, this mechanism of universal exchange. In other words, the life of society really depends upon this principle. And the necessity of this liberal ideology lies solely in its expression of this fact. Thus it is only when you also acknowledge this moment of objective truth in liberalism that you can properly recognize the moment of untruth that it equally involves – and that alone would represent a case of genuinely dialectical thinking. Anything else would fall back even behind the concept of mere ratiocination upon which Hegel had already justifiably poured his scorn and contempt.[14]

But I think that I also owe you a few further remarks at least on the concept of ideology itself, and its prospects today, and on the essence of ideology in the contemporary context. I not feel it would be right if we merely contented ourselves with the history of dogma, or simply engaged in reflections on the past here, and avoided the issue regarding the status of the concept of ideology and the question of ideology today. You will not of course expect me to offer you a fully developed theory of ideology at this point. You can certainly find many of the elements that would contribute to such a theory if you take a look at our *Dialectic of Enlightenment*, and especially the chapter dedicated to 'The Culture Industry'.[15] The thoughts that I would like to offer you on this subject here are really just arabesques to what you can read there, for I generally like to avoid, if possible, simply regurgitating for you what is already contained in our published theoretical texts. So now we are all basically clear that ideologies also change along with history itself, although we have seen that this change in ideologies proceeds more slowly than that of the social-economic base, and although we have seen – if we look at history more closely – that it is the *functions* of certain fundamental claims persisting from the age of the Stoics through to bourgeois society as a whole which have actually changed, rather than that these fundamental claims as such were radically replaced by quite different ones. But you must bear in mind here – since bourgeois society has always been internally divided and the identity between the universal and the particular which it affirmed has never actually been realized – that the theoretical interpretations of this society have also contradicted one another. In this sense there is no such thing as *one* bourgeois ideology precisely because there is no *one* bourgeois society; or, to put this more exactly, because *the one* bourgeois society is defined precisely by the internal fracture, by the class relationship, which it involves. And the lack of identity, the unreconciled character of the relationship between universal and particular, is decisively reflected in the form assumed by the ideologies in question. Thus in a rather striking way we can distinguish between those theoretical positions which effectively uphold the side of the universal – in the history of modern thought these are the rationalistic positions – and those which uphold the side of the particular – which are the empiricist positions. Nonetheless, after what we have heard, it proves impossible, in terms of a theory of social class, to establish an unambiguous coordination between one or other of these philosophical positions and one or other specific class. This is because the whole, with all of its internal fractures, actually reveals itself in both of these theoretical positions, and that is why they also change their functions historically and are also mediated with one another in multiple ways. If we approach these things in a philosophical way we soon discover – since each such form of philosophy tries to grasp the whole, however inadequately – that the whole also presents itself, in however fractured a fashion, in every one of these philosophies. So, for example, you will be able to find elements of conceptual realism within empiricist approaches and also find that the reverse is true. Thus we may consider our old friend Bacon, whom I mentioned earlier (though I should perhaps say Bacon the younger, since of course we are talking of Francis Bacon here rather than of the scholastic or pre-scholastic Roger Bacon).[16] For it has often been pointed out that, even in the case of Bacon, who played his cards quite openly, what we find is a radically empiricist programme that is nonetheless combined with a completely unshaken faith in the essences of the Aristotelian tradition, and to that extent Bacon might be described as a half medieval and a half modern thinker. In response to this, I think we should recognize that this is not because he lived in what is ominously described as a 'time of transition' – a rather childish notion that I would be happy to see you dispense with altogether. For the real reason is that empiricist thought, even here in its very early modern phase, was already faced with the double task of doing justice to the particular aspects of experience while also trying to grasp them as an integrated whole. Where the changing role of ideologies is concerned, we see a constant process of selection taking place between these two ideal types or extreme possibilities. Yet, whichever of these theoretical approaches is selected, we always find that one also contains elements of the other. This is because one approach on its own – one of these divided halves of reality, if I can put it that way – is not sufficient to grasp the whole; yet, at the same time, under the conditions of an antagonistic and divided world, no genuine internal synthesis is possible. The most impressive attempt at such a synthesis in fact is that of Hegel. I would just remark in passing that the considerations I have been suggesting to you here might also become clearer and easier to grasp if you bear in mind that certain invariant features of bourgeois society qua market society have persisted since ancient times and still continue to manifest themselves. Thus when we are talking about substantive questions with regard to ethics, law and the state, i.e. when we are talking about the relationship of philosophy to society, we find that the actual divergences between thinkers who are emphatically opposed to one another in terms of their fundamental epistemological or metaphysical positions turn out to be far less striking than we would ever have imagined. In the field of ethics, for example, you will find that the rejection of compassion as a ground for how we should relate to each other is shared by thinkers who are otherwise utterly different from one another, such as Spinoza in the early bourgeois age, Kant in the age of revolution, or Nietzsche in the age of imperialism. Yet the radical differences of fundamental approach here would seem to have had little influence on the idea that one should try and follow reason rather than give in to the heart. This is naturally connected with the fact that all these thinkers can actually be seen as ideological[17] in the specific sense that the necessary demands of false bourgeois consciousness are reflected in their case too, that they are all forced to expect a certain kind of rationality from human beings if the latter are to function in this society precisely as they are required to do. The identity of the social structure here makes itself felt in all these theoretical positions, even in the face of the narrower ideological, i.e. the abstractly philosophical, difference that defines the starting point of each thinker. You can apply this observation to countless other categories beyond that of 'compassion', and it would be an excellent subject for a dissertation if someone could show how philosophies which utterly contradict one another officially may still frequently agree on what may look like rather eccentric ideas. And you can be sure, when you stumble on these paradoxical points of agreement, that you have actually come upon a very fundamental stratum, or bedrock, of bourgeois civilization itself.

But when I speak of the essentially historical character of ideologies, it should be quite clear – if I may emphasize this once again – that it belongs to the essence of ideology that, although the various conditions, insights, forms of behaviour, whatever it is, have been historically produced and have come to be what they are, all of this – in the context of ideology – is almost always presented as something that exists in itself or possesses some intrinsic being as such. One might say that the fetishization of the historical – in other words, the absolutizing of what has become what it is and the forgetting of how it came to be what it is – is a necessary characteristic of ideology. And one can even show that forgetting as such is a constitutive category for the overall form that modern epistemology has assumed.[18] Thus we might say that something like the 'consciousness of things' in the context of philosophy is only possible when the undiminished actuality of the phenomena to be synthesized is no longer present to us, and we thus forget or neglect certain aspects of these phenomena. And it is only through what is no longer present in the phenomena, in other words through a kind of *sterēsis* (στέρησις)[19] or deprivation, that they first become susceptible to what metaphysical and epistemological theories have so lauded under the name of 'synthesis'. The cognitive achievement involved in such theories of knowledge is an achievement of forgetting, for something which has become what it is here appears as an absolute. This alone helps you to understand the relationship of ideology to history itself: while ideology is constitutively dependent on history, it must nonetheless deny the latter precisely in order to uphold the absolute truth content it claims. History is the scar, the critical point, of ideology as such. Once we can expose the historical origin of a particular ideology, it forfeits that illusory appearance of absoluteness which is essential to its existence.

Now when you recognize that ideologies are intrinsically entwined with history, this seems to open up an extremely important aspect that points in another direction as well. For it is not just that ideologies themselves change; the essence of ideology also changes, if I can put it that way. In other words, the contents of consciousness are not equally ideological at all times – there is a more or a less where ideology is concerned. In the course of our earlier reflections on the theory of ideology I have already spoken at various points about the way that ideology has become more tenuous and more fragmented today. It is either merely a duplication of what already exists or nothing but the kind of naked lie currently propagated by dictatorships. I have thereby already indicated that one cannot just take over the concept of ideology as if it were a constant that is equally valid for all epochs. Now there is a subjective and an objective side to this. On the objective side, it seems that ideology in an emphatic sense presupposes a highly developed society. An ideology as such can really emerge only where the base is articulated enough to provide a closed motivational context to which the superstructure then corresponds. Now in primitive nomadic or hunter-gatherer societies of one kind or another one certainly cannot speak of ideologies at all, for the concept of ideology presupposes a certain kind of social objectification, a kind of alienation on the part of socialized subjects. It is only where society has taken on a certain weight or power of its own in relation to socialized subjects, only where society is no longer immediately identical with socialized human beings themselves but has already become extended and objectified, that something like the formation and development of an ideology is really possible. And on the other side, namely the subjective side, I would say that ideology presupposes a relatively highly developed level of rationality. Ideology in an emphatic sense can arise only where the claim to the rational, legitimate or justifiable character of society has already in some sense become universal. Now if you have developed a certain sensitivity, a good ear, as it were, for these things, you will notice that there is not really much point in talking about something such as feudal ideology. For where a genuinely feudal society exists, where such a society is relatively unproblematic and actually functions, the human mind will certainly attempt to derive and justify the prevailing hierarchical conditions in some way by appealing to philosophy or principles of natural law. But no one will try and prove these structures themselves as a thorough expression of rationality. That is why there are no such things as legitimating ideologies of feudalism in the feudal period itself, nothing which could really be compared with bourgeois ideologies. Now I would say that, today, in a world where bourgeois society is trembling or already broken in so many ways, there can no longer be ideologies in the sense of attempts to show the coherent rational character of society. Thus if we think about Sorel or Nietzsche's vitalism in this connection, and both thinkers actually have an extraordinary amount in common here, you can see that the real basis of ideology as an attempt to show the immanent rationality of society has effectively been shattered. Now if we try and make these things intelligible at all, I believe it may perhaps be somewhat exaggerated – though no more so than one actually has the right to exaggerate here – to say that the concept of 'ideology' is not an abstract universal concept but one that strictly applies only to bourgeois society. Thus there are no feudal ideologies but only feudalistic ones, or what we might call restorationist ideologies, and it is no accident that the great theoretical formulations in this regard – we might think here of Plato's glorification of the hierarchical system of Spartan society as a kind of utopia, or of the glorification of absolutism that you find in de Maistre[20] – belong to times of attempted restoration. In other words, they belong to times in which, as Hegel says, the irrational and traditional forms of social order which are glorified in this way no longer enjoy substantial existence, or even are no longer actually present.[21] For what is common to all these great restorationist thinkers is that they are all confronted with the genuinely paradoxical task of justifying the irrational itself, the irrational character of those societies themselves, precisely by appeal to rationality – in other words, there is really only something such as feudal ideology under the form of romanticism.

LECTURE 15
19 July 1960

Ladies and gentlemen,
[...]¹
Now allow me to come to the central issue, and let me try today, if at all possible, to bring together our hitherto fragmentary reflections on the problem of ideology as the principal site where sociology and philosophy essentially intersect with each other. In our last session I pointed out that it is not just that ideologies and the functions of these ideologies undergo change over time, but also that ideologies can be said to exist to a different extent in different historical periods. Thus one cannot simply take all forms of consciousness – even insofar as they could be described as false consciousness – and subsume them all to the same extent under the classical concept of ideology. For this concept essentially relates to the model from which it was originally derived, namely that of classical liberalism, and thus cannot just be applied without further ado to feudal society, as I pointed out earlier. Now I did not mention this solely through an anxious desire for historical accuracy or through a somewhat formalistic need to make the concept of ideology as tight and secure as possible, although in an age when such concerns have been seriously weakened this would hardly seem particularly contemptible to me. On the contrary, I mentioned it on account of certain things which we need to bear in mind when we think about the role of ideology today. For I wanted to bring out for you that the concept of 'ideology', in the specific sense of a necessary kind of false consciousness, is really beginning to dissolve today. On

one side we are confronted with something that can no longer properly be described as ideology precisely because it no longer harbours any claim to objective truth, irrespective of whether this claim is redeemed or not. Thus to speak of National Socialist ideology in this context would be quite wrong, for the kind of theory propagated in the Third Reich was no longer remotely concerned with expressing the truth about society. And there is something utterly useless and inadequate, as I would put it, about expressing contempt or intellectual superiority with regard to such so-called theory. For that was simply to mock something that was actually invulnerable at the very spot where this mockery sought to strike. In this kind of National Socialist theory – in its racial doctrines, for example, or in its doctrine of the organic articulation of the people as a national body in the face of the unprecedentedly visible concentration of capital and thereby increasing dissolution of so-called natural and spontaneous bonds and relations between people – there was really no question of anyone ever seriously believing these things. I would even think that such a truth claim was not taken seriously as a truth claim even in the innermost circles of the movement. Anyone who ever took a look, as I occasionally did in the period of the Third Reich, at the party newspaper *Das schwarze Korps*[2] – which expressed the core content of such doctrines – would also find a barely concealed scorn regarding the cult of German antiquity, including caricatures of the ancient Germans with their long beards and so on, even though one would hardly have expected this in something published on the authority of Himmler. And, in fact, the word 'Blubo' was widely used in Germany at the time as shorthand for the ideology of *Blut und Boden* [Blood and Soil], and no one expected to end up in a concentration camp for using the expression. But I am not telling you this, ladies and gentlemen, in order to make light of National Socialism in any way. And I believe that is indeed the very last thing you would expect of me. I mention this here only to show you how little these things were taken seriously at the time in terms of supposed objective content. All that mattered was to provide propagandistic slogans which were extremely memorable and extraordinarily easy to adopt and exploit, and which in the simplest and most primitive way gave people to understand: 'This is how we do things! This is the praxis we are after.' Nobody seriously claimed to be offering something akin to a theory of society or even, as I see it, a theory of 'the People' or of anything else. And, indeed, Goebbels had already proceeded in much the same way, presenting himself explicitly as the minister of propaganda rather than as any kind of real theorist, while the only one among the Nazis who offered up something resembling a self-contained world view or *Weltanschauung*, whatever that is supposed to be, namely Rosenberg,[3] always found himself rather on the sidelines and was not really taken very seriously by those who occupied the key positions of power. He was basically used as a kind of propagandist against the church, and it could not be said that his orthodox fascist views, if I could put it that way, ever provided anything like a real theoretical basis for the whole movement. I believe that the awareness that what Herr Goebbels was saying was a simple lie, that this consciousness was in fact extraordinarily widespread in Germany, and that the denunciations to which Goebbels gave voice were simply heard with a knowing wink, as if to say: 'Yes, he brought that off well again, didn't he?; he's really clever at doing that, isn't he?' – but all with the implicit understanding that he is simply lying for reasons of pure Realpolitik. In a world where the authority of reason has been neutralized by the immediate application of power or the immediate reality of oppression, the mind forfeits even that aspect or moment of independence that makes it into the kind of necessarily false consciousness that I spoke to you about before. And the widely recognized interchangeability of slogans in totalitarian states, as we can also observe in Russia, where the once idolized Stalin could suddenly be publicly denounced – and rightly denounced – as a murderer at the Twentieth Party Congress,[4] without this leading anyone even remotely to question what kind of political system effectively permits the substitution of one individual for another in such a way that the idolized 'Leader' of today can become the demented murderer of yesterday. This also serves to demonstrate how this actual decay of ideology in the classical sense, if I may put it this way, is becoming ever more widespread. On the other hand, however, we see that it is not as if truth were now somehow immediately replacing ideology. For if we observe what is happening in relation to ideologies today – apart from this tendency to become nothing but pure lie or simple deception, to become a consciousness that is not necessarily or intrinsically obfuscating but actually almost transparent once more – I would describe this in the following terms. I would say that ideologies today are no longer really developed in the same way as the doctrine of human rights in the past, and here I am referring to the whole complex of bourgeois ideology which leads from Locke through Montesquieu and the French Enlightenment to Jefferson's conception of the constitution.[5] For this relative independence of ideology, as a philosophical construction developed to legitimate or complement real social relations, is something that is increasingly beginning to disappear today. In place of these relatively independent ideologies, what we see more and more these days is that the existing order itself, in other words the totality of productive relations and productive forces as they are given today, is now taking over the function of ideology. The existing order is thus accepted as such, and that which exists is experienced as so inescapable that it is effectively raised into a justification of itself in its mere factual existence. I believe that the veil beneath which human beings exist today, beneath which consciousness exists today, is – to put this in an extreme way – the veil of complete unveiledness. It is the veil that consists in the way that human beings certainly experience in themselves the power of the reality that confronts them, without this power being particularly dressed up in any way, although the power in question, through its sheer disproportion to the power and to a considerable extent even the insight of any individual, appears as if it were not itself something that has become what it is, as if it were not itself mediated in and through human beings themselves, as if it were not society itself that ultimately lay behind this power. For this power appears as if it had literally become what Hegel had already said it was at a much earlier stage of the development of bourgeois society as an emerging system of complete socialization, namely a kind of 'second nature'.[6] And even here we might speak of the formation of a necessarily false consciousness insofar as society[7] in fact here still appeared to the individual, in accordance with the model of individual initiative and the free active agent of the eighteenth and early nineteenth century, as something that could be changed. Today, by contrast, society no longer even allows the thought that it might be changed on the part of individuals to arise in the first place. That élan which was bound up with the emancipation of the bourgeois class and with the relatively dispersed and independent property-owning individuals of middling means who constituted it is something that has been driven out of people by a social order where every individual, in order to live at all, is effectively forced to seek some little hole or other to crawl into in the hope of somehow surviving the permanent catastrophe in which we find ourselves. Now conditions such as these are not just unfavourable for the emergence of ideologies but deeply unfavourable for any independent movement of thought whatsoever. And behind the increasing loss of intellectual vigour, the increasing loss of interest for theoretical issues more generally, that we see today there are further reasons beyond those I have already discussed with you, namely reasons on the subjective side of things. That no one any longer takes any real pleasure in thinking actually reflects something objective – namely the pressure which weighs upon every individual, and the danger to which every individual is exposed simply by trying to exercise independent thought, and, above all, that feeling of hopelessness and powerlessness which every thought now tends to assume.

I believe that in a sense all this is an illusion. In other words, I believe that, just as 'second nature' is in reality nothing but society in a bewitched form, so too the powerlessness of human beings themselves, who ultimately constitute this very society, is only an illusion. But I also believe that we cannot resolve this simply by invoking the idea of humanity and appealing to human spontaneity in an empty and declamatory fashion or just by exhorting people to all imaginable kinds of wonderful things, thoughts and deeds. For we need first of all to go back and consider the conditions of that weakening and that kind of resignation under which we suffer so much today. It is not by denying our current state but only by comprehending it as such, by seeing through it precisely as a piece of ideology, that there is any possibility of moving beyond it. Now on the objective social side of things, the gradual extinction of ideology as an independent factor may in turn be connected with the way that, in the present phase of social concentration, we see that those individual spheres of economic life which were once relatively independent of one another – namely the spheres of production, of distribution, of the circulation of capital – are now more or less being fused together. It has often been pointed out – thus Spengler already clearly formulated this,[8] although the observation actually goes back much earlier – that the intellectual development of the mind, the development of rational consciousness itself, is very closely connected with the function of circulation, and especially with the function of money, in human society. And when we consider how journalists and writers, who have long upheld the affairs and concerns of the mind in the course of social development, are also closely involved with development of trade and commerce, it is evident that this sphere of independent, relatively unregimented, but still ideologically functioning intellectual labour has also been growing weaker insofar as this relatively independent sphere of commerce and economic circulation no longer really exists at all. The impressive and overwhelming power of the productive apparatus, and especially of the accompanying technology, to which we are all bound is to some extent also taking over the intellectual function which was once exercised by the relatively independent means and sources of information, and then also of the thinking which springs from reflecting upon such information. In our time, as we all know, the realm of information itself has produced what we now describe with terms such as 'mass communication' and the 'mass media'. And the word 'mass' in this connection is also a case of *hysteron proteron*, in other words, an inversion of the order of cause and effect. For what actually characterizes these mass media is not so much the way they adapt to the existing power structures – in fact, the so-called free production of the so-called things of the mind probably adapted itself to an even greater extent in earlier times – but the way that the central agents involved are also directly connected or even utterly entwined with the centres of economic power themselves, and that the views and attitudes which are thereby communicated to the masses directly correspond above all to the interests of the prevailing order. And in this connection – I would just like to add – the content of what these mass media hammer home to us is actually no longer even essential in relation to their own existence, to the impressive and imposing power of this whole technological apparatus to which we find ourselves constantly exposed. It actually seems more important to the amateurs and hobbyists in this technological world – who represent a characteristic social-psychological type in this respect – that they can access some short-wave radio programme or other from Arab countries than that they should understand something about the anti-European or anti-American tirades of a minor Arab leader in terms of any actual content. What I want to say, in other words, is that ideology today rests upon the way that the social order and, above all, the technological apparatus under which we live, together with the technical means and productive forces on which that order depends, have themselves acquired a kind of halo and suggestive power of their own, where the very powerlessness of the individual in relation to these media is in truth reflected. It is very much as Aldous Huxley anticipated in what I would have to call his prophetic dystopian novel *Brave New World*[9] about thirty years ago. There he imagines a future humanity for which the cross has had its top section removed to leave a simple T as a universal symbol, so that 'Model T' – the first Ford model that went into mass production – is a car that now stands in directly for religion. However critical we may otherwise be regarding the overall intention of his novel, I believe that Huxley was nonetheless remarkably acute in perceiving the direction in which ideology itself was moving. In other words, ideology is polarized between an idolization of technology and of institutions on the one hand and sheer deception on the other. I would say there is an essential conclusion to be drawn from this: the critique of ideology today, if it is to avoid focusing on what is actually inessential, must concern itself less with the intellectual and cultural products of the mind – and with confronting ideological products with the *cui bono* question as we used to do in the good old days – but should attempt instead to recognize ideology precisely in the realism seemingly devoid of ideology and the practice of naked deception to which human beings have subjected themselves.

This brings me to the problem of the so-called sceptical generation, or what is often described as the generation without ideology – an idea that has been widely disseminated through a book by my colleague Schelsky.[10] And I imagine that many a disillusioned young person may well recognize themselves in this description. The question whether the criteria of a sceptical generation do in fact apply to the youth of today, and whether a general scepticism is therefore the characteristic feature of the period that is now emerging, is surely an open one. And I do not think I am interpreting Herr Schelsky inaccurately when I say that he himself shows no desire to cling to this particular description as a magical formula for understanding the youth of today or what is to come in the future. There are countless investigations which have also revealed certain contrary tendencies, such as very strong, albeit backward-looking ideological elements of an elitist kind that emphatically appear to contradict this idea of a so-called sceptical generation. There are also certain investigations undertaken under the auspices of the Institute of Social Research[11] which have completely disproved an essential thesis upon which the concept of the sceptical generation relies, namely the thesis that asserts a general levelling down on the part of consciousness. These investigations have shown that we do indeed discover ideological differences which are very strikingly related to the social situation of the specific groups being investigated, and which certainly cannot be taken as lightly as they generally have been for some time now. This tendency to pay insufficient attention to such differences, and to assume a generally prevailing scepticism instead of recognizing a more specific form of consciousness, has a specific intellectual source, if I am not much mistaken, which sheds considerable light on the question at issue here. For it actually ties in with a critique of a somewhat misunderstood concept of proletarian class consciousness. I am referring to an approach which has been around for some time now and which began with social democratic revisionism,[12] was further developed in the writings of the later fascist leader Hendrik de Man,[13] and still finds an echo in specific works such as that of Bednarik on the young worker today.[14] Defenders of this approach expended considerable effort to show that members of the proletariat never actually possessed anything like a proletarian consciousness but, in reality, exhibited nothing but a petit bourgeois consciousness. And this claim was greeted with something like a howl of triumph because of the conclusion it seemed to imply: 'Surely if the workers are not explicitly workers in their own eyes, if the famous class consciousness to which socialism had once appealed does not actually exist, then the whole socialist conception is evidently built on ideological ground, and the reality of the workers fundamentally diverges from the form of consciousness that has been ascribed to them.' Now, as far as this triumphant conclusion is concerned, I believe that it actually involves a misunderstanding of the concept of class consciousness itself. For class consciousness is not – and in the classical theory of ideology itself was never conceived as – something that would just accrue to human beings by nature as it were, simply in accordance with their class position. And there was a very obvious reason for this. For you must not forget that, even on the classical conception, which sees the proletariat as essentially an object of social processes, the proletariat itself does not somehow stand beyond society. For the proletariat too, insofar as it sells its labour power and keeps the bourgeois process of production in motion, is already incorporated into bourgeois society from a relatively early point of time. It would therefore be quite absurd to suppose that the consciousness of this class, which in terms of its own interests is certainly opposed to the prevailing order but still lives in and from this order and is shaped down to its innermost impulses by the totality of this order, would a priori possess an expressly oppositional and entirely distinctive class consciousness of its own. And the great theorists of socialism in particular were the last people to harbour illusions in this respect, for they were always convinced that class consciousness was something that needed to be encouraged and produced precisely through insight into the objective social situation. And in the history of socialism theory was always essentially understood specifically as the means to help bring about such consciousness.

I do not really want to go into this controversy about class consciousness any further at this point, but I simply wanted to show how it actually starts from the wrong place, and an ideological place at that. Here I would just like to take up in substantively sociological terms a thought that I tried to develop for you earlier in a much more formal way in terms of general philosophical reflections. For the ideological core which this approach basically shares with the idea of the sceptical generation derives from the way that everything here is framed in the context of a form of thought which attempts to conceptualize ideology in essentially subjectivist terms. We saw the same thing, as you will recall, with the so-called total concept of ideology which effectively dissolved all ideologies in a mere psychology of interests, and where any attention to the objectivity of social relations or the objective social determinations of particular groups simply falls away.[15] What I want to bring out here is that this subjectivism, this subjectification, and thus the evacuation or flattening of the concept of ideology, also takes place when we go beyond merely showing that the proletarians now love to ride motorbikes,[16] which I can hardly regard as a tremendous achievement (whether we are talking about the insight or the motorbikes). For it also evident when people go even further and claim that humanity as a whole is free of ideology today. Now if you take away anything from these lectures either directly for yourselves or for your own general experience of social reality, then I believe this is a point where you may already have good reason to feel suspicious in this regard. For it is not really a question of whether human beings, where their own subjective consciousness is concerned, actually doubt whether they possess or recognize certain values or fail to possess or recognize any values at all. For if ideology is really a necessary form of false consciousness, as I think we ought to interpret the concept of ideology if it is not to become vague and flabby, then what truly decides whether a given consciousness is ideological or not is not the subjective attitude of the relevant subject but the structure of the categories in terms of which a human being actually thinks. Thus, to put it rather crudely, a person may believe in nothing at all, may be an utterly hardened sceptic who walks down the street with his elbows sticking out, just waiting to bump or push into someone he doesn't like the look of, with a general attitude that says: 'So what, it's all crap anyway!' He may even pride himself on being a hero of universal scepticism, a man who endorses a distinctively modern attitude of disenchantment towards things. Yet he may, for all that, still be thoroughly caught up in ideology. And I would actually be tempted to argue that this particular kind of scepticism is itself a form of ideology, precisely because it tends to be closely associated with a narrow-minded attachment to one's own merely individual interests: 'So what, even if I don't believe in anything, I do believe' – at least this is what you usually hear – 'that I have to earn lots of money, that I have to do well in life, that I have to get a decent job' – and all kinds of similar things. Yes, indeed, but this completely blind and unreflective acceptance of the category of the maximization of gain, which is of course the theoretical goal of higher bookkeeping, this naive acceptance of the notion of maximization, already implies that the individual concerned is still completely caught up in the prevailing order, even if he spits contempt on what are called values – the values which he encounters in the existing shape or set up of that same contemporary society which respects those who achieve economic success and causes problems for those who do not. Such an individual falls victim to an entire context of delusion insofar as he fails to recognize – and this can be indicated in a very precise way – that the very principle of the unreflective pursuit of merely particular interests can only end in the destruction of the whole, the collapse of the totality. Thus the narrow-minded realism or lack of naivety and the supposedly disenchanted attitude with which this now widespread type of person pursues their particular interests finally turns against even these interests themselves – and this is not to mention the tremendous inner damage which is suffered by people who adopt the kind of outlook which I have just outlined for you and which is probably all too familiar to you from your observation and experience. And if there should be anyone here today who basically shares this outlook – something which is socially produced and not really a matter of individual blame – and I were perhaps capable of shaking their naive and dogmatic trust in this particular kind of scepticism, then that alone would be one good thing to come out of these reflections. In this connection we should also point out that technology itself also functions as a kind of veil in the sense that we are no longer capable of perceiving the human productive forces behind the technology which they have created.[17] We thereby reify technology and simply treat it under the category of consumer goods, which only leads us to lose sight of the relation between the consumer goods which appear to promise happiness or satisfaction for our own recognizable needs and what, to be blunt, we actually get from these so-called consumer goods.

In short, I would like to show you that this consciousness of the so-called sceptical generation, insofar as there really is such a thing, is an ideological or false consciousness – in other words, a consciousness which mistakes a series of surface phenomena which directly claim our attention – above all the immediacy of our own particular interests – for what is essential here, namely the structure of society itself. Once we realize that the immediacy of the individual and of particular interests is itself mediated by society as a whole, we can no longer really endorse the standpoint that the individual is always what is closest to itself, simply because this is not actually true. For the whole is present in every individual person, even in what strikes us as the most naive and self-evident human need. Thus the truly sceptical approach should actually be aimed at this very tendency to absolutize the standpoint of immediacy. For it is just here that the so-called sceptical generation tends to be entirely unsceptical, to reveal instead what I would call an intransigent naivety which is then reflected in the typically refractory attitude which has already been described in connection with this scepticism. For this refractory attitude – the attitude which exclaims: 'We don't want to know about ideology, we don't want to be troubled by anything' – implies the desire to ward off any thought that would threaten the kind of comforting immediate consciousness that I have described for you. For then one would have to recognize that what is expressly taken to be non-ideological is itself actually ideology, to recognize that if I am fortunate enough to ignore all ideologies, to have enough money to go to the cinema every night, then I thereby become the victim of that ideology which cinema already is and represents – and the ideological character of which outdoes anything that the classical forms of ideology, whether in religion, philosophy or anything else, ever succeeded in producing. I believe therefore that this scepticism which is supposedly free of ideology, if it actually exposes itself to such critical self-reflection, can hardly fail to recognize itself as ideology and thus come up against a concept of binding truth that it otherwise struggles to resist. Then at last it will realize that the obsession with merely immediate consciousness serves only to conceal the objective social structures on which this individual consciousness depends.

LECTURE 16
21 July 1960

Ladies and gentlemen,

In the last session we spoke in connection with ideology about the problem of the contemporary generation which is supposedly free of all ideologies and therefore relates to things in a purely sceptical way. And you will recall how I showed you that a consciousness which is sceptical in terms of subjective attitude certainly cannot be accounted free of ideology simply for that reason. For it is actually the dogged immediacy with which one's ends are pursued, without any theoretical reflection or any thought that goes beyond what currently exists, that itself constitutes a certain ideology and weaves a kind of veil. I would like to continue this idea here and share certain thoughts which may help you somewhat to refine the concept of ideology and dispense with certain all too naive conceptions which readily arise when this concept is employed – although I am well aware, given the general tendency of the age to reduce all such concepts to the lowest formula or common denominator, that this attempt to resist the kind of absurd or disastrous approach which is specifically adopted where the concept of ideology is concerned may also appear rather quixotic.

I believe that what is all too often neglected in discussions of the concept of ideology is precisely that ideologies in the strict or emphatic sense are mediated by the totality of society. In other words, ideological categories are those which appear in an a priori way as essential forms of our consciousness yet are basically defined or determined by the entire structure of our society – and thus do not represent merely interests or views which are characteristic of particular groups and would be specific to some particular social class. When we discussed the concept of class consciousness I took the opportunity of distinguishing the concept of ideology from the kind of psychology of interests to which it has often been reduced, and I believe that we can properly understand this point only once we are quite clear that ideology is not a sort of thinking, or is not necessarily a sort of thinking, that is imposed on some individual within the overall social structure essentially by the group to which the individual in question happens to belong. For the veil which I spoke about arises through the way that the entire social structure within which we are bound does not merely appear to us as a kind of second nature but also actually produces us, as you might say, as a kind of second nature out of itself, and provides us with the means, forms and categories in terms of which we think and act. Hence it is also extraordinarily difficult to reduce ideologies today to the special interests of particular groups. I do not want you to misunderstand me here. For I am not trying to defend the thesis of some entirely undifferentiated consciousness that simply pervades the whole of society, a thesis that has actually become dangerously widespread especially today. We know perfectly well, in direct contradiction to this idea, that certain essential differences do prevail within different groups of the population as a whole. Thus an investigation carried out at the Institute for Social Research[1] – and we are talking specifically about subjectively directed questions and investigations here – has shown that there is a significant difference in attitude and consciousness between the members of the higher social groups – including employees of these groups who also feel they have some possibility of identifying with them – on the one hand, and the 'underlying population',[2] in other words, ordinary workers and employees, and people of lower social status generally, on the other. Where the consciousness of the individuals in question is concerned, this shows itself as a difference between the distinct realism of the lower social group, which is less likely to let itself be hoodwinked and thus corresponds much more closely to that image of the so-called sceptical generation that we talked about in the last session, and the attitude of the higher social group, which at least sees itself in more idealistic terms – in other words, believes that it is inspired by a consciousness of higher things, by values that are more or less independent of the material basis of life, and thus feels it can also justify its privileges by reference to these same higher values which it endorses. So I certainly have no intention of denying differences such as this, but I really believe that we are talking here about more or less surface phenomena of a social-psychological kind. Whereas the mechanisms of reification, or the mechanisms of reifying consciousness – the hypostatization of immediate private interest as the only relevant criterion, the nationalistic ideologies that have spread to so many countries in the world, and other things of this kind – are mediated by the totality of society itself, and in this sense they reach down below the specific forms of social differentiation and constitute a kind of fundamental stratum which human beings basically have in common today. Hence these mechanisms weigh infinitely more heavily upon people than the kind of differences we have just mentioned. People themselves are also far less conscious of these mechanisms, for they function at a preconscious level and are much more difficult to resist and challenge precisely because they have taken on the character of a second nature. I would also like to add here that the attempt to reduce ideologies to the needs of particular groups obviously becomes more difficult the further removed the cultural and intellectual spheres are from the immediate interests of the material base of society. Thus if you think about the famous controversy between Sir Robert Filmer and John Locke about the divine justification or otherwise of the structure of political rule based on different estates,[3] it is fairly easy to recognize the latter as the ideology of a specific social group which attempted to legitimate its claim to rule and to its particular privileges in relation to other social groups on the basis of a supposedly divine right, or even in terms of an authority inherited from Adam himself as the first ruler over nature.[4] And now the representative of a bourgeois class that in principle espoused an egalitarian approach – although we may suspect that the ideology of this class was always far more egalitarian than its practice – challenged that specific group ideology that was defended by the old privileged nobility. But when you hear people say today that the human being as such is what counts, that the sole end or goal is man himself, and that specific social relations are irrelevant to this notion of man, we can certainly say that such an ideology only helps to maintain the current order and thus ultimately works to the advantage of those who benefit from this order. But these people cannot specifically be said to represent this ideology in contrast to other social groups, for it is also expressly shared by the less advantaged members of society and various other groups which certainly have no special interest in propagating it. Nor can we say that this ideology, in terms of its content, is specifically designed to justify any particular identifiable differences within society. For in terms of actual content it does not serve class differences in a direct or immediate way. It does so only indirectly in the sense that, by presenting society as it exists as a truly human society, this approach assumes an ideological character precisely as a whole. Let me just add here that it would probably be a worthwhile task, though one that sociology has never undertaken in this way, to differentiate the concept of ideology in a quite different manner from before, namely in terms of the structure which ideologies assume in relation to the existing order and the essential variations in the way they do so. I imagine, if I am thinking once again of a good subject for a doctoral dissertation, that one of you here might consider the idea of developing a typology of such ideologies. I hardly need to say, of course, that a typology of this kind could not be framed as a theory of unchanging 'idols', for the relevant types of ideology themselves would have to be related in essential ways to specific historical phases and historical forms of production.

Here I would just like to suggest at least two possibilities where the formation of such ideology is concerned, both of which seem to me to be quite fundamental. One of these possible types of ideology could perhaps be described as an extremely broad type of legitimating ideology. This type of ideology interprets certain relations in terms of an ideal concept of the same and thereby legitimates these relations in the process. Thus the theory of liberal society as a domain of free and equal exchange is a typical legitimating ideology of this kind. Or we might think of a legitimating ideology such as that of conservative or restorationist thought during the bourgeois era, an ideology which theoretically tries to defend the privileges which have already fallen victim to rational critique by arguing that a system of rule based on such privileges is justified because human beings, the masses, the people are not in a position to understand their own interests and are thus also incapable of properly judging the measures undertaken by governments. In other words, the mass of people must be excluded in their own interest from participating in any discussion and particularly from any process of political will formation. This kind of ideology played a very significant role in the seventeenth century especially – but also in the eighteenth century in Britain and France – and finally passed into the particularly backward form of conservative thought that we find in nineteenth-century Germany.

Now I would contrast legitimating ideologies of this kind with what I call complementary ideologies, namely ideologies which really experience some aspect of things in their negative character. Instead of trying to justify or legitimate the prevailing order of things itself directly, ideologies of this sort attempt to supplement the latter by recourse to some kind of cultural or intellectual argument, some form of consciousness, which that order itself does not possess. You could say that such ideologies stretch from the consumption of opium practised by subjugated peoples under barbaric forms of rule in Central and South American lands before the time of the Spanish conquest, and which – as some of you may know – has persisted in certain South American countries to this day,[5] all the way to far more elevated things. Thus there is absolutely no question, for example, that one of the social functions of religion has been to console human beings who have suffered in this life with the prospect of some recompense in the next life where their lot will be very different. And it is difficult to say what is cause and what is effect here, when through a certain internalization of religious processes connected with the whole movement of the Reformation this motif of consolation and what is deemed a better world beyond has actually receded considerably as a form of social cement or as a complementary ideology. But of course there are still such complementary ideologies at work today, when it is constantly hammered into us that 'the human being' stands at the heart of things precisely because every one of us is actually treated today as little more than a function within the social totality and when less and less really depends on our own spontaneity or individuality. One might say that 'the human being' is just the complementary ideology to ubiquitous dehumanization.[6] And I suspect we encounter something very similar – if you will allow me to pursue a somewhat speculative thought here – with those metaphysical explorations of temporality which flourish so much today, in other words, with all those attempts to turn time into the metaphysically crucial and essential thing as such. It is very interesting to observe how this metaphysical elevation or glorification of time has emerged precisely in an epoch when something such as the consciousness of temporal continuity, of a continuous, coherent and meaningful course of life, can no longer really be found. And in terms of cultural and intellectual history it is indeed the case that these metaphysical explorations of time first arose in the context of *Lebensphilosophie*, namely the philosophy of life which emerged in reaction to the causal-mechanistic form of thought which reflects the reification in which something like the experience of temporal continuity no longer exists. And in fact Bergson, in his extremely important work *Matière et mémoire*, specifically related the thought of irrational and spontaneous experience directly to the notion of what he called 'living time'.[7] And it is from this stratum of thought that all the other metaphysical philosophies of time actually emerged. And we also find that all of the philosophies which, in a certain sense, were reacting against a rationalistic approach espoused the idea of the stream of consciousness – that is, of the essentially temporal character of subjectivity as something immediately lived – until the metaphysical construction of time itself finally arose out of this specific aspect of experience.⁸ In other words, I believe that if you genuinely engage with ideologies you will also have to ask about the specific kind of ideology you are dealing with in each case.

I may just also ask here whether in our time – and in this regard the ideological structure of the present time may perhaps remind us of pre-bourgeois periods of history – the complementary ideologies are not beginning once again to prevail over the legitimating kind of ideologies. This seems to me to be the case everywhere that the order of things itself, whether as first or second nature, is taking on such power that it seems simply to be beyond all discussion. The feudal order, as long as it actually existed, was essentially beyond discussion and just had to be accepted. And, to facilitate this acceptance, the consolatory ideology always added the complementary reflection which, when repeated in later bourgeois times in order to keep the poor peasantry in line, assumed the touchingly philistine form of the old saying 'Keep ever true and honest'.⁹ But the structure of ideology is quite different in genuinely bourgeois phases of development when *ratio* is sanctioned as the criterion of the social and political relations themselves, when these relations are open for rational discussion and can be rationally justified in some way. One might say that the legitimating form of ideology is characterized by the notion of discussion, is characteristic of the classes where ideas are contested, and specifically in the form that certain more or less particular interests are required to justify themselves as universally binding ones. Today, on the other hand, when the preponderant power of the existing relations is so firmly established that this kind of discussion no longer takes place in a genuine or emphatic sense, when it has become illusory or, I would almost say, itself ideological, we see that complementary ideologies are rising up again in a quite new way. Yet they now appear only really as parodies of what once existed. Thus, whereas the great religions still offered human beings something like the hope for a better life, now we are told that this life only has to be re-enacted in a special higher kind of way, that its merely reflected form is immediately identical with true meaning that such a life itself possesses. Thus if we have grasped life in its meaninglessness, and then repeated and seized hold of it as such, if we have truly discovered its constitutive factors, then we have thereby also discovered its own inner meaning – this at least is what is wisely imparted to us.¹⁰ In other words, what is nothing but what it merely is basically gets duplicated in order to find its complement through this very duplication, and thus to appear as more than what it is. In general this is possible only when the objectively established social relations are effectively presented and reflected back to us in forms of false immediacy as if they really were immediate, and immediately human relations at that. Now it should be evident that such complementary ideologies, like those we see all around us today, no longer possess any substance of their own, and precisely on account of this abstractness end up resembling the kind of lie which I spoke to you about in the last session and described as the decaying form of ideology. Thus the one eventually passes over directly into the other. That is basically all I wanted to say to you about these types of ideology.

But allow me to return to the question about the basic character of ideology – in relation to the social totality and the extraordinary difficulty of identifying and correlating those ideologies which cannot directly be situated in the context of the struggle between specific social groups but are further removed from that context. In the first place, I would say that where this distance is rather large, as in the case of works of art, the task of identifying the relevant ideological correlations is very difficult indeed. Generally speaking it is not possible to explain given works of art in terms of the particular social group from which the artists who produced the works in question originally emerged – at least of today; nor is it possible to correlate the effect which such works of art have, if they have an effect at all, or indeed the content which they express with some such specific social group. For what is actually reflected in all this, admittedly from the specific angles which society assumes through the particular ways in which it is concealed and refracted in the process, is just the whole and actually only the whole of society as such. Now I once engaged in a lengthy controversy on this very point with my long departed friend Walter Benjamin, some of whose writings may well be familiar to at least some of you. I am talking here about a text that has not yet been published, part of a larger work on Baudelaire,[11] where he attempted to explain certain poems from *Les Fleurs du mal*, from the cycle 'Le Vin',[12] in relation to the wine tax which was imposed in France in that period.[13] What I said in response at the time was: 'Well, the question is not that simple, for it is naturally the case that empirical elements of an immediate kind generally find their way into an important work of art too.' And in this controversy, I would have to say, Benjamin certainly did not acquit himself badly, for he raised the emphatic objection against me that recourse to the totality of society could only import a kind of abstractness into the theory of ideology which would essentially drain all living colour from the latter.[14] On the other hand, I would say something rather different about why this cycle of poems might allude to a problem such as that of the wine tax and the possibility, in the Paris of 1840 or 1850, that wine could be obtained more cheaply in the banlieue, in other words outside the limits of the city proper,[15] and that this was the reason the proletarians of Paris tended to venture beyond those limits in order to drink. Thus I would say that what is reflected in Baudelaire's wine poems is that peculiar fusion of self-destructiveness and self-intoxication which itself can only be understood in terms of the totality of social conditions, of the social totality itself, rather than in terms of this particular situation of the workers who were forced to go into the suburbs to look for wine. And I say this neither to pour scorn on the activity of the workers here nor in order to suggest that Baudelaire specifically attempted to express their predicament – something that would be very difficult to show given the highly complex political outlook of Baudelaire, which was anything but simply revolutionary in the sense of the bourgeois protagonists of 1848. I believe that it is important for me to draw your attention to these things on account of the mischief perpetrated in the name of the theory of ideology in the Eastern bloc where Diamat duly celebrates its triumphs. For that is essentially connected with the way that the concept of ideology here is no longer mediated in terms of the social totality, and ideologies are now simply and immediately identified with group interests of any kind or even with national interests, namely those of the supposedly socialist states and of the imperialist states on the other side. And that gives rise to this horrifying distortion, this instant identification of cultural and intellectual products as either sheep or goats, something which, on account of its primitivism, is not merely repellent to our perhaps overly discriminating bourgeois consciousness but, perhaps more importantly in this context, also obscures the meaning of the concept of ideology itself.

I have tried to develop a relatively strict concept of ideology for you, one that is free of the usual tendencies to water this concept down in one way or another.[16] And, just as I warned you earlier about the manner in which Mannheim applied the concept of ideology, here I would also like to warn you about another way of applying the concept of ideology. I am talking about what Brecht described as 'Murxism'[17] – when he still trusted himself to say what he really thought, as he often did in earlier days. I believe that there is no greater danger than this way of thinking for people who are genuinely concerned with the interpretation of cultural and intellectual products. But since I take this question extraordinarily seriously and feel a distinct obligation in this respect as I discuss these things with you now, I cannot avoid alerting you, as best I can, to the enormous threat of simplification and vulgarization where the concept of ideology is concerned. Thus I cannot avoid offering you some clear examples of the kind of thinking I am talking about, and which do not derive from recent second-rate literature on the subject in the Eastern zone but were actually developed in the Western sphere of influence. I take these examples from an essay by Leo Löwenthal entitled 'On the Social Situation of Literature', which appeared in 1932 in a volume which also contains my own first contribution to the sociology of music, which was an essay on the social situation of music.[18] The Löwenthal essay actually seems to me to be a classic example of how not to go about these things. I think it is necessary to mention this here since I noticed that, in a basically very sympathetic piece that appeared in your student journal a while ago, Löwenthal's efforts were clearly likened and brought into relation to my own,[19] although our approaches to these things even then, when those essays were published, were in truth entirely opposed to one another. I believe you have only to take a brief look at both texts to realize this. To begin with I would just like to read you a couple of sentences from this essay, 'On the Social Situation of Literature', to show you just something of the problems and difficulties I have been talking about. Thus in the essay we read: 'Other class relations come to light once we compare the function of the framing narrative in Storm and Meyer respectively.'[20] He is referring to Conrad Ferdinand Meyer here.[21] Then we read:

> This principle of artistic composition possesses an opposite meaning in the two writers. It allows Storm to assume an attitude of resignation, a kind of retrospective renunciation. He is the weary petit bourgeois rentier for whom the world in which he could mean something has effectively collapsed. Time has passed. The only foothold in life which the present still has to offer is one of recollection. The transfiguring function of such recollection is also clearly revealed by the specific technique Storm deploys in handling his images, where memory is only capable of reproducing fragments of the past, specifically those which do not relate directly to the dismal reality of the present and thus need not fall victim to a process of psychological repression.[22]

Now in the first place what I would like to say, even if we accept that the kind of consciousness that finds expression in Storm really is that of a petit bourgeois rentier[23] – which strikes me as a rather arbitrary assumption that can hardly be justified on the basis of the texts themselves – is that such a consciousness, and thereby the conscious awareness of the impotence of the bourgeois individual, is not simply to be rejected out of hand but should be recognized as a true consciousness of the position of those condemned to impotence in their private individual existence, and thus as something anti-ideological in character. We would thereby already discover something eminently critical in the grief and melancholy that we do indeed encounter in the highly significant novellas of Theodor Storm. But in adopting this abstract schema and regarding the petit bourgeois merely as something already condemned to death, in thereby devaluing something which in a particularly impressive way really expresses the impotence of bourgeois reality, the negativity of bourgeois individualism, we simply turn the blind optimism of the proletariat into the criterion for a genuine work of art. This treats any work of art as good as long as it expresses the triumph of the newly emergent class, whereas anything that expresses suffering and negativity, anything which lends voice or expression to the true state of things, is specifically devalued. Now this attitude already basically implies the schema of the kind of thinking we subsequently find in Diamat, which would have us believe that everything that is weary, decadent, alienated from life, everything that does not already stand on the side of the big battalions, is thereby already condemned as backward and obsolete. On the other hand, we find that abstract and quite vacuous glorifications of a proletariat which is threatened by saboteurs, yet manages to discover and despatch these saboteurs and then undertakes to achieve even higher levels of livestock or potato production, is supposed to represent not merely a higher form of life but a higher form of literature as well. With this kind of straightforwardly correlating approach to ideology, even when it is still pursued in a relatively academic and respectable way, so to speak, you can basically see how it already clearly prefigures that regression of consciousness which has become so widespread today. But there is something else at work here too. For Storm is specifically being reproached for the way the process of[24] recollection in his work involves a certain highly selective principle of literary composition, for the way that only those specific moments or aspects emerge which have carefully been selected or emphasized by the author for a very particular purpose. In short, he has been reproached for not trying to present life as a seamless and meaningful whole. Now if you reflect for a second – and here I appeal to the students of the history of literature among you, whatever your particular speciality – you will recognize that Storm's literary technique of presenting life solely in retrospect, of describing life in terms of excerpts or segments rather than in terms of continuity, already anticipates that later tendency to dissolve all of the obvious surface connections of life which eventually find decisive and objective expression in the great novels of Proust and Joyce. Yet the literary form here, which is extraordinarily modern and progressive from a technical point of view, is also turned into an object of censure. Thus we are confronted with a quid pro quo which already derives a negative judgement on the work of art itself from the fact that the artistic technique involved represents the collapse of the appearance of life as something self-contained, and thus also expresses the negative character of that life. What is so important here is that all this becomes a pretext for devaluing the new technique itself, the development of the artistic productive forces, which allows the writer to break down a life into fragments and reassemble it out of these fragments rather than describing it as if it possessed a self-evident meaning – in other words, for devaluing everything that is eminently modern, progressive and forward-looking abut Storm's practice as a writer. And this is also how the members of KUBA, or whatever they happen to call themselves, in the Eastern bloc presume to pass judgement on avant-garde literature today.[25] In other words, the sort of wretched denunciations of modern art and culture that we find there are already anticipated in reflections like those of Löwenthal here, even when they appear to maintain a certain level of quality.

But things become even worse, as you can see, if I just read you a couple more sentences from what he says about Conrad Ferdinand Mayer. In his work, so Löwenthal tells us, the framing narrative serves 'in the precise sense as the splendid frame of a magnificent painting and thereby fulfils two functions'.[26] Here the author is obviously confusing the description of the splendid life style which may have prevailed at the court of the Borgias or other dissolute potentates with the splendid form of the work of art itself. You can already see here that typical blindness to the genuine value of a work, that lack of attention to the specific substance and quality of a work of art, which later found its way into the kind of vulgar Marxist approach we talked about and has become so widespread there today. These two functions are thus supposed to point to the worthiness, as he puts it, of the subject matter, and to emphasize the important singular aspects over against the indifferent multiplicity of surface appearances.[27] What we are dealing with here, to put it bluntly, is an attempt to correlate Theodor Storm with the world of the petit bourgeois and Conrad Ferdinand Meyer with the world of the haute bourgeoisie, on the schema of the parlour and the drawing room respectively. Storm is petit bourgeois because he talks so much about the cosy parlour room, and Meyer is haut bourgeois because he talks so much about magnificent Renaissance interiors, if not exactly about bourgeois drawing rooms. Now I would just point out that this class-conditioned kind of reaction, which is so concerned with what is grand and splendid, is generally more likely to be encountered among the maidservants than among the members of the haute bourgeoisie themselves. I do not know whether I am as familiar with the upper classes as Herr Löwenthal, but as far as my own perhaps more modest experience goes I think the upper classes were generally more drawn to Knut Hamsun and so-called literature of the native land,[28] or perhaps with the world of fishermen[29] and figures of this kind, whereas the maidservants would prefer to read about the life of the upper classes. Thus there is a tremendous naivety about this kind of attempt to correlate ideology and social position, which effectively inverts the actual class relations and the actual social consequences of these relations. But I would certainly not wish you to misunderstand me here, for I have no desire to impugn the lyrical artistry of Conrad Ferdinand Mayer or the very beautiful and refined prose which he has bequeathed to us. Yet to proceed in the way I have indicated, to note that one author published his pieces in a very stylish journal while the other allowed his writings to appear with 'Westermann',[30] and to infer the specific class significance of both writers from this, seems to me to be the crudest possible simplification of the relationship between base and superstructure, between society and culture. And the ubiquitous vehicle for such vulgar simplification is the concept of the 'petit bourgeois',[31] a notion which can always be applied as an easy stopgap whenever we find literary tendencies where victims of progress and the collectivized world also find some kind of voice, where the language in question suggests that they have not been forgotten either. This whole approach to literature betrays the worst thing that can be said of it, for it instinctively identifies with the stronger and picks on whatever it sees as weaker and more hopeless than itself. And there is something very interesting here: if you take a look at the wretched DDR film of Heinrich Mann's novel *Der Untertan*,[32] you will see how the unfortunate petit bourgeois character, basically already broken in childhood, is picked on, while most of the attention in this film falls on the powerful president with his huge beard and body, although he is actually the expression of crass autocratic power. Now I do not think I have to say any more about these things here. Perhaps these examples have shown you what I really wanted to bring out today and may serve as warnings where the concept of ideology is concerned. For this is precisely not how to approach this concept, and if you wish to do any serious work on it you should avoid such an approach entirely.

LECTURE 17[1]
26 July 1960

Ladies and gentlemen,
In the last session we basically concluded our discussion with regard to what I wanted to say to you in particular about the concept of ideology. I would just like to add a couple of further points here. And the first is this: I would certainly not wish you to regard these two types of ideology which I mentioned in terms of a possible typology as somehow exhaustive or as something you could simply apply to everything. Now the curious thing about typologies, if I may just point this out here, is that it is really difficult to get by without some kind of typological thinking if we wish to concretize a specific concept, and that the 'types' involved even generally end up assuming a certain independence in relation to what they are supposed to render intelligible; but when we seriously engage with the latter, we immediately face the danger that the types crumble in our hands or dissolve into thin air. It would be a very interesting task, in terms of the philosophy of knowledge, to say something illuminating about the epistemological foundations and the general epistemological problematic involved in the production of such types, at least in the context of the social sciences. In this regard Max Weber employs an entirely nominalistic concept of types – one to which he therefore ascribes no special status or substantive character – but what he says on this question is quite insufficient in relation to the very specific types that we actually come up against time and time again.[2] Any serious treatment of the problem of typologies would really have to unfold and explore the following antinomy: we generally find that

typical structures do reveal a certain substantial character, and also a certain theoretical justification, and cannot therefore be regarded as merely heuristic devices, while, on the other hand, they also threaten to dissolve on account of the problem of so-called intermediate cases and transitional phenomena. I imagine I hardly need to add here that any meaningful typology must also be indexed historically. Thus if we are thinking of a typology of drama, we should not proceed as if everything basically stood on the same level and thus compare ancient comedy, the comedy of character, and Shakespearian comedy simply as various types of 'the comic'. For the task would be to show how philosophical-historical structures enter into the formation of the type in each case.

In material terms I would just like to say that, in addition to those two types of legitimating ideology and complementary ideology, as I described them, we should really also add the type of ideology that one might call obfuscatory ideology in the emphatic sense, although you may find it rather difficult in practice to separate obfuscatory ideologies clearly from legitimating ideologies. A typical expression of obfuscatory ideology would be the frequently encountered claim that human beings are actually unequal and that therefore the inequality of property is anthropologically grounded in essential characteristics of nature itself. Thus it is said that, even if there were some drastic currency reform in Germany and everyone had to start off with exactly the same salary, we would still end up with Herr Flick[3] on one side and the famous last unemployed person on the other, and this is supposed to prove the ominous inequality of nature. Yet that is just an obfuscatory ideology to conceal the fact that, even on such a day as that, some human beings enter the labour process and the process of exchange with more to call on than the conscientious work of their own hands, and that control over the means of production proves more decisive than any formal rights to earn money. That would be a good example of an obfuscatory ideology in the strong sense.

Since I have already alluded to the difficulty of strictly distinguishing such an obfuscatory ideology from a legitimating ideology, I would just like to emphasize that, where concept formation in the sciences is concerned, our concepts can really meaningfully be formulated only by reference to their extremes; they should be maintained in their extreme formulation but cannot be maintained at all when they are already framed in such a way as to incorporate so-called transitional phenomena. Thus, if we want to capture the difference between plant and animal, it is better to talk about a palm tree and an elephant – I do not believe they are particularly related to each other in Heine's poem,⁴ but they do seem to go very well together – than about bacilli and bacteria, for example, where we already need a microscope and a good deal of specialist knowledge to determine in this context what is vegetable and what is animal. It may be quite important to stress this here when we consider the prevailing tendency I have already mentioned, namely the tendency to turn positivism into an ideology itself and discredit every kind of theory by simply appealing to the facts, for we see this combined with the desire to disqualify every firmly determined concept and thus every form of theory by drawing attention to whatever transitional phenomena or whatever limiting cases we can find that cannot be accommodated entirely within the concept in question. Thus I remember a philosophical seminar many years ago now when we were exploring the phenomenology of particular concepts, and we identified the concept of landscape in phenomenological terms as a part of the earth's surface as seen from the specific perspective of someone who synthesizes and subsumes the scene in question. And one rather wilful student who always liked to stand apart, as it says in *Götz*,⁵ objected and said, 'But then what are we to say about lunar landscapes?' In other words, one can take a cheap pleasure in discrediting theoretical ideas by invoking transitional cases of this kind and showing that an extreme example of some phenomenon or other cannot readily be accommodated in a given concept. In truth, however, concepts must be developed in such a way that they organize, from a central theoretical perspective, the mass of phenomena which are subsumed under them. Thus within the continuum that, in a sense, any actual thing really represents, it can never be the task of a concept to include every possible detail in a totally clear and unambiguous way. For that only sabotages thinking by expecting or demanding too much of the concept of a concept.

The other thing that I wanted to say here by way of supplementing our earlier remarks – although I have already mentioned it in passing⁶ – is that the historical dynamics of the concept of ideology seem to suggest that ideologies themselves are becoming ever more abstract, i.e. that the dominant ideologies of today involve infinitely less specific positive content than was formerly the case. Thus the concept of 'man' – which has become one of the most decisive theoretical vehicles of this development today⁷ – is already infinitely thinner and more abstract than the principal ideological concept deployed by the National Socialists, namely that of race or blood, and I think we can expect that this attenuation of ideological substance will become more and more conspicuous in future. For you must remember that, in spite of the ever-increasing concentration and centralization of power and capital in modern society, the potential pressure that weighs on the masses who show increasing levels of awareness – even if the political structures leave them very little room to express this or allow them to do so only indirectly – is so great that one can expect less of them in ideological terms than was once the case. If you just recall Sir Robert Filmer's theory,[8] that we mentioned earlier, which traces the differences of the fundamental social groups or estates all the way back to the will of God, since such differences were supposedly inherited from the descendants of the very first human beings, it is obvious that we can no longer invoke things of this kind where people today are concerned, even in the context of totalitarian states. In this regard it is particularly interesting to note that the National Socialists, while they certainly espoused an elitist theory which emphatically scorned the bourgeois concept of equality, in no way endorsed a theory that expressly privileges a specific minority. For their own concept of the elite – as Karl Mannheim once acutely pointed out[9] – is itself a plebiscitary concept of the elite. In other words, the elite the Nazis were talking about is simply the majority, namely all those who did not have Jewish grandmothers, so that one was allowed to feel like the chosen people over against a tiny minority of the general population. The reason for this, of course, is that, had the Nazis openly and widely declared – as quite a few of them must have thought – that it was really only blond people with the right size of skull who make up this elite, while brown-haired people with larger heads are regarded as less than human, they would probably have encountered such serious difficulties that they would never have proved as successful as they did. Thus the pressure I mentioned just now, which inevitably leads to a relatively abstract production of ideology – for which I offered you a rather grotesque example, although less grotesque ones could easily be found – may increase so much that it generates that abstractness and attenuation of ideologies I was referring to earlier. This is a change of consciousness which, as I have already remarked, amounts in a way to the end or the obsolescence of ideology. Of course, I do not mean this in the sense that the unveiled truth finally takes the place of ideology. On the contrary, what I mean is just that – as we experience this in the East today – naked and immediate domination now simply joins hands with a lie in order to impose a certain situation on people and hammer it home to them as something both inescapable and legitimate – even though they are not actually expected to accept what the ideology offers them as if it were a genuine explanation or rational principle. I believe that these structural changes in the concept of ideology cannot be seen in terms of intellectual and cultural history in the same way as the transition from the classical concept of ideology to what I called the total concept of ideology. They are dependent on fundamental structural changes in society which would have emphatically to be taken into account in any attempt to produce something like a theory of ideology appropriate to our current situation.

Now, ladies and gentlemen, although we have been able to carry out only part of the programme that I originally set for myself – as so often happens with such lecture courses – I would at least just like to say something to you about the problem of genesis and validity, which, as I have already suggested on several occasions, constitutes one of the central problems as far as the relationship between philosophy and sociology is concerned. You will often enough be presented with a rather crude and primitive polarization here, where sociology is generally supposed to address issues about the content of knowledge in essentially genetic terms, while philosophy by contrast – on the traditional view – is expected to deal with pure issues of validity. It is obvious that this question of genesis and validity is intimately connected with the problem of ideology which we have been discussing in many of these lectures. I need only to remind you of Mannheim's concept of our so-called connection with being,[10] which basically means that the question of validity is effectively rejected or is decided in terms of the genetic question. Now a certain confusion easily arises here because Mannheim proceeds as if his own approach were really supposed to resolve the antinomic and antagonistic problem of genesis and validity, whereas in truth, when we look more closely, we can see behind the obtrusive terminological veil and recognize his one-sided decision in favour of the genetic moment. The concept of ideology itself – if I can just clarify this point for you in one particular detail – already involves the priority of the genetic moment. For with the vaguer and less precise sense that the idea of ideology often bears, even in Marx or among the Marxists in comparison to the strict concept of ideology, we are simply talking about the hypostasis of something that has historically become what it is. In this looser and broader sense, ideological thinking is a kind of thinking that in the case of a particular concept ignores the conditions of its production and turns the congealed product of a dynamic process into something that simply exists in itself, and thus fetishizes it in the process. In this sense ideology and fetishism are identical with each other. Thus in bourgeois society, given the universality of the exchange principle which underlies all processes, we no longer even reflect on the principle of exchange itself and thereby look upon its results, namely exchange values, as if it were a natural given. And if relations between human beings are thus reflected back to us as if they were properties of things in themselves, as Marx puts it,[11] then this reification of the products of labour at the same time represents a characteristically ideological form of thinking – a thinking in which false consciousness necessarily prevails because, in truth, the reified value which is here ascribed to objects themselves is nothing but a human product, namely congealed labour. And this ideology arises when we turn what has become or has been produced – the genetic moment – into a truth as such, into something that exists absolutely in itself. This may suffice to show you just how intimately the problem of genesis and validity is actually connected with the problem of ideology. And I believe we could probably go so far as to claim that, to a certain extent, all of the efforts which philosophy and also sociology have taken upon themselves in order to clarify and articulate the relationship between genesis and validity basically arose from their argument with the concept of ideology, and that the tendency of both philosophy and sociology to ward off the concept of ideology wherever possible has played a truly decisive role here.

Now I believe, ladies and gentlemen, that it is important you should be clear from the start about something essential to the positions we are talking about here, namely the position which appears to regard all truth, all that is binding, all that claims to possess reality, in a genetic way as something mediated, something that has become, and the position which maintains that there are pure forms or kinds of validity. And this is that both approaches are characterized by their dichotomous character, in other words, by the fact that they present themselves as simple alternatives. This way of formulating the problem of genesis and validity already forces us to respond to the question as follows: 'Well, either there is no truth, for if truth is conditioned by certain processes, then it enjoys no absolute validity, or it does enjoy absolute validity, in which case the processes through which it has been brought forth are irrelevant.' Here, ladies and gentlemen – if I may speak once again in a pedagogical vein – I would expressly warn you to beware of such alternatives which are aimed at you like a pistol in order to force a decision, as the charming phrase has it. Thus you are told: 'Come on, either you believe in values, validity, truth, or you believe in becoming, process, mediation, genesis!' But you should not allow these alternatives to be imposed on you. On the contrary – if I may go back and draw on the results of an earlier lecture course here[12] – I hope you have learned that what really matters to the scientific or philosophical consciousness – and I disdain to distinguish between the two – is precisely not to let such alternatives be foisted upon you. For the task is to reflect on these very alternatives and recognize them as nothing but the expression of the reified consciousness I have been talking about. For this consciousness of the world is wonderfully clear and everything runs very smoothly. On one side you have the people with their eternal values, preoccupied with validity or pure being, who look down contemptuously, on the other side, on all the pernicious relativists and historicists, on the corrosive thinkers so concerned with change and process; and in the opposite corner you have the people who consider themselves as enlightened and claim that everything turns on the question of genesis, on tracing things back, on identifying the origin, and the idea of validity is nothing but mythology. And in comparison with those who insist on the concept of truth, they see themselves as terrifically enlightened and progressive, although both parties to the dispute fail to see that the concepts which in each case they themselves deploy in a sense intrinsically presuppose the opposed position. And that is the key thing you should realize here, rather than believing, as Mannheim claimed, that you have somehow already solved the problem of validity if you insist on taking up the perspective of genesis only in a unilateral way. And, God knows, that is just what he does. But the important thing for you is to realize that this bifurcation, this alternative, which is forced upon you, is rigidly framed in advance, like the box to be ticked for rival political parties which you might easily find on a questionnaire. This is precisely the kind of thinking you need to be on guard against, and you should summon all the autonomous thought you can in order to see through it.

Now I claim that validity is not something pure which is conceivable independently of questions of genesis; on the other hand, the sociological position that genesis is just validity, the idea behind what we called the total concept of ideology, is not defensible either. Thus everything comes down to mediation. But when I say 'mediation' here I must also warn you about a misunderstanding that it is always easy to fall into, and perhaps especially easy to fall into here since we have not really been able to unfold the philosophical problematic of the problem of mediation here on account of the specific thematic focus of these lectures. When I speak of 'mediation', I am not talking about a middle way, about an approach that would acknowledge the right that is due to genesis and validity in each case. To a certain extent we might say that the sociology of knowledge which was developed by Max Scheler did represent a theory of mediation somewhat along those lines, although, as you will all know, he still basically came down rather one-sidedly on behalf of the theory of validity. He argued that the issue of genesis, or the genetic perspective, prevails within the order of being, so to speak, which is also where we deal with ideologies, with the psychology of interests, with everything like that. And here he even provided entire lists which correlated particular cultural and intellectual forms with particular social factors and conditions. But then he goes on to claim, as if by decree, that in the intellectual realm as such, in the realm of ideas – and here he was a good Husserlian – everything is quite different and enjoys a validity which holds quite independently of any specific social conditions.[13] Now I believe it is fairly clear that this type of solution, which simply appeals to two orders of justification or levels of connection, is quite inadequate. For basically all it does is to treat the problem in question – namely, how genesis and validity come together or relate to each other – as its own solution. In other words, this approach just says: 'There you are, on the one side you have genesis, on the other side you have validity, and they basically have nothing to do with each other.' Now this is nothing but the hypostasis of the scientific division of labour. Thus the issue of genesis is referred to the factual sciences, especially to the historical and sociological disciplines, while the question of validity becomes an exclusive matter for the discipline of philosophy, which has itself through the division of labour now effectively been divorced from the substantive content of the other disciplines. We fail to see that this actually exposes us to a really quite rudimentary objection. For if certain types of ideas are intrinsically coordinated or connected with a ruling class and the interests of that class, it is far from evident how at the same time we can continue to regard these ideas as subsisting in themselves as absoluta in the Platonic sense – just as ontology, which Scheler certainly qualified yet never entirely abandoned, has always wanted to do. This problem was never really solved by Scheler, and he believed that he could somehow avoid it by arguing 'on the one hand this' and 'on the other hand that'.[14] Thus the answer is not the kind of mediation which just accepts there is genesis on the one hand and validity on the other, and then seeks to balance out or accommodate both perspectives. For where the philosophical concept of mediation is concerned – and I believe this is fundamental for any genuine understanding of dialectical method, and something one must really already learn from Hegel if one wants to understand the whole approach that is adopted here – we need to see that the problem of mediation lies in the concept itself, which has to be conceived as essentially mediating in character. We are not talking about a general relationship between concepts that is external to individual concepts, about something intermediate that somehow balances out these concepts. We are talking about the recognition that the moments which intrinsically belong to and are presupposed by the individual concepts also appear to be excluded or indeed specifically excluded by these same concepts.[15] You can see here just how closely the idea of dialectic as a process in which extremes pass over into one another is connected with the thought of mediation. This means that, if you just question the concepts thoroughly enough in terms of their own intrinsic meaning, you will actually stumble on the very moments which they appear to exclude and see that the mediation involved here cannot be understood as a kind of connecting link between concepts. Here I should perhaps just mention one of the misunderstandings, and not the least important, to which Hegel was subjected at the hands of his successors, especially with Kierkegaard but to a certain extent with Marx as well.[16] This is the idea that the concept of mediation in Hegel implies a kind of moderating or levelling process which is external to the matter itself, and we generally make things very easy for ourselves with Hegel precisely because we assume a form of thinking which mediates in this external way, although this is exactly what robs his thought of its savour, namely of dialectic itself.

Now I believe that the easiest and clearest way to show you what I mean by this inner mediation of the two opposed concepts of genesis and validity is the following. For in a certain – and admittedly very superficial – sense we can see that the mutually opposed positions that I shall here call the nominalist and the realist positions, namely the sociological approach on the one hand and the idealizing or Platonizing approach on the other, are also completely at one with each other. For they both share the view that truth and history have nothing essentially to do with each other, that truth and history are external to each other. One might also put this by saying that truth has its history, that truth advances and becomes more adequate, as it were, or that in and through its changing historical phases the concept of truth and the inner composition of truth undergo change. But the two categories do not really come together, for truth still finds itself as something fixed and congealed, or, let me repeat, something thing-like that lies within history and encounters history only as external to itself. And the whole difference, where this reified and external way of opposing concepts to one another is concerned, is simply that one party comes down on the side of truth, which is supposed to contrast with history and to have nothing essentially to do with it, while the other comes down on the side of history, which is supposed to have nothing essentially to do with truth. But the really important thing is for you to get beyond this rigid antithesis altogether. We could perhaps express this – and I am no longer sure whether this formulation originally comes from Benjamin or from me, though I imagine that we came up with it together at some point[17] – by saying it is not just that truth exists within history, which is a commonplace, but that history itself inhabits truth. In other words, the concept of truth itself – and the concept of judgement itself – in its innermost meaning and not in any merely external sense already refers to history. It is only once you fully grasp this, I believe, that you will be able to get beyond the dichotomous conception of genesis and validity. Now it is quite true, heaven knows, that I have often criticized Edmund Husserl,[18] but in a certain sense he also deserves the greatest credit. For although, as you will all know, he began by defending the idea of pure validity in contrast to issues of genesis in the most emphatic possible way,[19] he still found himself compelled, through the immanent demands of his own thought, to concede that there are, as Husserl puts it, genetic meaning-implications involved in acts of judgement, implications which he nonetheless interpreted in a traditional Kantian manner as problems of constitution.[20] In other words, he later retreated from his famous thesis regarding the validity of propositions in themselves independently of their origin and now claimed that it was part of their meaning that we can follow them back to their origin. But then he looked for this origin in universal reason, in other words, in the transcendental structure of the mind itself, which he attempted in turn to distinguish and split off from anything that factically exists.

I believe I should really say something more here about this thesis of the genetic meaning-implications, about this claim that the genetic moment is inextricably involved in the truth itself. But then again perhaps that is unnecessary at this point, since I imagine I may already have said enough in our earlier discussion of ideology when I emphasized that the concept of ideology itself, if it is to possess any meaning, actually presupposes the concept of truth; that it is intrinsically contradictory, and an utterly meaningless undertaking, to speak about ideology in an emphatic sense, and thus about what is supposedly the simply conditioned character of knowledge, unless we possess a concept of truth itself in this regard. For if I say that a thought or idea is simply conditioned, or can be understood only in terms of its simply conditioned character, and thus lacks any truth moment whatsoever, I thereby deny that the concept in question has truth, or I relativize the truth claim that it raises. But that is only possible if one possesses a concept of truth that is not exhausted in the process, i.e. a concept of truth against which a notion such as 'simply conditioned' or 'absolute' can be measured. In other words, without a concept of validity it is quite impossible to grasp the concept of any conditioned truth. I am basically just repeating this from an earlier lecture[21] and importing it into this one. But now I would also like to look at the other more difficult and opposed moment, namely the genetic meaning-implications within the idea of truth itself, and say at least a few words about this aspect of the question. So if you just think of the content or state of affairs captured in a judgement, say a very simple judgement such as: two times two equals four. It will be immediately evident to you, if you reflect phenomenologically for a moment on the concept of a 'judgement', that this concept has a double meaning. Thus there is the judgement which I enact – in other words, my act of judging – and there is the judgement as an objective affirmation, as something valid in itself. Thus the classic definition of the judgement in the philosophical tradition tells us that a judgement is an affirmation in reference to which the predicates 'true' and 'false' can meaningfully be applied, an affirmation that can be said to hold, or otherwise.[22] At least this is the definition of the concept of judgement which philosophy has become accustomed to using when it needs to refine this concept in a critical way. Now, when you distinguish and contrast these two meanings of the idea of judgement, you will also discover that they are reciprocally implicated in each other. This is not just a matter of equivocation, or simply a semantic question of double meaning. In other words, independently of the process of comparing or collating, i.e. unless I compare or collate something – and by 'I' here I mean all of us or each and any possible thinking mind – unless the diversity of the elements 'two', 'two', and 'four' is brought together, without the moment of synthesis – if you like, without a genetic moment – unless a process is actually performed here, then a proposition such as 'two times two equals four' has no valid justification. If I do not bring 'two', 'two' and 'four' together, if I do not synthesize these elements, then no statement regarding their synthesis, i.e. this synthetic judgement itself, is even possible. On the other hand, however, if nothing answers to this – or if I may put this tautologically – if two times two does not really equal four, then I cannot for my own part accomplish the synthesis that expresses this. You might object that I have committed a logical blunder here, for in saying that two times two really equals four it looks as if I had once again simply turned the affirmation back into something merely objective, whereas before I specifically said that it presupposes synthesis as its subjective condition. Well, ladies and gentlemen, I have indeed committed this mistake, but the mistake does not lie with me. The mistake really lies in the circumstance that the matter itself is internally constituted in such a way that it is not possible for me to express one of these aspects or moments unless I also presuppose the other. Thus the judgement is true only if the state of affairs which it expresses answers to the judgment in question. But the state of affairs is only present or available when I pronounce the judgement. Thus both of these moments – and here you can see what I am driving at – are mediated through each other. One cannot be thought without the other, and any attempt to isolate one of these moments alone inevitably discovers that I am thereby arbitrarily hypostasizing or absolutizing that aspect or moment. Or it discovers that, if I think thoroughly consistently enough about one aspect or moment, I end up thinking about the other as well. But the great difficulty which arises here – and this is the difficulty of all dialectical thinking – is that although both of these moments are reciprocally related to one another, and neither can exist without the other, they are by no means simply the same. For, when I make a judgement, I aim at something objective which is other than my judgement, other than my act of judging; but then again, when I enquire into the validity of the judgement itself, I am also required to consider the subjective moment, namely that act of judging. Thus there is a synthesis of subjective and objective aspects or moments which cannot be separated from one another but which nonetheless cannot be collapsed into a simple identity with one another. Now I believe that, if you have understood this, then you will also have understood what I mean when I speak of genesis as something already implied in the meaning of judgement and validity itself. And the conclusion that should be drawn here is simply that, once this subjective moment has been brought into the field of validity itself, we find that history as a whole has also been brought into the question as a condition of truth, just as we find in turn that something such as history is not even possible unless the concept of validity or truth itself is posited as well. And that is essentially what I wanted to get over to you, at a relatively high level of philosophical abstraction, where the question of resolving the problem of validity and genesis is concerned. So I think we should just try in the next session to give somewhat more concrete form to these considerations, and thus address the social aspects of this problem in closer detail. Thank you all for your attention.

LECTURE 18
28 July 1960

Ladies and gentlemen,

Perhaps I should begin by reminding you that the idea that I was trying to recommend to you during our last few sessions was not the thought that genesis should enjoy some kind of priority over validity, or that the demands of validity should somehow be diminished. For what I actually wanted was to enable you to see through this rigid antithesis between genesis and validity itself as an expression of reification, and to understand that these two concepts are not simply opposed to each other after all. It is perhaps necessary to emphasize this because there is a subtle point at issue here which can easily give rise to misunderstanding. For by relativizing this antithesis – which appears so obvious to our usual, traditional way of thinking – we may simply seem to be endorsing relativism. But that is not what I want to argue at all. What I want to argue is that the opposition between the relativist position, which regards everything as merely ephemeral precisely because it is something that has come into being, and the position usually described as absolutism, which makes an absolute and objective truth claim – that this antithesis itself cannot be sustained. In other words, neither of these aspects or moments, the genetic moment and the moment of objective truth, can be thought without the other. I would ask you to bear this distinction clearly in mind, especially given the way in which the problem of genesis and validity has been formulated in Mannheim's very influential version of the sociology of knowledge. For while it looks as if Mannheim also claims to bring these two moments together, the synthesis which he offers simply works to the detriment of the question of validity and thus effectively denies any kind of autonomy. And by 'autonomy' here I mean the autonomous character that belongs to intellectual forms and products of the mind: the autonomy of knowledge and, ultimately, the autonomy of logic itself. In that sense, Mannheim's claim to reach back even behind the process of thought is simply an empty assurance on his part. But I actually hope to show you that these categories are reciprocally implicated in each other, which does not mean that the concept of validity simply vanishes or dissolves in the idea that everything has a history or has become what it is. Thus I think it would be a good idea if I try at least to indicate – and indeed specifically with reference to the field of cultural and intellectual development: the so-called realm of 'spirit' – how genetic moments already involve aspects or moments of validity.

Now if you understand the history of the human mind or spirit as the history of 'enlightenment' in the broadest sense – as we tried to formulate this concept in *Dialectic of Enlightenment*[1] – you will discover that this history, the genetic aspect of the mind itself, already involves an essentially critical aspect. The historical movement of the mind, where the various intellectual stages interact with, differ from, and transcend one another, cannot be grasped as a mere temporal sequence or simply as a change of so-called styles of thought, or again as a change of different socially determined world views. For there is a certain material logic at work here, and I hope to say at least a few more words about this, and about its relation to the logic of society, at the end of the lecture. Thus in the change which marked the difference between the bourgeois ideology and the hierarchical ideas of the feudal-medieval period it is impossible to overlook such a material moment alongside or in conjunction with the new social tendencies that were emerging here. I would simply draw your attention to the fact that the majority of the fundamental concepts of bourgeois thought, such as the concept of freedom or that of equality, in a certain sense actually emerged from the ideas of the feudal age – in the sense that these ideas were compared with their own actual reality. The bourgeois ideal of freedom is nothing other than that concept of freedom which the feudal order had already attained by developing the concept of a free owner of property who is not directly bound to the land. And once this concept of freedom was recognized, at least as the privilege of one particular group of human beings, the internal logic of this concept promoted further reflection on the idea of freedom, encouraged questions about the source and justification of existing limitations, and eventually turned this idea of freedom against those to whom it had once exclusively been reserved. Thus with some considerable exaggeration – though I hope you will see what I am driving at – we might say that from this point of view the bourgeois ideal of freedom already understands itself as an essentially critical relationship to what preceded it, so that this ideal now appears as the realization of a freedom that had somehow already been envisaged and projected. In other words, the genesis or process of development that leads from one form of society to the other cannot actually be separated from the issue of validity or justification – from the question about the degree to which concept and reality genuinely correspond with each other. In a very similar way, the concept of equality emerged from reflection upon the natural relationship between human beings in the context of the family – and it is indeed entirely characteristic of feudal thought to regard the familial relationship as the fundamental one for human beings; it was then perfectly plausible to ask whether this natural relationship is really restricted simply to those who own property and are able to inherit property by virtue of belonging to certain social groups, and indeed to ask whether the recognition of this natural relationship among human beings does not already harbour some kind of appeal to the natural relations and connections of the human being as a species. In other words, we may ask, to put this very paradoxically, whether an appeal to the concept of equality is not ultimately implicit precisely in our fundamental connection to nature and our relations of kinship. For the relationship to nature as a whole in which human beings find themselves, so far as we are capable conceiving it, pertains of course to the species itself rather than to any particular group. And this theme came to be explored ever more strongly in the context of the early bourgeois struggle against the remnants of feudal ideology. You will recall what I undertook to show you in the last session, or at least managed to outline for you in a rather summary fashion – for a detailed presentation of the argument I must refer you to the discussion in the *Metacritique of Epistemology*.[2] I showed that genetic moments are already implicit in the question of validity and went on to argue that, by virtue of such critical moments – and critique always involves a reference to truth, to the genuine relation between judgement and thing, to *adaequatio rei atque cogitationis*[3] – it is equally impossible to separate genetic moments from the claim to validity or justification. It follows from this that the two categories of 'genesis' and 'validity' – and I can present this to you here only in terms of models – are not actually opposed to each other in the rigid way that is so often suggested. Rather, and I would like to put this carefully here, the claim is that genetic connections cannot be thought of without reference to concerns about validity, while, at the same time, the categories of validity already involve and contain the question of genesis as their own meaning. There is no truth which, as truth that *appears* to us, has not *come to be*; on the other hand, there is nothing pertaining to the mind or spirit, whatever it may be, which qua judgement – whether directly or indirectly – could shirk the question of its truth, of its own validity or justification.

Now there is a very deeply rooted habit of thought which recoils from this thesis – a habit of thought which was already objectively and fatally challenged by Hegel's theory of universal mediation,[4] although it only became an explicit target of philosophical critique in Nietzsche, and especially in his magnificent late text *Twilight of the Idols*,[5] a work that I would strongly recommend all of you to read. There are really very few things that are so directly relevant to the questions we have to address here. For we are talking about a prejudice – which is precisely what I have to call it – which has marked the entire course of intellectual history, especially with the elevation of mathematical truth to the status of truth par excellence which became so common after Plato's time. I am referring to the idea, which was first articulated by Plato in a prototypically brilliant way, it has to be said, that what has become cannot be true, that only that which directly or immediately 'is', or that to which everything that 'becomes', can ultimately be traced back, can properly raise the claim to truth.[6] I do not wish to investigate the source of this prejudice with you here today. After all we have heard so far about reified consciousness, it will probably come as no surprise to you if I say that this way of thinking – the idea that nothing which has become is really capable of truth – is the primal phenomenon, the very prototype, of reifying thought, for which truth must be always tied to what remains or persists. Perhaps this is because human beings originally, and rightly, saw the concept of truth as the antithesis to the phenomenon of death and their own ephemeral existence, as an end to all that untruth and illusion to which our life is exposed by virtue of its transience. Perhaps they believed that this conception of truth offered them a remedy for all this, without actually recognizing that this moment of emergence or becoming is already contained in the idea of truth. It is one of the most curious aspects of philosophy that those philosophers, like the great German idealists after Kant, who placed the idea of spontaneity, function, activity and becoming at the centre of philosophy – all of them concepts in which time is implicated as a necessary moment – still clung to this thing-like concept of truth. So although they essentially saw the a priori itself as a generative and generated process – and at this relative level I would not really wish to distinguish between the two – they continued to hold on to a rigid and static concept of truth in spite of this insight into the essential relationship between truth and process or becoming; in other words, they still held on to the idea that, while truth is something produced or brought about, it is nonetheless supposed to be entirely independent of time. And this philosophical tradition, which is vulnerable even to the criticisms of the most ordinary human understanding, criticisms which any uncorrupted consciousness – and I mean any consciousness that has not been corrupted by philosophy – is capable of endorsing, this philosophical tradition has actually persisted right up to all those contemporary expressions of ontology, of the metaphysics of temporality, in which time itself is de-temporalized and converted into an invariant condition. Now this condition as such is indifferent to history, so that the aspect of becoming, of what has become, and thus of facticity itself, is just re-ontologized, and thereby forfeits that relation to movement and mutability which belongs to its innermost meaning. This is the really important thing, it seems to me, where the liberation of consciousness is concerned. In short, you must relinquish the belief that the truth cannot have 'become'.

But in order to avoid the danger of remaining too abstract here – in the usual non-dialectical sense of the word – I would just like to illustrate what I mean with a particular example, although I fear it is certainly one I have already used on other occasions. Thus it is quite possible to show – and you will forgive me if I turn to art here – that what we call great autonomous art originally arose from an art that served all sorts of more or less external purposes. We can also show, for example, that the great tradition of free instrumental music originated in *Gebrauchsmusik*, namely the kind of music that was used for various celebratory or accompanying purposes in the courts of absolutist monarchy. Richard Wagner once observed, and I think correctly in this case – he was surely thinking of the minor rather confected products of Mozart, of which there are certainly a number of examples – that with these pieces he could not help thinking of the clatter of dishes coming in and out at the great banquets of princes and archbishops.[7] He was thereby drawing attention to the origins of great instrumental music in the need for entertainment, in the desire to kill time, as we say, and indeed aspects of this kind are not wholly alien to very great music. I only have to mention that specific aspect which the music historian Georgiades has described as the 'festive' character of music, something which certainly belongs to the great symphonic music of the classical Viennese composers.[8] At the same time a certain aspect of compulsion or even coercion, a self-contained sense of necessity, can be observed in such music, which is nothing but the aesthetic sublimation or secularization of that disciplinary element, that disciplinary compulsion, which music is supposed to exercise on human beings, as you may discover from Saint Augustine's treatise on music.[9] Now anyone who strictly adhered to the prejudice that truth cannot have come into being could simply say: 'Well, there you are, what is all this great music you keep talking about, what is your Mozart, your Beethoven, your Brahms, or your Schoenberg? It's all basically nothing but a descendent of the art once used to entertain the privileged, and it's basically no better than the popular hits we take such pleasure in.' Now in America this kind of argument would not sound nearly as shocking as it does to us, simply on account of our so-called cultural heritage. But it is not a question of springing to the defence of so-called higher cultural things and values in the face of the barbarism which is documented by such words and sentiments. And I am certainly not tempted to indulge in apologetics of that sort. What is at stake here is actually quite different. For we may fail to see that what sprang from those earlier things – and let us exaggerate here and say that it sprang solely and entirely from those things – that what emerged from this lowly and heteronomous *Tafelmusik* – this background music to eat to – eventually turned into the symphonies and late quartets of Beethoven. And these works not only speak the language of humanity, not only represent the most consummate expression of the ideal of humanity that has ever been achieved in artistic form, but are also structures which have developed an autonomous logic, a wholeness, and an internal coherence which down to the subtlest details can stand comparison with the logic of philosophy – and you know that I am thinking specifically of Hegel here.[10] In other words, the high quality of this great music – and in order not to complicate things unnecessarily I am taking here about music from the classical tradition around 1800 – certainly did arise from this lowly, dependent, heteronomous material that we mentioned before. But it contains within itself, in the language of its own forms and structures, everything that points beyond that origin. And there clings to it that same emphatic concept of truth which was articulated by the great modern philosophical tradition, and to which we also rightly appeal when confronted by the question of genesis. You can already see from this that the true can in fact have 'become', that the idea of truth itself is something which has arisen, something which has been laboriously achieved. And I believe that the power of truth, that which compels us to hold on to the idea of truth, lies in this element of emergence, this process of becoming, in which it seeks to find expression – in stark contrast to any conception of truth which looks upon it as simply rigid, fixed and given. So if you really want to get beyond this antithesis between genesis and validity – which is crucial not only for understanding the true relationship between the disciplines of sociology and philosophy but for the tasks which any really productive consciousness has to confront – the decisive thing is to try and free yourself as resolutely as possible from the idea that truth cannot be something that has become; from the idea that truth stands motionless on one side, while the realm of factical existence, of change, of becoming, stands on the other, and the task is somehow to bring them both together. Only once you have seen through this notion – the antithesis between objectivity qua truth and mere subjectivity qua becoming – as illusory, or as simply provisional, will you be able to escape the spell of ideology. For ideology always basically consists in denying any truth-character to what has become; and it is only another way of saying the same thing when that which has become is absolutized, and something longer in the process of becoming is regarded as if it enjoyed a simply objective kind of being in itself. The critique of ideology has rightly and repeatedly recognized the fixated and reified forms of what exists as something that has emerged and come to be. I could also point out – though only in passing for reasons of time – that it is not a question of either accepting or rejecting the absolutist position, which our own ideal notion of culture has usually defended against the allegedly corrosive effects of relativism. For the task is to recognize this antithesis itself, this opposition between the absolute and the relative, as a kind of deceptive appearance. The problem here is that some partial, particular and objectified truth takes itself to be absolute, when of course it is not, whereas the totality of interconnected moments, once they are grasped precisely as such, does indeed go beyond the merely contingent appearance and relativity of particular instances of knowledge.

I have only been able to say a little of what I actually wanted to say to you today, and I am well aware – even more than is usually the case with such lectures – of the rather fragmentary character of this series of lectures. But by way of conclusion I would just like to say something more about the problem of mediation between the aspect of genesis and the aspect of validity, and especially about the problem of mind itself. I do not know whether many of you – although I imagine you did – were present at our last sociological seminar, when Herr Massing spoke to us about the relationship between philosophy and sociology in the work of Mannheim.[11] Now one of Mannheim's principal theses is the emphatic denial that there is any immanent logic at work where the mind or cultural and intellectual products are concerned. For he integrates all such things directly into the broader context of the interests at work in society and, indeed, reduces them to this play of interests.[12] This view of Mannheim's is too superficial. Thus I would just point out to you that, in the field we are directly concerned with here, that of philosophy, there are entire complexes of ideas which extend over generations and reveal something like an internal logical connection with one another – a self-contained motivational and argumentational structure as Mannheim himself would incorrectly express it. Thus, to give an example that will be familiar to all of you, there is just such a connection that runs from Bacon's empiricist programme, through the materialism of Hobbes, to the first methodical self-reflection of epistemology in Locke, and ultimately ends up with the subjectivist position of Berkeley and the extreme nominalist scepticism of Hume. Here you can see very clearly how problems that are thrown up in one philosophy are addressed and resolved in another. And believe me when I say that it is not only in philosophy that we can find motivational connections of this kind, for they are evident in every intellectual and cultural field, certainly in art, and I would even think in religion as well, if you consider the whole problem of demythologization in religion generally. Now just try for a moment to imagine the situation of Plato and Aristotle. Plato was criticized by Aristotle in much the same immanent way we have just mentioned. In other words, Aristotle examined Plato's theory of ideas and honed in on certain serious intellectual errors with a directness of which we would be incapable today, burdened as we are with so much historical knowledge. And when Americans, for example, approach certain cultural and intellectual things with the same directness, and bluntly ask about their truth or falsity, we easily shrink back in horror, without realizing that in a sense such naivety does greater honour to the mind than the kind of respect for the cultural and intellectual achievements of the past which is so respectful that it dispenses with the question concerning truth altogether. Thus assume that there is indeed a substantive and critical relationship between the metaphysics of Aristotle and that of Plato. At the same time it is impossible to deny that the two philosophers also represent different social standpoints or, as I would prefer to say, different stages of the general tendency of social development. In Plato we find a highly conservative form of thought which arises in the context of the dissolution of Greek democracy during, and especially after, the Peloponnesian War and undertakes to restore the formerly binding values of Greek religion in a way that is compatible with critical consciousness, and thus in the shape of a purely spiritual and demythologized philosophy. In Aristotle, by contrast, we already find something more like reason in a bourgeois sense, a sense of equity and fairness, even an appeal to reason as a universal standard – in a way that is quite close to Stoicism – a notion of ordinary everyday understanding, a tendency to mediate between opposed positions, however you want to put it. Now you might well ask, how does all this fit together? – and with this I should like to bring things to a close, since it bears directly on the answer to the most central question of all as far as the relationship between philosophy and society is concerned. For there is, after all, something quite remarkable here. It looks as if there were some kind of pre-established harmony between the logic of the matter – the purely philosophical critique of the Platonic *chōrismos* at the hands of Aristotle's mediating ontology – and the move from a conservative metaphysics to a moderately enlightened almost bourgeois and scientific mentality.[13] Again we might ask, how does this all fit together? The problem cannot possibly be solved on the basis of Mannheim's theory because he does not even recognize the problem of an immanent logic of the matter itself. Whereas I would say that the real task of a sociology of knowledge would precisely be to grasp the immanent logic of the matter in social terms as well, to see how we come socially to something like the formation of an autonomous intellectual sphere, rather than simply trying to deny such a logic even when it stares us in the face, or to make sense of these motivational connections by trying to coordinate with one another in external and more or less arbitrary ways. Now, if we are to remain faithful to our own principles here, the mediation we are seeking cannot be found in some third term; it can be found only at the heart of the matter itself. In other words, society already lies within the shape of the problem itself. In Plato, the Ideas are objective essences that are supposed to govern and regulate society, as this was concretized in his discussion of the state – in other words, in Plato's *Republic* – but they are faced by a subjective reason that is supposed to grasp these ideas.[14] And this expresses the contradiction of a society which has certainly developed and emancipated the concept of reason but, in the course of doing so, forfeited the objectively binding character of truth itself, on which reason had indeed once been modelled. Now assume – and here I must speak in more formal terms than I generally like to do so that you can go off on your holidays with this fundamental thought – that society and all its implications is really already bound up in the very shape of the problem that Aristotle inherited from his teacher Plato. Then to pursue this problematic, and to address everything that remained unresolved, unclarified and contradictory there in a serious intellectual way, would also be to realize, albeit unconsciously, the social tendency that is implicit in a thesis such as the Platonic one regarding the objective and independent existence of the Ideas – *chōris* (χωρίς) – and the non-being – *mē on* (μὴ ὄν) – of the empirical world.[15] Yet a problem that that inherited from Plato is not an absolutely self-contained one. For neither should we reify intellectual problems by imagining that the solutions we are trying to find for them are already simply and immediately inscribed in those problems. For if we really want to resolve these problems, we discover that we are thrown back on our own spontaneity and subjectivity. In a sense the problem lies waiting in the matter itself, but it also lies waiting for us, and without the requisite intellectual activity on our part it cannot be picked up in the first place. But insofar as subjects are inevitably required to resolve the hidden or implicit problem – and therewith actual living social human beings – it is clear that society in turn also leaves its mark on these problems. For the human beings which these problems intrinsically require if they are to be resolved are the same human beings who belong in turn to a social totality, who are pre-formed through the categories of this social totality which they bring to the problems. Thus human beings impress something of the shape of the society to which they themselves belong upon the problems with which they are involved. In this way I believe you can get some sense of the overall relationship I am talking about without appealing to some third term. Thus, to conclude, the mediation between philosophical thought or intellectual products as such and society lies in the totality – in the totality of society, in the whole that is actually implied by every cultural or intellectual product, rather than in any single, particular or interacting interests. To put this another way: the unfolding rationality which prevails within the products of the mind, which distinguishes what is right and what is false, which drives one intellectual structure, one philosophy, one principle on towards the next, is itself identical with the unfolding principle of the society which – as a thoroughly interconnected society bound together by the principle of exchange – obeys this moment of rationality to the point where it might finally drive beyond the form of exchange society altogether. Thus we might say that the history of mind and culture is a self-contained and internally motivated and coherent history to the extent that the interconnected character of society is internally motivated and coherent; on the other hand, it is just as fractured, arbitrary and afflicted in itself as society, for all its systematic unity, has remained fragmented, afflicted and destructive to this day. Thus if you take this idea of the totality truly seriously, it is not so much that society touches and affects intellectual and cultural things in an external sort of way. On the contrary, society appears in a 'windowless' way in the so-called cultural and intellectual problems. Mind or spirit is the shape of society, is society as appearance, rather than something motivated by or dependent on society. And validity or justification would ultimately be nothing but the appearing necessity of genesis. It is with this thought that I would like to close today, and indeed close with a significant question mark. All I would ask is that you continue to pursue these things in future, in the hope that the way in which we have posed these questions has at least furnished you with a model that suggests how you can avoid throwing philosophy and sociology into the same pot or simply persisting in a reified and unfruitful antithesis between the two.

ADORNO'S NOTES FOR THE LECTURES

Lecture Course Philosophy and Sociology[1]

Summer Sem. 1960

Main Issues

1) the basic problem from the perspective of both disciplines
2) critique of philosophy purged of substantive content
3) problem of genesis and validity
4) critique of sociology that would dispense with philosophy
   sub-themes: against the idea of pure disciplines
   critique of sociologism
   empirical sociology and self-reflection
   reply to Schelsky + König
   truth and ideology

NB analogous to the warning regarding apologetic philosophy – a warning regarding unreflective sociological empiricism.

Provide detailed sociological analysis of fundamental ~~logical~~ ontological categories (thrownness, care; the relation to death?)

Insert critical analysis of the concept of value.

I

10 May 1960

stating the problem: no general introduction to the 2 fields, better to address one key problem – the conflict between these fields.
Cast light on the whole from one critical point.
An acute moment: philosophers and the 'right philosophy'.
        sociologists and the scientific ideal

General form of the problem:
Philosophy supposed to show the possibility of experience (Kant), thus not permitted to anticipate particular material deriving from experience. – This is an insufficiently unreflective premise taken over from tradition
Kant's rejection of psychology   (Premise ⎯⎯⎯→
Since the Kantian subject not individual but subj. 'in general', what he calls psychology could meaningfully be extended to sociology.
But the social nexus would also belong to the constituted in his sense, would be 'merely empirical'.
Thus it was necessary to separate sociology strictly from phil
He certainly admitted the rights of empirical psychology, but not transcendental doctrine of the soul. The modern Kantians anti-sociological without exception. The anti-empirical tendency of phil. also spreads to fields remote from philosophy.

10. V. 60

Sociology, on the other hand, arose from the struggle against philosophy. ✗ Insertion a)
If we look closely at Comte, the founder of the discipline, he is particularly keen to challenge metaphysics above all, i.e. speculation that cannot yield solid results and fails to follow the

✗ Ins. a   rules of natural scientific method (evidence for this).
Thought not fully covered by the facts already subversive to him.
In the history of sociology one generation is always for the next

1 a Insertion a)

And that in an <u>authoritarian</u> rather than a critical spirit.
Comte's critique of metaphysics 49. also vol. I 45
    organized society contra freedom of conscience. Point of contact with Hegel
        the premise: affirmation of society.

<u>79</u>   Imagination privileged over observation.
    Contempt for facts = inadequate accommodation to existing order, 12.V.60
    Contra freedom of subject. – Implication: the channelling of social thought.
        Functioning immanent to the system

159   The charge against philosophers: 'they weaken social power' (capacity for
        integration) Already some pragmatism here. Measuring by effects.

(464   'healthy philosophy') Accommodation. The dogmatism of common sense,
        Healthy means affirmative, playing along

Cult of the <u>practical</u> III 642²

17. V.   More on imagination and observation. The plausible. But:
    Imagination brings the immediate into <u>relationships</u>
    Comte's argument suggests such contexts and relations are fictive
    and only facts are true
    He underestimates the possibility that the overall relationship is prior i.e. the <u>system</u> of society.

But all individual social acts are <u>interwoven</u>.
There is no whole without the individual moments, and vice versa.
We <u>know</u> about this priority:
    contrainte sociale
    Folkways (e.g. taboo about political opinions)
    Wages (value, collective agreements, economic situation, social system).

17. V.60

159

19. V. ad Comte v 79 Turning explanation in terms of principles into the 'abstract names of processes', i.e. tautologies. Something similar in Hegel.

464 the charge of <u>vanity</u>.

My quotation about the self-renouncing labour of the scholar

'Healthy', i.e. well-adapted, no wilful notions the 'readily intelligible' elevates
healthy = normal, non-aberrant, self-reliant prevailing consciousness into a criterion
    further p. 2 below

2

already metaphysics. Evidence from Durkheim. X insertion
Fundamental opposition here to any substantalized concepts.
The conflict of phil. and soc. as modern form of nominalist controversy.
take this further on 14 June 1960
 For philosophy sociology is essentially nominalist, devoid of concepts, relativistic, sceptical, lacking in truth.
 For sociology philosophy is essentially realist, dogmatic, its concepts are unclarified remnants.
 In both cases concept and fact remain unmediated.

UnMmediated~~ion~~ means something like substance in Descartes: quod nulla re indiget ad existendum.³
 A theory which can only conceive both poles <u>through</u> one another, or does not rigidly oppose two worlds to one another, cannot rigidly oppose phil. and soc. to one another either; nor can it simply identify them. This is precisely what has to be shown.
  further p. 3
 [The opposition of philosophy and sociology is not merely metaphysical or epistemological but substantive in character.

Sociology is ^ destructive in the eyes of traditional philosophy as philosophy is in the eyes of early
    as
sociology. Thinking out the premises.
Heidegger's formulation from the pre-fascist period about climbing up the façade.]
For traditional philosophy, despite the criticisms of Hegel and Nietzsche in
            truth
this regard, ^ is something rigid and fixed – a 'pronouncement', and sociology has largely taken over this idea only then to attack it – like Comte, for example, who accuses philosophy of hypostasizing concepts
as
      eternal truths. – The liberated facts are just as rigid and reified.
Sociology supposed to destroy what presents itself as ultimate, / choses as unconditioned, by revealing it to be conditioned, i.e. by deriving it from something factical and mutable.

Durkheim Règles

Durkheim contra Comte ^ pp. 19f. / Ambiguity of idée. D handles C as if he
Objection against conceptuality / were handling ideas, but he still makes use
Indicate it is only through concepts of concepts.
that data are given to science as it rises from mere observation, and that observation already presupposes
some conceptual framework. XX excursus on chosisme
Substantive objection: progress.

D sees rightly that this concept springs from that same ~~phil~~
metaphysics against which Comte rails. – Also right that there is no unilinear
progress.
As wrong to deny progress as to assume it.

Denial of progress 20.

The argument from bottom of 19 to top of 20
D's pluralism would condemn sociology to complete sterility
[xxx]

Attack on the law of three stages 117 (lack of conceptual clarity)
The theory a) the process as inevitable. As self-consuming. start here on 31.V
then on to 3a
b) no thought without concepts, everyone exposed to charge of
unfulfilled concepts.
There is no such thing as pure immediacy ~~XX excursus on chosisme~~
ad progress. There is progress in the domination of nature, in particular

→

progress in Comte   rationality, – technical progress. Relief of want and distress
not absolute. In
tension with order.   Also potential for progress of the whole.
Progress itself blind, step by step, not with social consciousness.
(forcibly produced   But 1) the violence of natural domination is continued
by the mechanism)   thus pressure + drive for destruction
                             within human beings themselves. Persisting danger.
                                                                    Regressions

                             2) Rationality embedded in irrationality.
                             But still blind play of force. now international. Tendency [?]Contradictions
                             No general social subject.   and threats
                             3) particular rationality as disaster. Le prix de
                                                                defective rationality
                             progrès. Devastation of life.   means: not
                                                                          rational enough
                             4 fetishism of means, i.e. of production.
                                                        today: growth in quantity of goods
                                                         along with a decline in human self-determination.

Result: growth of antagonisms

Sociology is thus identified with relativism.
In fact there have been relativistic sociologies, like that of Du Pareto and that of Mannheim, considerably influenced by the former.
The principal theses of their sociologies.
Max Weber was also relativistic insofar as he exempted the decisions which appear in his work under the concept of values from the scientific rationality and abandoned them to the individual's private world view – and thus to chance. He too was pluralistic in outlook, like his antipode Durkheim. This is characteristic of a form of thought which attempts to escape the problem of philosophy and sociology by ascribing them pluralistically to 2 different worlds.
This is most marked in Scheler, for whom, qua philosophy, there is an eternal realm of ideas, and qua factual science certain logical determinants, in other words, the dependence of ideas on social conditions, without the one interfering particularly with the other.

Scheler's great merit is to have let the cat out of the bag.

The overall phenomenological <u>tendency</u>: the more extremely, the more purely the ideas are separated as propositions in themselves from subjective conditions, the more material falls to positive science: 'renunciation of the empirical'.[4] (Husserl)

Already evident in Kant, where transcendental philosophy expels everything psychological from itself, only to become so narrow that even more of the 'I' is handed over to empirical psychology

<u>continued on 14 July</u>

The position of phil. and soc.; in a sense both depend on each other.
This is not the only reason why unreflective dualism unsatisfactory.
That something absolutely fixed and isolated should at the same time

chosisme XX 3a
chosisme. Things.   Criterion of impenetrability and resistance. The analogy
with physical nature.   24. V 60

Motifs 1) Contra the notion of 'understanding'. Charge of projection. Contrast to German philosophical sociology, esp. that of Weber + Dilthey
Individual psychology as model. Weber's appeal to means–end rationality

2) negative experience, society as <u>compulsion.</u>
Society actually possesses thing-like and congealed character
Relations between people appear as relations between things.
This is registered by D and turned into a norm by science.

Critique 1) faits sociales qua things have emerged as such and are transient.
31.V.60 Their thing-like character <u>itself</u> to be explained, not just duplicated.
But to clarify the faits sociales <u>is</u> to understand them

2) Not to be absolutized, for they are realized through individuals. Statistics derived from them

| Theory. | Clear from D that social understanding does <u>not</u> mean, in contrast to Weber, tracing it back to the meaningful, i.e. purposive, action of subjects. Hence the significance of primitive people in Durkheim's school.

'Cultural anthropology' as starting point

These things not just to be accepted, but grasped in terms of the objective tendencies of a society. Thing-like character = the way these tendencies are realized behind the backs of human beings. Yet they are understandable.

<u>Begin on 3I. V.</u>

NB Durkheim's *motif*: Comte's thought is a philosophy of history in sense that he ascribes a <u>meaning</u> to history. This lies behind the impossible polemic against concepts, which he <u>himself</u> is forced to employ.
Distinguish between meaning in positive or justificatory sense and meaning as overall interconnection reflected through the individual.

be something that has become, is incompatible with its concept.
Only someone who knows the conditions for the emergence of an idea, who knows, like Scheler, for example, that conceptual realism is a form of thought characteristic of the upper classes (as documented in
173
Excursuses ^)⁵ will ever challenge its absoluteness.
Impossible to rest contented with the peaceful coexistence of both spheres, for it is their relationship that needs to be further explored.
Relativism is not implied by the <u>concept</u> of sociology.
Thus the otherwise highly positivistic thought of Durkheim, who was also influenced by Kant among others, was strongly anti-relativist.
He absolutized the object of sociology – as the individual sciences are always inclined to do – just as Comte had already done.
The book on the division of labour is a paean to organized society insofar as it organic, i.e. characterized by division of labour.

                The question about the justification of organized society and its continued
                existence is not raised.

The victims which society requires threaten to destroy it
With him the concepts organic + mechanical almost always mean the opposite of what they usually do (also true of Marx).
Hypostasis of organized society, the 'collective mind' becomes truth.

Philosophy today, in the face of totalitarian collectivism, must be especially critical of that aspect of his thought. It must reflect critically on the individual and on society.
All this as evidence of the complex relationship of philosophy and society.

X

17.
~~12.~~ May
On the other side, sociology variously interwoven with critique of philosophical theories as false insofar as they are conditioned by specific interests.
This is what is meant, in the broad sense, by theory + critique of ideology.

Insert at p. 4.
Against apologetic thought.
That thought might destroy something is not a priori an argument against it. Against fixed premises, positivity.
That we want to see the benefit, that we desire to bind ourselves to something, is no criterion.
Science in an emphatic sense begins when we free ourselves from such ideas.
If we measure thought by what it leaves untouched, we fall back into dogmatism.
Kant already identified the close affinity between dogmatism + scepticism.
If we halt the process of thought in order to preserve or keep something back – these days usually something as
                                                                   arbitrariness
tenuous as 'being' – we abandon thought to arbitrariness and work against its possibilities.
Truth that is simply assumed implies rationalistic approach: truth may just as well turn out to be quite different.

Reified consciousness as correlate of the administered world.
It concerns our relationship to <u>all</u> theory.
The apologetic mentality always indicates a <u>weak</u> consciousness.
The repression of anxiety exacts an even greater price.
Freeing oneself from all criteria alien to the matter itself.
Reified consciousness means:
{ a) looking upon objectivity as something rigid and alien, conventionalism
  b) turning oneself into a thing, becoming equivalent to things. Incapacity for experience, hardening the self.
The need for something safe and secure reflects the very condition it laments.

This concept covers some very different things, so that the social <u>function</u> of critique also changes constantly. It is by no means, as the anti-sociological approach assumes, always revolutionary in intent; on the contrary, in its specifically scientistic sense, sociology was usually the opposite insofar as its critique of philosophy ended up enthroning the factual sciences. X Insertion 5a
Refer to Hans Barth.
Overview of the most important theories of ideology

    Bacon
    the Enlightenment
    the idéologues
    Marx
    the total concept of ideology.

The problematic character of the concept of ideology

1) the <u>immediate</u> inference from process of becoming to the matter in question. That which has 'become' need not be false. 2 + 2 = 4.
2) the abstract expectation of untruth. Suspecting presence of ideology
3) the concept of truth is both exploited and rejected, although the relation of both aspects or moments is left unexplored.

This is also why self-reflection regarding the relationship between philosophy and sociology is necessary. Perhaps supplement discussion of the problem of ideology from the Excursuses at this point.

17. May. The separation from sociology is originally <u>alien</u> to philosophy.
This is a result of the social <u>division of labour</u>.
Knowledge and the division of labour not mutually indifferent.
This easily shown with respect to the relationship of phil. and soc.
Philosophy as a <u>branch</u> that now hands over more and more to the particular disciplines,

5a Any theory can misunderstand its own function.
There is no unilateral relationship here.
Sociology in particular knows that identical theories can assume different meanings in a different social context.
<u>Scepticism</u> can be critical in a social sense (eighteenth century), but also apologetic in character when it questions all truth.
Today the <u>Marxian</u> theory has assumed an apologetic role for the dictatorship in Russia.
It has been deformed by exploiting certain elements, such as the theory of dictatorship, which were already present in the original version itself.

turns into method, but becomes pure and timeless, excludes any relationship to that which transpires in time, and declines into irrelevance.

Soc. becomes a question of establishing the facts, as social technology. It ceases to reflect on its own most central concept, that of society, and even tries to manage without it altogether. No longer asks about the right form of society, about basic structural problems, etc.

What is essential sinks from view.

In <u>Plato</u> we still find an identity, indeed an <u>immediate</u> identity; in other words, the problem of a <u>distinction</u> between the philosophical and social sphere does not appear at all. The theory of Ideas in the context of Plato's state.

This seems paradoxical here in light of the theory of Ideas, and especially given the lack of reality that is ascribed to everything but the Ideas.

But then it appears that the Ideas are hypostasized general concepts, i.e. are acquired by abstracting from existing things.

The Ideas, as Aristotle complained, are a repetition of the real. But that also allows him a social theory. He needs only to follow his method of abstracting and then distinguishing concepts in order to arrive at what are social concepts.

The <u>interest</u> of philosophy for P + A is intrinsically substantive, an interest in the right kind of society, which is not ignored. These thinkers remain within the context of the society of their time, of the city state – they do <u>not</u> talk about humanity or society as such.

Phil. reflects <u>more</u> upon institutions than upon human beings.

In this sense Plato falls behind the Greek Enlightenment.
Phusis (φύσις) + thesis (θέσις), the critique of slavery.⁶
The core construction – the coordination of the Ideas, the parts of the soul, and the social classes.
Equilibrium as an exchange relation.
The highest Idea, that of justice, is defined by Plato in terms of the social relationship of equivalence, without any shame on the part of philosophy.

[xxx] Aristotle's critique of thought which is remote from experience, and his objections to any abstract utopia. First example of 'social research': the comparative study of Greek city states.⁷

Basic features of Aristotle's Politics in contrast to Plato's approach.
Humanity, i.e. the idea of a universal state only in the middle Stoa. Panaetius.[8]
In the service of Rome.
Thesis of the different functions which any theory may assume: humanity and imperialism. Cf. far right radicalism + 'The Nation of Europe' today.[9]
The decline of social thought in late antiquity. Not just empirically, but through a growing interest in the individual.
The correspondence between individualism qua atomization and the power of the state.
The decline of the individual in individualistic society.
Theoretical claim: that thinking loses its vigour and forfeits its object when the possibility of real consequences with respect to that object begins to fall away.

2 June. Holding on to the difference between sociology and philosophy.
This is necessary in order to understand unity and mediation.
Essential to start from the traditional concepts of both disciplines.
1) Sociology a special science in intentione recta, concerned with facts and connections within society, or with society itself.

In the first instance this is its _object_, irrespective of how it is constituted.
Sub-divided into special areas (hyphen); the question arises as to the relationship between these areas. Max Weber's definition, p. 5. /

    Reason for the difficulty: agglomeration of elements
    Social theory, individual disciplines
    Hyphen-sociology etc., institutions.

Social research in the narrow sense. Collection of material data for the tasks defined by MW. In a sense this is an auxiliary science or propaedeutic for sociology.

Relationship to philosophy in the context of self-reflection, then in the context of sociology of knowledge.
2) Philosophy is concerned with essence.
    It is not directly concerned with facts.
    Society not primarily the object of philosophy.

Philosophical thematic, e.g.: God, freedom, immortality.
   That which truly is, being and beings.
   The Good, the True, the Beautiful.
   The possibility of knowledge.
      This thematic changes in the course of the history of philosophy
Intentio obliqua. Reflection upon substantive claims.
      No immediate object here.
      Science is not taken for granted either; the task is to reflect on the possibility of scientific truth.
      Philosophy is both the theory and critique of science.
      Soc.

It comes into contact with phil. through self-reflection:
      The subject as social
      the pure separation of fact and essence problematic.
      In taking up facticity it establishes a relation to the mightiest and most all-embracing facticity: society.

The changing character of the conflict between disciplines. In Comte phil. is seen as corrosive, today sociology is widely seen as such. Further p. 2 above.
Principal reason why mediation is <u>required</u>:
    philosophy becomes a branch of abstraction and denies its own intrinsic relationship to what actually exists. – The materialist element has become the social one.
    Soc. needs a critical theory of society if it is not to misunderstand its own object.
        Critical = seeing if something measures up to its concept.
        Reflection is always critical.
Dissolution of all that is that is fixed.
    Supplement with 4a

28 June 1960
Theory of ideology the field where philosophy and sociology intersect.
On the one side sociology, as sociology of knowledge, is concerned with cultural and intellectual forms and structures. Evidence from Durkheim
Mind not something with independent existence in itself, but intimately bound up with the life process of humanity.
Its absolute independence is itself a socially necessary illusion. This reflects the separation of mental labour, and ultimately the class relationship.
Whether the sphere of the mind is socially <u>determined</u> and socially <u>conditioned</u>, i.e. whether it is <u>absolutely</u> dependent, is where the theories differ.
We discover here that the sociological theory of ideology also comes up against philosophical problems. In Hegel the process of spirit – the substrate of philosophy – is already identified with the life process of society. The concept of socially necessary illusion in Marx presupposes the concept of truth.
Derivation from ~~surplus value~~ exchange relation.
Reminder how it all seems to be a matter of real things. Max has told you that the matter appear one way to the employer and another way to the worker.
The reason: congealed labour and control over natural resources already contained in what the employer appropriates.
Thus the total social subject is <u>prior</u> to the individual economic subject.

The question about ideology becomes a question about the theory of society, not an isolated question that can be directly decided on its own. This confirms Hegel's insight that the truth is the whole, not a single assertion. Theory as a whole is the critique of society as a whole. The crucial role of the category of totality.

—In the face of such critique the
whole may prove untrue

This category is not exhausted by the facts and cannot simply be derived from them. In that sense the theory of ideology is specifically philosophical and not purely sociological.

28. VI. 60

Start from the point that we can only speak of ideology if we hold fast to the concept of truth. The distinction points back to the Platonic one of objectivity and subjectivity, of alētheia (ἀλήθεια) and doxa (δόξα).
On conventionalist account of truth the theory of ideology in its strict form derives consciousness from the objectivity of the social process, from the sphere of production, from the relationship between forces of production + relations of production (explain both). The 'legacy of great philosophy'
  positivistic / of the forms of consciousness
By contrast sociology ^ is ~~the narrowest~~ subjectivistic in the narrow sense:
In the epistemological sense this is true of positivism generally, but specifically in 2 aspects:
  a) sociology concentrates on the individual subjects, rather than their interconnection and the laws which govern it. Also the case with statistics, which are abstracted from individual findings.
  b) as theory of consciousness it starts from the consciousness of individual subjects. Emphasize tremendous danger of hypostasizing this consciousness and elevating it to the norm. The customer as model.
Problem of public opinion. Respect and contempt in this regard.
Subjective consciousness not an ultimate point of reference but something mediated.
  Largely socially determined (consumer culture, mass media)

30. VI.

The significance of motivational studies, and their limits: the total system, the problem of constitution.
Controversy between philosophy and sociology fundamentally centred on the theory of ideology.
Sociology taken to be destructive since it transforms every truth from something that exists in itself into something that exists for another.
everything eternal, every 'in itself', becomes transient
^

The standpoint of sociology essentially taken to be one of philosophical <u>scepticism</u>.
Our analysis shows that for the <u>strict</u> form of theory of ideology the opposite is the case. X insert 10a
So much so that Durkheim, through (?) misunderstanding, even described himself as an apriorist.[10]
It is <u>remarkable</u> that the alternative versions of the theory of ideology which are expressly directed <u>against</u> Marx are actually the relativistic

'Everything is ideology' = everything equally true. Power decides.
ones, especially the total theory of ideology in Pareto. ^
Clear from this that the equation: revolutionary = nominalist, conservative = realist is not. No theory possesses an absolute social function <u>in itself.</u>

No social order is unambiguously bound in itself to a particular theory.
The relation between both is a functional one.

5. VII. 60

10a

This is why cultural and intellectual creations deserve our serious attention. The claim to truth is inseparable from every expression of the mind. This cannot be decided externally, by 'aligning' ideas or by raising the suspicion

otherwise merely abstract

of ideology in relation to them, but only immanently. ^ This view opposed both to the theories of Mannheim + Pareto and to the way heterodox views are treated in the East.
It is not the critique of ideology that is relativistic, but the prescribed absolutism itself. NB Mussolini

Continue here with 4a

Bourgeois society does not simply change its ideology. There is a slower process of transformation (only explicable through unconscious factors)

Explain: the apologetic interest of society turns against any fundamental critique of society. [over the last 100 years]
It tends to dissolve the categories of critical truth directed against society by appeal to nominalism, the same nominalism which early bourgeois thought had deployed to criticize the feudal hierarchical
            here retained
order. The same theory ^ now signifies the precise opposite.
            The mere fact, which always diverges from the
            totality, sabotages the concept X 11a
            here retained

In Russia by contrast the critical theory of society ^ has become a dogma, dispensed from any confrontation with reality.

E.g. socialist realism, picture theory, etc.   Judgement not a picture.
      'Ideology'   Problem of the copula.
                                           Violence involved here.[11]

Diamat is the arrested and reified form of dialectic as a 'world view', which is a contradiction in itself. Decreed as ideology, it falls back into subjectivism, a mere assertion on the part of those in power.

– Dialectic not a rigid method but a consciousness that escapes reification and relativism. Against the clatter of triplicity.

12. VII. 60

Reference to Hans Barth, Truth and Ideology, Zürich, Manesseverlag 1945.
History of the concept of ideology which passes from Bacon's subjectivism through to the objectivity of Helvetius, before relapsing into subjectivism once more.
Subjectivism of the Idola fori: 'human beings', 'the many', employ a false conception of values.
    The decisive thing in the concept of ideology is its <u>objectivity</u>. Not a psychology of interests. The truth moment of ideology always lies in this objectivity, e. g. the reproduction of society in liberalism.
Some theoretical observations on ideology.
    1) The nature of ideologies changes as the ideologies change.
        Ideology in the specific sense is bourgeois rather than feudal. It

14. VII.

presupposes a unity of rationality and irrationality.
Ideology only where there is a <u>claim</u> to rationality   NS not ideology
    There is no feudal ideology in proper sense   but lies
    only a feudalistic mentality | base and superstructure |
    historically there is certainly greater or less dependency ↓

                                      function of the
                                      degree of socialization

    2) today ideology is moving over into the productive apparatus itself

Insertion 11a

The truth moment should not be underestimated here.
Disinterest in theory not just ideological, not just an expression of a weakened merely adaptive consciousness.
Despite rationalization, society becomes ever more irrational through growing antagonism.
The more it moves from the exchange relation to increased economic on the one hand, blind relations of power on the other, direction, the less it can be measured against the rationalist conception that was modelled on the relation of equivalence, and the more it eludes theory, for theory is the question concerning immanent rationality. Positivism corresponds to the decay of bourgeois society. 7. VII. 60
  in a sense   To understand the matter
Once something is abandoned by ratio, ^ it loses its right to be understood. On the other hand, the processes are so transparent that one no longer requires theory – which always involves mediation.
Politically managed distribution is taking the place of the economy.
Role of special investment.
Theory increasingly concentrated on the question about what still weaves the veil.
The impossibility + redundancy of theory as 2 sides of the same situation.
– The old disparity of universal and particular is actually intensified. Always marked by antagonism, it is unmediated today.

And the old distinction falls away. But it remains ideology nonetheless.

> Ideology an expression of the process of circulation. 'Money and spirit'.

Ideology today is the appearance of ineluctability, which also finds its truth content in the relationship of power and powerlessness.

> Hence the abstract
> concept of 'being'
> today

Yet this is also very close to the truth

3) The problem of the so-called sceptical generation which is free of ideology. An open question how far this is true, as even Schelsky suspects. This is complemented by the need for something to 'hold on to'. (The role of right-wing radicalism)

> It is not a matter of whether we have doubts, but of the categories in which we think

The whole question is subjectivistic.

Issue of class consciousness (De Man. Bednarik)

One can believe in nothing, yet remain caught up in ideology.

The youth who says: 'It's all rubbish', but sticks rigidly to the idea of pursuing his own advantage whatever is not free of ideology. The role of technology and consumption. 'Technological veil'.[12] 19.VII

This rigid focus on one's own immediate interest conceals things, is a case of false consciousness.

4) Ideology in strong sense is mediated through the <u>totality</u>, and is very difficult to reduce to the specific interests of social groups the more remote it is from the immediate social basis.
The Filmer–Locke controversy; the idea that the people cannot
                Example of Baudelaire and the wine tax.
understand their own interests.
The ideology that man is essentially what matters is false.
NB Distinguish between legitimating ideology (exchange of equivalents) and complementary ideology.
                   formerly: reward after death

The latter is dominant today

5) concept of ideology more difficult the more remote from the base, the more constant it is.
Difficulty of ideologically locating significant artistic works. Example of
        Storm
F. C. Meyer and **Keller**.[13] 12a. 21.VII.60
<u>Abstractness</u> of ideology today. The constant gossip about film stars is more important than any message in the films.
The constant advertising of life complements the malaise.
Ideology today is the culture industry, now fused with the productive apparatus.
In the end the ideology we profess is simply an expression of conformity and reliability. The person who claimed: 'My ideology is man'.[14]

Examine Löwenthal, p. 97 of vol. 1 of ZfS
Nonsense on p. 98
Lack of perception here p. 99.[15]

12a

Remarks on genesis and validity.   ~~Begin with 13a~~

1) Together with problem of ideology; the 'connection with being' in Mannheim. Ideology = hypostasis, thought blind to its own process of becoming.

13a

2) That what has become cannot be really true is a philosophical prejudice, as has been evident since Nietzsche. Model of eternal, static truth. Regression of thought which lost the idea of universal mediation.

3) Completely static <u>separation</u> of genesis and validity.   Genesis implicit in the <u>meaning</u>
No truth that has not come to be.   of judgement, not external to it.

There is nothing pertaining to the mind that, as a judgement, could avoid – directly or indirectly – exposing itself to the question of truth.

Critique of concepts of the absolute and the relative.

4) Durkheim and Husserl as extreme cases

a) Husserl fetishistic, i.e. blind to the subjective moment. The proposition in itself, logical absolutism. Enormous influence of his doctrine. The doctrine of 'being' depends on it.

Mind, subject, appears as object, as proposition in itself.
An idea later revised, but to no avail: the whole of ontology is based upon it.
The pseudos (ψεῦδος) of the critique of logical absolutism: the dogmatic thesis of the unconditional validity of logic.

Overemphasis of the absolute precisely here: logic too is appearance.

Relativism is the correlate of this over-emphasis

The demonstration is effectively tautological, but we <u>have</u> no other logic – no logic of the angels.[16]
Counter-argument: inadequacy of predicative logic revealed in the particular, the 'is' of the copula is untrue.

Basically a form of identity thinking

Dialectic the attempt to grasp this irrational aspect, to address it in a rational way.

b) Durkheim subjectivized objectivity. His sociologism has to be rejected.

When we proceed in a realist fashion, and turn categories into

13a ~~Beginning~~ 26.VII.60

Genesis and validity.
Positions: dichotomous.
   a) validity is pure, independent of genesis.
      Scheler's makeshift solution and the difficulties involved.
   b) sociologism: genesis = validity; the total concept of ideology.

Everything depends on mediation here. But this cannot just be a middle term between the two, it must be internal to the matter itself.
Guard against misunderstanding (natural in case of Mannheim) that such mediation just is sociologism.
Thesis of the history of truth. 26.VII.
Critical of the abstractness of this antithesis.
The moments of genesis contain the moments of validity within themselves:

thus the entire history of enlightenment ^ a <u>critique</u>, and this extends right into bourgeois ideology (freedom = the free man versus the serf; equality over against the mythologization of all natural relations and contexts.

(^ also)

he <u>must</u> do so to escape the Kantian problem, i.e. genesis the mere analysis of consciousness <u>from within</u>, not just forms of consciousness as such
into things, it proves impossible to understand how they can have emerged or come to be.
The theory of social genesis and the theory of the 'in itself' come apart
<s>example of entwinement; the situation of</s>
<s>the judgement</s>

in his work just as they do in Husserl. –
With him genetic analysis remains on the side of the constituted.
Subject and object themselves a necessary form of false consciousness
  Necessary as expression of a real rift, the world <u>is</u> as riven as it appears to be in these concepts.
  False: because neither exists immediately, i.e. without the other.
  Thus immediacy, qua moment, does not forfeit its meaning.
  Motif of the priority of objectivity.
Yet this is not be ontologized in turn. It is a <u>negative</u> determination, namely that of suffering.
The subject as something that is yet to be.
    in terms of
The decision <s>concerning</s> / genesis etc. always presupposes an immanent decision concerning truth, cannot be accomplished abstractly.

The priority of immanent critique, i.e. confronting a judgement with its own content. Concluding remarks on the problem of <u>mediation</u>. | What follows here extremely important.

Mannheim's denial of any immanent logic in relation to things of the mind. On the contrary – there is such a logic (Plato + Aristotle)
Mediation not to be sought in some third term, but in the matter itself.
                        the Ideas = objective insight
                        contra subjective reason.

Society already contained in the very form of the problem.
To pursue and resolve this problem is to realize, in an unconscious way, a movement that belongs to society.
Yet the problem is not absolutely self-contained.
Insofar as spontaneity, the contribution of the subject, is required, then society in turn, through the subject, makes its presence felt from without.

Mediation lies in the totality.
The self-unfolding rationality of mind or spirit is that of society.
History of thought and culture is as self-contained as the nexus of society is self-contained.
Society appears in the problems themselves.
The question of validity is the appearing necessity of genesis.

EDITOR'S AFTERWORD

In the context of the series of *Nachgelassene Schriften* which is published by the Theodor W. Adorno Archiv in Frankfurt, since 2003 under the general editorship of Christoph Gödde and Henri Lonitz, the lecture course *Philosophy and Sociology* (given in the summer semester of 1960 at the Johann Wolfgang Goethe University in Frankfurt) is the first of three courses which Adorno dedicated specifically to the relationship between philosophy and sociology. It would be followed by the lecture course *Philosophical Elements of a Theory of Society* in the summer semester of 1964 and the lecture course *Introduction to Sociology* in the summer semester of 1968.

Although Adorno never entertained any illusions about the fundamental separation between these two disciplines which had already transpired, he does not simply accept this separation as a given. On the contrary, he directly challenges the prejudice that, 'with philosophy and sociology, we are essentially dealing with two at least disparate, if not downright irreconcilable, spheres of thought' (Lecture 1, p. 2). The present lecture course, therefore, does not attempt to offer an introduction to philosophy as well as an introduction to sociology. Rather, it tries to 'unfold ... something about the conflict, the problematic, that has historically prevailed in the relation between the two fields of philosophy and sociology, and which is becoming even stronger at the present time, and indeed from both of the sides involved' (Lecture 1, p. 1). After Adorno has presented a general historical account of the origins of sociology as a science – here he basically follows the account provided by Hans

Barth in his book *Truth and Ideology* (published in 1945), which had also furnished the material basis for the discussion in the *Sociological Excursuses* (see Lecture 1, note 21) – he pauses in Lecture 8 and turns directly to the theory of ideology as a sphere 'where philosophy and sociology are both equally involved, since sociology here clearly finds itself confronted with philosophical questions, while at the same time it makes certain demands on the understanding and sometimes even the explanation of philosophical questions' (Lecture 8, p. 94). In this section of the lecture course Adorno presents his listeners with that critique of sociology and its object, namely society, which in more elaborated form would feed into of his subsequent publications, from the *Introduction* to Emile Durkheim and the lecture 'Late Capitalism or Industrial Society?'.

Insofar as the concept of ideology also presupposes the concept of truth, we are immediately confronted with the question whether truth, with which knowledge is essentially concerned, is something that has only come to be historically or is given in a timeless way. In other words, we are confronted by the problem of genesis and validity which 'constitutes one of the central problems as far as the relationship between philosophy and sociology is concerned. You will often enough be presented with a rather crude and primitive polarization here, where sociology is generally supposed to address issues about the content of knowledge in essentially genetic terms, while philosophy by contrast – on the traditional view – is expected to deal with pure issues of validity' (Lecture 17, p. 189). Against the dominant view in sociology, which sees this as a problem where we simply have to decide for one of these alternatives, namely for the priority of the genetic aspect, Adorno tells his listeners that genesis and validity are always reciprocally mediated, that neither can be conceived independently of the other. Here he takes up the thesis of Walter Benjamin that 'it is not just that truth exists within history, which is a commonplace, but that history itself inhabits truth. In other words, the concept of truth itself – and the concept of judgement itself – in its innermost meaning and not in any merely external sense already refers to history. It is only once you fully grasp this, I believe, that you will be able to get beyond the dichotomous conception of genesis and validity' (Lecture 17, pp. 193–4). Adorno reveals how a one-sided appeal to the genetic aspect which shows how the social has come to be as it is, an appeal which no longer admits the concept of valid or binding truth, is just as much a function of a reified and disempowered consciousness as is the epistemological absolutism that insists on the eternal and immutable character of truth.

EDITOR'S AFTERWORD

Adorno delivered these lectures twice a week, on Tuesdays and Thursdays between 4 and 5 pm, on the basis of notes outlining the subject of each lecture. The lectures were tape-recorded and then transcribed for Adorno's own use. The present edition of this lecture course is based on 221 pages of transcripts of the tape recordings which are kept in the Theodor W. Adorno Archiv, catalogued as Vo 5451–5670. With the present edition the only exception in this regard concerns Lecture 11 of 5 July, Lecture 12 of 7 July, and Lecture 17 of 26 July 1960. In these cases the original recordings have survived on two audio tapes, along with the relevant transcriptions. The tapes are held by the Institute for Social Research in Frankfurt and have been catalogued as TA 35 and TA 380 by the Theodor W. Adorno Archiv. These three lectures have been edited directly on the basis of these tape recordings.

The presentation of the text follows the general editorial principles adopted with other posthumously published lecture courses by Adorno. In other words, the aim was to offer an edition of the lectures for general readers rather than trying to provide anything resembling a critical edition of these materials. The editor has attempted to retain the free character of the spoken word, along with some of Adorno's own stylistic and linguistic peculiarities. Obvious grammatical errors and certain mistakes that crept into the transcriptions have been silently corrected where there is no doubt about Adorno's intended meaning. The use of punctuation, for which of course the editor is directly responsible, is designed to clarify as far as possible the articulation of some of Adorno's longer sentences and periods which are often interrupted by digressions, qualifications and parenthetic explanations of one sort or another. Occasional gaps in the transcription, due to technical problems or simply the process of turning over the tapes during a lecture, are indicated in the text by ellipses and are signalled in the Editor's Notes. In a couple of places the same device is also used to indicate Adorno's omissions in certain texts that he cites in the lectures.

After the text of the lectures themselves this edition also includes a facsimile-style transcription of Adorno's handwritten notes for this course of lectures (these notes are kept in the Theodor W. Adorno Archiv, catalogued as Vo 5671–5686). Adorno's notes reveal two phases in the elaboration of the material for these lectures: his initial notes are presented here in normal type, while his subsequent insertions and additions have been reproduced in slightly smaller type. Where the original is not completely clear, the editor's conjectured reading is followed by [?]. Two places where the original could not be deciphered at all are marked [xxx]. Further information is provided with regard to this material in note 1 of the concluding section of the Editor's Notes.

The Editor's Notes are intended to explain or clarify various names, texts and historical events that are mentioned by Adorno in the course of the lectures. Without claiming to provide a detailed reading or commentary on the lectures, they are also intended to provide some initial orientation for readers who may not already be familiar with Adorno's writings or his overall theoretical approach.

The 'overview' or outline table of contents which has been provided by the editor is intended merely as a general orientation for the reader with regard to various issues and questions that are discussed in the course of these lectures and is not meant to suggest some principle of organization or even overall systematic structure that the lectures do not possess.

The editor would like to thank all those who have assisted the preparation of this edition by providing important information of various kinds: Heine von Alemann, Andreas Arndt, Amalia Barboza, Manuel Baumbach, Simon Duckheim, Simone Faxa, Hans-Helmuth Gander, Regula Giuliani, Christoph Hesse, Oliver König, Martin Koerber, Beate Kotar, Klaus Lichtblau, Michael Maaser, Otwin Massing, Stephen Roeper, Nicole J. Saam, Hans-Ernst Schiller, Michael Schwarz, Christa Sonnenfeld, Thomas Welt, Martina Werth-Mühl and Christoph Ziermann.

EDITOR'S NOTES

Lecture 1

1   T. W. Adorno was appointed Assistant Professor of Philosophy and Sociology in the Faculty of Philosophy at the University of Frankfurt in 1953; four years later he became Full Professor, a position which he held until his death in 1969.
2   Max Horkheimer (1895–1973) had been Professor of Social Philosophy at the University of Frankfurt between 1930 and 1933. After his return from exile in the USA he held the post of Professor of Philosophy and Sociology from 1949 until 1959.
3   In his lecture course *Introduction to Sociology* delivered in the summer semester of 1968, however, Adorno specifically says that 'the career prospects for sociologists are not good.' He continues:

> It would be highly misleading to gloss over this fact. And far from improving, as might have been expected, these prospects have actually got worse. One reason is a slow but steady increase in the number of graduates; the other is that, in the current economic situation [Adorno is referring to the period of recession in 1966 and 1967], the profession's ability to absorb sociology graduates has declined. I should mention something that I was not aware of earlier, and have only found out since becoming closely involved in these matters. It is that even in America, which is sometimes called the sociological paradise, and where sociology does, at least, enjoy equal rights within the republic of learning, it is by no means the case that its graduates can effortlessly find jobs anywhere. So that if Germany were to develop in the same direction as America in this respect, as I prognosticated ten years ago, it would not make a significant difference. (NaS IV.15, p. 9; *Introduction to Sociology*, trans. Edmund Jephcott, Cambridge, 2000, pp. 1–2)

4   See Adorno's essay 'On Statics and Dynamics as Sociological Categories' (GS 8, pp. 217–37), which was first published in this form in 1962, although an earlier version of the piece had appeared in 1956 under the title 'Observations on Statics and Dynamics' (See *Kölner Zeitschrift für Soziologie und Sozialpsychologie*, 8/2 [1956], pp. 321–8).

5   Reading 'nicht' for 'wach'.

6   Adorno's essay 'Sociology and Empirical Research' was originally published in Klaus Ziegler (ed.), *Wesen und Wirklichkeit des Menschen: Festschrift für Helmuth Plessner*, Göttingen, 1957, pp. 245–60. In a note to that essay Adorno says: 'The text which is published here is a revised and expanded version of theses which were originally presented in a discussion between German social scientists which took place on 1 March 1957 at the Institute for Social Research at the Johann Wolfgang Goethe University of Frankfurt' (ibid., p. 245). The text can now be found in GS 8, pp. 196–216; see the Editor's Afterword in GS 9.2, p. 407.

7   See Helmut Schelsky, *Ortsbestimmung der deutschen Soziologie*, Düsseldorf, 1959. In this book Schelsky (1912–1984) engages in detail with Adorno's critique of empirical social research (see, in particular, pp. 28f., 50–2, 67–89; see also NaS IV.15, p. 81; *Introduction to Sociology*, Jephcott, p. 105).

8   See René König, 'On Some Recent Developments in the Relation between Theory and Research', in *Transactions of the Fourth World Congress of Sociology*, Vol. II, London, pp. 275–89. Adorno's personal library included an offprint of this essay (Nachlaßbibliothek Adorno 5694). See also the letter from König (1906–1992) to Adorno of 7 January 1959 and Adorno's letter to König of 29 September 1959 (René König, *Schriften: Ausgabe letzter Hand*, ed. Heine von Alemann et al., vol. 19: *Briefwechsel*, vol. 1, ed. Mario König and Oliver König, Opladen, 2000, pp. 506 and 512).

9   See the opening section of the 'Introduction' to the *Critique of Pure Reason*: 'On the Distinction between Pure and Empirical Knowledge' (Immanuel Kant, *Werke in sechs Bänden*, ed. Wilhelm Weischedl, Wiesbaden, 1956, vol. II: *Kritik der reinen Vernunft*, pp. 45f. (B 1–3); *Immanuel Kant's Critique of Pure Reason*, trans. Norman Kemp Smith, Macmillan, 1933, pp. 41–3).

10 In his lectures on Kant's *Critique of Pure Reason*, delivered in the summer semester of 1959, Adorno discusses this 'problem of constitution' in detail and notes that 'quotidian existence, factuality, is just as much a precondition of the possibility of thinking about mere forms as is its claim that without these forms the contents of experience could not come about at all' (NaS IV.4, p. 239; *Kant's Critique of Pure Reason*, trans. Rodney Livingstone, Polity, 2001, p. 157). This recognition leads Adorno at the end of the lecture to propose

> a variation of the famous Kantian project of 'the critical path that alone is open'. We shall indeed adopt this Kantian project of the critical path.

What I have been doing was very consciously carried out in the spirit of an immanent critique of the *Critique of Pure Reason*. My arguments have been moving within the conceptual apparatus and the lines of thought developed by Kant. At the same time, their aim was to break out of the prison of the so-called problem of what constitutes what. They terminate in the proposition that the *dialectical* path alone is open. (Ibid., p. 241; Livingstone, p. 159)

11 Adorno ascribes the concepts of the 'constituting' and the 'constituted' to Kant in other places too (*Drei Studien zu Hegel*, GS 5, pp. 258–69, and *Negative Dialektik*, GS 6, p. 239; see *Hegel: Three Studies*, trans. Shierry Weber Nicholsen, Cambridge, MA, 1993, pp. 9–22, and *Negative Dialectics*, trans. E. B. Ashton, Routledge, 1973, p. 241). In fact, these specific terms are not actually used by Kant himself. Adorno discusses the concepts in question and the problem he takes to be involved here in lecture 14 of the aforementioned course on the first *Critique* (NaS IV.4., pp. 226–41; *Kant's Critique of Pure Reason*, trans. Rodney Livingstone, Cambridge, 2001, pp. 149–59).

12 Reading 'nicht diskursiven' for 'den kursiven'.

13 Edmund Husserl (1859–1938) distinguished between 'sensuous intuition' and what he called 'categorial intuition'. See *Husserliana: Gesammelte Werke*, ed. H. L. von Breda et al., The Hague, 1956–, Vol. XIX.2, *Logische Untersuchungen. Zweiter Band. Untersuchungen zur Phänomenologie und Theorie der Erkenntnis. Zweiter Teil*, ed. Ursula Panzer, pp. 657–963; *Logical Investigations*, Vol. II, trans. J. N. Findlay, Routledge, 2001, pp. 271–92. Adorno also refers to this issue in his *Metakritik der Erkenntnistheorie*:

> We may perhaps surmise that this is one of the causes for Husserl's effect. His philosophy codifies an objectively historical experience without deciphering it, viz. the withering away of argument. Consciousness finds itself at a crossroads. Though the call to insight [*Schau*] and the scorn of discursive thought may furnish the pretext for a commandeered world view and blind subordination, it also exhibits the instant in which the correctness of argument and counter-argument disappears, and in which the activity of thought consists only in calling what is by its name. Namely, what everyone already knows, so no more arguments are needed, and what no one wants to know, so no counter-argument need be heard. ... Husserlian analyses, and even the paradoxical construction of categorial intuition, remain, in Hegelian terms, completely mired in mere reflection. (GS 5, pp. 212f.; *Against Epistemology: A Metacritique*, trans. Willis Domingo, Cambridge, MA, 2013, pp. 209–10)

14 See Adorno's remarks in *Jargon der Eigentlichkeit: Zur deutschen Ideologie*:

> The notion of the double character of Dasein, as ontic and ontological, expels Dasein from itself. This is Heidegger's disguised idealism. For the dialectic in the subject between the existent and the concept becomes

being of a higher order; and the dialectic is brought to a halt. Whatever praises itself for reaching behind the concepts of reflection – subject and object – in order to grasp something substantial, does nothing but reify the irresolvability of the concepts of reflection. It reifies the impossibility of reducing one into the other, into the in-itself. This is the standard philosophical form of underhanded activity, which thereupon occurs constantly in the jargon. It vindicates without authority and without theology, maintaining that what is of essence is real, and, by the same token, that the existent is essential, meaningful, and justified. (GS 6, pp. 493f.; *The Jargon of Authenticity*, trans. Knut Tarnowski and Frederic Will, London, 1973, pp. 120–1)

15 In the following winter semester of 1960/61 Adorno did indeed offer a lecture course entitled 'Ontologie und Dialektik' (NaS IV.7; *Ontology and Dialectics*, trans. Nicholas Walker, Cambridge, 2019).

16 The quotation comes from scene 2 of Wagner's opera *Das Rheingold*, where Fricka addresses her spouse Wotan in the following words: 'Concern for my husband's fidelity, / drives me to ponder in sadness / how yet I might bind him to me / when he is drawn to roam afar: / a glorious dwelling, / splendidly furnished / was meant to hold you here / in tranquil repose' (Richard Wagner, *Sämtliche Schriften und Dichtungen*, Leipzig, 1911, vol. 5, p. 215).

17 In a series of lectures delivered in the winter semester of 1929/30 Martin Heidegger (1889–1976) had declared that a

transformation of seeing and questioning is always the decisive thing in science. The greatness and vitality of a science is revealed in the power of its capacity for such transformation. Yet this transformation of seeing and questioning is misunderstood when it is taken as a change of standpoint or shift in the sociological conditions of science. It is true that this is the sort of thing which mainly or exclusively interests many people in science today – its psychologically and sociologically conditioned character – but this is just a facade. Sociology of this kind relates to real science and its philosophical comprehension in the same way in which one who clambers up a facade relates to the architect or, to take a less elevated example, to a conscientious craftsman. (Martin Heidegger, *Die Grundbegriffe der Metaphysik*, ed. Friedrich Wilhelm von Hermann, Frankfurt, 2004, p. 379; *The Fundamental Concepts of Metaphysics: World, Finitude, Solitude*, trans. Nicholas Walker and William McNeill, Bloomington, IN, 1995, p. 261)

Adorno could not have had direct knowledge of these lectures (which were first published in 1983) but probably heard these remarks on sociology going the rounds.

18 See Max Weber, *Soziologische Grundbegriffe*, Tübingen, 1960 (an offprint from: Max Weber, *Wirtschaft und Gesellschaft*, 4th edn, ed. Johannes Winckelman, 1956, pp. 1–30). This opening chapter from *Economy and Society* is included in Max Weber, *The Theory of Social and Economic Organization*, ed. Talcott Parsons, New York, 1964, pp. 87–157.

19 On the introduction of the term 'sociology' by Auguste Comte (1798–1857), see Adorno's footnote in the opening chapter of *Soziologische Exkurse*:

> The term 'sociology' can be found in Comte in his letter to Valat of December 25, 1824 (*Lettres d'Auguste Comte à Monsieur Valat*, Paris, 1870, p. 158). The term was made public in 1838 in the fourth volume of Comte's chief work. Up to that point he had designated the science at which he was aiming *'physique sociale'*. He justified the introduction of the new term as follows: 'I believe that at the present point I must risk this new term, *physique sociale*, in order to be able to designate by a single word this complementary part of natural philosophy which bears on the postivie study of the totality of fundamental laws proper to social phenomena.' (*Soziologische Exkurse*, ed. Theodor Adorno and Walter Dirks, Frankfurt, 1956, p. 18; *Aspects of Sociology, by The Frankfurt Institute of Social Research*, trans. John Viertel, London, 1973, pp. 11–12)

20 Claude-Henri de Rouvoy, Comte de Saint-Simon (1760–1825), is generally regarded as one of the founding fathers of sociology as a specific discipline. From 1817 to 1824 Saint-Simon was Comte's student, secretary and confidante.

21 Claude Adrien Helvétius (1715–1771) and Paul Thiry d'Holbach (1723–1789) both regarded themselves as followers of John Locke (1632–1704). Like Locke, they espoused the theory of innate ideas and regarded human beings as essentially the products of their environment. In the essay referred to in the previous note, Adorno says that

> Thus the left-wing encyclopedists Helvetius and Holbach proclaim that prejudices of the sort which Bacon attributed to man universally have their definite social function. They serve the maintenance of unjust conditions and stand in opposition to the realization of happiness and the establishment of a rational society. ... To be sure, the Encyclopedist too did not as yet attain a comprehensive insight into the objective origin of ideologies and the objectivity of their social function. For the most part prejudices and false consciousness are traced back to the machinations of the mighty. In Holbach it is said: 'Authority generally considers it in its interest to maintain received opinions [*les opinions recues*]: the prejudices and errors which it considers necessary for the secure maintenance of its power are perpetuated by this power, which never reasons [*qui jamais ne raisonne*]' At approximately the same time, however, Helvetius, perhaps the thinker among the Encyclopedists endowed with the greatest intellectual power, had already recognized the objective necessity of what was attributed by others to the ill will of camarillas: 'Our ideas are the necessary consequence of the society in which we live.' (Institut für Sozialforschung, *Soziologische Exkurse*, pp. 164f.; *Aspects of Sociology*, pp. 184–5)

The quotation is from d'Holbach's *Système de la nature ou des lois du monde physique et du monde moral* and is cited in German translation by Hans Barth in his book *Wahrheit und Ideologie*, Zurich, 1945, p. 69. In the same essay Adorno quotes a passage from Helvétius, *De l'esprit*, also in Barth's German translation, p. 62. In this connection, see also Adorno's *Beitrag zur Ideologienlehre*, GS 8, pp. 457–77.

22 The concept of 'ideology' can be traced back to Antoine Louis Claude Destutt de Tracy (1754–1836). He used the term in his work *Eléments d'idéologie* (Paris, 1801–15) to describe the exact theory of ideas (in the sense of mental 'representations'). This Enlightenment theory was expressly taken over by the philosophical 'School of the Ideologists' and exerted considerable influence in the French educational system until the doctrine was attacked and discredited by Napoleon Bonaparte. In a passage from the *Soziologische Exkurse* we read that:

> Although his dictatorship was itself linked in so many respects to the bourgeois emancipation, Napoleon, in a passage which Pareto cites, already raised the accusation of subversion against the ideologues, even if he did so in a more subtle manner, an accusation which ever since has attached itself like a shadow to the social analysis of consciousness. In this reproach he emphasized the irrational moments – in a language with Rousseauean colorations – to which a continual appeal was made subsequently, against the so-called intellectualism of the critique of ideology ... Napoleon's denunciation charges: 'It is to the doctrine of the ideologues – to this diffuse metaphysics, which in a contrived manner seeks to find the primary causes and on this foundation would erect the legislation of the peoples, instead of adapting the laws to a knowledge of the human heart and to the lessons of history – to which one must attribute all the misfortunes which have befallen our beautiful France. Their errors had to – and indeed this was the case – bring about the regime of the men of terror. Indeed, who was it who proclaimed the principle of insurrection as a duty? Who misled the people by elevating them to a sovereignty which they were incapable of exercising? Who has destroyed the sanctity of the laws and all respect for them, by no longer deriving them from the sacred principles of justice, the essence of things, and the civil order of rights, but exclusively from the arbitrary volition of the people's representatives, composed of men without knowledge of the civil, criminal, administrative, political, and military law? If one is called upon to renew a state, then one must follow principles which are in constant opposition to each other [*des principes constamment opposés*]. History displays the history of the human heart; it is in history that one must seek to gain knowledge of the advantages and the evils of the various kinds of legislation.' ... The later usage too, which employs the expression 'unworldly ideologues' against allegedly abstract utopians in the name of '*Realpolitik*,' is discernible in Napoleon's pronouncements. But he failed to realize that the ideologues' analysis of consciousness was by no means so irreconcilable with the interests of the rulers. Already then a technical manipulative moment was associated with it. (Institut für Sozialforschung, *Soziologische Exkurse*, pp. 166f.; *Aspects of Sociology*, pp. 187–8)

23 The other 'force' was the rationalism defended by Gottfried Wilhelm Leibniz (1646–1716) and Christian Wolff (1679–1754) as an alternative

to British empiricism. Kant sought to overcome both of these schools with his philosophy of transcendental idealism, which claimed that knowledge depended upon both sensible experience and the 'concepts of the understanding'. For Kant, the opposition between rationalism and empiricism was equivalent to that between dogmatism and scepticism; he was concerned principally with the question concerning the possibility of metaphysics as a science, an idea which dogmatism simply affirmed and empiricism denied. For Kant, genuine metaphysical knowledge is simply knowledge that holds independently of experience and comes about through the formation of pure synthetic a priori judgements. In his view, 'the dogmatists' were never able to explain how the formation of such judgements is even possible. See NaS IV.4, p. 89; *Kant's Critique of Pure Reason*, Livingstone, p. 56.

24 The description of empiricist philosophy and psychology as the 'analysis of consciousness' can already be found in Hegel:

> Psychology, like logic, is one of those sciences which in recent times have still derived least profit from the more general cultivation of the mind and the deeper concept of reason. It is still in an extremely poor condition. The turn effected by the Kantian philosophy has indeed attached greater importance to it, even claiming that it should (and that in its empirical condition) constitute the foundation of metaphysics, a science which is to consist of nothing but the empirical apprehension and analysis of the facts of human consciousness, merely as facts, just as they are given. (Georg Wilhelm Friedrich Hegel, *Werke*, ed. Eva Moldenhauer and Karl Michael Markus, Frankfurt, 1969–, vol. 10: *Enzyklopädie der philosophischen Wissenschaften im Grundrisse, Dritter Teil: Philosophie des Geistes*, p. 238; *Philosophy of Mind*, trans. William Wallace and A. V. Miller, rev. Michael Inwood, Oxford, 2010, §444, p. 171)

See also aphorism 39, 'Ego is Id', from *Minima Moralia* (GS 4, pp. 70–2; *Minima Moralia*, trans. Edmund Jephcott, London, 1974, pp. 63–4).

25 In his lecture 'The Virginity Taboo', delivered in 1917, Sigmund Freud (1856–1939) had spoken for the first time of 'the narcissism of small differences' (S. Freud, *Gesammelte Werke*, London, 1940–, vol. XII, p. 169; Pelican Freud Library, vol. 7, Harmondsworth, 1977, p. 272.) In his late text *Civilization and its Discontents* of 1939, Freud returned to this form of narcissism:

> I once discussed the phenomenon that it is precisely communities with adjoining territories, and related to each other in other ways as well, who are engaged in constant feuds and in ridiculing each other – like the Spaniards and Portuguese, for instance, the North Germans and South Germans, the English and Scotch, and so on. I gave this phenomenon the name of 'the narcissism of small differences', a name which does not do much to explain it. We can now see that it is a convenient and relatively harmless satisfaction of the inclination to aggression, by means of which cohesion between the members of the community is made easier. In this

respect the Jewish people, scattered everywhere, have rendered most useful services to the civilizations of the countries that have been their hosts; but unfortunately all the massacres of the Jews in the Middle Ages did not suffice to make that period more peaceful and secure for their Christian fellows. (S. Freud, *Gesammelte Werke*, vol. XIV, pp. 473f.; *Standard Edition of the Complete Psychological Works of Sigmund Freud*, vol. XXI, London, 2001, p. 114)

26 In §46 of his *Prolegomena*, Kant says that 'in all substances the subject proper, that which remains after the accidents (as predicates) are abstracted, hence the substantial itself, remains unknown'; and a little further on he continues:

Now we appear to have this substance in the consciousness of ourselves (in the thinking subject), and indeed in an immediate intuition; for all the predicates of an internal sense refer to the ego, as a subject, and I cannot conceive myself as the predicate of any other subject. Hence completeness in the reference of the given concepts as predicates to a subject – not merely an idea, but an object – that is, the absolute subject itself, seems to be given in experience. But this expectation is disappointed. For the ego is not a concept, but only the indication of the object of the internal sense, so far as we cognize it by no further predicate. Consequently, it cannot be itself a predicate of any other thing; but just as little can it be a determinate concept of an absolute subject, but is, as in all other cases, only the reference of the internal phenomena to their unknown subject. (Kant, *Werke in sechs Bänden*, vol. III: *Schriften zur Logik und Metaphysik*, pp. 204–5; *Prolegomena to any Future Metaphysics that Will Be Able to Come Forward as Science*, trans. Paul Carus, rev. James W. Ellington, Indianapolis, 1977, p. 75)

27 See Kant's discussion of 'The Original Synthetic Unity of Apperception', in §16 of the *Critique of Pure Reason* (B 131–6; *Immanuel Kant's Critique of Pure Reason*, trans. Norman Kemp Smith, London, 1970, pp. 152–5).
28 'The Deduction of the Pure Concepts of the Understanding' is the title of chapter 2 of Book 1 of the *Critique of Pure Reason* (Kemp Smith, pp. 129–75).
29 In §16 of the *Critique of Pure Reason* Kant writes:

It must be possible for the 'I think' to accompany all my representations; for otherwise something would be represented in me which could not be thought at all, and that is equivalent to saying that the representation would be impossible, or at least would be nothing to me. That representation which can be given prior to all thought is entitled intuition. All the manifold of intuition has, therefore, a necessary relation to the 'I think' in the same subject in which this manifold is found. (*Kant's Critique of Pure Reason*, Kemp Smith, pp. 152–3)

In *Negative Dialectics* Adorno provides a critique of the constitutive function of the pure 'I think' (GS 6, pp. 63f., 98, 184f., 213, and 228f.;

Negative Dialectics, trans. E. B. Ashton, London, 1973, pp. 53, 91, 182f., 213, 229).
30   Reading 'Einheit' for 'Eigenheit'.
31   In the *Prolegomena* Kant writes:

> The uniting of representations in a consciousness is judgment. Thinking therefore is the same as judging, or referring representations to judgments in general. Hence judgments are either merely subjective when representations are referred to a consciousness in one subject only and are united in it, or they are objective when they are united in a consciousness in general, that is, necessarily. The logical moments of all judgments are so many possible ways of uniting representations in consciousness. But if they serve as concepts, they are concepts of the necessary unification of representations in a consciousness and so are principles of objectively valid judgments. (*Werke in sechs Bänden*, vol. III, p. 171 (A 88); *Prolegomena to Any Future Metaphysics that Will Be Able to Come Forward as Science*, trans. Paul Carus, rev. James W. Ellington, Indianapolis, 1977, §22, p. 47)

32   An allusion to a line from the final strophe of Schiller's 'Rider's Song': 'Youth dashes, life sparkles' (Friedrich Schiller, 'Reiterlied', in *Sämtliche Werke*, ed. Gerhard Fricke and Herbert G. Göpfert, 3rd edn, Munich, 1962, vol. 1, p. 414).

33   In §7 of the introduction to the second volume of the *Logical Investigations* ('The Principle of the Presuppositionless Character of Epistemological Investigations') Husserl wrote: 'An epistemological inquiry which makes a serious claim to be regarded as scientific in character, must, as has indeed often been said, satisfy the principle of presuppositionlessness. But in our view this principle can only mean the strict exclusion of all assertions that cannot be fully and completely realized *phenomenologically*' (Husserliana, *Gesammelte Werke*, vol. IX.2: *Logische Untersuchungen. Zweiter Band*, p. 24; *Logical Investigations*, vol. 2, Findlay, p. 11). Adorno always strongly criticized philosophies which appealed to some kind of first or original principle, and thus rejected 'the idea that we must begin from something which is primary and entirely certain, upon which everything else must subsequently be based in a transparent way.' For this approach already decides key questions in advance – like the question concerning the possibility or necessity of some such original principle in the first place. These questions

> can only be resolved in the context of philosophy itself. The concept of presuppositionlessness in particular is a fantasy and has never actually been realized by any philosophy. Anyone who genuinely engages with philosophy must leave this idea of presuppositionlessness outside ... In short, the only appropriate thing where philosophy is concerned is to give oneself over to it without recourse to any kind of authority, but also without anticipating the result by imposing rigid demands on it from the start, while still retaining one's own capacity for thought. There can be no

rules for this, but only modest suggestions for how to go about it. (*Zum Studium der Philosophie*, GS 20.1, pp. 318f.; see also NaS IV.4, pp. 30f.; *Kant's Critique of Pure Reason*, trans. Rodney Livingstone, Cambridge, 2001, pp. 15–17)

34   The 'Dasein analysis' to which Adorno refers was developed by Ludwig Binswanger (1881–1966), a student of C. G. Jung (1875–1961), in the early 1940s. It attempted to develop a therapeutic approach that was not specifically based on psychology – i.e., on an analysis of the subjective development of the patient – but drew instead on the so-called analysis of existence undertaken by Heidegger.

Lecture 2

1   Adorno is alluding to an aphorism of Walter Benjamin (1892–1940) from the little section 'Hardware' in his *One Way Street*: 'Quotations in my work are like wayside robbers who leap out, armed, and relieve the idle stroller of his conviction' (Walter Benjamin, *Gesammelte Werke*, ed. Rolf Tiedemann and Hermann Schweppenhäuser, Frankfurt am Main, 1991, vol. IV.1, p. 138; Walter Benjamin, *Selected Writings*, ed. Michael W. Jennings, Cambridge, MA, vol. 1, *One Way Street*, p. 481).

2   Comte formulates his 'law of the three stages' as follows:

> Every branch of our knowledge passes, in this order, through three different theoretical states (stages), namely the theological or fantastical state, the metaphysical or abstract state, and the scientific or positive state. In other words, in all of its investigations the human mind employs, as it advances, quite different and even opposed methods when it philosophizes; firstly the theological method, then the metaphysical method, and finally the positive method. The first method is the point where knowledge begins; the third represents the secure and final state, whereas the second serves simply as a transition from the first to the third. (Auguste Comte, *Die Soziologie: Die positive Philosophie im Auszug*, ed. Friedrich Blaske, Leipzig, 1933, p. 2. See also NaS IV. 14, p. 15. *Metaphysics: Concept and Problems*, trans. Edmund Jephcott, Polity, 2000, p. 5; NaS IV, 15, pp. 219f.; *Introduction to Sociology*, trans. Edmund Jephcott, Cambridge, 2000, p. 131.)

There is a partial English translation of some of the texts to which Adorno refers in these lectures in Auguste Comte, *The Positive Philosophy*, trans. H. Martineau, New York, 1974.

3   Adorno may be thinking here of a passage from Hegel's early Jena essay *Differenz des Fichteschen und Schellingschen Systems der Philosophie*:

> The only aspect of speculation visible to common sense is its nullifying activity; and even this nullification is not visible in its entire scope. If common sense could grasp this scope, it would not believe speculation to be its enemy. For in its highest synthesis of the conscious

and the non-conscious, speculation also demands the nullification of consciousness itself. Reason thus drowns itself and its knowledge and its reflection of the absolute identity, in its own abyss: and in this night of mere reflection and of the calculating intellect, in this night which is the noonday of life, common sense and speculation can meet one another. (G. W. F. Hegel, *Werke*, Michel and Moldenhauer, vol. 2, p. 35; *The Difference between Fichte's and Schelling's System of Philosophy*, trans. H. S. Harris and Walter Cerf, New York, 1987, p. 103)

4   In fact three years later Oskar Negt (b. 1934), a student of Adorno's, obtained his doctorate under Adorno and Horkheimer with a dissertation on this very subject. See Oskar Negt, *Strukturbeziehungen zwischen den Gesellschaftslehren Comtes und Hegels*, Frankfurt am Main, 1964. In their joint introduction to the published version, Adorno and Horkheimer wrote:

> The merit of Negt's book is to provide a close comparative analysis of the Hegelian and Comtean theories of society. The results of this analysis diverge significantly from the current view on these issues. Even in the past it was by no means clear that one could simply locate positivism on the side of emphatic progress and speculative philosophy on the side of ideology ... The parallels and the contrasts between Hegel and Comte are actually so striking that it is astonishing that the discipline of sociology has paid so little attention to this question to the present day. As an exception one could only really mention Gottfried Salomon-Delatour's article 'Comte ou Hegel', published in the *Revue positiviste internationale*, Paris 1935/6. (See GS 20.2, p. 660; see also NaS IV.15, p. 218; *Introduction to Sociology*, trans. Edmund Jephcott, Cambridge, 2000, p. 178, n. 6)

5   'In the metaphysical state, which is only a mutation of the previous one, supernatural powers are replaced by abstract forces or entities which are supposed to inhere in the different beings in the world' (Auguste Comte, *Die Soziologie: Die positive Philosophie im Auszug* (see note 2 above), p. 2.
6   Comte, *Die Soziologie: Die positive Philosophie im Auszug*.
7   Adorno is referring to the German edition of Comte, *Die Soziologie*, 3 vols, trans. Valentine Dorn, 2nd edn, Jena, 1923.
8   Emile Durkheim (1858–1917) founded the journal *L'Année Sociologique* in 1898. He acted as the editor for the next twelve years, and it effectively became an organ for disseminating the ideas of his own school of sociology. See Adorno, *Einleitung zu Emile Durkheim, Soziologie und Philosophie*, GS 8, p. 246.
9   Adorno formulates this idea in a very similar way in his essay 'The Current State of German Sociology': 'The National Socialists were not remotely disturbed by the fact that sociology, their bogeyman, had often claimed, by virtue of scientific objectivity, to occupy a social standpoint beyond the play of social forces and to be able to direct society from that position, something that Plato had already recommended' (GS 8, p. 501).

10 See NaS IV.15, pp. 27f. Adorno claims that society as a totality, despite its internal social dynamics, still 'always remains the same – the persistence of "prehistory" – but is realized as constantly different, unforeseen, exceeding all expectation, the faithful shadow of developing productive forces' (GS 4, pp. 267f.; *Minima Moralia*, Jephcott, p. 234). This constant development of productive forces is itself the expression of the 'remorseless domination of nature' and a blind aspect of the ever-same, which Adorno sees in terms of mythic repetition (Adorno, *Philosophische Terminologie: Zur Einleitung*, vol. 2, ed. Rudolf zur Lippe, Frankfurt am Main, 1974, p. 187).

11 In his lecture 'Late Capitalism or Industrial Society?', Adorno pointed out how 'Hegel's Philosophy of Right, where bourgeois ideology and the dialectic of civil society are so deeply intertwined, had once invoked the state, allegedly beyond the play of social forces, as an agency that could intervene from without, applying special administrative measures, to ameliorate the antagonisms produced by the immanent dialectic of a society which, according to Hegel, would otherwise disintegrate' (GS 8, p. 367). On this question, see also Adorno's lecture of 21 February 1963 on the character of philosophical terminology (*Philosophische Terminologie*, vol. 2 [see note 10 above], pp. 305–19).

12 In his book *Ideology and Utopia* (first published in Bonn in 1929) Karl Mannheim (1893–1947) described the 'socially unattached intelligentsia' as that 'relatively classless stratum' whose members were best placed, through reflection on their own position, to effect the 'synthesis' between the socially conditioned character of knowledge on the one hand and the search for truth – conceived as independent of spatial and temporal factors – on the other *(Ideologie und Utopie*, 3rd edn, Frankfurt am Main, 1952, p. 135; *Ideology and Utopia*, trans. Louis Wirth and Edward Shils, London, 1991, pp. 137–8).

13 The human being can neither be inherited, nor sold, nor given away; he cannot be the property of anyone because he is his own property, and must remain so. Deep within his breast he bears a spark of divinity which raises him above the animals and makes him a fellow citizen in a world the highest member of which is God – this is his conscience. It commands him utterly and unconditionally – to will this and not that, to do so freely and on one's own initiative, without external compulsion of any kind. (Johann Gottlieb Fichte, *Zurückforderung der Denkfreiheit von den Fürsten Europas, die sie bisher unterdrückten*, in *Johann Gottlieb Fichte's sämtliche Werke*, ed I. A. Fichte, Bonn, 1834–, and Berlin, 1845–, vol. 6, p. 11.

14 See, for example, J. G. Fichte, *Beitrag zur Berichtigung der Urteile des Publikums über die französische Revolution*, ibid., pp. 37–79, and especially p. 61.

15 In the preface to the *Phenomenology of Spirit*, Hegel describes 'ratiocination' [*das räsonnieren*] as 'freedom from all content and an attitude of vanity in regard to it' (Hegel, *Werke*, vol. 3, *Phänomenologie des*

Geistes, p. 56; *Hegel's Phenomenology of Spirit*, trans. A. V. Miller, Oxford, 1970, p.35 (translation modified).

16 'The history of mankind can be seen, in the large, as the realization of Nature's secret plan to bring forth a perfectly constituted state as the only condition in which the capacities of mankind can be fully developed, and also bring forth that external relation among states which is perfectly adequate to this end' (I. Kant, *Idee zu einer allgemeinen Geschichte in weltbürgerlicher Absicht*, in *Werke in sechs Bänden*, vol. 6, p. 45 [A 403]; *Idea for a Universal History from a Cosmopolitan Point of View*, trans. Lewis White Beck, in *Kant Selections*, ed. L. W. Beck, New York, 1988, p. 422.

17 In his book *Spirit of the Laws* of 1748, Montesquieu (1689–1755) had developed John Locke's constitutionalism and argued for the division of powers between the legislative, the judiciary and the executive.

18 Auguste Comte, *Soziologie* (see note 7 above), vol. 1, p. 45. Contrary to what Adorno says, this passage is included in the Blaschke edition of excerpts from Comte (pp. 47f.).

19 In his book *Système de politique positive* (Paris, 1851–4) Comte presented his conception of a 'religion of humanity'. Thus he writes:

> The positivist priesthood must also renew all those functions which refer to our own perfection, in calling upon science to study humanity, poetry to produce song, morality to cultivate love, in order that, through the irresistible cooperation of all three, politics may unceasingly serve humanity. The cult endorsed by the positivists, in contrast to that of the theologians, is by no means directed towards an absolute, isolated and unintelligible being, whose existence cannot be proved and which brooks no comparison with anything else. No mystery shall impair the spontaneous self-evidence which attaches to the new Supreme Being. The latter can only be celebrated, and loved, and served, in accordance with a proper knowledge of the different natural laws which govern its existence, and which are the most complex laws we are capable of observing. (Auguste Comte, *System der positiven Politik*, trans. Jürgen Brankl, Vienna, 2004, pp. 341f.)

20 In his lectures on Kant's first *Critique*, Adorno characterizes the kind of 'Yes, but' objection which prevents us from asking the questions that really need to be asked as 'infantile': 'For that is precisely what children do when they reply, Yes, but …, to every explanation you give, and when they find that they cannot stop asking questions because they do not understand the matter in hand, but instead just keep on asking questions mechanically. That is to say, they just keep on asking for the sake of asking without ever responding to the resistance in the matter in hand, the resistance created by what it actually refers to' (NaS IV.4, p. 31; *Kant's Critique of Pure Reason*, Livingstone, p. 16).

21 Adorno goes into more detail in this regard in his 'Introduction' to *The Positivist Dispute in German Sociology*:

Comte, whose sociology reveals an apologetic, static orientation, is the first enemy of both metaphysics and fantasy simultaneously. The defamation of fantasy, or the way it is forced to become a field for specialists subject to the division of labour, is a primal phenomenon of the regression of the bourgeois spirit – not however, as some avoidable error, but more in thrall to that fatal character that couples instrumental reason, which society indeed requires, with the taboo on fantasy. That the latter is only tolerated in reified form, as abstractly opposed to reality, weighs no less heavily on art than it does on science. Legitimate fantasy seeks despairingly to lose this burden. Fantasy is less a question of free invention than of working with a free mind without instant recourse to a realized facticity. (GS 8, p. 336; Adorno et al., *The Positivist Dispute in German Sociology*, trans. G. Adey and D. Frisby, London, 1976, p. 51)

22 For the 'very important concept of second nature', see T. W. Adorno/ Walter Benjamin, *Briefwechsel 1928–1940*, ed. Henri Lonitz, Frankfurt am Main, 1955, p. 145; Theodor W. Adorno and Walter Benjamin, *The Complete Correspondence 1928–1940*, trans. Nicholas Walker, Cambridge, 1999, p. 110. The concept of 'second nature' had been employed by Georg Lukács (1885–1971) – who perhaps derived it from §4 of Hegel's *Philosophy of Right* – in his early *Theory of the Novel* to describe the nature-like appearance of what has been socially produced (G. Lukács, *Theorie des Romans: Ein geschichtsphilosophischer Versuch über die Formen der grossen Epik*, 2nd edn, 1963, p. 61; *The Theory of the Novel*, trans. Anna Bostock, London, 1978, pp. 62f. See also G. W. F. Hegel, *Werke*, Michel and Moldenhauer, vol. 7: *Grundlinien der Philosophie des Rechts oder Naturrecht und Staatswissenschaft im Grundrisse*, p. 46; *Outlines of the Philosophy of Right*, trans. T. Malcom Knox, rev. and ed. Stephen Houlgate, Oxford, 2008, p. 26). Adorno used the expression very early on to describe 'the world of things created by human beings and also lost by them' (GS 1, p. 355). See also *Negative Dialektik*, GS 6, pp. 350f.; *Negative Dialectics*, trans. E.B. Ashton, London, 1973, pp. 356f.
23 Adorno underlined the word 'political' here.
24 See Lecture 1, note 2.

Lecture 3

1 Reading 'biology' for 'philosophy' here.
2 Since Herbert Spencer (1820–1903) expressly defended an evolutionary theory of society, he has often been seen as a forerunner of Social Darwinism. In his later lecture course 'Introduction to Sociology', Adorno recommended that the students should take a look at Spencer's 'system of sociology', since his *'Principles of Sociology*, although long-winded, contains, unlike the work of Comte, an abundance of concrete social insights and real social perceptions. I would recommend Spencer as extremely worthwhile. I would think that very many of the great

sociological systems of later times, if one may call them such – even Durkheim's – cannot be understood without a knowledge of Spencer.' (NaS IV. 15, p. 72f.; *Introduction to Sociology*, Jephcott, p. 40).

3 In accordance with the distinction between the 'intelligible' and the 'empirical' character, Kant and Fichte expressly distinguished between the supra-empirical or transcendental subject and the empirical or material individual. Adorno argues that 'the chorismos [i.e. separation] between subject and individual belongs to a late stage of philosophical reflection that was conceived for the sake of exalting the subject as the absolute' (GS 7, p. 297; *Aesthetic Theory*, trans. Robert Hullot-Kentor, London, 2004, p. 263). In *Negative Dialectics* he formulates this idea as a criticism of Hegel: 'He who seeks to liquidate Kant's abstract concept of form keeps nonetheless dragging along the Kantian and Fichtean dichotomy of transcendental subject and empirical individual. The lack of concrete determinacy in the concept of subjectivity is exploited for the sake of a higher objectivity on the part of a subject cleansed of contingency; this facilitates the identification of subject and object at the expense of the particular' (GS 6, p. 343; *Negative Dialectics*, Ashton, p. 350, translation slightly modified).

4 Adorno often uses this expression, although it is not actually found in Hegel.

5 Reading 'Desiderat' for 'ein ewiger Rat'.

6 In his influential and widely read introduction to the *Fischer Lexikon* on sociology, König had defended a concept of the discipline from which 'in the first instance all philosophically motivated reflections' were said to have been 'expunged'. In this way we are 'finally able to envisage a sociology which is nothing but sociology, namely the systematic and scientific treatment of the general structures of social life, the laws that govern their movement and development, their relations to the natural environment, to culture in general and to the specific fields of human life, and finally to the social-cultural character of the human being as a person' (René König, 'Einleitung', in *Fischer Lexikon – Soziologie*, Frankfurt am Main, 1958, p. 7). In his introduction to *The Positivist Dispute in German Sociology*, Adorno also refers explicitly to the 'concept of society which many positivists, such as König and Schelsky in Germany, would happily eliminate' (GS 8, p. 314).

7 Reading 'jeder' for 'kein'. In a radio discussion with Ernst Bloch (1885–1977) broadcast on 6 May 1964, Adorno alludes to Kant's discussion of the ontological proof of the existence of God to clarify the sense in which utopia is harboured in every concept. He explains that we cannot have any concept, including any concept of what does not as yet exist,

> unless there were some ferment, or some seeds, of what this concept genuinely intends. I would actually think that, if there were no trace of truth in the ontological proof for the existence of God, in other words, if the moment of its reality were not also already contained within the power of the concept itself, then there could not only be no utopia, but

there could be no thought either. (Theodor W. Adorno and Ernst Bloch, *Etwas fehlt ... Über die Widersprüche der utopischen Sehnsucht*, in Ernst Bloch, *Viele Kammern im Welthaus: Eine Auswahl aus dem Werk*, ed. Friedrich Dieckmann and Jürgen Teller, Frankfurt am Main, 1994, p. 702)

The hope that, if the concept is already there, then there is also already a trace of what that concept intends – in other words, a real possibility of realizing the concept in question – is also strongly endorsed in Adorno's lecture course on 'History and Freedom'. There he says that 'we can only speak meaningfully of freedom because there are concrete possibilities of freedom, because freedom can be achieved in reality. And in contrast to the entire dialectical tradition of Hegel and Marx, I would almost go so far as to say that actually this has always been possible, that it has been possible at every moment' (NaS IV.13, p. 249; *History and Freedom*, trans. Rodney Livingstone, Cambridge, 2008, p. 181).

8 The Latin expression, the origin of which is unknown, means: 'Live first, and then philosophize'.
9 The words cited come from Friedrich Hölderlin's poem 'An die Parzen' of 1799 (Friedrich Hölderlin, *Poems and Fragments*, trans. Michael Hamburger, London, 1980, p. 15: 'To the Fates').
10 Adorno is quoting the last two verses ('I know not what this should mean') from Heinrich Heine's poem 'Die Lorelei' from the cycle of poems entitled *Heimkehr* (*Homecoming*), composed in 1823–4.
11 Adorno is thinking of the remark 'The discovery of truth is only fatal for the one who declares it.' See Claude Adrien Helvétius, *A Treatise On Man; His Intellectual Faculties and his Education*, London, 1810. See also Adorno's essays 'Kultur und Verwaltung' (GS 8, p. 139) and 'Zur Bekämpfung des Antisemitismus heute' (GS 20.1, p. 382).
12 In the *Republic*, Plato identifies the rational element, the courageous element and the desirous element as the three parts of the soul, which correspond in turn to the three classes that constitute his ideal state (*Republic*, Bk IV, 437b–441c). See NaS IV.15, p. 217; *Introduction to Sociology*, Jephcott, pp. 129f.
13 See note 6 above.
14 See below, Lecture 4, pp. 44–6.
15 Adorno repeats this characterization of his own theoretical approach almost word for word in his introduction to *The Positivist Dispute in German Sociology*:

> The assertion of the equivalence of what is exchanged, the basis of all exchange, is repudiated by its consequences. As the principle of exchange, by virtue of its immanent dynamics, extends to the living labours of human beings it changes compulsively into objective inequality, namely that of social classes. Forcibly stated, the contradiction is that exchange takes place justly and unjustly. Logical critique and the emphatically practical critique that society must be changed simply to prevent a relapse

into barbarism are moments of the same movement of the concept. (GS 8, p. 307; *The Positivist Dispute in German Sociology*, Frisby, p. 25)

16 Reading 'etablierten Wissenschaft' for 'Etablierungswissenschaft'.
17 The transcript indicates a gap in the tape recording of the lecture at this point.
18 Durkheim writes:

> the public conscience exercises a check on every act which offends it by means of the surveillance it exercises over the conduct of citizens, and the appropriate penalties at its disposal. In many cases the constraint is less violent, but nevertheless it always exists ... Here, then, is a category of facts with very distinctive characteristics: it consists of ways of acting, thinking, and feeling, external to the individual, and endowed with a power of coercion, by reason of which they control him. These ways of thinking could not be confused with biological phenomena, since they consist of representations and of actions; nor with psychological phenomena, which exist only in the individual consciousness and through it. They constitute, thus, a new variety of phenomena; and it is to them that exclusively that the term 'social' ought to be applied. And this term fits them quite well, or it is clear that, since their source is not in the individual, their substratum can be no other than society ... (Emile Durkheim, *Les règles de la méthode sociologique*, 7th edn, Paris, 1910, pp. 7f.; *The Rules of Sociological Method*, trans. Sarah A. Solevay and John H. Mueller, New York, 1964, pp. 2–3)

19 The concept goes back to William Graham Sumner, *Folkways: A Study of the Sociological Importance of Usages, Manners, Customs, Mores, and Morals*, Boston, 1906. In his book, the American sociologist Sumner (1840–1910) describes 'folkways' as the habits and customs through which social groups attempt to realize their interests in relation to nature and other groups of people. In his *Introduction to Sociology*, Adorno says that 'wherever there is a manifestation of what ... was called "folkways", you come up against what is called "society" quite directly. You encounter modes of behaviour which neither have rational causes nor – perhaps this is all too true – are derived from individual psychology. These are long established rites ...' (NaS IV.15, p. 65; *Introduction to Sociology*, Jephcott, p. 36.
20 In Lecture 5 and Lecture 6 Adorno explores Durkheim's concept of '*chose sociale*' in more detail. See pp. 48f., 59f., and 64f. above.

Lecture 4

1 Auguste Comte, *Die Soziologie: Die positive Philosophie im Auszug*, p. 159 (see Lecture 2, note 2).
2 Compare Nietzsche's remarks in Book 3 (section 151) of *The Gay Science*:

> The metaphysical need is not the origin of religion, as Schopenhauer has it, but only a late offshoot of it. Under the rule of religious ideas, one has got used to the idea of 'another world (behind, below, above)' and feels an unpleasant emptiness and deprivation at the annihilation of religious delusions – and from this feeling grows now 'another world', but this time only a metaphysical and not a religious one. (Friedrich Nietzsche, *Werke in drei Bänden*, ed. Karl Schlechta, Munich, 1954, vol. 2, p. 138; *The Gay Science*, trans. Josephine Nauckhoff, Cambridge, 2001, p. 131)

3   Comte, *Die Soziologie: Die positive Philosophie im Auszug*, p. 159 (see Lecture 2, note 2).
4   Adorno's personal library included a copy of John Dewey's (1859–1952) *Intelligence in the Modern World: John Dewey's Philosophy*, ed. Joseph Ratner, New York, 1939 (Nachlaßbibliothek Adorno 369).
5   Compare Kant's remarks:

> A great, perhaps the greatest, part of the business of our reason consists in analysis of the concepts which we already have of objects. This analysis supplies us with a considerable body of knowledge, which, while nothing but explanation or elucidation of what has already been thought in our concepts, though in a confused manner, is yet prized as being, at least as regards its form, new insight. But so far as the matter or content is concerned, there has been no extension of our previously possessed concepts, but only an analysis of them. Since this procedure yields real knowledge a priori, which progresses in an assured and useful fashion, reason is so far misled as surreptitiously to introduce, without itself being aware of so doing, assertions of an entirely different order, in which it attaches to given concepts others completely foreign to them, and moreover attaches them a priori. And yet it is not known how reason can be in a position to do this. Such a question is never so much as thought of. (Kant, *Werke in sechs Bänden*, vol. 2: *Kritik der reinen Vernunft*, pp. 51f. [B 9f., A 5f.]; *Critique of Pure Reason*, Kemp Smith, pp. 47–8)

6   According to Talcott Parsons (1902–1979) it is not so much the systems themselves as the actions of individuals that should be seen as functional or dysfunctional in terms of maintaining a given social system: 'The obverse of the functional prerequisite of meeting a minimum proportion of the needs of the individual actors is the need to secure adequate participation of a sufficient proportion of these actors in the social system, that is, to motivate them adequately to the performances which may be necessary if the social system in question is to persist or develop' (*The Social System*, Glencoe, IL, 1951, p. 29). In his essay 'On the Current Situation in German Sociology', Adorno expressed his view of this distinction between the 'functional' and the 'dysfunctional' in Parsons even more sharply:

> In renouncing any broader form of thinking which would go beyond what can be directly verified – and thus the critical thinking which is indispensable here – this distinction submits all too readily to that

limited state of consciousness which it registers, and which is precisely what calls out to be explained in social terms. Preoccupied with the superior functioning of the social machinery in this way, he conjures up precisely what is desired. It is not by chance that the dichotomy between the functional and the dysfunctional is the highest point attained by the work of Talcott Parsons, which is already beginning to exert an influence in many places in Germany today. (GS 8, p. 507)

7   Hernán Cortés (1485–1547) conquered the Aztec Empire for the Spanish Crown between 1519 and 1522.
8   Comte, *Die Soziologie: Die positive Philosophie im Auszug*, p. 159 (see Lecture 2, note 2).
9   Ibid.
10 The 'on the other hand' refers to the following: 'on the other hand, the organic weakness of such a philosophy in political terms prevents the gradual transformations of the theological regime into a comparable force that could oppose the positive spirit' (ibid.).
11 Ibid.
12 Thus Kant specifically criticizes what he calls idle reasoning or easy speculation (*vernünfteln*). See *Werke in sechs Bänden*, vol. 2: *Kritik der reinen Vernunft*, p. 33 (B XXXI); *Critique of Pure Reason*, Kemp Smith, p. 30. Hegel sometimes speaks about those who reason solely on the level of the finite understanding (*die Räsoneurs*) in a similar derogatory way (Hegel, *Werke*, vol. 5: *Wissenschaft der Logik I*, p. 147; *Hegel's Science of Logic*, trans. A. V. Miller, London, 1969, p. 136). Adorno suspects that aspersions of this kind betray an unreasonable attempt to ward off unwelcome criticism:

> Even the 'all-destroying one', as Kant himself was called two hundred years ago, often gave the appearance of one who chides criticism as somehow unbecoming. There are signs of this in his vocabulary when he uses spiteful expressions such as 'idle reasoning' [*vernünfteln*], which are not meant simply to punish the tendency of reason to overstep its boundaries but would also like to rein in its employment more generally, which, as Kant himself recognized, has an irresistible urge to go beyond those boundaries. And Hegel in particular, who marks the culmination of the movement initiated by Kant, and who in many places identifies thought with negativity itself and thus with the activity of critique, in a rather similar way also reveals the opposite tendency, namely the tendency to extinguish critical reflection. He describes a person who relies on the limited activity of his own understanding with a politically loaded word as a mere *raisonneur*, thus accusing him of vanity because he fails to acknowledge his own merely finite perspective and consequently proves incapable of comprehending and subordinating himself to the higher perspective of the totality. (*Dialektische Epilogomena: Marginalien zu Theorie und Praxis*, GS 10.2, p. 786)

13 Adorno is referring to the discussion of 'ground' in the second volume of Hegel's *Logic* (Book II, section 1, chapter 3). See Hegel, *Werke*, vol.

6: *Wissenschaft der Logik II*, pp. 80–123; *Science of Logic*, Miller, pp. 444–78. The 'interesting passage' Adorno mentions here is probably the 'Remark: Formal Method of Explanation from Tautological Grounds' in the section entitled 'Formal Ground' (*Werke*, vol. 6, pp. 98–102; *Science of Logic*, Miller, pp. 458–61).

14 See Lecture 2, note 2.
15 See Lecture 2, note 22.
16 See Lecture 2, note 19.
17 In his study *On the Elementary Forms of the Religious Life*, originally published in 1912, Durkheim offers a detailed examination of the totemism of the indigenous Australian peoples, but in the introduction he already states his general conclusion 'that ... religion is something eminently social. Religious representations are collective representations that express collective realities; the rites are a manner of acting which take rise in the midst of the assembled groups and which are destined to excite, maintain or recreate certain mental states in these groups' (*The Elementary Forms of the Religious Life*, trans. J. W. Swain, 2nd edn, London, 1976). Adorno himself possessed a French edition of the work: *Les formes élémentaires de la vie religieuse: le système totémique en Australie*, 3rd edn, Paris, 1937 (Nachlaßbibliothek Adorno 2332).
18 Durkheim himself alluded to Comte's idea of founding a positivist religion: 'In a word, the old gods are growing old or already dead, and others are not yet born. This is what rendered vain the attempt of Comte with the old historic souvenirs artificially revived: it is life itself, and not a dead past that can produce a living cult' (*The Elementary Forms of the Religious Life*, Swain, p. 427).
19 Comte, *Die Soziologie: Die positive Philosophie im Auszug*, p. 464 (see Lecture 2, note 2).
20 See the beginning of Zarathustra's Prologue: 'When Zarathustra was thirty years old he left his home and the lake of his home and went into the mountains. Here he enjoyed his spirit and his solitude, and for ten years did not tire of it' (Friedrich Nietzsche, *Werke in drei Bänden*, vol. II, p. 277; *Thus Spoke Zarathustra*, in *The Portable Nietzsche*, trans. Walter Kaufmann, New York, 1968, p. 121).
21 See the chapter title 'Subjective Truth, Inwardness; Truth is Subjectivity', in Søren Kierkegaard, *Concluding Unscientific Postscript*, trans. H. V. Hong and E. H. Hong, Princeton, NJ, 1992, p. 189.
22 See Lecture 1, note 6.
23 See Lecture 1, notes 8 and 7.
24 At this point Adorno reads from a manuscript that has been preserved (Theodor W. Adorno Archiv, Vo 5687). The passage also appears in Adorno's essay *Soziologie und empirische Forschung* (GS 8, pp. 211f.).
25 Adorno is alluding to the figure George Follansbee Babbitt in the novel *Babbitt* (1922) by Sinclair Lewis (1885–1951). The character represents a narrow-minded and unimaginative member of the American middle class.
26 See Theodor W. Adorno, 'Theorie der Halbbildung', in Deutsche

Gesellschaft für Soziologie, *Verhandlungen des vierzehnten Deutschen Soziologentages*, Berlin, 20–24 May 1959, Stuttgart, 1959, pp. 169–91 (a lecture delivered on 23 May 1959); now in GS 8, pp. 93–121.

27 Adorno is probably alluding to the 'ordinary language philosophy' that emerged as a particular branch of analytical philosophy after the perceived failure of the Vienna Circle to formulate the kind of logically structured ideal language to which they had originally aspired. Their attempt was widely believed to have foundered on the kind of paradoxes that also attach to ordinary language. This critical reaction to the positivist project was spearheaded in the 1940s and 1950s by the Oxford philosophers Gilbert Ryle (1900–1976), John L. Austin (1911–1960) and Peter Strawson (1919–2006). They defended a broader 'philosophy of ordinary language' on the grounds that, since 'ideal language' was itself also a part of ordinary language, the latter could not really be regarded as somehow more deficient in comparison to the former. Three letters from the correspondence between Adorno and Ryle have survived, the first of which dates from February 1938 (Theodor W. Adorno Archiv, Br 1275).

Lecture 5

1 The usual opening address is missing in the transcription of the tape recording. It has been supplied by the editor both here and in the following lecture.
2 According to a note in the transcription, the first twenty minutes or so of the lecture are also missing.
3 At the time this lecture course was delivered there was still no German translation of Durkheim's *Règles de la méthode sociologique*. A German translation, by René König, actually appeared the following year. It is clear that Adorno provided his own free translation of the relevant passages in this and the following lectures. Durkheim had written: 'Nous ne disons pas, en effet, que les faits sociaux sont des choses matérielles, mais sont des choses au même titre que les choses matérielles, quoique d'une autre manière' (*Les règles de la méthode sociologique*, 7th edn, Paris, 1919, p. xi; *The Rules of Sociological Method*, Solovay and Mueller, p. xliii: 'We assert not that social facts are material things but that they are things by the same right as material things, although they differ from them in type.' Thus in Adorno's view Durkheim holds 'that sociology differed essentially from psychology ... in that real social facts – *faits sociaux* – cannot be understood, are impenetrable and opaque and ought, as he put it without himself quite realizing the implications of what he said, to be treated as "things", as *choses*; thus, Durkheim's sociology was also called *chosisme*' (NaS IV.15, pp. 132f.; *Introduction to Sociology*, Jephcott, p. 77).
4 'Comte, il est vrai, a proclamé que les phénomènes sociaux sont des faits naturels, soumis à des lois naturelles. Par là, il a implicitement reconnu

leur caractère de choses ...' (*Les règles de la méthode sociologique*, p. 25; *The Rules of Sociological Method*, Solovay and Mueller, p. 18: 'Comte, it is true, declared that social phenomena are natural facts, subject to natural laws. He thereby implicitly recognized their character as things.')

5 '[C]ar il n'y a que de choses dans la nature' (ibid., p. 25; *The Rules of Sociological Method*, Solovay and Mueller, p. 18: '[F]or in nature there are only things').

6 'Mais quand, sortant de ces généralités philosophiques, il tente d'appliquer son principe et d'en faire sortir la science qui y était contenue, ce sont des idées qu'il prend pour objet d'études' (ibid., p. 25; *The Rules of Sociological Method*, Solovay and Mueller, pp. 18–19: 'But when he passes beyond these philosophical generalities and attempts to apply his principle and develop from it the science implied in it, he too, takes ideas for the subject matter of study').

7 See Wilhelm Dilthey, *Gesammelte Schriften*, ed. Karlfried Gründer and Frithjof Rodi, Stuttgart, 1957–, vol. VIII: *Der Aufbau der geschichtlichen Welt in den Geisteswissenschaften*, pp. 93–106.

8 'En effet, ce qui fait la matière principale de sociologie, c'est le progrès de l'humanité dans le temps' (Durkheim, *Les règles de la méthode sociologique*, p. 25; *The Rules of Sociological Method*, trans. Sarah A. Solovay and John H. Mueller, New York, 1964, p. 19: 'It is the course of human progress that forms the chief subject of his sociology').

9 'Il part de cette idée qu'il y a une évolution continue du genre humain qui consiste dans une réalisation toujours plus complète de la nature humaine et le problème qu'il traite est de retrouver l'ordre de cette évolution' (ibid., pp. 26f.; *The Rules of Sociological Method*, Solovay and Mueller, p. 19: 'He begins with the idea that there is a continuous evolution of the human species, consisting in an ever more complete perfection of human nature; and his problem is to discover the order of this evolution').

10 'Or, à supposer que cette évolution existe, la réalité n'en peut être établie que la science une fois faite ...' (ibid., p. 26; *The Rules of Sociological Method*, Solovay and Mueller, p. 19: 'Now, the existence of this assumed evolution can be established only by an already completed science ...').

11 '[O]n ne peut donc en faire l'objet même de la recherche que si on la pose comme une conception de l'esprit, non comme une chose' (ibid., p. 26; *The Rules of Sociological Method*, Solovay and Mueller, p. 19: '[I]t cannot, then, constitute the immediate subject of research, excepting as a conception of the mind and not as a thing').

12 In their comprehensive collective work on *Authority and the Family* (Paris, 1936), Max Horkheimer, Herbert Marcuse (1898–1979), Erich Fromm (1900–1989) and others had come to the conclusion that, under the prevailing relations of production, i.e. under current conditions of exploitation, the institution of the family was just as caught up in a process of decline as the culture as a whole. Adorno brings out

the dialectical consequences of this experience in the aphorism 'Grassy Seat' in *Minima Moralia*:

> One realizes with horror that earlier, opposing one's parents because they represented the world, one was often secretly the mouthpiece, against a bad world, of one even worse. Unpolitical attempts to break out of the bourgeois family usually lead only to deeper entanglement in it, and it sometimes seems as if the fatal germ-cell of society, the family, were at the same time the nurturing germ-cell of uncompromising pursuit of another. With the family there passes away, while the system lasts, not only the most effective agency of the bourgeoisie, but also the resistance which, though repressing the individual, also strengthened, perhaps even produced him. The end of the family paralyses the forces of opposition. The rising collectivist order is a mockery of a classless one: together with the bourgeois it liquidates the Utopia that once drew sustenance from motherly love. (GS 4, p. 23; *Minima Moralia*, trans. Edmund Jephcott, London, 1974, pp. 22–3)

See also the report of the session on the sociology of the family that was convened on 7 January 1955 in the Institute for Social Research in Frankfurt (in *Kölner Zeitschrift für Soziologie und Sozialpsychologie*, 1955, pp. 334–6). The report begins as follows:

> The discussion which involved Adorno, [Walter] Dirks, [Ludwig] von Friedeburg, Horkheimer, König, [Ludwig] Neundörfer, Schelsky, and [Gerhard] Wurzbacher developed into a controversy centred on the central question of whether the family is in a process of decline as an essential social category today, or whether it can expect to survive, given its fundamental character, as the sole persisting intimate social group or minimum form of humanity in the face of a society which increasingly dissolves anything that resists it or refashions it in its own image. The former position was defended by Adorno and Horkheimer, the latter by Schelsky, Wurzbacher, König, Neundörfer, and, with considerable qualifications, Dirks. (Ibid., p. 334)

13 Oswald Spengler (1880–1936) introduced the distinction between an absolute and a relative way of measuring time with respect to the investigation of history. He believed that his '*Copernican discovery* in the field of historiography' was a systematic conception of history which 'admits no sort of privileged position to the Classical or the Western Culture as against the Cultures of India, Babylon, China, Eygpt, the Arabs, Mexico – separate worlds of dynamic being which in point of mass count for just as much in the general picture of history as the Classical, while frequently surpassing it in point of spiritual greatness and soaring power' (Spengler, *Der Untergang des Abendlandes: Umrisse einer Morphologie der Weltgeschichte*, Munich, 1923, p. 24; *Decline of the West*, trans. Charles F. Atkinson, New York, 1965, p.14).

14 *in statu pupillari*: in a still undeveloped state.

15 'En effet, il s'agit si bien d'une représentation toute subjective, en fait,

ce progrès de l'humanité n'existe pas. Ce qui existe, ce qui seul est donné à l'observation, ce sont des sociétés particulières qui naissent, se développent, meurent indépendamment les unes des autres' (Durkheim, *Les règles de la méthode sociologique*, p. 26; *The Rules of Sociological Method*, Solovay and Mueller, p. 19: 'And indeed, this "representation" is so completely subjective that, as a matter of fact, this progress of humanity actually cannot be said to exist at all. It is only the individual societies which are born, develop, and die that can be observed, and therefore have objective existence').

16 Reading 'vernachlässigt' for 'bewältigt' here.
17 See above, Lecture 2 (pp. 14–15) and Lecture 4 (pp. 41–2).
18 Durkheim, *Les règles de la méthode sociologique*, pp. 1495f.; *The Rules of Sociological Method*, Solovay and Mueller, p. 119. The transcription has a lacuna here where Adorno reads out the French text. The passage has been identified and inserted by the editor on the basis of the translation Adorno immediately provides in the lecture.
19 The paragraph in question concludes as follows: 'Fût-il vrai que nous tendons actuellement à chercher notre bonheur dans une civilisation industrielle, rien n'assure que, dans la suite, nous ne le chercherons pas ailleurs. Or, ce qui fait la généralité et la persistance de cette méthode, c'est qu'on a vu le plus souvent dans le milieu social un moyen par lequel le progrès se réalise, non la cause qui le détermine' (ibid., p. 146; *The Rules of Sociological Method*, Solovay and Mueller, p. 119: 'If it were true that we tend at present to seek our happiness in an industrial civilization, nothing assures us that, in epochs to follow, we shall not seek it elsewhere. The prevalence and persistence of this method may be accounted for by the fact that we have usually seen in the social milieu a means by which progress is realized, not the cause which determines it').
20 In the introduction that he wrote for a German edition of Durkheim's texts, Adorno described him in these terms: 'In France he was the head of a whole school of thought and summed up the tendencies that were opposed to the Bergsonianism of the time; his general scientific attitude was fundamentally hostile to intuitionism' (Adorno's introduction can be found in GS 8, pp. 245–79; the remarks in question, p. 245).
21 See above, Lecture 3, pp. 32–5.
22 The philosophical position generally known as empirio-criticism was developed by Ernst Mach (1838–1916) and Richard Avenarius (1843–1896), although they worked more or less independently of each other. See Ernst Mach, *Erkenntnis und Irrtum*, 5th edn, Leipzig, 1926, and Richard Avenarius, *Kritik der reinen Erfahrung*, Leipzig, 1888–90. The empirio-critical theory holds that all perception must be traced back to irreducible sensory elements such as colour, heat, and spatial and temporal locations.
23 See V. I. Lenin, *Materialism and Empirio-Criticism*, London, 2021.
24 See Lecture 3, note 19.
25 The 'damned compact, liberal majority' which unites in the face of

non-conformity is actually the enemy of freedom and truth in Henrik Ibsen's play *En Folkefiende* (*An Enemy of the People*).

26 In his *Meditationes de prima philosophia*, René Descartes (1596–1650) sets out his causal-mechanical world view in which *res cogitans* – the active thinking being – is strictly separated from *res extensa* – the world of bodies or passive matter – which is described as follows: 'by a body I understand whatever has a determinable shape and a definable location and can occupy a space in such a way as to exclude any other body; it can be perceived by touch, sight, hearing, taste or smell, and can be moved in various ways, not by itself but by whatever comes into contact with it' (*Meditations on First Philosophy*, trans. John Cottingham, Cambridge, 2017, p. 22).

27 John Locke distinguished between the primary qualities of things, those qualities which essentially belong to things themselves, and the secondary qualities, namely those which appear to us in a particular way because we apprehend them through our particular senses. The former qualities are taken by Locke to be objectively real, while the latter are regarded as subjectively constructed through the way in which we perceive them.

Lecture 6

1 The lectures were normally delivered twice a week, on Tuesdays and Thursdays. Ascension Day, a public holiday in Germany, happened to fall on the Thursday between the last lecture and this sixth lecture in the series.

2 For 'the fury of disappearance', see Hegel, *Werke*, vol. 3: *Phänomenologie des Geistes*, pp. 435f.; *Phenomenology of Spirit*, Miller, p. 359.

3 Nietzsche specifically discusses this issue among others in *Human, All Too Human* of 1878. In Aphorism 30, 'Bad habits in making conclusions', he writes:

> The most common false conclusions of men are these: a thing exists, therefore it is legitimate. Here one is concluding functionality from viability, and legitimacy from functionality. Furthermore, if an opinion makes us glad, it must be true; if its effect is good, it in itself must be good and true. Here one is attributing to the effect the predicate 'gladdening,' 'good,' in the sense of the useful, and providing the cause with the same predicate 'good,' but now in the sense of the logically valid. The reversal of the proposition is: if a thing cannot prevail and maintain itself, it must be wrong; if an opinion tortures and agitates, it must be false. The free spirit, who comes to know all too well the error of this sort of deduction and has to suffer from its consequences, often succumbs to the temptation of making contrary deductions, which are in general naturally just as false: if a thing cannot prevail, it must be good; if an opinion troubles and disturbs, it must be true. (Friedrich Nietzsche, *Werke in drei Bänden*, vol. I, p. 469; *Human, All Too Human*, trans. Marion Faber and Stephen Lehman, London, 2004, p. 34)

4 See the remarks by Weber (1864–1920) in his essay *'Objectivity' in Social Science and Social Policy*: 'There are, to use the words of F. Th. Vischer, "subject matter specialists" [*Stoffhuber*: gluttons for facts] and "interpretative specialists" [*Sinnhuber*: gluttons for meaning]. The fact-greedy gullet of the former can be filled only with legal documents, statistical work-sheets and questionnaires, but he is insensitive to the refinement of a new idea. The gourmandise of the latter dulls his taste for facts by ever new intellectual subtleties' (Max Weber, *Gesammelte Aufsätze zur Wissenschaftslehre*, ed. Johannes Winkelmann, 7th edn, 1988, p. 214; *The Methodology of the Social Sciences*, trans. Edward A. Shils and Henry A. Finch, New York, 1949, p. 112). Friedrich Theodor Vischer (1807–1887) had introduced this distinction between the 'gluttons for facts' and the 'gluttons for meaning' in his satirical work *Faust Part III*. See also NaS IV. 15, p. 184; *Introduction to Sociology*, Jephcott, p. 181.

5 Kierkegaard rejects the idea that doubt and despair can be regarded as

> coordinate, and that is not the case. Despair is precisely a much deeper and more complete expression; its movement is much more encompassing than that of doubt. Despair is an expression of the total personality, doubt only of thought. The supposed objectivity that doubt has, and because of which it is so exalted, is a manifestation precisely of its imperfection. Thus doubt is based on differences among people, despair on the absolute. (Søren Kierkegaard, *Either/Or, Part II*, trans. H. V. Hong and E. H. Hong, Princeton, NJ, 1987, p. 212)

6 In this regard, see the relevant quotation from Weber that Adorno introduces in Lecture 8 above, p. 88.

7 Wilhelm Dilthey (1833–1911) and Ernst Troeltsch (1865–1923) both attempted to overcome the problem of historicism and historical relativism through a hermeneutic or interpretative approach to history and society.

8 > For the purposes of a typological scientific analysis it is convenient to treat all irrational, affectually determined elements of behaviour as factors of deviation from a conceptually pure type of rational action. For example a panic on the stock exchange can be most conveniently analysed by attempting to determine first what the course of action would have been if it had not been influenced by irrational affects; it is then possible to introduce the irrational components as accounting for the observed deviations from this hypothetical course ... Only in this way is it possible to assess the causal significance of irrational factors as accounting for the deviations from this type. The construction of a purely rational course of action in such cases serves the sociologist as a type ('ideal type') which has the merit of clear understandability and lack of ambiguity. By comparison with this it is possible to understand the ways in which actual action is influenced by irrational factors of all sorts, such as affects and errors, in that they account for the deviation from the line of conduct which would be expected on the hypothesis that the action were purely rational. (Max Weber, *Soziologische Grundbegriffe*, p. 7;

'The Fundamental Concepts of Sociology', in *Max Weber, The Theory of Social and Economic Organization*, ed. Talcott Parsons, trans. A. M. Henderson and Talcott Parsons, New York, 1964, p. 92)

Weber goes on to define his general concept of 'understanding' [*Verstehen*] as follows: 'In all these cases "understanding" involves the interpretive grasp of the meaning present in one of the following contexts: (a) as in the historical approach, the actually intended meaning for concrete individual action; or (b) as in cases of sociological mass phenomena the average of, or an approximation to, the actually intended meaning; or (c) the meaning appropriate to a scientifically formulated pure type (an ideal type) of a common phenomenon' (ibid., p. 9; *The Fundamental Concepts of Sociology*, Henderson and Parsons, p. 96).

9   Henri Hubert (1872–1927) also participated in Durkheim's journal *L'Année Sociologique*, sometimes in close collaboration with Marcel Mauss. See, for example, Henri Hubert and Marcel Mauss, 'Essai sur la nature et la fonction du sacrifice', *L'Année sociologique*, II (1899), pp. 29–138.

10 The most famous ethnological study by Marcel Mauss (1872–1950) is his 'L'essai sur le don: forme et raison de l'échange dans les sociétés archaïques', which appeared in *L'Année Sociologique* in 1925; *The Gift: The Form and Reason for Exchange in Archaic Societies*, trans. W. D. Halls, London: Routledge, 1990.

11 While cultural and social anthropology in the European context originally signified the empirically oriented study of the origins of human culture in general, in the USA the term 'cultural anthropology' came to mean the particular branch of ethnology that was concerned with the theory of social organization. See Adorno's short essay 'Kulturanthropologie', which was written in around 1951 and published only posthumously (GS 20.1, pp. 135–9).

12 See Margaret Mead, *Growing Up in New Guinea: A Comparative Study of Primitive Education*, New York, 1930.

13 See, for example, Geoffrey Gorer, *The Americans: A Study in National Character*, London, 1948.

14 Adorno is alluding here to the well-known section on 'The Fetishism of the Commodity and its Secret' in the first volume of Marx's *Capital*:

> The mysterious character of the commodity-form consists therefore simply in the fact that the commodity reflects the social characteristics of men's own labour as objective characteristics of the products of labour themselves, as the socio-natural properties of these things. Hence it also reflects the social relation of the producers to the sum total of labour as a social relation between objects, a relation which exists apart from and outside the producers. (Karl Marx and Friedrich Engels, *Werke*, Berlin, 1956–, vol. 23: *Das Kapital: Kritik der politischen Ökonomie*, vol. I, book 1, Berlin, 1962, p. 86; *Capital: A Critique of Political Economy*, vol. I, trans. Ben Fowkes, Harmondsworth, 1976, pp. 164–5)

Adorno heavily underlined this passage in his own copy of *Capital* and added *ff* (for 'fortissimo') alongside the text (Nachlaßbibliothek Adorno 279).

15 See Wilhelm Heinrich Riehl, *Die Naturgeschichte des Volkes als Grundlage einer deutschen Sozial-Politik*, Stuttgart, 1854. The first volume of the work is entitled 'The Land and The People'. Riehl, a disciple of Lorenz von Stein (1815–1890), described how he had felt impelled 'over many years to roam the beautiful German regions to find, through immediate contact with the people, a natural social order [*eine natürliche ständische Gliederung*] in his travels', a social order which he wishes to present in his 'outline for a *social ethnography of Germany*' (ibid., pp. vff.). On the basis of speculative interpretations of the individual findings that he gathered during his travels, Riehl (1823–1897) developed an organic folk conception of society which, as might be expected, also fed into the National Socialist ideology of 'blood and soil'.

16 In his *Ortsbestimmung der deutschen Soziologie* (Düsseldorf, 1959, p. 9), his discussion of the current state of sociology in Germany, Helmut Schelsky calls for the sort of 'sociological self-determination through self-reflection' that he claims to see at work 'in Comte, Saint Simon, Marx, Riehl, and also in Mannheim, Alfred Weber, [Pitirim] Sorokin, [Hans] Freyer, [Eugen] Rosenstock-Hessy or the American sociologists associated with the New Deal'. In his own copy of this text Adorno underlined the names of Riehl and Marx, which Schelsky had mentioned in a single breath, and added an exclamation mark in the margin here (Nachlaßbibliothek Adorno 2420).

17 In the 'first book' of his work *De la division du travail social* (Paris, 1930), Durkheim specifically discusses the connection between social solidarity, morality and the division of labour. See Durkheim, *The Division of Labor in Society*, trans. George Simpson, New York, 1964.

Lecture 7

1 See the section 'Trend and Facts', in *Negative Dialektik* (GS 6, pp. 295–7; *Negative Dialectics*, Ashton, pp. 300–3).

2 Adorno is obviously thinking here of what Marx called 'the law of the tendential fall in the rate of profit' (Marx and Engels, *Werke*, vol. 25: *Das Kapital*, vol. 3, book III, 9th edn, Berlin, 1964, pp. 221–77; *Capital*, vol. 3, trans. David Fernbach Fowkes, London, 1991, p. 317). In his lecture 'Philosophische Elemente einer Theorie der Gesellschaft' [Philosophical Elements of a Theory of Society] Adorno writes: 'Marx speaks of a tendency for the rate of profit to fall. It may be questioned whether that is an adequate expression for what are supposed to be social laws' (NaS IV.12, p. 38).

3 See Emile Durkheim, *Le suicide: étude de sociologie*, Paris, 1897; *Suicide: A Study in Sociology*, trans. J. A. Spalding and George Simpson, London, 1972.

4   The discipline of 'statistics' emerged at the end of the eighteenth century, especially in Britain, France and Germany, and sprang from the administrative needs of governments to gather reliable data about the general population. The role of statistics took a new and political theoretical direction in 1834 when the Royal Statistical Society (founded in London in 1834) announced the separation of specifically political motivations from the collection of the mathematical data as such. This process led to the distinction between political economy and statistics per se and thereby established the latter as a field of scientific research in its own right.

5   In this regard, see book 2, chapter 2, of Durkheim's study on suicide, where he investigates the specific connections between suicide and membership in particular religious confessions. Durkheim, *Le suicide*, pp. 149–73; *Suicide*, trans. John A. Spalding and George Simpson, London, 1970, pp. 152–70.

6   See the relevant titles of chapters 2 to 5 in book 2: 'Egoistic Suicide', 'Altruistic Suicide', and 'Anomic Suicide' (Durkheim, *Le suicide*, pp. 149–311; *Suicide*, pp. 152–276).

7   In Adorno's introduction to his edition of Durkheim he writes:

> If in Durkheim's sociology individuals are effectively reduced to the status of mere atoms, while the totality he glorifies prevails behind their backs, and they are unable to do anything about it, his conception does justice to reality. For it names the nature-like character which has persisted and continues to persist in society despite the increasing rationality of the latter, to the point where rationality is no longer merely a means but has become an end. The sociological validity of the law of magnitudes cannot be refuted against Durkheim. Yet its validity does not follow, as he and his school have suggested, from the essence of the social as such. The reason is that society has not as yet assumed control of it. To this day the action of conscious individuals has not succeeded in wresting the social process from a heteronomous fate. Inasmuch as Durkheim ignores or fails to recognize this, he becomes unwittingly complicit in the same myth that prevails, unilluminated, in the religions of nature which he interrogates with respect to the collective mind that they embody. That is his expression of solidarity with false consciousness; yet his achievement is the way in which he revealed, willingly or not, just how much modern human beings still remain under this ancient spell. (GS 8, p. 278)

8   'If anyone were able to do this, he would have supplemented Marxism so that it was made into a genuine social science. For sociology too, dealing as it does with the behaviour of people in society, cannot be anything but applied psychology. Strictly speaking there are only two sciences: psychology, pure and applied, and natural science' (Sigmund Freud, *Gesammelte Werke*, vol. XV: *Neue Folge der Vorlesungen zur Einführung in die Psychoanalyse*, p. 194; *The Standard Edition of the Complete Psychological Works of Sigmund Freud*, vol. XXII: *New Introductory Lectures on Psycho-Analysis and Other Works*, trans. James Strachey et al., London, 2001, p. 179).

9 The concept in question derives from the social researcher Elisabeth Noelle-Neumann (1916–2010), who wrote: 'The careful distinction between the "singular sphere" and the "plural sphere" seems to me the first step required if we are to understand the statistical-representative survey method and its results, to define its place, and to dispel any sense of unease that these methods and their results do not bear on the individual, on the human personality' (Noelle-Neumann, 'Anmerkungen zu L[eopold] v. Wieses Rezension v. Friedeberg, Ludwig: Die Umfrage in der Intimsphäre', *Kölner Zeitschrift für Soziologie*, 6 (1954), p. 633). Noelle-Neumann was specifically responding here to a review by von Wiese of vol. 4 of 'Beiträge zur Sexualforschung' [Stuttgart, 1953], ibid., pp. 121–2. See GS 8, p. 277, and NaS IV.15, p. 129; *Introduction to Sociology*, trans. Edmund Jephcott, Cambridge, 2000, p. 75 and pp. 173–4.

10 This concept was developed by Herbert A. Simon (1916–2001), who employed it for the first time in his essay 'Spurious Correlation: A Causal Interpretation' (*Journal of the American Statistical Association*, 49 (1954), pp. 467–79). It refers to a correlation between two or more events or phenomena which, in spite of appearances, actually have no causal relation to one another.

11 See Lecture 8, pp. 87–90.

12 See Lecture 5, pp. 49–52.

13 Compare the theologico-political treatise *De civitate Dei* (*The City of God*) by Saint Augustine (354–430).

14 Jacques-Bénigne Bossuet (1627–1704) was a French bishop and theologian. His most famous contribution to a theological philosophy of history was his *Discours sur l'histoire universelle* of 1681.

15 Marie-Jean-Antoine-Nicolas de Caritat, Marquis de Condorcet (1743–1794), presented a theory of progress in his posthumously published work *Esquisse d'un tableau des progrès de l'esprit humain*. His concept of progress involved not only the question of nature but also the progress of the human mind and its characteristic expressions. In his book Condorcet tells us that he wants 'to show by appeal to reason and fact that nature has set no term to the perfection of human faculties; that the perfectibility of man is truly indefinite; and that the progress of this perfectibility, from now onwards, independently of any power that might wish to halt it, has no other limit than the duration of the globe upon which nature has cast us' (*The Sketch*, in *Political Writings*, ed. Steven Lukes and Nadia Urbinati, Cambridge, 2012, p. 2).

16 Adorno opened his lecture series 'History and Freedom' (delivered in the winter semester of 1964/5) with the programmatic claim that, 'Objectively, Hegel takes over the idea of working one's way forward through the conflict' between ideal freedom and actual history from Kant's philosophy of history, 'but, by adding the idea of the cunning of reason, he intensifies it into a metaphysics, a theory of progress in the consciousness of freedom. History becomes a radical movement in the direction of freedom. "Consciousness of freedom" does not refer

to individual, subjective consciousness, but to the spirit that objectively realizes itself through history, thus making freedom a reality' (NaS IV.13, p. 11; *History and Freedom*, Livingstone, p. 5).

17 The use of organic-vegetative vocabulary is extremely common in Spengler's work. Thus he writes, for example:

> A culture is born at the moment when a mighty soul awakens from the primordial soul-state of an eternally child-like humanity, separates itself, and assumes form out of the formless, becomes something limited and transient out of something unlimited and enduring. It blooms upon the soil of a very particular landscape to which it remains bound in a vegetative way. A culture dies when this soul has realized the entire sum of its possibilities in the form of peoples, languages, religious confessions, arts, polities and sciences, and thereby returns once more to its primordial soul-state. (Oswald Spengler, *Der Untergang des Abendlandes*, vol. 1: *Gestalt und Wirklichkeit*, Munich, 1923, p. 144)

18 Herbert Spencer's theory of adaptation (see Lecture 3, note 2) led to the notion that so-called primitive societies were not in principle different from modern societies, but simply less advanced on the path that continuous social evolution had already inevitably prescribed. On this basis it was possible for Durkheim and his followers – and subsequently for cultural anthropology as a whole – to believe that the investigation of archaic peoples and their rituals could yield insights about bourgeois society as well. As Adorno put it, the relations of primitive society 'are taken to be prototypical for the social realm as such' (GS 8, p. 251).

19 Reading 'affirmierte' for 'diffamierte' here.

20 John Maynard Keynes (1883–1946) laid the foundation for what would soon be described as 'the Keynesian revolution', and a specifically Keynesian conception of economics, in his work *The General Theory of Employment, Interest and Money*. His analysis marked a turning away from laissez-faire liberalism, which was seen as one of the causes of the worldwide economic crisis, towards a political approach that sought to influence and channel national economic policy. (See J. M. Keynes, *The General Theory of Employment, Interest and Money*, London, 1936.)

21 In his lecture series on the 'Philosophical Elements of a Theory of Society' (delivered in the summer semester of 1964), Adorno returned to the implications of state intervention in the context of contemporary society. In this connection he mentions

> a series of modifications which must be understood largely as unconscious reaction-formations in response to the gap between rich and poor, between the powerful and the powerless, and so on, which have only been fantastically exacerbated by the tendency towards increasing monopolization. Here we should have to mention direct state intervention in the economy, financial support for the unemployed, special work programmes, etc., things which the most advanced states in the world can hardly conceive of doing without today. But these things no

longer have the function simply of supporting the unemployed, which itself has something rather problematic and explosive about it, for they increasingly involve expenditure on major public works and the like which create a safety valve in the event of serious economic crises and mass unemployment. All these institutions – and that is the entire sphere of what is also often referred to in this country as the social market economy – are of course violations of the pure principle of competition as conceived by the liberal model, and no longer permit us to explain the whole of social life and the reproduction of the life of society according to the classical formulae of a liberal exchange society. In other words, unless society openly or covertly gave its members to understand that they will be supported by public means if they can no longer support themselves by their own means – without this understanding, which suffuses the entire climate of the major capitalist countries like an ether – then the continued existence of society in its current forms would hardly be conceivable. And the interventionist approach to the economy which derives from Keynes and has assumed a highly developed form in the meantime is the theoretical expression of all this, and indeed also an expression of farewell to an inwardly coherent and strictly maintained liberal model. (NaS IV.12, pp. 51f.)

22   See the beginning of the final paragraph of this text by Freud:

The fateful question for the human species seems to me to be whether and to what extent their cultural development will succeed in mastering the disturbance of their communal life by the human instinct of aggression and self-destruction. It may be that in this respect precisely the present time deserves a special interest. Men have gained control over the forces of nature to such an extent that with their help they would have no difficulty in exterminating one another to the last man. (Sigmund Freud, *Gesammelte Werke*, vol. XIV: *Das Unbehagen in der Kultur*, p. 506; *The Standard Edition of the Complete Psychological Works of Sigmund Freud*, vol. XXI: *Civilization and its Discontents*, London, 2001, p. 145)

23   One may reject philosophical speculations in principle or simply in some particular case or other; however, one cannot fairly do so by appealing to features which define meaning or correctness in the context of scientific knowledge that is based on experience but are ones which metaphysics excludes in the context of its own approach to problems. The legitimate rights of speculation correspond precisely to those pertaining to historical laws: they are either situations on a path that cannot be foreseen and that leads towards the laws of movement of historical elements and to the identification of the energies directly involved in them, a path which in the meantime can only anticipate its conclusion – and here is the point where historical laws become quite false, when they dogmatically arrest what is actually a momentary stage of development and then claim to be entirely right; or, alternatively, they construct a world from the actual historical givens on the basis of categories which have no place and desire no place in the context of factual or empirical investigation, for they spring from entirely autonomous needs concerned with the organization of material, with its translation into concepts, with the demands of

synthetic unity. (Georg Simmel, *Die Probleme der Geschichtsphilosophie: Eine erkenntnistheoretische Studie*, 4th edn, Munich, 1922, pp. 153f.)

24 Adorno was obviously thinking of a posthumously published aphorism of Feuerbach's: 'To be not *against* religion, but *above* it. Knowledge is more than faith. However little we know, that definite little is more than the nebulous more which faith has in advance of knowledge' (Ludwig Feuerbach, *Sämtliche Werke*, ed. Wilhelm Bolin and Friedrich Jodl, vol. 10, Stuttgart, 1911, p. 326). Adorno alludes to these remarks, in adapted form, elsewhere: NaS IV.4, p. 206 (*Kant's Critique of Pure Reason*, Livingstone, p. 136), and NaS IV.15, p. 134 (*Introduction to Sociology*, Jephcott, p. 78).

25 Given the pause Adorno mentions in the next lecture (Lecture 8, p. 81), he does not actually go on to discuss the problem of statics and dynamics as 'fundamental sociological-philosophical categories' in these particular lectures. However, he does provide a detailed discussion of these categories in the essay '*Über Statik und Dynamik als soziologische Kategorien*' (GS 8, pp. 217–37; see Lecture 1, note 4).

Lecture 8

1 Fritz Mauthner (1849–1923) mentions 'the old philosophical joke' that plays with the supposed connection between the similar sounding words 'concrete' and 'concave'. Hermann von Helmholtz (1821–1894) is said to have enjoyed telling the following story: 'After Kant's successor had delivered a popular lecture on Kant's philosophy, the ladies of the committee came up afterwards and were allowed the opportunity to ask about something that had not been entirely clear. Thus they confessed, for example, that the distinction between *concrete* and *concave* was still deeply obscure to them' (Fritz Mauthner, *Wörterbuch der Philosophie: Geschichte der Philosophie*, 2nd edn, Leipzig, 1923, vol. 3, p. 388). In 1932 Adorno had written a little piece with the title 'Abstract or concave' (GS 20.2, p. 521).

2 Adorno specifically discusses this point in his lecture course 'Einführung in die Dialektik', delivered in 1958 (NaS IV.2, pp. 275–90; *An Introduction to Dialectics*, trans. Nicholas Walker, Polity, 2017, pp. 194–205). Adorno's most detailed discussion of the problem of 'definition' and the process of 'defining' terms generally can to be found in the lecture course delivered in the summer semester of 1962. (See Theodor W. Adorno, *Philosophische Terminologie: Zur Einleitung*, vol. 1, ed. Rudolf zur Lippe, Frankfurt am Main, 1973, pp. 9–32.)

3 See NaS IV.2, p. 275; *An Introduction to Dialectics*, Walker, p. 194.

4 Reading 'Verengung' for 'Versenkung' here.

5 The term refers to the communication of knowledge in a didactic context.

6 See Plato's *Republic*, 433a8–b4 and 443b7–444a9. See also Adorno's remarks in *An Introduction to Dialectics*:

For the idea that we can lay hold upon an essentially stable and reliable truth first in individual concepts, and then in the highest generalizations and in the highest fields of scientific knowledge, is itself nothing but the projection of the social division of labour upon knowledge as such and ultimately upon metaphysics. In other words, the particular contributions to knowledge which have been facilitated through the necessary specialization of human experience in terms of highly specific roles and professions, and without which the progress of human civilization itself would not even be conceivable, have been hypostasized into a very limited conception of intrinsically stable truth ... It is indeed no accident ... that the specific philosophy in which the claims of limited particular truth, and above all the claims of a limited form of concept which has been specifically developed and scrupulously distinguished from all other concepts, and the claims of definition itself, were first expressly defended, namely the philosophy of Plato, is the same philosophy in which the concept of the social division of labour first expressly appears as an issue of political philosophy ... (NaS IV.2, pp. 295f.; *An Introduction to Dialectics*, Walker, p. 209)

7   See Goethe, *Faust*, Part 1, verses 354–7.
8   Reading 'früher' for 'später' here.
9   The French sociologist of law Georges Gurvitch (1894–1965) went into exile in 1941 and worked at the New School for Social Research in New York. From 1942 onwards he edited the *Journal of Legal and Political Sociology*. His most significant contribution to the sociology of law was the ground-breaking monograph *Sociology of Law* (1942).
10 The purpose of 'institutional analysis', strongly influenced, among other things, by the theoretical approach of Emile Durkheim and Max Weber, is to investigate the ways in which society is specifically organized by means of institutions of one kind or another.
11 See chapter VIII, 'Sociology and Empirical Social Research', in *Soziologische Exkurse* (Lecture 1, note 19), pp. 106–15.
12 On the social-political origins of 'statistics' as a scientific discipline, see above, Lecture 7, note 4.
13 As a political exile in New York, Adorno had begun working for the Princeton Radio Research Project at the end February 1938 (under the direction of the sociologist Paul F. Lazarsfeld (1901–1976), who had emigrated to the United States from Austria). The Radio Research Project was set up to investigate the particular preferences and listening habits of American radio audiences. See the foreword by Robert Hullot-Kentor in NaS I.3, pp. 7–71.
14 See Paul Felix Lazarsfeld, 'Remarks on Administrative and Critical Communications Research', *Studies in Philosophy and Social Science*, IX/1 (1941), pp. 2–16. See also GS 8, p. 535.
15 Rudolf Gunzert (1906–1981), along with Adorno and Ludwig von Friedeburg (1924–2010), was one of the three directors of the Institute for Social Research. He was Honorary Professor for Statistical Methods in Empirical Social Research in Frankfurt from 1956 until 1977. For

the summer semester of 1960 he had announced a lecture course on the 'Statistical Analysis in Empirical Social Research', which was held between 5 and 7 pm on Mondays.

16 See Theodor W. Adorno, Else Frenkel-Brunswik, Daniel J. Levinson and R. Nevitt Sandford in collaboration with Betty Aron, Maria Hertz Levinson and William Morrow, *The Authoritarian Personality*, New York, 1950. The chapters which were specifically written by Adorno alone or in collaboration with one of the other contributors can now be found in GS 9.1 (pp. 143–509).

17 In the first chapter of *The Authoritarian Personality* the authors suggest that the personality structures of individuals are shaped principally by individual factors, and not so much by socio-economic ones:

> [I]t was considered that economic motives in the individual may not have the dominant and crucial role that is often ascribed to them. ... There is only the most general similarity of opinion among people of the same socio-economic status, and the exceptions are glaring, while variations from one socio-economic group to another are rarely simple or clear-cut. To explain why it is that people of the same socio-economic status so frequently have different ideologies, while people of a different status often have very similar ideologies, we must take account of other than purely economic needs. (GS 9.1, pp. 158f.)

18 See Lecture 1 above, p. 7.
19 See Max Weber, *Soziologische Grundbegriffe*, p. 5; *The Fundamental Concepts of Sociology*, Henderson and Parsons, p. 88.
20 In fact this is the first time in the lecture course that Adorno mentions the category of 'alienation.'
21 See the conclusion of Lecture 5 above, pp. 56f., and Lecture 6, pp. 63–8.
22 The Latin terms that Adorno uses here ultimately derive from a very important distinction in the theory of knowledge that was defended by the scholastic tradition in particular. Thus *intentio recta* designates the direct perceptual relation of consciousness to the object of knowledge, whereas the *intentio obliqua* designates the apperceptive relation to the inward act of representing the object, i.e. a reflexive relation to the process of knowledge itself.
23 See Plato, *Apology*, 20e6–23c1.
24 In a letter to Hans Magnus Enzensberger (b. 1929) of 22 September 1965, Adorno referred to analytical philosophy as

> a new form of obscurantism. The defaming of any genuine thinking as unscientific, the hypostasis of scientific methods in their established form in place of the very thing that matters to philosophy – in other words, a shortcut towards barbarism. If the Marxists didn't really know what to do with it (Korsch and Brecht worked some appalling mischief with certain neo-positivist motifs), that it is all to their credit. ... Since it is possible to detect strong symptoms in Germany that this nonsense

– which promises an absolute feeling of security because it has no content – is also spreading here, I really believe it is imperative that something decisive be done to counter this. (Theodor W. Adorno Archiv, Br 361/20)

25 In the announcement for his journal *Die Horen* in 1794, Schiller described the purpose of the journal as follows:

> In the midst of all this political turmoil, it is meant to create a close and faithful circle to cultivate the Muses and the Graces, one that shall banish everything that is stamped with an impure and merely partisan spirit. Yet though it excludes all immediate reference to the current course of the world and the immediate expectations of humanity, it will look to philosophy in the context of the earlier history of the world and the world of the future, to gather up the particular features of that ideal and ennobled humanity which is given over to us as a task by reason, though it is so easily lost from view in the field of experience. It will thus concern itself, to the best of its powers, with quietly building up those better concepts, purer principles, and nobler morals from which all true improvement in our social condition ultimately depends. (Friedrich Schiller, *Ankündigung: Die Horen*, in *Sämtliche Werke*, vol. 5, pp. 870f.)

Lecture 9

1 Both of the lectures that Adorno was to have delivered the previous week were actually taken over by Max Horkheimer. Adorno was in Vienna at the time, where he had been invited to give a lecture on 21 June in the context of the upcoming centenary celebration (on 17 July 1960) of the birth of Gustav Mahler. (Adorno's lecture was first published in the *Neue Züricher Zeitung* on 2 July 1960 under the title 'Gustav Mahler: Zur Feier des hunderten Geburtstags'; the text can now be found under the title 'Mahler: Wiener Gedenkrede' in GS 16, pp. 323–38.) From a letter to Horkheimer of 19 June 1960, written in Vienna, in which Adorno thanks him 'on account of the lectures', it is clear that Horkheimer must have taken over both the lecture scheduled for 23 June and that for 21 June. (Theodor W. Adorno, *Briefe und Briefwechsel*, vol. 4: *Theodor W. Adorno und Max Horkheimer: Briefwechsel 1927–1969*, vol. IV: *1950–1969*, ed. Christoph Gödde and Henri Lonitz, Frankfurt am Main, 2006, p. 629). According to information from the relevant archives, the only thing to have survived in relation to these substituted lectures, apart from a few notes by Horkheimer, is a two-page typescript in which Adorno attempted to inform his friend of the progress of the lectures up to this point. The typescript reads as follows:

> TWA Lectures
> In the last lecture I discussed the difference between philosophy and sociology in cursory terms. Sociology is a factual science of the social,

in *intentione recta*. I criticized Max Weber's definition of economy and society on the grounds that the subjectivistic concept of understanding cannot do justice to the alienated objectivity of society. Sociology is not a unified science but an agglomeration of various disciplines. It is drawn towards philosophy on the one hand – like every particular science – through reflection upon its own object and its own method; on the other hand, because it tries to understand philosophies as dependent on social aspects or moments, and because the subject matter of philosophy itself has something essential to do with society.

There is no attempt to define the concept of philosophy, and it is illustrated instead by reference to its traditional themes or objects, such as Aristotle's metaphysics, or God, or freedom and immortality. Philosophy is driven beyond the immediate engagement with these objects by the objects themselves and finds itself compelled to exercise self-reflection. Hence the question concerning the possibility of knowledge, rather than just a direct knowledge of things.

It is very hard to identify the difference between philosophy and sociology since they initially seem to be completely alien to each other; there is no shared ground from which the difference could be derived. All the more so because philosophy cannot simply be subsumed under the concept of science. While philosophy does include a theory of science and a method, it is also a theory of the possibility of the sciences themselves and a critical interrogation of science.

The self-reflection of philosophy compels it to move beyond those questions about being and about essence, the issues to which it was originally oriented, but also beyond questions about thought alone. It recognizes that its concepts are as much mediated through facticity as facticity is mediated through concepts. But this mediation is essentially social in character. It can be shown that philosophy does not depend on social conditions in a merely external way, where that dependence would not essentially touch its inner meaning, for social moments actually inhere in its own meaning (illustrated by reference to Kantian ethics, which is particularly suitable in this regard precisely because it expressly claims to exclude such a connection as something merely empirical).

The task for the next lecture is to maintain the difference of the two disciplines, but also to show how they are reciprocally mediated, i.e. to show that a sociology without categories like that of the totality which points beyond mere facticity, or that of the social system itself, mistakes its object; on the other hand, it must show that philosophy itself has a temporal core, by virtue of which its own determinations are also essentially social. This can be shown in an entirely unforced way by reference to Hegel and Marx, but the line of thought pursued in your own piece on 'Philosophy and Sociology' could also easily take this up with the addition of a few introductory remarks on the problem of mediation. (Nachlaß Max Horkheimer, Archivzentrum der Universitätsbibliothek Frankfurt am Main, Na1: X.67.5a-5b)

The allusion to Horkheimer's piece on 'Philosophy and Sociology' relates to an essay which originally appeared under the title 'Sociology and Philosophy' in *Soziologie und moderne Gesellschaft*, Proceedings of the 14th German Sociological Conference, Berlin, 20–24 May

1959, ed. Alexander Busch, Stuttgart, 1959, pp. 27–37; now available under the later title 'Philosophy and Sociology', in Max Horkheimer, *Gesammelte Schriften*, ed. Alfred Schmidt and Gunzelin Schmid Noerr, Frankfurt am Main, 1985–, vol. 7, pp. 108–21.

2   Horkheimer had expressed this thought in a conversation with Adorno on 3 February 1939. In this discussion he suggests 'the economic formula for the objective origin of ideology as a necessary illusion ... the employer, on account of his position in society, must believe that the social surplus also comes through c and not merely through v' (Max Horkheimer and Theodor W. Adorno, [*Diskussionen über die Differenz zwischen Positivismus und Materialistischer Dialektik*], in Max Horkheimer, *Gesammelte Schriften*, vol. 12: *Nachgelassene Schriften 1931–49*, ed. Gunzelin Schmid Noerr, pp. 469f.). See the chapter on 'The Rate of Surplus Value' in Marx's *Capital*: 'The capital C is made up of two components, the sum of money c laid out on means of production, and the other the sum of money v expended on labour power; c represents the portion of value which has been turned into constant capital, v that turned into variable capital' (Marx and Engels, *Werke*, vol. 23, *Das Kapital*, vol. 1, p. 226; *Capital*, vol. 1, Fowkes, p. 320).

3   In his essay 'Beitrag zur Ideologienlehre' Adorno writes: 'In the work of Scheler and Mannheim we see how the theory of ideology has given rise to the sociology of knowledge as an academic field. The name "sociology of knowledge" is revealing enough: all consciousness, not just false consciousness but true consciousness as well – i.e. "knowledge" – is meant to be exposed as subject to social conditioning' (GS 8, pp. 471f.).

4   See Georg Lukács, *Geschichte und Klassenbewußtsein: Studien über marxistische Dialektik*, Berlin, 1923; *History and Class Consciousness: Studies in Marxist Dialectics*, trans. Rodney Livingstone, London, 1961. In his lecture course 'Fragen der Dialektik', delivered in the winter semester of 1963/4, Adorno identifies this book as 'the most important Marxist publication on Hegel'. He writes:

> It is, and the chapter in question is very interesting, an attempt, one might say a particularly extreme attempt, to produce a Hegelianized version of the Marxian dialectic. And it is quite remarkable how this book managed to establish the most intimate connection between seemingly idealistic theses and a self-confessedly extreme communist position. ...; let me say right away that the universality which is derived from the concept of reification here, and the way that the problem involved in the concept of reification and that of alienation is expressly brought into relation with the theory of knowledge in its entirety, is eminently fruitful – and that no one who wants to think seriously about questions of the dialectic can afford to neglect what Lukács does with the concept of reification in this book. On the other hand, I also have to say that the exaggerated Hegelianism, the idealist extremity of this book, so to speak, also led to the most remarkable construction of the Communist Party, which is then,

as in many of the later writings of Lukács too, almost identified with the World Spirit, with all the sinister consequences you can see in the political world today. (Theodor W. Adorno Archiv, Vo 8831)

5   In his book *The Elementary Forms of the Religious Life* Durkheim writes as follows:

> For example, try to represent what the concept of time would be without the processes by which we divide it, measure it or express it with objective signs, a time which is not a succession of years, months, weeks, days and hours! This is something almost inconceivable. We cannot conceive of time, except on condition of distinguishing its different moments. ... The divisions into days, weeks, months, years, etc., correspond to the periodical recurrence of rites, feasts, and public ceremonies. A calendar expresses the rhythm of the collective activities, while at the same time its function is to assure their regularity.
>
> It is the same thing with space. As Hamelin has shown, space is not the vague and undetermined medium which Kant imagined it to be: something purely and absolutely homogeneous. It would then be no use to us, and could not even be conceived by the mind. (Emile Durkheim, *The Elementary Forms of the Religious Life*, trans. Joseph Ward Swain, London, 1976, pp. 10–11)

In the last sentence here Durkheim is referring to Octave Hamelin (1856–1907) and his *Essai sur les éléments principaux de la répresentation* (Paris, 1908). Durkheim goes on to say:

> Analogous proofs will be found presently in regard to the concepts of class, force, personality and efficacy. It is even possible to ask if the concept of contradiction does not also depend upon social conditions. What makes one tend to believe this is that the power which this idea has exercised over humans has varied with different times and societies. Today the principle of identity dominates scientific thought; but there are vast systems of representations which have played a considerable role in the history of ideas where it has frequently been set aside: these are the mythologies from the crudest up to the most elaborate ones. (Ibid., p. 12, translation modified)

A year earlier than this series of lectures, in his lecture course on Kant's *Critique of Pure Reason*, Adorno had also reflected upon the relationship between Durkheim and Kant that is explored in this paragraph and the following one of this lecture:

> Durkheim made a serious attempt to give a sociological explanation of space, time and a series of categories and, above all, the forms of logical classification. For example, he derived temporal relations from the sequence of the generations and thus described them as something entirely social in origin. Durkheim's account is just as antinomic as Kant's ... But if sociologism is really doomed to failure at this its most radical point, the point where it has really tried its hardest, then the entire enterprise

must be extremely problematic. My view would be that the objectivity of time – which appears in Kant as a transcendental condition, a pure form of intuition – should be separated from reflections on time or the creation of a concept of time. ... On the other hand, however, we must repeat that without subjectivity, and that means: *without* real subjects interacting with one another, all talk of an objective concept of time as a concept which is prior to the mere consciousness of time would be meaningless. Instead, the truth is that these two aspects or moments are mutually interdependent. (NaS IV.4, pp. 255–7; *Kant's Critique of Pure Reason*, Livingstone, pp. 168–9, translation slightly modified)

6   In the *Critique of Pure Reason* Kant writes: 'Space is not a discursive or, as we say, general concept of relations of things in general, but a pure intuition. For, in the first place, we can represent to ourselves only one space; and if we speak of diverse spaces, we mean thereby only parts of one and the same unique space' (Kant, *Werke in sechs Bänden*, vol. II: *Kritik der reinen Vernunft*, p. 73 [A 24f./B 39]; *Kant's Critique of Pure Reason*, Kemp Smith, p. 69).

7   Reading 'initiiert' for 'irritiert'.

8   Hegel already emphasizes the social dimension of mind or spirit: 'With this, we already have before us the concept of Spirit. What still lies ahead for consciousness is the experience of what Spirit is – this absolute substance which is the unity of the different independent self-consciousnesses which, in their opposition, enjoy perfect freedom and independence: "I" that is "We" and "We" that is "I"' (Hegel, *Werke*, vol. 3: *Phänomenologie des Geistes*, p. 145; *Hegel's Phenomenology of Spirit*, Miller, p. 110).

9   In accordance with the programme announced by Engels in his essay *Ludwig Feuerbach and the End of Classical German Philosophy* (namely that of taking 'the Hegelian dialectic, which was standing on its head, and putting it back on its feet again'), Marx says in a similar vein:

> My dialectical method is, in its foundations, not only different from the Hegelian, but exactly opposite to it. For Hegel, the process of thinking, which he even transforms into an independent subject, under the name of the 'Idea', is the creator of the real world, and the real world is only the external appearance of the idea. With me the reverse is true: the ideal is nothing but the material world reflected in the mind of man, and translated into forms of thought. (Marx and Engels, *Werke*, vol. 21, p. 93, and vol. 23: *Das Kapital*, vol. 1, p. 27; *Capital*, vol. 1, Fowkes, p. 102)

10 Both Marx and Engels rejected all talk of Hegel as the Prussian State Philosopher, a view that was once defended by the 'liberal' critics of Hegelian thought. Thus Marx reacted angrily to certain remarks of this kind that were expressed by Wilhelm Liebknecht: 'I wrote to him and said that, if all he wanted to do was to repeat this old garbage about Hegel, it would be better if he just kept his mouth shut altogether'

(Marx in a letter to Engels of 10 May 1870, in Marx and Engels, *Werke*, vol. 32, Berlin, 1965, p. 503).

11 Compare the following passage from Hegel's *Phenomenology*:

> But essence that is *in* and *for itself*, and which is at the same time actual as consciousness and aware of itself, this is *Spirit*.
>
> Its spiritual *essence* has already been designated as ethical *substance*; but Spirit is the *actuality* of that substance. It is the *self* of actual consciousness to which it stands opposed, or rather which it opposes to itself as an objective, actual *world*, but a world that has completely lost the meaning for the self of something alien to it, just as the self has completely lost the meaning of a being-for-self separated from the world, whether dependent on it or not. Spirit, being the *substance* and the universal self-identical and abiding essence, is the unmoved solid *ground* and *starting-point* for the action of all, and it is their purpose and goal, the in-itself of every self-consciousness expressed in thought. (Hegel, *Werke*, vol. 3: *Phänomenologie des Geistes*, p. 325; *Hegel's Phenomenology of Spirit*, Miller, pp. 263–4)

12 The talk of basis [*Basis*] – and not so often of substructure [*Unterbau*], as Adorno suggests – and of superstructure [*Überbau*] was much more common in Marxist-Leninism than in the work of Marx or Engels themselves. The principal passage where Marx does use both of these concepts is to be found in his *Critique of Political Economy*:

> In the social production which men carry on they enter into definite relations that are indispensable and independent of their will; these relations of production correspond to a definite stage of development of their material powers of production. The sum total of these relations of production constitutes the economic structure of society – the real foundation, on which rise legal and political superstructures and to which correspond definite forms of social consciousness. The mode of production in material life determines the general character of the social, political and spiritual processes of life. It is not the consciousness of men that determines their existence, but, on the contrary, their social existence determines their consciousness. At a certain stage of their development, the material forces of production in society come in conflict with the existing relations of production, or – what is but a legal expression for the same thing – with the property relations within which they had been at work before. From forms of development of the forces of production these relations turn into their fetters. Then comes the period of social revolution. With the change of the economic foundation the entire immense superstructure is more or less rapidly transformed. (Marx and Engels, *Werke*, vol. 13, Berlin, 1961, pp. 8f.; *A Contribution to the Critique of Political Economy*, trans. N. I. Stone, Independently published, 2020, p. 6)

13 In his lectures on 'Philosophical Terminology', Adorno pointed out that the

> category of exchange also harbours something conceptual and mind-like: the exchange of equivalents, of equal exchange values, actually presupposes, as Marx showed in detail, that it is possible to abstract from the particular quality of use value which is grounded in the sensuous immediacy of the individual things or objects that are to be exchanged for one another. There is exchange value, there is something such as exchange in general, only insofar as there is something conceptual; to that extent, the aspect or moment of the concept – in other words, the non-material moment – lies not only in the construction of concepts and not merely in the observer, as it were, but also just as much in the actual social objectivity itself which Marx seeks to analyse. (Adorno, *Philosophische Terminologie*, vol. 2, pp. 22f.)

14 In the *Critique of the Gotha Programme* (Marx and Engels, *Werke*, vol. 19, Berlin, 1962, pp. 11–32), Marx had rightly seen, according to Adorno, that, 'in contrast to the customary litany of vulgar socialists, labour was not the sole source of wealth.' In this sense,

> at a time when his official interest in philosophical questions already lay behind him, he was philosophically proclaiming nothing less than that labour should not be hypostasized in any form, either in that of manual work or that of intellectual production. Such hypostasis merely extends the illusion of the predominance of the productive principle. It comes into its truth only in relation to the moment of the non-identical which Marx, so disdainful of epistemology, chose to call at first by the crude and far too narrow name of 'nature', and later on by 'natural material' and other less loaded terms. (GS 6, p. 179; *Negative Dialectics*, Ashton, pp. 177–8, translation amended)

15 See note 1 above.
16 In *Ideology and Utopia*, Karl Mannheim (1893–1947) had spoken about the concept of ideology in the 'particular' sense of the term (see Lecture 15).

> The particular conception of ideology makes its analysis of ideas on a purely *psychological* level. ... If it is claimed for instance that an adversary is lying, or that he is concealing or distorting a given factual situation, it is still nevertheless assumed that both parties share common criteria of validity – it is still assumed that it is possible to refute lies and eradicate sources of error by referring to accepted criteria of objective validity common to both parties. The suspicion that one's opponent is the victim of an ideology does not go so far as to exclude him from discussion on the basis of a common theoretical frame of reference. The case is different with the total conception of ideology. When we attribute to one historical epoch one intellectual world and to ourselves another one, or if a certain historically determined social stratum thinks in categories other than our own, we refer not to the isolated cases of thought-content, but to fundamentally divergent thought-systems and to widely differing modes of experience and interpretation. (Karl Mannheim, *Utopie und Ideologie*, pp. 54f.;

Ideology and Utopia, trans. Louis Wirth and Edward Shils, London, 1991, pp. 50–1)

See Adorno's essay *Dialektische Epilogomena: Marginalien zu Theorie und Praxis*, GS 10.2, p. 779.

17 What Adorno says here largely concurs with Horkheimer's conception of the complementary roles that can be performed by different fields of research. See Horkheimer's remarks in his address on 'The Contemporary Situation of Social Philosophy and the Tasks of an Institute for Social Research' (delivered in 1931 when he assumed the chair for social philosophy at the University of Frankfurt and simultaneously became director of the Institute for Social Research). He argues that the task of the institute would be

> to draw on contemporary philosophical approaches and organize investigations in which philosophers, sociologists, political economists, historians and psychologists can join together in ongoing collaboration. Thus they can do together what in other fields only one person can do in solitary research, and what all genuine researchers have always done: namely to pursue their large-scale philosophical questions in close conjunction with the most sophisticated scholarly and scientific methods, to refine and reconfigure their questions in the process of exploring and working on the objects in question, and to develop new methods, but without losing sight of a universal overall perspective in the process. In this way, there would be no question of providing simple 'yes' or 'no' answers to the philosophical questions involved. Rather, these very questions would be dialectically integrated into the empirical process of scientific research. In other words, the answer to those questions lies in the progress of knowledge which is achieved by the specialist disciplines, and through which the form of those questions is in turn affected. Where the theory of society is concerned, such an approach cannot possibly be undertaken by any one individual, both on account of the sheer wealth of the material involved here and on account of the differences between the various sciences and disciplines which make their own indispensable contribution. (Horkheimer, *Gesammelte Schriften*, vol. 3, ed. Alfred Schmidt, pp. 20–35, in particular, pp. 29f.)

18 This Hegelian idea is clearly expressed in the introduction which Hegel wrote for the *Critical Journal of Philosophy* (co-edited with F. J. Schelling): '*Über das Wesen der philosophischen Kritik überhaupt und ihr Verhältnis zum gegenwärtigen Zustand der Philosophie insbesondere*'. See Hegel, *Werke*, vol. 2: *Jenaer Schriften*, pp. 171–87; 'On the Essence of Philosophical Critique', trans. H. S. Harris, in *Between Kant and Hegel*, ed. H. S. Harris and George di Giovanni, Indianapolis, 2000, pp. 272–86.

19 'The True is the whole. But the whole is nothing other than the essence consummating itself through its development. Of the Absolute it must be said that it is essentially a *result*, that only in the *end* is it what it truly is; and that precisely in this consists its nature, viz. to be actual,

subject, the spontaneous becoming of itself' (Hegel, *Werke*, vol. 3: *Phänomenologie des Geistes*, p. 24; *Hegel's Phenomenology of Spirit*, Miller, p. 11). Adorno reacted directly to this claim with his own much quoted reformulation: 'The whole is the false' (GS 4, p. 55; *Minima Moralia*, Jephcott, p. 50).

Lecture 10

1 In Plato the word *alētheia* signifies the genuine or justified truth of discourse, in contrast to *doxa*, which signifies mere subjective opinion. See Plato's *Republic*, Book VI, 489e3–490b8, and Book VIII, 533e7–534a5.
2 See Lecture 1, note 21.
3 See Hans Barth, *Wahrheit und Ideologie*, Zurich, 1945.
4 According to the notes taken from a seminar discussion, Adorno said that Engels was right to invoke 'the heritage of German philosophy' ('Theodor W. Adorno über Marx und die Grundbegriffe der soziologischen Theorie: Aus einer Seminarmitschrift im Sommersemester 1962', in Hans-Georg Backhaus, *Dialektik der Wertform: Untersuchungen zur Marxschen Ökonomiekritik*, Freiburg im Breisgau, 1997, pp. 501–15, specifically p. 511). But Adorno also describes 'the chapter on fetishism' from Marx's *Capital* as part of 'the heritage of classical German philosophy' (GS 6, p. 190; *Negative Dialectics*, Ashton, pp. 189–90), so we may assume that 'the critical theory of society' is essentially concerned with the critique of political economy in Marx's sense. In the foreword to the second German edition of his book *The Condition of the Working Class in England*, Engels wrote in 1892 that the work 'everywhere reveals traces of the origins of modern socialism in one of its predecessors – namely in German classical philosophy' (Marx and Engels, *Werke*, vol. 2, Berlin, 1957, p. 641). This interpretation became programmatic for the theoretical approach adopted under the Second International at the end of the nineteenth and the beginning of the twentieth century.
5 See Hegel's 1802 essay *Glauben und Wissen oder Reflexionsphilosophie der Subjektivität in der Vollständigkeit ihrer Formen als Kantische, Jacobische und Fichtesche Philosophie* (Hegel, *Werke*, vol. 2, pp. 287–432; *Faith & Knowledge*, trans. Walter Cerf and H. S. Harris, New York, 1977).
6 In *An Enquiry concerning Human Understanding*, David Hume (1711–1776) writes that 'we may divide all the perceptions of the mind into two classes or species, which are distinguished by their different degrees of force and vivacity.' Thus we have '*Thoughts* or *Ideas*' on the one hand and '*Impressions*' on the other. Both of these furnish the material for the human understanding: 'In short, all the materials of thinking are derived either from our outward or inward sentiment: the mixture and composition of these belongs alone to the mind and will. Or, to

express myself in philosophical language, all our ideas or more feeble perceptions are copies of our impressions or more lively ones.' (Hume, *Enquiries concerning the Human Understanding and concerning the Principles of Morals*, ed. L. A. Selby-Bigge, Oxford, 1972, pp. 18–19).

7 Adorno discusses Kant's conception of the objectivity of knowledge in some detail in Lecture 9 of his 1959 lecture course on Kant's first *Critique* (NaS IV.4, pp. 143–59; *Kant's Critique of Pure Reason*, Livingstone, pp. 93–104). In support of his argument there, Adorno cites the third section of §26 on 'Transcendental Deduction of the Universally Possible Employment in Experience of the Pure Concepts of the Understanding' (Kant, *Werke in sechs Bänden*, vol. II: *Kritik der reinen Vernunft*, pp. 156f. [B 163–165]; *Critique of Pure Reason*, Kemp Smith, pp. 172ff.).

8 In the first of his three studies on Hegel ('Aspects of Hegel's Philosophy') Adorno writes as follows:

> In Hegel the tendency of idealism is to move beyond itself. ... In Kant, the idea that a world divided into subject and object, the world in which, as prisoners of our own constitution, we are involved only with phenomena, is not the ultimate world, already forms the secret source of energy. Hegel adds an un-Kantian element to that: the idea that in grasping, conceptually, the block, the limit that is set to subjectivity, in understanding subjectivity as 'mere' subjectivity, we have already passed beyond that limit. Hegel, who in many ways is a Kant come into his own, is driven by the idea that knowledge, if there is such a thing, is by its very idea total knowledge, that every one-sided judgment intends, by its very form, the absolute, and does not rest until it has been sublated in it. (GS 5, p. 255; *Hegel: Three Studies*, trans. Shierry Weber Nicholsen, Cambridge, MA, 1993, p. 6)

9 Bertrand Russell (1872–1970) and Alfred North Whitehead (1861–1947) published *Principia Mathematica* in three volumes between 1910 and1913. Adorno pointed out that logic as a philosophical discipline – which had undergone little significant change since Aristotle – was 'rendered supple again' in the work of Russell and Whitehead. (*Zur Metakritik der Erkenntnistheorie*, GS 5, p. 76; *Against Epistemology: A Metacritique*, Willis Domingo, p. 69).

10 In the so-called Vienna Circle there was some largely unofficial discussion of the thought of Ludwig Wittgenstein and indeed some direct contact with him. In the course of the 1930s the members of the Vienna Circle developed a particular form of positivism which became known as 'logical empiricism'. The core of the group was made up by philosophers, mathematicians and physicists, principally Moritz Schlick (1882–1936), Hans Hahn (1879–1934), Philipp Frank (1884–1966), Otto Neurath (1882–1945) and Rudolf Carnap (1891–1970).

11 In *The Social Contract* Rousseau had distinguished between the will of all (*la volonté de tous*) and the general will (*la volonté générale*): 'the latter considers only the common interest, while the former takes

private interest into account, and is no more than a sum of particular wills: but take away from these same wills the pluses and minuses that cancel one another, and the general will remains as the sum of the differences' (Jean-Jacques Rousseau, *The Social Contract and Discourses*, trans. G. D. H. Cole, rev. J. H. Brumfitt and John C. Hall, London, 1973, p. 185).

12 'Thirteen million Americans can't be wrong' is a popular advertising slogan which is a more faithful echo of the spirit of the epoch than the segregated pride of those who regard themselves as the cultural elite. The average opinion – with all the social power that is condensed in it – becomes a fetish to which the attributes of truth are transferred. It is infinitely easier to detect the wretchedness that lies in this, to become indignant about it or to despise it, than it is to confront it in a truly rigorous way. (*Meinung Wahn Gesellschaft*, GS 10.2, p. 584; in this connection see also *The Psychological Technique of Martin Luther Thomas's Radio Addresses*, GS 9.1, p. 52)

13 See Hegel, *Werke*, vol. 7: *Grundlinien der Philosophie des Rechts*, pp. 483–6 (§§ 316–18). In §318 Hegel says: 'Public opinion therefore deserves to be as much *respected* as *despised* – despised for its concrete expression and for the concrete consciousness it expresses, respected for its essential basis, a basis which only appears more or less dimly in that concrete expression' (ibid., p. 485; Hegel, *Outlines of the Philosophy of Right*, trans. M. Knox, rev. and ed. Stephen Houlgate, Oxford, 2008, p. 301).

14 In various places Adorno refers to the experience that 'proletarians hardly feel themselves to be proletarian any more' (*Anmerkungen zum sozialen Konflikt heute: Nach zwei Seminaren*, GS 8, p. 187). Again in the 1968 lecture course on sociology, Adorno says:

> If there really is a gradual process whereby those who are objectively defined, according to some threshold value, as proletarians are no longer conscious of themselves as such, and even whereby they emphatically reject such a consciousness, then, as a tendency, no proletarian will finally be left knowing that he is a proletarian. In that case, despite the objective situation, the use of the traditional concept of class can easily become a dogma or a fetish. There comes a point – and I believe that this is a case in which the empirical aspect of sociology comes into its own – where a concept such as class-consciousness must be simply confronted with the reality of individual consciousness. But if the proletarians, who allegedly have everything to gain and nothing to lose but their chains, no longer even know that they are proletarians, the practical appeal to them takes on an ideological moment. Sociological knowledge must, unquestionably, take account of this. (NaS IV.15, pp. 43f.; *Introduction to Sociology*, Jephcott, p. 23)

15 Adorno clearly does not want to say that the lack of class-consciousness on the part of the workers suffices to refute the Marxian theory of

surplus value. But he thinks that knowledge about this theory cannot help the proletariat to develop any sort of revolutionary consciousness if there is no longer a proletariat that expressly experiences itself as such. As he says elsewhere: 'Sociologists ... ponder the grimly comic riddle: where is the proletariat?' (GS 4, p. 221; *Minima Moralia*, Jephcott, p. 194).

16 Punchcards were formerly used for storing data in electronic form, but in the mid-1960s magnetic tapes came to be employed for this purpose instead. The 'Hollerith card' goes back to Hermann Hollerith (1860–1929), who first used punchcards in conjunction with a specially developed technology for gathering census information in the USA.

17 It has not been possible to identify a film with this particular title or one resembling it. Adorno may simply have come up with it as a typically kitsch sort of title in order to use it, *pars pro toto*, as an illustration of the point he wants to make here. It is also possible that he was thinking of a once popular rather sentimental poem by Emanuel Geibl (1815–1884) with the title 'Hope'. The first strophe reads: 'And though the winter rages, / Displays its fearsome visage, / And scatters ice and snow on every side / Yet spring *must* come' (Emanuel Geibl, *Werke*, ed. Wolfgang Stammler, Leipzig, 1918, vol. 1, p. 176). At the beginning of the twentieth century Geibl, with his trite artistic ideals, was frequently derided, among others by Thomas Mann in his novel *Buddenbrooks*. The lack of artistic vision and the nationalist pathos in his work eventually made him into one of the most favoured poets among the National Socialists.

Lecture 11

1 Of the tape recordings from which Adorno's secretary originally transcribed this entire series of lectures, the recordings for this lecture, for lecture 12 (7 July) and for lecture 17 (26 July) have in fact survived (see the editor's Afterword). In the case of these three lectures, the present edition is based directly on the tape recordings.

2 Adorno is probably thinking of his recently published book *Klangfiguren* (Berlin, 1959; now in GS 16, pp. 7–248). It has not been possible to identify the critic Adorno mentions at the beginning of his lecture.

3 'The works of individual composers, however strictly they are concerned with solving technical problems as well, breathe the spirit of the society of their age – who could think of denying the ideas of the revolutionary bourgeois period in Beethoven, of expansive imperialism in Wagner, of the late liberal era and its museum-like relationship to so-called cultural commodities in Strauss?' (*Über Technik und Humanismus*, GS 20.1, p. 313).

4 See Franz Mehring, *Karl Marx: Geschichte seines Lebens*, Leipzig, 1918. Mehring was a prominent journalist and social democrat. The considerable influence which his book exercised on the German

working-class movement helped to give a strong social-democratic inflection to German Marxism. 'In the working-class movement it has become a habit, especially since the time of Mehring, to view naturalistic and realistic tendencies in art which tend to reflect social life in its immediacy as being inherently progressive and everything opposed to this as reactionary. Any artist who does not depict backyards, pregnant mothers and, more recently, prominent figures, is deemed a mystic' (GS 10.1, p. 227; *Prisms*, trans. Samuel Weber and Shierry Weber, London, 1967, p. 217). On 10 November 1941 Adorno wrote to Horkheimer: 'I have also been reading a good part of Mehring's biography of Marx – all I can say is that it is exactly as I imagined it to be – appalling' (Theodor W. Adorno, *Briefe und Briefwechsel*, ed. Theodor W. Adorno Archiv, vol. 4: Theodor W. Adorno/Max Horkheimer, *Briefwechsel 1927–1969*, vol. II, Frankfurt am Main, 2004, p. 286).

5 Thus in 1920 Pareto spoke of the principle

> that seems to me of fundamental significance for this science [i.e. sociology], namely the principle of the usefulness of certain world views in relation to praxis and of their damaging effect as far as our knowledge of reality is concerned. Thus one should not oppose faith to the sceptical outlook of science, as people so often do, for both are useful, depending on the purposes we have in view. (Vilfredo Pareto, from the Epilogue to his *Trattato di Sociologia Generale*, Rome, 2010)

For Adorno's critique of Pareto, see *Beitrag zur Ideologielehre*, where he writes:

> What Hans Barth says about Pareto in his book *Truth and Ideology* is quite right, namely that, for Pareto, the world of the mind, so far as it claims to be anything more than the investigation of causal connections conceived in mechanical terms, possesses no principles of its own and no genuine cognitive value. The seemingly scientific reformulation of the theory of ideology simply gives rise to an essentially resigned version of science in the face of its object. In blinding himself to the element of reason within ideologies, something that was always also part of the Hegelian conception of historical necessity, Pareto thereby relinquishes the legitimate right of reason to pass any critical judgement on ideologies. This theory of ideology lends itself particularly well to the ideology of the total state that is based simply on power. In already subsuming all that belongs to the mind to the purposes of propaganda and domination, it provides cynicism with a very good scientific conscience. The connections between the declarations of Mussolini and Pareto's treatise are well known. The late form of political liberalism, which already revealed a certain affinity to relativism on account of its emphasis on freedom of thought, in the sense that everyone is allowed to think what he likes irrespective of whether it is true, since everyone thinks only what serves his own interest or his own need for self-preservation anyway – this form of liberalism was hardly immune to these perversions of the concept of ideology. This too confirms that the totalitarian domination of mankind

is not just externally imposed by a few *desperados*, is not just some technical malfunction on the straight motorway of progress. Rather, we see how the forces that will destroy are already growing at the heart of culture itself. (GS 8, pp. 469f.)

Hans Barth described Pareto's theory of ideology as follows: 'The world of the mind, insofar as it claims to be anything beyond the investigation of causal relations conceived in mechanical terms, possesses no principles of its own and no genuine cognitive value. It offers nothing but a confused welter of pseudo-rationalizations through which the social struggle for power is concealed and morally legitimated by particular groups and strata of society as the case may be' (Hans Barth, *Wahrheit und Ideologie*, Zurich, 1945, p. 345).

6 It is not clear which early writings by Mussolini (1883–1945) Adorno has in mind here. But in the first issue of *Il Popolo d'Italia*, the newspaper which he founded, Mussolini wrote a major article which evokes the collapse of traditional certainties and concludes with an appeal to violent action:

> Since I am certain that time will prove me right and will destroy the foolish dogma of absolute neutrality [that of Italy at the beginning of the First World War], just as it has already destroyed many other no less venerable dogmas of every religion and of every party, I could just have sat back and waited in this proud certainty with an easy conscience. The time would surely have come fast enough, but it is sometimes also necessary to advance towards it. In a time such as ours, when everything is dissolving before us, it is not merely the dead who hasten, as the poet says, for the living must hasten even more than the dead. ... The call lies in a word that I would never have uttered in normal times, but which today I proclaim in a clear strong voice, without hypocrisy and with utmost conviction – the fearful and fascinating word: War! (Benito Mussolini, *Il Popolo d'Italia*, 15 November 1914)

7 In *Human, All Too Human*, Nietzsche writes: 'We believe instinctively that the religiously tinged sections of a philosophy are better proved than the others. But basically it is the reverse; we simply have the inner wish that it might be so – that is, that what gladdens might also be true. This wish misleads us into buying bad reasons as good ones' (*Werke in drei Bänden*, vol. 1, p. 531; *Human, All Too Human*, trans. Marion Faber and Stephen Lehmann, London, 1994, p. 90). See also Adorno, *Ohne Leitbild: Anstelle einer Vorrede*, GS 10.1, p. 296.

8 'Thus the critique of reason, in the end, necessarily leads to scientific knowledge; while its dogmatic employment, on the other hand, lands us in dogmatic assertions to which other assertions, equally specious, can always be opposed – that is, in *scepticism*' (Kant, *Werke in sechs Bänden*, vol. II: *Kritik der reinen Vernunft*, p. 61 [B 23f.]; *Kant's Critique of Pure Reason*, Kemp Smith, p. 57).

9 See Lecture 4, note 26.

10 Adorno undertook to provide a detailed account of such reified consciousness in the first part of *Negative Dialectics* under the title 'Relation to Ontology' (GS 6, pp. 67–136; *Negative Dialectics*, Ashton, pp. 61–131) and earlier in *Jargon of Authenticity* (GS 6, pp. 413–526; *Jargon of Authenticity*, Tarnowsky and Will, passim).

11 In a review of Karl Korn's *Die Sprache in der verwalteten Welt* (Frankfurt am Main, 1958), Adorno spoke of 'some of my own hobby-horses about language, such as the curious phrase "in some sense"' (GS 20.2, p. 520). He regarded this formulaic phrase as one the 'basest clichés' which 'are used without the least embarrassment, indeed with gusto, as though the employment of such catchphrases meant that one is absolutely up-to-date' (*Critical Models: Interventions and Catchwords*, trans. Henry W. Pickford, New York, 1998, p. 29).

12 In fact the concept of reification, i.e. the term *Verdinglichung*, appears only twice in Marx's work, and both times in the posthumously published third volume of *Capital* (see Marx and Engels, *Werke*, vol. 25: *Das Kapital*, part 3, p. 838 and p. 887; *Capital: A Critique of Political Economy, Volume Three*, trans. David Fernbach, Harmondsworth, 1981, pp. 969 and 102.) Marx also uses three different words that have also been rendered by 'objectification' or 'reification' in English, namely *Vergegenständlichung*, *Versachlichung* and *Objektivierung*. Thus in the first volume of *Capital* we read:

> There is an antithesis, immanent in the commodity, between use-value and value, between private labour which must simultaneously manifest itself as directly social labour, and a particular concrete kind of labour which simultaneously counts as merely abstract universal labour, between the conversion of things into persons and the conversion of persons into things; the antithetical phases of the metamorphosis of the commodity are the developed forms of motion of this immanent contradiction. (*Marx and Engels, Werke*, vol. 23: *Das Kapital*, vol. 1, p. 128; *Capital: A Critique of Political Economy Volume One*, trans. Ben Fowkes, Harmondsworth, 1976, p. 209)

One can really speak only of 'the central role' of the concept of reification (*Verdinglichung*) by the time we get to Lukács's book *History and Class Consciousness*.

13 Max Scheler (1874–1928) was nominated as Professor for Philosophy and Sociology at the University of Frankfurt in 1928 but died in May of the same year.

14 In the *Soziologische Exkurse*, Scheler's book *Die Wissensformen und die Gesellschaft* (Leipzig, 1928) is specifically cited as 'a kind of typology, or even an ontology of ideologies. Today, after not quite thirty years, his much-admired attempt strikes one as astonishingly naive.' Adorno excerpts the relevant claims as follows:

> The contemplation of becoming – lower class; the contemplation of being – upper class ...

Realism (the world predominantly as 'resistance') – the lower class; idealism – upper class (the world predominantly as the 'realm of ideas) ... Materialism – lower class; spiritualism – upper class ... (Institut für Sozialforschung, *Soziologische Exkurse*, p. 173; *Aspects of Sociology*, trans. John Viertel, London, 1973, p. 195)

In his own notes for the lecture course, Adorno references this material from Scheler as evidence for his general argument (see p. 223).

15 Adorno is alluding to the twofold meaning of the concept of 'substance' in Aristotle, which is most clearly expressed in his work entitled *Categories*. There Aristotle introduces the idea of 'primary substance' (*prōtē ousia*; πρώτη οὐσία), which he describes as substance in the full and proper sense, i.e. it does not inhere in anything that underlies it and is not predicated of anything that underlies it (*Categories*, 2a11–14). Here Aristotle is clearly referring to manifest individual things, where each particular thing signifies an individual 'determinate this' (*tode ti*; τόδε τι), as Aristotle puts it (ibid., 3b10–13). Thus 'primary substance' in Aristotle's sense is ontologically independent, i.e. is not an accident or property of anything else: logically speaking, it is the ultimate subject of predication and therefore cannot itself be a predicate of anything else. What Aristotle calls 'secondary substances' (*deuterai ousiai*; δεύτεραι οὐσίαι) are the kinds and species under which 'primary substances' fall. They are the predicates which render first substances knowable, are therefore predicated of 'that which underlies', namely as accidental determinations that are not 'in that which underlies' (ibid., 2a14–19; 2b29–31; 3a7–a21).

16 In the first of his *Two Treatises of Government* of 1689 ('The False Principles and Foundation of Sir Robert Filmer, and His Followers, Are Detected and Overthrown'), John Locke undertook to refute the claims and assumptions which Robert Filmer (1588–1653) had defended in his work *Patriarcha* (written between 1620 and 1630). These involved the claim that human beings are unfree by nature and must therefore dutifully submit to patriarchal, princely, monarchical and divine authorities. (See Sir Robert Filmer, *Patriarcha and Other Writings*, ed. J. P. Sommerville, Cambridge, 1991, pp. 1–68.)

17 The concept of the *hypokeimenon* ('the substrate' or 'that which underlies') appears in two contexts in Aristotle. In his natural philosophy the word is used synonymously with *hylē* (ὕλη), the indeterminate matter which underlies all determinate manifestations of material being (*Physics* I, 9, 192a31f.). In the logical-ontological context, the word *hypokeimenon* appears in Aristotle's *Categories*: on the one hand, it signifies that which ontologically underlies 'accidents' and is itself independent and, on the other, the subject which underlies all predicates in a propositional statement (*Categories*, 1a20–b24).

18 Namely 7 July, which is when Lecture 12 was delivered.

19 The final word of the lecture was drowned in the applause of the audience as the lecture ended.

Lecture 12

1   See Lecture 11, note 1.
2   See Lecture 9, note 12.
3   The concept of 'cultural lag' – usually rendered in German as *kulturelle Phasenverschiebung* – was introduced into sociology by William Fielding Ogburn (1886–1959) in his book *Social Change with Respect to Culture and Original Nature* (New York, 1922).
4   'Money aims at the mobilization of *all* things. World economy is the economy that has become a fact, an economy of abstract and fluid values that have been completely emancipated from their ground' (Oswald Spengler, *Der Untergang des Abendlandes*, vol. 2, 1922, pp. 1167f.). In this connection compare the following note.

5   *Nobility and priesthood* first arose from land that was free, and constitute the pure symbolic expression of existence and vitality, of time and space. From a brooding and rapacious mentality there would subsequently emerge a second type of existence of less symbolic power, and which becomes predominant in later urban times in the form of *economy and science*. In these two streams of existence the ideas of fate and causality are thought through to the end in a ruthless way and in a manner that is hostile to tradition. There emerge two powers which a fatal enmity has separated from the social ideals of a heroic and a sacred culture – namely *money and spirit*. These two relate to the former just as the soul of the city relates to the soul of the land. (Ibid., p. 989)

6   In a similar vein, Adorno points out in *Minima Moralia* that 'the relation between matter and expression is severed, and just as the concepts of positivists should be seen as mere counters, those of positivistic humanity have become literally coins' (GS 4, p. 156; *Minima Moralia*, Jephcott, p. 137).
7   Compare the frequently cited observations of Marx in the *Economic and Philosophic Manuscripts of 1844*, where he describes logic as 'the *money* of the spirit' (Marx and Engels, *Werke*, vol. 40, p. 571; *Karl Marx: Early Writings*, trans. Rodney Livingston and Gregor Benton, London, 1992, pp. 211, 237, 238, 254, 264, 265).
8   Freud often refers to the notion that 'the unconscious' knows nothing of time. See the essay *Das Unbewußte* (Freud, *Gesammelte Werke*, vol. X, p. 286; Freud, *The Unconscious, Standard Edition*, vol. XIV, p. 187).
9   Adorno is probably thinking of a passage in Freud's encyclopaedia article *Psycho-Analysis* of 1922: 'Some analysts ... have reported too that the analytic treatment of gross organic diseases is not unpromising, since a mental factor not infrequently contributes to the origin and continuance of such illnesses. Since psycho-analysis demands a certain amount of psychical plasticity from its patients, some kind of age-limit must be laid down in their selection (Freud, *Gesammelte Werke*, vol. XIII, p. 226; *Standard Edition*, vol. XVIII, p. 250).

10 Adorno explores and elucidates this thought in his essay 'Beitrag zur Ideologielehre' (GS 8, pp. 457f.).
11 In the *Philosophy of Right* Hegel discusses the relation between wealth and poverty in the second section of part three ('Civil Society'). Thus in §243 he writes:

> When civil society is in a state of unimpeded activity, it is engaged in *expanding* internally in *population* and *industry*. The *amassing of wealth* is intensified by *generalizing* (a) the linkage of people by their needs and (b) the methods of preparing and distributing the means to satisfy these needs, because it is from this double process of generalization that the largest profits are derived. That is one side of the picture. The other side is the *subdivision* and *restriction* of particular work. This results in the *dependence* and *distress* of the class [*Klasse*] tied to work of that sort, and these again entail the inability to feel and enjoy the broader freedoms and especially the spiritual benefits of civil society. (Hegel, *Werke*, vol. 7: *Grundlinien der Philosophie des Rechts*, p. 389; *Elements of the Philosophy of Right*, Houlgate, pp. 220–1)

12 See Lecture 1, p. 4 above.
13 Wilhelm Windelband (1848–1915) founded the so-called South-Western School of Neo-Kantianism, which was subsequently continued by Heinrich Rickert (1863–1936).
14 Talcott Parsons proved extremely influential in encouraging the view that Weber never succeeded in developing a fully coherent sociological theory, and especially not a coherent theory of the prevailing capitalist system: 'Weber never developed a unified theory of capitalism. In spite of the fact that a very large proportion of his sociological work was devoted to this problem, he left only a number of fragments which from our points of view are to be regarded as special investigations' (Parsons, '"Capitalism" in Recent German Literature: Sombart and Weber – Concluded', *Journal of Political Economy*, 37/1 [1929], p. 34).
15 See Lecture 4, note 17, and Lecture 6, note 16.
16 It has not been possible to discover anything more precise about the conversation in question.
17 See Lecture 3, note 6.

18 It is quite conceivable that contemporary society eludes any internally coherent theory. It was easier for Marx in the sense that the developed system of liberalism, in theoretical form, already lay before him. He needed only to ask whether capitalism and its own dynamic categories corresponds to this model in order for him to develop something like a systematic theory of his own as a determinate negation of the theoretical system that confronted him. In the meantime the market economy has become so weakened that it scorns any such confrontation. (*Spätkapitalismus oder Industriegesellschaft*, GS 8, p. 359)

19 Friedrich Pollock (1894–1970), the principal economist of the Institute

for Social Research, had used the expression 'pseudo-market' to characterize the command economies at work in the Soviet Union, in National Socialist Germany, and in the United States after the initiation of Franklin D. Roosevelt's New Deal. See Friedrich Pollock, 'State Capitalism: Its Possibilities and Limitations', *Studies in Philosophy and Social Science*, IX/2 (1941), pp. 200–25.

20 The metaphor of 'the invisible hand' derives from Adam Smith's *An Inquiry into the Nature and Causes of the Wealth of Nations* of 1776. He used this vivid image to underline the advantages of economic liberalism and to suggest how the socio-economic order in question was maintained without reference to the conscious intentions of individuals.

21 In his later article 'Society' (1965), Adorno would revise this view and identify the exchange relation as the central element that holds society together:

> The process of increasing social rationalization, of universal extension of the market system, is not something that takes place beyond the specific social conflicts and antagonisms, or in spite of them. It works through those antagonisms themselves, the latter, at the same time, tearing society apart in the process. For in the institution of exchange there is created and reproduced that antagonism which could at any time bring organized society to ultimate catastrophe and destroy it. The whole business keeps creaking and groaning on, at unspeakable human cost, only on account of the profit motive and the interiorization by individuals of the breach torn in society as a whole. (GS 8, pp. 14f.; 'Society', trans. Frederick Jameson, in *Critical Theory: The Essential Readings*, ed. David Ingram and Julia Ingram, New York, 1992, p. 65)

22 In his 'Reflections on Class Theory' (written in 1942 and published posthumously), Adorno already defended the view that the development of class consciousness was 'objectively blocked and ultimately hindered by certain measures expressly undertaken by those who exercise power in the name of the great totality from which they are indistinguishable' (GS 8, p. 380). One such measure, which was required to help prevent the further material impoverishment of the proletariat, according to Adorno, was 'improvement of the standard of living by means that could be described as external to the economic system' (ibid., p. 88) in the form of 'gratuities' (ibid., p. 386) that are paid not as part of the regular wage but 'out of the income or monopolistic profits themselves'. 'The dynamic of misery is appeased by accumulation. The amelioration of the economic position at the bottom, or at least its stabilization, is external to the economic system' (ibid., p. 385). In other words, those who exercise power made this strictly extra-economic support of the working class into their own private matter, though not of course through any personal benevolence: 'Good intentions and psychology have nothing to do with it.' The workers themselves, the only ones who guarantee the continued existence of those who exercise power, must be looked after in the sense that 'we "safeguard the existence to the slave

in his slavery" precisely in order to secure our own existence' (ibid., p. 386).

Lecture 13

1 See Lecture 12, note 20.
2 In speaking of products here, Adorno is thinking not of economic products but of the socially separated individuals who are actually produced by society itself.
3 Adorno is referring to the 'Iron Curtain' which divided the West European countries and the Eastern bloc countries throughout the Cold War period.
4 Reading 'jenseits' for 'diesseits' here.
5 'Diamat' is an abbreviated expression for dialectical materialism. The term was used, along with 'Histomat' for historical materialism, to characterize the official doctrine of Marxist-Leninism that prevailed in the Eastern bloc.
6 See Lecture 7, note 23.
7 It was not possible to identify this thesis in so many words in the work of Ernst Mach. According to Mach, a '*complete theory* ... is the ultimate goal of investigation .... But as long as this ultimate goal has yet to be achieved, theory always signifies ... a progress, an approximation ... inasmuch as it provides a more complete picture of the facts than it would be possible to provide without its assistance' (*Die Prinzipien der Wärmelehre*, Leipzig, 1896, p. 459).
8 It was not so much Marx as Engels who first really defended the 'reflection theory' which would become characteristic of Marxist-Leninism. In his work *Ludwig Feuerbach and the End of German Classical Philosophy*, he talked about his own and especially Marx's transformation of Hegel's conceptual dialectic:

> We comprehended the concepts in our heads once more materialistically – as images [or reflections: *Abbilder*] of real things, instead of regarding the real things as images of this or that stage of the absolute concept. Thus dialectics reduced itself to the science of the general laws of motion, both of the external world and of human thought – two sets of laws which are identical in substance, but differ in their expression in so far as the human mind can apply them consciously, while in nature and up to now for the most part in human history, these laws assert themselves unconsciously ... Thereby the dialectic of concepts became merely the conscious reflex of the dialectical motion of the real world. (Marx and Engels, *Werke*, vol. 21, p. 292; Karl Marx and Friedrich Engels, *Selected Works in One Volume*, London, 1968, p. 609)

9 In the *Prolegomena*, Kant wrote: 'we have long been accustomed to seeing antiquated knowledge produced as new by taking it out of its former context, and fitting it into a systematic dress of any fancy

pattern under new titles. Most readers will set out by expecting nothing else from the Critique' (Kant, *Werke in sechs Bänden*, vol. III, p. 120 [A 16f.]; *Prolegomena*, Ellington, p. 7). And in the preface to Hegel's *Phenomenology* we read:

> The intelligible form of Science is the way open and equally accessible to everyone, and consciousness as it approaches Science justly demands that it be able to attain to rational knowledge by way of the ordinary understanding ... Science in its early stages, when it has attained neither to completeness of detail nor perfection of form, is vulnerable to criticism. But it would be as unjust for such criticism to strike at the very heart of Science, as it is untenable to refuse to honour the demand for its further development. This polarization seems to be the Gordian knot with which scientific culture is at present struggling, and which it still does not properly understand. One side boasts of its wealth of material and intelligibility, the other side at least scorns this intelligibility, and flaunts its immediate rationality and divinity. Even if the former side is reduced to silence ... it is by no means satisfied regarding the said demands; for they are justified but not fulfilled. Its silence stems only half from the triumph of its opponent, and half from the boredom and indifference which tend to result from the continual awakening of expectations through unfulfilled promises. (Hegel, *Werke*, vol. 3: *Phänomenologie des Geistes*, p. 20; *Hegel's Phenomenology of Spirit*, Miller, pp. 7–8)

10 See Lecture 9, note 19.
11 See NaS IV.7, p. 15; *Ontology and Dialectics*, trans. Nicholas Walker, Polity, 2019, p. 6.

12 > When I make use of the term dialectics I would ask you not to think of the famous scheme of thesis, antithesis and synthesis in the usual sense, as you encounter it in the most superficial account of school dialectics. Hegel himself, who after all did possess something like a system that aspired as a system to be a synthesis, did not adhere consistently to this scheme. In the Preface to the *Phenomenology* ... he spoke of this creaking triadic scheme with utter contempt. (NaS IV.16, p. 16; *Lectures on Negative Dialectics*, trans. Rodney Livingstone, Cambridge, 2008, p. 6)

For further criticism of this schematically reduced conception of dialectics, NaS IV.16, p. 27, and GS 5, p. 314; *Hegel: Three Studies*, Nicholsen, p. 75. See also 'Einleitung in dialektisches Denken: Stichworte zur letzten, abgebrochenen Vorlesung SS 1969', *Frankfurter Adorno Blätter* VI, ed. Rolf Tiedemann, Munich, 2000, p. 174.

13 The lectures that would have been delivered on 7 and 9 July were dropped and not rescheduled, like those for the 26 May (Ascension Day) and 16 June (Corpus Christi). The lectures scheduled for 21 and 23 June were taken over by Max Horkheimer (see Lecture 9, note 1).
14 Lecture 18, pp. 197–207.
15 This paragraph was crossed out by Adorno in the lecture transcript.

Lecture 14

1. See Lecture 1, note 23.
2. In this regard, compare the words of Heraclitus:

   Of the Logos which is as I describe it men always prove to be uncomprehending, both before they have heard it and when once they have heard it. For although all things happen according to this Logos men are like people of no experience, even when they experience such words and deeds as I explain, when I distinguish each thing according to its constitution and declare how it is; but the rest of men fail to notice what they do after they wake up just as they forget what they do when asleep. (Fragment 1)

   Or again: 'Therefore it is necessary to follow the common; but although the Logos is common the many live as though they had a private understanding' (Fragment 2). See G. S. Kirk and J. E. Raven, *The Presocratic Philosophers: A Critical History with a Selection of Texts*, Cambridge, 1970, pp. 187–8.
3. See Lecture 10, note 1.
4. In his *Novum Organum*, Francis Bacon (1561–1626) identified numerous reasons for what he regarded as the poor state of the sciences and of human knowledge in general, such as the adoption of false aims and methods, the constant overvaluation of the classical world, and a widespread and harmful deference towards religion and theology. Francis Bacon, *Novum organum*, trans. M. Silverthorne and L. Jardine, Cambridge, 2008 (see in particular Aphorisms XIX, LVI and LII).
5. Such references to 'the many' (*hoi polloi*) can already be found in the fragments of Heraclitus (see note 2 above). Plato's contempt for democracy was directly connected with his derogatory attitude to 'the many' (see *Republic*, 491e–492c).
6. Adorno mistranslates Bacon's *Idola specus* here, confusing the Latin *specus* (cave or den) with *speculum* (mirror).
7. Aphorism XXXIX of the *Novum organum* named the 'idols' and 'false notions' which 'have taken possession of the human mind and are deeply rooted there.' In Aphorism XXXIX he writes: 'Quatuor sunt genera Idolorum quae mentes humanas obsident. Iis (docendi gratia) nomina imposuimus; ut primum genus, Idola Tribus; secundum, Idola Specus; tertium, Idola Fori; quartum, Idola Theatri vocentur.' In translation: 'There are four kinds of illusions which block men's minds. For instruction's sake, we have given them the following names: the first kind are called *idols of the tribe*; the second *idols of the cave*; the third *idols of the marketplace*; the fourth *idols of the theatre*.' Bacon explained the *Idola specus* as follows:

   The *idols of the cave* are the illusions of the individual man. For (apart from the aberrations of human nature in general) each man has a kind of individual cave or cavern which fragments and distorts the light of nature. This may happen either because of the unique and particular nature of each man; or because of his upbringing and the company he keeps; or because of his reading of books and the authority of those whom he respects and admires; or because of the different impressions things make on different minds, preoccupied and prejudiced perhaps, or calm and detached, and so on. (Bacon, *Novum organum*, Aphorism XLII)

8   Meyers *Großes Konversations-Lexicon* (Leipzig, 1907) explains the 'personal equation' as 'an imperfection of the human senses that was first discovered in the context of astronomical observations, namely that two simultaneous phenomena could not be registered by the senses of vision and hearing at exactly the same moment but only one after the other.'

9   'Finally there are the *illusions* which have made their homes in men's minds from the various dogmas of different philosophies, and even from mistaken rules of demonstration. These I call *idols of the theatre*, for all the philosophies that men have learned or devised are, in our opinion, so many plays produced and performed which have created false and fictitious worlds' (*Novum organum*, Aphorism XLIV).

10 There are also *illusions* which seem to arise by agreement and from men's association with each other, which we call *idols of the marketplace*; we take the name from human exchange and community. Men associate through talk; and words are chosen to suit the understanding of the common people. And thus a poor and unskilled code of words incredibly obstructs the understanding. The definitions and explanations with which learned men have been accustomed to protect and in some ways liberate themselves, do not restore the situation at all. Plainly words do violence to the understanding, and confuse everything; and betray men into countless empty disputes and fictions. (Aphorism XLIII)

11 See Lecture 8, note 24.

12 Adorno's 'Beitrag zur Ideologielehre' first appeared in the *Kölner Zeitschrift für Soziologie und Sozialpsychologie*, 6 (1954), pp. 360–75; GS 8, pp. 457–77.

13 See Lecture 11, note 5.

14 See Lecture 2, note 15.

15 See GS 3, pp. 141–91; *Dialectic of Enlightenment*, Jephcott, pp. 94–136.

16 Adorno is referring to the Franciscan philosopher Roger Bacon (c. 1214–1294). Whether he can properly be described as a scholastic philosopher is debatable, since in his work *Opus maius* (1265) he reacted to the growing conflict between faith and knowledge by insisting – in contrast to the scholastic position – on a strict separation between the two spheres.

17 Reading 'ideologisch' for 'Ideologie'.

18 In a letter to Benjamin of 29 February 1940, Adorno spoke about 'forgetting' as an epistemological category:

In a certain sense 'forgetting' is the foundation for both these things, for the sphere of experience or *mémoire involontaire*, and for the reflex character of a sudden act of recall that already presupposes the forgetting. Whether an individual human being is capable of having such experiences depends in the last instance upon how that person forgets. ... Is it not the case that the real task here is to bring the entire opposition between sensory experience and experience proper into relation with a dialectical theory of forgetting? Or one could equally say, into relation with a theory of reification. For all reification is a forgetting: objects become purely thing-like the moment they are retained for us without the continued presence of their other aspects: when something of them has been forgotten. (Theodor W. Adorno, *Briefe und Briefwechsel*, vol. 1: Theodor W. Adorno/Walter Benjamin, *Briefwechsel 1928–1940*, p. 417; Theodor W. Adorno and Walter Benjamin, *The Complete Correspondence 1928–1940*, trans. Nicholas Walker, Cambridge, 1999, pp. 320–1. See also NaS IV. 1.2, p. 71; *An Introduction to Dialectics*, Walker, pp. 46–7)

19   In Aristotle's philosophy, *sterēsis* signifies 'lack' or 'privation', a negation of some feature or attribute of a thing. Thus 'blindness' is the privation of the power of vision with respect to the eye. See Aristotle, *Metaphysics*, Book V, 22, and *Categories*, 12a26–31.

20   Joseph de Maistre (1753–1821) was a member of the Catholic nobility who fled to Saint Petersburg during the French Revolution and became the most important theological thinker of the counter-revolutionary movement. He vigorously opposed the French Republic as an incarnation of all evil and defended the absolutist claims of the sovereign as the representative of divine power on earth, who was supposed to lead human history towards salvation in the Christian sense.

21   Adorno is referring not so much to the idea of a substantial or traditional social order in Hegel as to his use of the word 'substantial' in the sense of 'that which exists independently' or 'that which has being in and for itself' (Hegel, *Werke*, vol. 2: *Phänomenologie des Geistes*, p. 110; *Hegel's Phenomenology of Spirit*, Miller, p. 82).

Lecture 15

1   The transcription of the lecture indicates a gap immediately after the opening address. It seems likely that Adorno made certain introductory remarks at this point which were omitted because they had nothing specifically to do with the substance of the lecture that follows.

2   Under Gunter d'Alquen (1910–1998) the weekly newspaper and Nazi propaganda sheet *Das schwarze Korps: Zeitung der Schutzstaffeln der NSDP – Organ der Reichsführung SS* enjoyed a circulation in National Socialist Germany second only to the *Völkischer Beobachter*.

3   Alfred Rosenberg (1893–1946) was a leading ideologist for the 'Third Reich' who published his anti-Semitic text *Der Mythus des 20. Jahrhunderts* in 1930. He was condemned to death at the Nuremberg Trials and executed in 1946.
4   This was actually a speech delivered behind closed doors at the Twentieth Party Congress of the Soviet Union (14–26 February 1956, in Moscow). Nikita Khrushchev (1894–1971) used this as an opportunity to accuse Stalin (1878–1953) of crimes against the people, while proclaiming Lenin (1870–1924) as a shining example to the nation. The speech is generally regarded as the beginning of the process of de-Stalinization in the Soviet Union.
5   In contrast to Filmer and in some respect even Hobbes, thinkers such as Locke and Montesquieu sought to legitimate specific forms of government by reference to the idea of citizenship itself rather than by recourse to the Bible. They thought that representative government was best suited to ameliorate the tension between the exercise of political authority and the demand for the greatest possible degree of freedom. It was on the basis of liberal ideas of this kind that the statesman Thomas Jefferson (1743–1826), later to become the third president of the United States, composed the federalist-republican Declaration of Independence, which proclaimed the separation of the original thirteen 'states of America' from Great Britain in 1776 and thereby affirmed the sovereignty of the new nation.
6   See Lecture 2, note 22.
7   Reading 'Gesellschaft' instead of 'Möglichkeit' here.
8   See Lecture 12, note 5.
9   *Brave New World by* Aldous Huxley (1894–1963) was published in London in 1932. In the same year the novel was translated into German by Herberth E. Herlitschka under the title *Welt – wohin?* (Leipzig). See Adorno, 'Aldous Huxley und die Utopie', GS 10.1, pp. 97–122; *Prisms*, Weber, pp. 95–117, specifically p. 103.
10 See Helmut Schelsky, *Die skeptische Generation*, Dusseldorf, 1957.
11 Adorno is thinking of the study which was put together between 1957 and 1959 by Jürgen Habermas (b. 1929), Ludwig von Friedeburg, Christoph Oehler (1928–2001), and Friedrich Weltz (b. 1927). In the chapter entitled 'Democratic Potential' they write:

> Empirical observations such as those assembled here cannot smoothly be extrapolated to form the picture of a more levelled-out form of middle-class society. There is no question of the dissolution or reduction of the structure of authority and thus also of prestige in contemporary society. The tendencies towards such processes of levelling out have only advanced in the sphere of consumption. In spite of this, the differences in levels of income of particular groups are still considerable and remain relatively fixed. (Habermas et al., *Student und Politik: Eine soziologische Untersuchung zum politischen Bewußtsein Frankfurter Studenten*, 2nd edn, Neuwied, 1967, p. 225)

According to the Archiv des Instituts für Sozialforschung, the manuscript submitted as the basis for the published edition was corrected and supplemented by Adorno.

12   The debate over so-called revisionism in the context of German social democracy began from around 1896 in connection with the Erfurt Programme of 1891, when Eduard Bernstein (1850–1932) and those associated with him challenged the revolutionary Marxism that was based on the appeal to ongoing class struggle and argued instead for a more moderate and reformist approach to socialism. Prominent opponents of the revisionist approach included Rosa Luxemburg (1871–1919), Clara Zetkin (1857–1933) and Karl Kautsky (1854–1938).

13   Hendrik de Man (1885–1953) was a nationalistically inclined religious 'socialist' who later adopted an openly fascist outlook and collaborated with the authorities during the Nazi occupation of Belgium. He had taught social psychology at the University of Frankfurt between 1929 and 1933.

14   See Karl Bednarik, *Der junge Arbeiter von heute – ein neuer Typ*, Stuttgart, 1953.

15   In his book *Ideology and Utopia*, Karl Mannheim had distinguished the limited or 'particular' concept of ideology from the 'total' concept of ideology, although not precisely in the way that Adorno presents it here. 'Whereas the particular conception of ideology designates only a *part* of the opponent's assertions as ideologies – and this only with reference to their content, the total conception calls into question the opponent's total Weltanschauung (including his conceptual apparatus), and attempts to understand these concepts as an outgrowth of the collective life of which he partakes' (Mannheim, *Ideologie und Utopie*, p. 54; *Ideology and Utopia*, Wirth and Shils, p. 50). Thus 'the particular conception of ideology operates primarily with a *psychology of interests*, while the total conception of ideology uses a more formal functional analysis, without any reference to motivations, confining itself to an objective description of the structural differences in minds operating in different social settings' (ibid., p. 55; Wirth and Shils, p. 51).

16   A theory of society that would try and ignore the fact that the predicament of the workers today has changed from that described in the classic analyses of Marx and Engels, the fact, to put it simply, that the proletariat today actually does have more to lose than its chains, namely its little car or its motorbike – though it is open to question whether these are not perhaps a more sublimated version of chains – such a theory is undoubtedly inadequate; and if we do not acknowledge these aspects or moments in our own theoretical reflection, the latter will remain damagingly abstract and fail to reach the phenomena themselves. (NaS IV.12, p. 65)

17   Reading 'hergestellt' for 'dargestellt'.

Lecture 16

1 See Lecture 15, note 11.
2 Adorno took over the concept of the 'underlying population' from Thorsten Veblen (1857–1929) (see Adorno, *Spätkapitalismus oder Industriegesellschaft?*, GS 8, p. 364). Veblen often used the term as it is explained by Adorno in this lecture, especially in his book *The Engineers and the Price System* (New York, 1921).
3 See Lecture 11, note 16.
4 See, for example, the opening chapter of Robert Filmer's *Patriarcha* (see Lecture 11, note 16): 'That the first kings were fathers of families.'
5 It has not been possible to identify exactly what Adorno is referring to here.

6 Man is the ideology of dehumanization. Conclusions are drawn from certain categories which remind us of somewhat primal social relationships, where the institutions of exchange do not yet have complete power over the relationships of men. From those categories it is concluded that their core, man, is immediately present among contemporary men, that he is there to realize his eidos. Past forms of societalization, prior to the division of labor, are surreptitiously adopted as if they were eternal. (GS 6, pp. 452f.; *The Jargon of Authenticity*, Tarnowski and Will, p. 59)

7 See Henri Bergson, *Matière et mémoire: essai sur la relation du corps à l'esprit*, Paris, 1896; *Matter and Memory*, trans. David G. Payne et al., Createspace Independent Publishing Platform, 2016.

8 Every form of cognition, including Bergson's own, needs the rationality he scorns, and needs it precisely at the moment of concretion. Absolutized duration, pure becoming, the actus purus – these would revert to the same timelessness which Bergson chides in metaphysics since Plato and Aristotle ... Bergson took his bearings, just like his positivistic arch-enemies, from the *données immédiates de la conscience*, as Husserl similarly did from the phenomena of the stream of consciousness. Both of them keep to the realm of subjective immanence. To be insisted upon, against both, would be what they pursue in vain: to say, against Wittgenstein, what cannot be said. (GS 6, pp. 20f.; *Negative Dialectics*, Ashton, p. 9; translation amended)

9 The first line of the poem 'Der alte Landman an seinen Sohn' by Ludwig Christoph Heinrich Hölty (1748–1776). The poem was set to music by Mozart in 1791.
10 Once again Adorno is referring to Martin Heidegger's conception of fundamental ontology:

The celebration of the meaningless as meaning is mythical, like the ritualistic repetition of natural relations by particular symbolic actions, as if this made them into something beyond nature. Categories such as *Angst*

– that we surely have no right to claim are everlasting – are transfigured into constituents of being as such, as if they came before existence, and were its a priori. They are installed as the very 'meaning' which at the present state of history cannot be positively or immediately named. What is meaningless is invested with meaning, for the meaning of being is supposed to be revealed precisely in its counterpart, in mere existence as its form. (GS 6, p.125; *Negative Dialectics*, Ashton, p. 119 [translation modified])

11 The text in question is Walter Benjamin's essay *The Paris of the Second Empire in Baudelaire* (Benjamin, *Gesammelte Schriften*, vol. I.2: *Abhandlungen*, ed. Rolf Tiedemann and Hermann Schweppenhäuser, pp. 511–604; an English translation of the essay is included in Benjamin, *Charles Baudelaire: A Lyric Poet in the Era of High Capitalism*, trans. Harry Zohn et al., Verso, 1997, pp. 9–106). Although Benjamin had composed this text in 1938, at Horkheimer's behest, for publication in the *Zeitschrift für Sozialforschung*, it was not accepted for publication in the end. In a letter of 10 November 1938 Adorno detailed certain criticisms of the piece and urged Benjamin 'to forgo publication of the present version' (Theodor W. Adorno and Walter Benjamin, *Briefwechsel 1928–1940*, p. 371; Theodor W. Adorno and Walter Benjamin, *The Complete Correspondence 1928–1940*, trans. Nicholas Walker, Cambridge, 1999, p. 285). Adorno explains one of his reasons as follows:

> Even though Baudelaire's wine poems may have been occasioned by the wine duty or the town gates, the recurrence of these motifs in his oeuvre can only be explained by the overall social and economic tendencies of the age – that is, in keeping with your formulation of the problem *sensu strictissimo*, through analysis of the commodity form in Baudelaire's epoch … The direct inference from the duty on wine to L'Ame du vin imputes to phenomena precisely the kind of spontaneity, tangibility and density which they have lost under capitalism. (Ibid., p. 368; p. 283). (See also NaS IV.2, p. 130; *An Introduction to Dialectics*, Walker, p. 88)

12 Baudelaire's cycle of poems 'Le Vin', from *Les Fleurs du mal*, comprises 'L'Ame du vin', 'Le Vin des chiffoniers', 'Le Vin du l'assassin', 'Le Vin du solitaire', and 'Le Vin des amants'.

13 See Benjamin, *Gesammelte Schriften*, vol. I.2, pp. 519–21; *Charles Baudelaire: A Lyric Poet in the Era of High Capitalism*, Zohn, pp. 17–20.

14 Benjamin had responded to Adorno's criticisms in a letter of 9 December 1938:

> The appearance of closed facticity which attaches to philological investigation and places the investigator under its spell, dissolves precisely to the degree in which the object is construed from a historical perspective. The base lines of this construction converge in our own historical experience.

In this way the object constitutes itself as a monad. And in the monad everything that lay formerly mythically petrified within the given text comes alive. Therefore, it strikes me as a misjudgement of the issue when you identify 'a direct inference from the wine duty to L'Ame du vin'. This conjunction was established quite legitimately in the philological context – just as we would also have to do in interpreting an ancient classical author. (Theodor W. Adorno and Walter Benjamin, *Briefwechsel 1928–1940*, p. 380; Walker, p. 292)

15 See NaS IV.2, pp. 130f., and corresponding note, p. 380 (*An Introduction to Dialectics*, Walker, p. 88, and note 16 on p. 281), where it is explained that 'what Benjamin was talking about here was not the suburbs (*banlieue*) but the town gate (*barrière*) which separated the suburbs from the city proper, and where the wine tax was levied', as Adorno had originally put it correctly in his letter to Benjamin of 10 November 1938 (see note 11 above).

16 Reading 'Aufweichungen' for 'Ausweichungen' here.

17 The earliest documented use of this word in Brecht is in 1943 (see Bertold Brecht, [Eine deutsch-jüdische Arztfamilie], in *Werke*, ed. Werner Hecht et al., vol. 22.1, Frankfurt am Main, 1993, pp. 32f.).

18 In the lecture Adorno refers mistakenly to the year 1931. In fact both the essays appeared in the *Zeitschrift für Sozialforschung* in 1932. See Leo Löwenthal, 'Zur gesellschaftlichen Lage der Literatur', *ZfS*, 1/1–2 (1932), pp. 85–102 (now under the title 'Zur gesellschaftlichen Lage der Literaturwissenschaft', in Leo Löwenthal, *Schriften*, ed. Henri Dubiel, Frankfurt am Main, 1980–, vol. 1, pp. 309–27); and T. W. Adorno, 'Zur gesellschaftlichen Lage der Musik, *ZfS*, 1/1–2, pp. 356–78 and 1/3, pp. 356–78 (now in GS 18, pp. 729–77; 'The Social Situation of Music', in Adorno, *Essays on Music*, ed. Richard Leppert, Oakland, CA, 2002, pp. 391–433).

19 An article which had appeared in the student newspaper *Discus* described Löwenthal (1900–1993) in the following terms:

> Leo Löwenthal, now sixty, was formerly involved with the Institute for Social Research, emigrated to the United States, where he is currently a professor at Berkeley, and published his pre-war contributions in the *Zeitschrift für Sozialforschung*, a journal that is very difficult to access today. ... His studies on serious and popular literature were principally concerned with the theory and method of the sociology of literature in relation to mass communication research. (Wolfgang Zapf, 'Zur Diskussion über Ziele und Grenzen der Literatursoziologie', *Discus*, 10/4 [1960], p. 6 [special number])

Löwenthal's writings on literature are collected in the first two volumes of Dubiel's edition of the *Schriften* (note 18 above): vol. 1: *Literatur und Massenkultur*, and vol. 2: *Das bürgerliche Bewußtsein in der Literatur*.

20 Löwenthal, 'Zur gesellschaftlichen Lage der Literatur', p. 97.

21　The Swiss poet Conrad Ferdinand Meyer (1825–1898) was regarded as one of the finest German-language poets of the *Gründerzeit*, the period of initial German economic growth after the establishment of the German Empire in 1870.

22　Löwenthal, 'Zur gesellschaftlichen Lage der Literatur', pp. 97f.

23　Adorno's suggestion that Löwenthal's essay takes Storm's work as the expression of a petit bourgeois consciousness springs from erroneously identifying the categories of author and narrator, something which cannot be laid at Löwenthal's door. The latter specifically pointed out, as Adorno's earlier quotation indicates, that the petit bourgeois figure is an aspect or moment that belongs to the deliberate literary shaping of the work and allows for the articulation of a specific outlook or perspective. If the narrator portrays a consciousness of this kind, this does not imply that Löwenthal ascribes this same consciousness to the author of the work.

24　Reading 'der' for 'zur'.

25　'KuBa' was the pseudonym adopted by the East German writer Kurt Barthel (1914–1967). In 1949 he had published a 'Cantata for Stalin'. As a member of the Central Committee of the Socialist Unity Party (the official name of the East German communist party), he was also a deputy in the *Volkskammer* (Parliament) of the former German Democratic Republic. His 'Karl Marx Cantata' was nonetheless attacked as 'formalistic' in character.

26　Löwenthal, 'Zur gesellschaftlichen Lage der Literatur', p. 98.

27　The passage Adorno is referring to reads: 'On the one side, it indicates the dignity of what is presented, while on the other it raises the quite singular aspect, which is essential, out of the otherwise indifferent multiplicity of phenomena' (ibid.).

28　The Norwegian writer Knut Hamsun (1859–1952) received the Nobel Prize for Literature in 1920 for a work that could be described as 'literature of the land', namely his novel *Markens Grøde* of 1917.

29　The daily life and the work of Norwegian fishermen is an idyllic element that permeates Hamsun's trilogy of novels: *Landstrykere*, *August* and *Men Livet lever*. All three novels were translated into German between 1927 and 1933.

30　Meyer frequently let his texts appear in the journal *Deutsche Rundschau* (Verlag der Gebrüder Paetel, Berlin) in advance of their more general publication; Storm similarly let his texts appear for the first time in *Westermanns Monatshefte* (Verlag von Georg Westermann, Braunschweig).

31　In Marxist-Leninist terminology, the concept of the petit bourgeois mentality or the petit bourgeois individual was often deployed to discredit certain cultural, intellectual and political currents and their representatives, which were not welcome to the official ruling ideology, but which could not unambiguously be ascribed to a merely bourgeois or even reactionary standpoint.

32 *Der Untertan* (DDR, 1951), a film directed by Wolfgang Staudte, to a screenplay by Wolfgang Staudte and Fritz Staudte, and based on the novel of the same title by Heinrich Mann (1917–1950). The novel appeared in English under the title *Man of Straw*, trans. Ernest Boyd, Penguin, 1984.

Lecture 17

1 See Lecture 11, note 1.
2 The transcription of the lectures indicates some missing material at this point.
3 The industrialist Friedrich Flick (1883–1972) at the height of his career was the richest man in Germany and one of the richest individuals in the world. He had made his wealth above all under National Socialism through the policy of 'Aryanization' and by the extensive use of slave labour in his various business enterprises, drawing on inmates of concentration camps, foreign workers and prisoners of war. In 1947 the American Military Court at the Nuremberg Trials sentenced him to seven years in prison on account of war crimes, among other things. However, he was at liberty once more by 1950, and in 1963 he was actually awarded the *Große Bundesverdienstkreuz* (Order of Merit of the Federal Republic of Germany).
4 It is possible that Adorno was thinking of Heinrich Heine's poem 'Friedrike' of 1823 (*Werke und Briefe in zehn Bänden*, ed. Hans Kaufmann, end edn, Berlin, 1972, vol. 1, pp. 269f.):

> Leave Berlin, with its sandy ground
> Its thin tea, and hyper-clever people
> Who know what God and World, and they themselves,
> Ultimately mean, instructed by Hegelian understanding.
>
> Follow us to India, the land of blazing sun
> ...
> There, where the palm trees waft and the waves glitter
> ...
> The Himalayas glow in the sunset,
> From nocturnal groves the elephant herd bursts forth and roars –
> An image! An image! My horse for a compelling image!

5 For the original context of the line from *Götz von Berlichingen*, see *Goethes Werke* (*Hamburger Ausgabe*), ed. Erich Trunz, Hamburg, 1948–, vol. 4, p. 88.
6 See Lecture 16, pp. 171–81.
7 Adorno often criticized the popular modern tendency to invoke 'the human being' as the ultimate point of reference, most emphatically perhaps in *The Jargon of Authenticity* (see GS 6, p. 453; Will and Tarnowski, p. 60).
8 See Lecture 16, pp. 175f.

9 In his book *Mensch und Gesellschaft im Zeitalter des Umbaus* (Man and Society in an Age of Reconstruction) (Leiden, 1935) Karl Mannheim had specifically talked about the connection between social development and the formation of elites. There he writes:

> It hardly needs pointing out that the recently proclaimed race-principle, interestingly enough, is no longer the same as the genuine blood-principle. It is no longer a matter, as it used to be, of the purity of aristocratic minority stocks and their traditions. For the principle has become democratic and quite suddenly offers to the great masses of the population the privilege of social ascendancy without any achievement. Formerly it was an often envied privilege of the aristocracy to lay claim to certain functions and positions primarily by virtue of their birth and blood, and it was only in a quite secondary sense that they justified their success in terms of achievement. Now the slightest individual who belongs to a particular group is allowed the advantage of appealing not to any achievement but simply to his origins ... It is now suddenly demanded that enormous masses of people should be privileged, that the man in the street should enjoy the privilege of a good racial background without regard to achievement. (Ibid., p. 69)

Adorno discusses this theory of elites in his essay 'The Sociology of Knowledge and its Consciousness', where he responds directly to this book:

> Mannheim designates 'blood, property, and achievement' as the selection principles of the elites. His passion for destroying ideologies does not lead him to consider even once the legitimacy of these principles; he is actually able, during Hitler's lifetime, to speak of a 'genuine blood-principle', which is supposed to have formerly guaranteed 'the purity of aristocratic minority stocks and their traditions'. From this to the new aristocracy of blood and soil it is only a step. Mannheim's general cultural pessimism prevents him from taking that step. As far as he is concerned, there is still too little blood. He dreads a 'mass democracy' in which blood and property would disappear as principles of selection; the all too rapid change of elites would threaten continuity. He is particularly concerned with the fact that things are no longer quite right with the esoteric doctrine of the 'genuine blood-principle'. 'It has become democratic and quite suddenly offers to the great masses of the population the privilege of social ascendancy without any achievement.' Just as the nobility of the past was never any more noble than anyone else, the aristocracy of today has neither an objective nor a subjective interest in really relinquishing the principle of privilege. (GS 10.1, pp. 31–46; *Prisms*, Weber, pp. 39–40)

10 In *Ideology and Utopia*, Mannheim does speak of a 'connection to being or existence' (*Seinsverbundenheit*) – an expression which has also been rendered in the English translation of the book as 'the existential determination of knowledge'. At the beginning of the final chapter Mannheim writes: 'The sociology of knowledge is one of the youngest branches of sociology; as theory it seeks to analyse the relationship

between knowledge and existence; as historical-sociological research it seeks to trace the forms which this relationship has taken in the intellectual development of mankind' (*Ideology and Utopia*, Wirth and Shils, p. 237; the following subsection 2a, which in the English translation appears as 'The Theory of the Social Determination of Knowledge', appears in the original as 'Die Lehre von der Faktizität der Seinsverbundenheit', ibid., p. 230; Wirth and Shils, p. 239. In the German, the expression in question also sometimes appears in a specifically qualified way in inverted commas as: 'die sogennante "Seinsverbundenheit"' ('what is known as the relationship to being').)

11   See Lecture 6, note 14.
12   See Lecture 7, pp. 73–6.
13   In his book *The Forms of Knowing and Society*, published in 1925, Scheler claims that 'it is a perfectly recognizable fact that class position *largely determines* both the *ethos* and the *mode of thought [Denkart]* – and by no means simply the object and content of thinking and knowing' (Max Scheler, *Die Wissensformen und die Gesellschaft*, in *Gesammelte Werke*, ed. M. Scheler and Manfred Frings, Berlin, 1954–, vol. 8, p. 171. On the same page at the bottom Scheler provides a list that is supposed to present the various 'modes of thought determined by social class'. See Adorno's specific discussion of this list in his *Beitrag zur Ideologielehre*, GS 8, p. 470). After his presentation of these 'modes of thought' Scheler continues as follows:

> These idols are absorbed by the classes in question *traditionally* – with their mother's milk, as it were. To that extent the economistic theory of knowledge is quite correct. But the mistake arises when we simply *identify* these class-determined systems of idols, firstly, with the forms of being and becoming which belong to things and, secondly, with the forms of thought, perception and evaluation which are content-independent, and when we judge these forms on analogy with these categorial perspectives as defined by particular class interests; and then, thirdly, when we not only regard these *tendencies* to think in a certain way and these *motivations* for perceiving things in a certain way as 'necessary' – which in fact they are – but also regard them as necessary in the causal sense, so that all individuals belonging to the social class in question *must* follow such tendencies and inclinations even where the conscious and spontaneous cognitive activity of the mind is concerned. The prejudices which derive from belonging to a particular class, and also the formal laws governing the formation of such class prejudices, are *in principle eliminable* for any individual of a given class. They can be neutralized – especially once their sociologically conditioned character is recognized on the basis of the sociological theory of idols itself – by any individual, whatever their class position may be. (Scheler, *Die Wissensformen und die Gesellschaft*, p. 172)

Adorno also alludes to this question in one section of his inaugural address of 1931, 'Die Aktualität der Philosophie' (GS 1, pp. 328f.).

14   Compare the following passage:

> But it is not really appropriate for intellectual representatives of any class to accuse one another, with regard to these and other questions, of simply defending an ideology of domination or an ideology of oppression, as the case may be ... If there really were no legitimate standpoint for the human mind which could rise above all class ideologies and the special interests and perspectives associated with them, then any possible knowledge of truth would be nothing but illusion. All knowledge would then ... *be merely a function of the outcome of class struggles of one kind or another*. ... On the other hand, it is a perfectly recognizable fact that class position *largely determines* both the *ethos* and the *mode of thought* ... We have already suggested how this apparent contradiction can be overcome: by seeing that the categorial systems of thinking, perceiving and valuing which form, develop and evolve through functionalizing the apprehension of essential forms may *also* be determined in class terms as far as specific *selection* and *application* is concerned, though certainly not in terms of their validity and possible origin. (Scheler, *Die Wissensformen und die Gesellschaft*, pp. 170f.)

15 For Adorno's understanding of Hegel's concept of mediation, see Lecture 3 of his *Einführung in die Dialektik* (NaS IV.2, pp. 28–42; *An Introduction to Dialectics*, Walker, pp. 15–25).

16 In the short text, 'Kierkegaard noch einmal', which was added to the later book version of Adorno's Habilitation (post-doctoral dissertation) on Kierkegaard, he says this:

> Kierkegaard's understanding of Hegel ... is problematic, remarkably similar, in this, to the situation with Marx. Hegel's central concept, which Kierkegaard contests so strongly, that of mediation, is crudely misinterpreted. In Hegel, mediation transpires in and through the extremes. The concept springs over into contradiction from out of itself, which means, in Hegelian language: the concept is mediated within itself. Kierkegaard, however, misread Hegelian mediation in a simplistic way as a middle path between concepts, as a kind of moderating compromise. (GS 2, p. 247)

17 Compare Adorno's remarks in *Metakritik der Erkenntnistheorie*: 'It is not, as relativism would have it, truth in history, but rather history in truth. Now is the time for decisive renunciation of the concept of "timeless truth". Yet truth is not, as Marxism claims, a temporal function of cognizing, but rather bound to a core of time which resides both in the cognized and the cognizer' (GS, p. 141; *Against Epistemology: A Metacritique*, Domingo, p. 135). Adorno is citing from the materials of Walter Benjamin's Arcades Project (*Gesammelte Werke*, vol. V.1., *Das Passagen-Werk*, ed. Rolf Tiedemann, p. 578 [N 3, 2]).

18 The relevant work here is *Metakritik der Erkenntnistheorie* (GS 5, pp. 7–245; *Against Epistemology: A Metacritique*.)

19 Adorno discussed this aspect of Husserl's thought in the *Metakritik der Erkenntnistheorie*: 'The first volume of the *Logical Investigations* propounds the thesis that logical propositions are valid for any and all

possible judgements. Since they apply to any thinking at all of any object at all, they attain "truth in itself"' (GS 5, p. 73; *Against Epistemology*, Domingo, p. 66). A little further on (GS 5, p. 81; Domingo, pp. 74–5) Adorno cites part of the following passage from the first volume of the *Logical Investigations*, where Husserl emphasizes the strict separation between genesis and validity:

> It is clearly an enterprise of considerable scientific importance to show the psychological ways and means through which this ... idea of a world as object of experience is developed and continued ... But this entire investigation is a matter of indifference from the epistemological point of view. ... The question is not how experience, whether naïve or scientific experience, arises but rather what content it must possess in order to be objectively valid knowledge; the question is what the ideal elements and laws are which found such objective validity of real knowledge (and more universally: of knowledge in general), and how this accomplishment is actually to be understood. In other words: we are interested not in the becoming or change of the world representation, but in the objective right with which the world representation of science is contrasted with every other representation of the world, with which it affirms its world as the objectively true one. (Edmund Husserl, *Husserliana*, vol. XVIII: *Logische Untersuchungen, Erster Teil: Prolegomena zur reinen Logik*, ed. Elmar Holenstein, pp. 208f.; *Logical Investigations, Part I*, trans. J. N. Findlay, see p. 207)

20 'Judgements as completed products of a "constitution" or "genesis" can and must be addressed in these terms. For it is an essential characteristic of such products that they are "senses" which, as genetic sense implicates, bear a kind of historicity within themselves' (Husserl, *Husserliana*, vol. XVII: *Formale und Transzendentale Logik*, ed. Paul Janssen, p. 215; *Formal and Transcendental Logic*, trans. D. Cairns, The Hague: Nijhoff, 1969, see pp 183f.). See GS 5, p. 140; *Against Epistemology*, p. 135).

21 In this particular regard, see Lecture 9.

22 In the lectures on Kant's first *Critique*, Adorno notes that, 'when we utter a judgement, a synthesising judgement, this synthesis is not simply something imposed on us arbitrarily by things external to us. Rather, 2+2 must actually *be* 4 in order for us to be able to express the judgement 2+2 = 4. For without that synthesis the proposition 2+2 could not even be thought' (NaS IV.4, p. 229; *Kant's Critique of Pure Reason*, Livingstone, p. 151).

Lecture 18

1 The authors of *Dialectic of Enlightenment* show how enlightenment and mythology have a shared primal history, namely the history of the domination of nature: 'Myth is already enlightenment, and

enlightenment reverts to mythology' (GS 3, p. 13; *Dialectic of Enlightenment*, Jephcott, p. xviii).
2 See GS 5, pp. 79–85; *Against Epistemology*, Domingo, pp. 72–8.
3 This expression, in the formulation 'veritas est adaequatio rei et intellectus' [lit.: truth is the agreement of thing and the intellect, or: the agreement of thought and being], goes back to Thomas Aquinas.
4 Adorno is talking about 'the idea of universal mediation, which in Hegel as in Marx produces the totality' (GS 10.1, p. 247; *Prisms*, Weber, p. 236), namely the thought that all the aspects or moments of the whole are mediated with the whole and with themselves in such a way that no one aspect or moment enjoys any special priority, whether epistemological or ontological, over any other.
5 In the chapter '"Reason" in Philosophy', from *Twilight of the Idols*, Nietzsche observes:

> The *other* idiosyncrasy of the philosophers is no less dangerous; it consists in confusing the last and the first. They place that which comes at the end – unfortunately! for it ought not to come at all! – namely, the 'highest concepts,' which means the most general, the emptiest concepts, the last smoke of evaporating reality, in the beginning, *as* the beginning. This again is nothing but their way of showing reverence: the higher *may* not [*darf* nicht] grow out of the lower, *may* not have grown at all. Moral: whatever is of the first rank must be *causa sui* [self-caused]. Origin out of something else is considered an objection, a questioning of value. All the highest values are of the first rank; all the highest concepts, that which has being, the unconditional, the good, the true, the perfect – all these cannot have become and *must* therefore be *causa sui*. (Nietzsche, *Werke in drei Bänden*, vol. 2, pp. 958f.; *Twilight of the Idols*, in *The Portable Nietzsche*, Kaufmann, pp. 481–2)

6 Platonic thought rests on a distinction between the ontic and the epistemic value of that which becomes and has become, namely 'the sensible', and that which possesses genuine being, namely 'the intelligible'. In Plato's philosophy it is quite true that mathematics enjoys a certain privileged status, but it is still regarded as merely the propaedeutic to dialectic. Thus numbers and geometrical objects are ontically secondary in relation to the Ideas, even though they too belong to the realm of that which has being. Mathematical entities are grasped by discursive thought (*dianoia*), while the Ideas are grasped by the higher faculty of the intellect (*nous*). The image of the line which Plato deploys in the *Republic* (Bk. 6, 509d4–511e5) is designed to exhibit these different levels with respect to the cognitive faculties, the philosophical method and the corresponding objects of knowledge. See also *Timaeus* 27d5–29c3 for Plato's explicit separation of 'that which becomes' (*to gignomenon*; τὸ γιγνόμενον) and 'that which is' (*to on*; τὸ ὄν), and his theoretical account of how the lower cognitive faculties are concerned with the realm of the former while the higher cognitive faculties are concerned with the latter. Thus truth is encountered solely in the realm

of 'that which is', while the realm of 'that which comes to be' remains the domain of 'opinion.'

7 Thus Wagner had written:

> Mozart, who was far closer in this regard to the Italian conception of melodic form, often and indeed usually fell back on the predictable musical phrasing which frequently reveals his symphonic movements to us in the light of so-called *Tafelmusik* [music played during meals or other social gatherings], namely music which in the midst all the attractive melodies also furnishes attractive sounds which simply serve as background for the conversation: with the ever so reliably recurring and slightly noisy cadences of a Mozartian symphony, it has always seemed to me at least that one can still hear the sound of the dishes being served and cleared away at the princely table. (Richard Wagner, *Zukunftsmusik*, in *Sämtliche Schriften und Dichtungen*, Leipzig [1911], vol. 7, p. 126)

8 See Thrasybulos G. Georgiades, *Das musikalische Theater*, Munich, 1965. See NaS I.1, p. 73 [fr. 107]; *Beethoven: The Philosophy of Music*, trans. Edmund Jephcott, Cambridge, 1998, p. 42.

9 In Book 6 of his treatise *De musica* (composed between 387 and 389 AD) Saint Augustine argues that music can only properly be regarded as valuable insofar as it serves to strengthen and deepen the Christian faith of the believer.

10 In his book on Beethoven, which was never brought to completion, Adorno had intended to show how the composer actually achieved in music what Hegel had essentially tried to do in his *Logic*: 'The Beethoven study must also yield a philosophy of music, that is, it must decisively establish the relation of music to conceptual logic. Only then will the comparison with Hegel's *Logic*, and therefore the interpretation of Beethoven, be not just an analogy but the thing itself' (NaS I.1, p. 31 [fr. 26]; *Beethoven*, Jephcott, p. 11).

11 On 19 and 26 July 1960 Otwin Massing (b. 1934) presented a seminar paper on 'The Relationship between Philosophy and Sociology in Karl Mannheim' in Adorno's sociology seminar that addressed 'Texts on the Relationship between Philosophy and Sociology'.

12 Karl Mannheim explains his theory of the 'Seinsverbundenheit des Denkens' ('the intrinsic relationship between thought and being' or 'the existential determination of thought' as Wirth and Shils translate it) in the following terms:

> The existential determination of thought may be regarded as a demonstrated fact in those realms of thought in which we can show (a) that the process of knowing does not actually develop historically in accordance with immanent laws, that it does not follow only from the 'nature of things' or from 'pure logical possibilities', and that it is not driven by an 'inner dialectic' [*einer inneren 'geistigen Dialektik'*]. On the contrary, the emergence and the crystallization of actual thought is influenced in many decisive points by extra-theoretical factors of the most diverse sort. These may be called, in contradistinction to purely theoretical factors,

'existential factors' [*Seinsfaktoren*]. This existential determination of thought will also have to be regarded as a fact (b) if the influence of these existential factors on the concrete content of knowledge is of more than mere peripheral importance, if they are relevant not only to the genesis of ideas [*von bloß genetischer Relevanz*], but penetrate into their forms and content and if, furthermore, they decisively determine the scope and the intensity of our experience and observation, i.e. that which we formerly referred to as the 'perspective' of the subject [*Aspektstruktur einer Erkenntnis*]. (*Ideologie und Utopie*, p. 230; *Ideology and Utopia*, London, 1991, Wirth and Shils, pp. 239–40)

A little further on Mannheim says: 'We may regard competition [*Konkurrenz*] as such a representative case in which extra-theoretical processes affect the emergence and the direction of the development of knowledge' (ibid., p. 231; Wirth and Shils, p. 241).

13 It was the Greek Sophists who first explicitly reflected upon the loss of normative validity which in many ways had started to befall traditional ideas and values in the fifth century BC. Thus religious and ethical ideas were increasingly regarded as something that was entirely dependent on and relative to the standpoint of the individual, or the standpoints adopted by different cultures. Plato's metaphysics begins with the distinction between two kinds of entities, the changeable objects of sensory perception and the unchanging Ideas (*Phaedo*, 79a6). In a way Plato takes up the anthropocentric conception that was advanced by the Sophists, but at the same time he locates this within a dualistic conception of the world and of knowledge, a conception which insists that truth can be attained only by looking towards the 'objective' nature of the Ideas. In this sense the philosophy of Plato could be understood as a deeply conservative reaction to the movement of 'enlightenment' inaugurated by the Sophists. It is this fundamental distinction between two kinds of entity – between the Idea and the particular or individual thing – that Aristotle attempts to challenge and to offer a mediating solution in the concept of substance (*ousia*; οὐσία) as developed in his own *Metaphysics* (especially Book VII–IX).

14 Plato's famous metaphor of the sun furnishes an exemplary image for the role of reason in his philosophy (*Republic*, Bk VI, 506d6–509b10). The Idea of the Good vouchsafes truth to what is known and vouchsafes the capacity to know it to the knower. It also bestows being and essence upon the thing known. It was precisely this attempt to essentialize and to ontologize ethics that Aristotle criticized so strongly.

15 By using the Greek word *chōris* [separated] here, Adorno is alluding to the whole problem of *chōrismos* [separation] as this emerged in the history of philosophy. One of the fundamental objections to the Platonic 'theory of Ideas' was the difficulty of understanding precisely how the Ideas could be utterly 'separated' or entirely remote from the very things they were supposed to constitute. Plato repeatedly emphasizes the transcendence of the world of the Ideas, although this transcendence also appears to be relativized by the essential concept of 'participation'.

Plato himself uses the word *chōris* to describe the separation involved in the Ideas (*Parmenides*, 129d7–129e1), although in that context he is actually talking about the distinction and separation of the Ideas from one another. The *mē on* in the sense of non-being, but also in the sense of 'that which becomes', of the sensible or 'the empirical world' as Adorno puts it, is expressly discussed, among other places, in the *Timaeus* (27d5–28a4).

Adorno's Notes for the Lectures

1 Adorno's preparatory notes for the lecture course were written in an A4 notebook, from which the pages were not detached, leaving the reverse side of each page free for further notes or jottings. Subsequent additions (with the page number and an added 'a' or, in the case of a second page, an added 'b') were written on the reverse side of the preceding page. This explains why *2b*, for example, is found on the reverse side of p. 1 rather than of p. 2. The arrangement as it appears in the notebook can basically be described as follows (the entries in parentheses designate the reverse of the page in each case): *Lectures on Philosophy and Sociology (1a insertion a)); 1 (2b); 3 (4a); 4 (5a); 5 (unused); 6 (unused); 7 (unused); 8 (unused); 9 (10a); 10 (11a); 11 (12a); 12 (13a); 13 (unused); 14 (unused); 15 (unused).* As the materials are printed here, the insertions which are sometimes made on the reverse side of the sheet, and which were added later, are given in numerical order immediately after the front pages. Thus 1a insertion a) follows on from 1, 2b follows on from 2, and so on. To read the outline of the lectures straight through without reference to the insertions, one should note that p. 212 is continued on p. 215; p. 216 is continued on p. 219; p. 220 is continued on p. 223; p. 224 is continued on p. 227; p. 228 is continued on p. 230; p. 239 is continued on p. 241; p. 242 is continued on p. 244; p. 245 is continued on p. 247; and p. 248 is continued on p. 250.

2 The passage from Comte which Adorno refers to here was not actually used in the lecture. It runs as follows:

> The typical intellectual attitudes assumed under the regime of the theological-metaphysical Absolute still convey to most thinkers of today a very confused idea of the power and character of observations pursued in an a priori manner; such observations, if intelligently organized and rationally applied, undoubtedly allow us to reach successful conclusions in the end on account of the indispensible pointers through which the study of nature cannot fail to illuminate our rational behaviour – on the condition, that is, that a practical sense never ceases to guide the often highly complex totality of any concrete undertaking, something which it achieves by correlating the scientific data solely with the prior elements of the particular combinations involved. Every subordination of the practical to the theoretical, which would go beyond this measure, would

soon find itself exposed to difficult and extensive difficulties. (Auguste Comte, *Soziologie*, vol. III, p. 642)

3   See GS 5, p. 39; *Against Epistemology*, Domingo, p. 31; and especially NaS IV.14, p. 47, and the corresponding note on p. 245; *Metaphysics: Concept and Problems*, trans. Edmund Jephcott, Polity, 2000, pp. 28 and 157 (note 10). 'Per substantiam nihil aliud intelligere possumus, quam rem quae ita existit, ut nulla re indigeat ad existendum' (*Oeuvres de Descartes*, Adam and Tannery, vol. VIII.1: *Principia Philosophiae*, Paris, 1964. 'By substance we can only understand a thing which so exists that it needs no other thing for its existence' (René Descartes, *Principles of Philosophy*, trans. V. R. Miller and R. P. Miller, Dordrecht, 1983, p. 23).

4   A self-citation from *Metakritik der Erkenntnistheorie*:

> The researcher imagines that he prescribes laws to the world. The 'ordinary man' must obey such laws in practice. He can do nothing about it, and it all may correctly seem arbitrary to him. The fact, however, that the world is composed of things such as are surrendered to accidents of that sort, and of other things which, though they may not make the law, can comfort themselves with its existence, is no accident. It is itself the law of real society. No philosophy which discusses the 'representation of the world' can overlook it. But the abandonment of the empirical does not grant Husserl undiminished insight into such connections. Rather, he repeats with a shrug of the shoulders the lixiviated prejudice that it is all a matter of point of view. (GS 5, pp. 92f.; *Against Epistemology*, p. 86)

5   See Lecture 11, note 14.
6   The Sophist 'enlightenment' had constantly reflected on the distinction between *physis* (nature) and *thesis* (that which is 'set' or 'posited' by tradition or convention) or *nomos* (law). Such considerations led them to recognize the difference between the posited character of 'positive law' and the necessity that belongs to what nature requires. For both Plato and Aristotle slavery was one of the natural conditions of the *polis*.
7   Aristotle had arranged for the collection – which has survived only in part – of 158 political 'constitutions' as part of the preparations for his *Politics*. He dedicates Book II of that work to a detailed critical examination of utopian, historical and contemporary constitutions of one kind or another. He argues against Plato's utopian idea of the state on the grounds that its fundamental tendency to privilege unity runs up against the fact that a state consists of human beings who are different in kind from one another. For Aristotle, the state involves multiplicity by nature, and any attempt to interpret it strictly in terms of unity can only destroy its character (*Politics*, Bk II, 2, 1261a13–b9).
8   Panaeteus of Rhodes (180–110 BC) was a leading representative of the middle Stoa in the first and second century BC. His ethical ideas

exerted enormous influence on the world of ancient Rome after Cicero canonized his account of the virtues in 44 BC by developing and incorporating them into his own treatise *De officiis*.

9 *Nation Europa: Monatzeitschrift im Dienste der europäischen Neuordnung* was a far-right journal which was founded in 1951 by former member of the Waffen SS Arthur Ehrhardt (1896–1971) and former member of the SA Herbert Böhme (1907–1971). The journal continued to be published up until 2009.

10 In his book *The Elementary Forms of the Religious Life* Durkheim had set himself the task of reconciling empiricism and apriorism in order to furnish an adequate sociological theory of investigation and knowledge: 'The fundamental proposition of the apriorist theory is that knowledge is made up of two sorts of elements, which cannot be reduced into one another, and which are like two distinct layers superimposed one upon the other. Our hypothesis keeps this principle intact' (*The Elementary Forms of the Religious Life*, Swain, p. 15). As early as 1924 Wilhelm Jerusalem argued, in the context of a series of sociological studies edited by Max Scheler, that Durkheim 'had clearly fallen victim to the frequently committed error of taking the a priori in a temporal sense. But this completely contradicts Kant's thought and that of his contemporary successors and those who undertake to renew and develop his thought.' On the other hand, we must expressly recognize that 'the belief in a timeless and unchangeable logical structure of reason is the most important foundation of apriorism. But Durkheim ... cannot bring himself to believe in such a structure, and thus his sympathies for apriorist thinkers ultimately rest on a misunderstanding' (Jerusalem, 'Die soziologische Bedingtheit des Denkens und der Denkformen', in *Versuche zu einer Soziolgie des Wissens*, ed. Max Scheler, Munich, 1926, pp. 182–207, specifically pp. 185f.).

11 Some notes from the beginning of the same year in which these lectures were delivered are relevant here: 'My earlier critique of *prima philosophia* [first philosophy] has never been radical enough. For the copula, the "is", always already involves the objectivity which is supposed to be grounded by reference to a "first" – and every "first" essentially consists in an "is". According to the mere *form* of mediation, therefore, the constitutive always leads back to the constituted, and vice versa' (Adorno, 'Graeculus [II]: Notizen zu Philosophie und Gesellschaft 1943–1969', *Frankfurter Adorno Blätter*, VIII [2003], p. 12).

12 Adorno explains the expression 'the veil of technology', which he and Horkheimer had developed in the period of their American exile in connection with their work on *Dialectic of Enlightenment*, in a vivid way in his address 'Education after Auschwitz': 'People are inclined to take technology to be the thing itself, as an end in itself, a force of its own, and they forget that it is an extension of human dexterity. The means – and technology is the epitome of the means of self-preservation of the human species – are fetishized, because the ends – a life of human dignity – are concealed and removed from the consciousness of people'

(GS 10.2, p. 686; *Critical Models: Interventions and Catchwords*, Pickford, p. 200).
13 Löwenthal's essay, which Adorno discusses in Lecture 16 (see pp. 181–4), does not simply compare Meyer and Storm but also brings in Gottfried Keller. In his work, according to Löwenthal, we find 'an almost striking disregard for the social distinctions of human life but an extraordinary attention to the significance of the political sphere' (Leo Löwenthal, *Zur gesellschaftlichen Lage der Literatur*, p. 100).
14 The origin of this expression, which Adorno does not actually use in the lecture itself, could not be traced.
15 In the lecture Adorno did not in fact quote from page 99 of Löwenthal's essay.
16 Georg Christoph Lichtenberg (1742–1799) had written the following aphorism in one of his notebooks: 'If an angel were to say anything at all about his philosophy, I imagine we would hear many sentences like 2+2 = 15' (Aph. B 328). Adorno used this aphorism as a motto for the first chapter of his *Metakritik der Erkenntnistheorie* (GS 5, p. 48; *Against Epistemology*, Domingo, p. 41). On 18 July 1960, at around the time when Adorno was making these notes for his lectures, he referred specifically to this 'Lichtenberg motto, the significance of which has hardly been exhausted' and observed

> that the insufficiency of formal logic – that it is *not* straightforward at all – repeatedly reveals itself as something negative, as the categorially posited inadequacy of the relation between judgment and thing. This is the gift of dialectic with regard to this controversy [i.e. the controversy over logical absolutism], i.e. we certainly know nothing about the logic of the angels, but we do know that the logic of human beings is not an absolute logic, and with that the absolutist claim collapses. (Adorno, Graeculus [II], p. 17)

INDEX

abstraction, method of, 40–1, 52, 73, 97, 100–1, 120, 179, 187–8, 235, 240, 245, 249
adaptation, 22, 25–6, 28–31, 45, 136, 213, 243
advertising, 79, 245
aesthetics, 90
alienation, 89, 122, 124, 160, 182
analytical philosophy, 154
anarchy, 15, 18–19
Ancien Régime, 19
Années Sociologiques, 16, 66
antagonism, of society, 19, 22, 218, 243
anthropology, 66, 153, 222
Aristotle, 90, 158, 204–5, 230–2, 251
art, 45, 117, 119–20, 179–80, 181–4, 201–2, 204, 245
Augustine, Saint, 74, 202
Authoritarian Personality (Adorno et al.), 87–8
authoritarianism, 17, 24, 87–8, 213
Avenarius, Richard, 54, 108, 127

Bacon, Francis, 152–5, 158, 204, 227, 242

barbarism, 78, 202
Barth, Hans, 105, 151, 227, 242
Barthel, Kurt ('KuBa'), 183
Baudelaire, Charles, 179–80, 245
Bednarik, Karl, 168, 244
Beethoven, Ludwig van, 117, 202
being, 6, 90, 189, 225, 244, 247
Benjamin, Walter, 13, 179–80, 193–4
Bergson, Henri, 54, 177
Berkeley, George, 204
Binswanger, Ludwig, 266
Blaschke, Friedrich, 15–16, 18
blind progress, 76–7, 218
Blut und Boden (Blubo), 163
Bossuet, Jacques-Bénigne, 74
bourgeois society, 10, 14, 17–20, 39, 65, 105, 117, 126, 128–33, 138, 140–5, 152–61, 164–5, 169, 175–6, 178–84, 188–90, 198–9, 205, 241–3, 249
Brave New World (Huxley), 167
Brecht, Berthold, 180

capitalism, 4, 76–7, 85, 101, 138
catastrophes, 76–7, 106, 129, 165
categorial intuition, 6

causality, 40, 53, 54, 70, 72, 88
China, 75
chosisme, 34, 48–9, 54–7, 63–4, 66–9, 73–4, 216, 217, 221
civil society, 19, 22, 133, 138
Civilization and its Discontents (Freud), 78
class, 18–20, 94, 98–9, 102, 126–32, 145, 153, 157–8, 165, 168–70, 174–84, 192, 223, 231, 236, 244
class consciousness, 168–9, 174, 244
classification, 31, 41, 53, 54, 56, 71, 72, 94, 141
collective mind, in Durkheim, 42, 54, 59, 72, 223
commodities, 50, 79–80, 111–12, 171, 218
common sense, 39, 112, 213
competition, 26, 156
complementary ideologies, 176–9, 186, 245
Comte, Auguste, 7, 13–25, 32, 36–53, 56–62, 71, 74–5, 92, 132–3, 145, 212–18, 222, 235
conceptual realism, 126, 140, 152, 158, 223
Condorcet, Marie-Jean-Antoine-Nicolas de Caritat, Marquis de, 74
congealed labour, 101, 190, 236
conscience, freedom of, 18, 21, 213
consciousness, 8–10, 29, 45–6, 55, 97, 105, 107–15, 131–3, 136, 153, 155, 162, 168–77, 181, 201, 238, 242–3, 250; *see also* class consciousness; false consciousness; reified consciousness; social consciousness
conservatism, 125–6, 176, 204, 239
consumption, 138, 171, 238, 244
contradictions, 22, 29–31, 61–2, 107, 137–8, 194, 241
Cours de philosophie positive (Comte), 15–16, 18, 22, 25

Critique of Practical Reason (Kant), 9
Critique of Pure Reason (Kant), 5, 9, 90, 109
cultural history, 50, 54, 117–18, 177, 188–9, 198, 206, 252
cultural lag, 129–32, 142
culture industry, 45, 157, 245
Cynics, the, 21

Darwin, Charles, 25–6
Daseinsanalyse, in Binswanger, 12
De civitate Dei (Augustine), 74
de Maistre, Joseph, 161
de Man, Hendrik, 168, 244
deception, 101, 107, 148, 152–3, 154, 164, 167–8, 179, 188, 242
definitions, 81–3, 88–90, 233
dehumanization, 177
democracy, 151, 204
Descartes, René, 15, 91, 215
destruction, 14, 18, 19, 20, 71, 78, 106, 122, 137, 216, 218, 239
Dewey, John, 37
dialectic, 20–1, 72, 82, 108, 138, 146–50, 156, 192–3, 196, 241–2, 248
Dialectic of Enlightenment (Adorno and Horkheimer), 157, 198
dialectical materialism ('Diamat'), 146–8, 180, 182, 241
dictatorship, 76, 160, 229
Dilthey, Wilhelm, 50, 64–5, 221
divine right, theory of, 175, 188
Division du travail (Durkheim), 135, 223
division of labour, 49, 68, 69, 84–5, 94, 192, 223, 228
dogmatism, 14, 36, 41, 50, 55, 123, 213, 215, 225, 241
domination, 76, 77–9, 83, 98–9, 106, 117, 130, 175, 188, 217–18
Durkheim, Emile, 16, 34–5, 42, 47–75, 81, 86–9, 94–7, 135, 145, 215–23, 236, 239, 247–8
dysfunctional social systems, 38–9

Eastern bloc, 100, 118, 120–1, 145–8, 180, 183, 188, 240
economics, 3, 26, 76–7, 94, 122, 138, 143–4, 166–7, 170, 214, 243
Economy and Society (Weber), 7, 88–9
elitism, 45, 131, 134, 168, 188
empirical research, 3, 4, 28, 31, 32, 44, 51–2, 73, 86–7, 111, 114, 135–6, 231, 233
empiricism, 8, 15, 55, 133–4, 158, 204, 210
empirio-criticism, 54–5
Enlightenment, 7, 10, 14–15, 19, 24, 36, 58–9, 74–5, 92, 105, 107, 152–3, 155, 227
equality, 14–15, 17, 19, 155–6, 188, 198–9, 249
equivalence, 33, 34, 101, 130, 138, 143, 155, 231, 243
Esquisse (Condorcet), 74
essences, 5, 15, 32, 90–1, 126–7, 141, 152, 158, 205, 233–4
eternal values, 63, 121, 191, 216
ethics, 90, 158–9
ethnology, 66
everyday language, 47
exchange, 17, 22, 33–4, 63, 67, 79, 83, 93, 100–2, 138, 155–6, 176, 186, 189, 206, 231, 236
existential ontology, 4, 6–7, 12
exploitation, 83, 106

facts, concept of, 11, 15, 21–8, 31–5, 39, 48–55, 61–3, 69–73, 82–3, 90, 103, 108, 124–8, 133–6, 141, 145, 149, 187, 192, 212–15, 230–4, 237
false consciousness, 118, 120, 147, 151, 159, 162–5, 170–1, 190, 244, 250
family, 51–2, 199
far right radicalism, 232, 244
fascism, 24, 87, 119, 163–4, 168
Faust (Goethe), 85

fetishism, 79–80, 98, 159, 189, 218, 247
feudalism, 17, 94, 126, 128, 153, 155, 161, 162, 178, 198–9, 241, 242
Feuerbach, Ludwig, 79
Fichte, Johann Gottlieb, 18, 26–7, 43
Filmer, Sir Robert, 175, 188, 245
films, 45, 114–15, 119, 172, 245
First Treatise (Locke), 126
Fischer, Gustav, 16
Les Fleurs du mal (Baudelaire), 179–80
Folkways (Sumner), 55
freedom, 14–15, 18, 21, 24, 43, 50, 74, 90, 155–6, 198–9, 213, 234, 249
French Enlightenment, 7, 19, 105, 164
French Revolution, 14–15, 17–20, 117, 128
Freud, Sigmund, 8, 72, 78, 131

Gebrauchsmusik, 201–2
genesis, 95, 120, 124, 189–96, 197–203, 207, 210, 247–50, 252
genetic meaning-implications, 194–5
Georgiades, Thrasybulos G., 201
German Idealism, 26–7, 134, 200–1
Germany, 3, 4, 6, 11–12, 26–7, 39–40, 64, 84–7, 92–4, 116–17, 119, 131–4, 163–4, 176, 221
God, 40, 74, 90, 188, 234
Goebbels, Joseph, 119, 163–4
Goethe, Johann Wolfgang von, 85
Gorer, Geoffrey, 66
Greek Enlightenment, 21, 231
Gunzert, Rudolf, 87
Gurvitch, Georges, 86

Hamsun, Knut, 184
Hegel, G. W. F., 14–19, 26, 40–3, 58, 60, 70, 74, 82, 86, 94, 99–100, 103, 107–9, 112–13,

126, 132, 140–1, 148, 150, 156, 158, 161, 165, 192–3, 200, 202, 213–16, 236–7
Heidegger, Martin, 6–7, 149, 216
Heine, Heinrich, 186–7
Helvétius, Claude Adrien, 7, 31, 105, 242
Heraclitus, 151
heteronomy, 122, 123, 147
Himmler, Heinrich, 163
History and Class Consciousness (Lukács), 94
Hobbes, Thomas, 15, 204
d'Holbach, Paul Thiry, 7, 105
Hölderlin, Friedrich, 30
Horkheimer, Max, 2, 93, 101, 118, 236
Hubert, Henri, 66
Hume, David, 8, 15, 108–10, 127, 142, 204
Husserl, Edmund, 6, 192, 194, 219, 247–8, 250
Huxley, Aldous, 167
hyphen-sociologies, 84, 233
hypostasis, 35, 53–4, 68, 72, 75, 111, 117, 175, 189, 192, 196, 216, 223, 230, 238

Ibsen, Henrik, 55–6
Idea for a Universal History with Cosmopolitan Intent (Kant), 19
idealism, 6, 14, 26–7, 53, 63, 99, 107, 134, 153, 174, 200–1
Ideologists, the, 7, 24, 227
ideology, concepts of, 14, 43, 93–4, 98–108, 111, 114–21, 125–32, 136, 138, 147, 151–90, 194, 203, 210, 224, 227–8, 236–49
illusion, 93, 98, 100–2, 107–8, 144, 153–4, 166, 170–1, 200, 236
imagination, 23, 25–8, 32, 213
immediacy, 110, 171–2, 173, 178–9, 217
immortality, 90, 121, 234
imperialism, 74, 117, 159, 180, 232

individual, concept of the, 9–10, 19, 24, 26–7, 38–9, 48, 55–6, 63–6, 69–73, 77–8, 89, 102–3, 111, 143–4, 153, 165–7, 170–1, 181–2, 221–2, 224, 232, 238
Institute of Social Research, 168, 174
intellectual freedom, 149–50
intellectual history, 50, 54, 90, 117–18, 177, 188–9, 198, 206, 252
intellectual labour, 30–1, 44–5, 94, 166, 214; *see also* mental labour
invisible hand, the, 138, 143–4
irrationality, 77–9, 106, 130, 137–8, 143–5, 161, 177, 218, 242–3, 248

Jefferson, Thomas, 164
Joyce, James, 182
judgement, concept of, 194–6, 199–200, 241, 247, 251
Jugendstil, 55–6

Kant, Immanuel, 4–12, 15, 18–19, 26–7, 38, 49, 82, 90, 94–6, 106–9, 123, 140, 148, 159, 211, 220, 223, 225, 250
Kantianism, 11–12, 109, 135, 194, 211
Keynes, John Maynard, 77, 138
Kierkegaard, Søren, 43, 62, 193
knowledge, 2, 5–10, 18, 24–31, 43–4, 49, 51, 64, 90–7, 106–11, 117–18, 121–4, 133–6, 140–2, 147, 151–3, 160, 185, 189, 191–4, 197–8, 205, 228, 234, 236
König, René, 4, 29, 32, 44, 136, 210

labour, 30–1, 34, 44–5, 79, 93, 97–102, 105–6, 113, 136, 155–6, 166–9, 186, 190, 214, 236
language, 47, 110, 153–4
Lazarsfeld, Paul, 86

Lebensphilosophie, 177
legitimating ideologies, 176, 178, 186, 245
legitimation, 98–9, 146, 155, 160–1, 164, 175–6, 178, 186, 188, 245
Leibniz, Gottfried Wilhelm, 15
Lenin, Vladimir Ilyich, 55
liberalism, 143, 155, 156, 162, 176, 242
Locke, John, 8, 15, 56, 126, 164, 175, 204, 245
logic, 94–5, 198, 202, 203–5, 247–8, 251
logical positivism, 12, 46–7, 127
Löwenthal, Leo, 181–4, 246
Lukács, Georg, 94

Mach, Ernst, 54, 108, 127, 146
Mann, Heinrich, 184
Mannheim, Karl, 18, 94, 120, 129, 180, 188–9, 191, 197–8, 203–5, 219, 240, 249, 251
market economy, 138, 143–4
market research, 86, 111
Marx, Karl, 70, 99–101, 105, 118, 120, 125, 135, 138, 146–7, 154–5, 189–90, 193, 223, 227, 229, 236, 239
Marxism, 99, 129, 183, 189
mass media, 112, 166–7, 238
mass production, 167
Massing, Otwin, 203
materialism, 99–100, 146–8, 204, 235
Matière et mémoire (Bergson), 177
Mauss, Marcel, 66
Mead, Margaret, 66
mediation, 73, 80, 81, 112, 115, 117–18, 143, 190–3, 200, 203–7, 215, 232, 235, 238, 243, 247, 249–52
Mehring, Franz, 118
memory, 181, 182
mental labour, 97–9, 236; *see also* intellectual labour

Metacritique of Epistemology (Adorno), 199
metaphysics, 14–15, 17–19, 22–3, 36–42, 53–4, 58, 60, 62–3, 71, 81, 99, 152, 177–8, 201, 204–5, 212–13, 215
Metaphysics (Aristotle), 90
Meyer, Conrad Ferdinand, 181, 183–4, 245
modernism, 182–3
money, 129–30, 166, 244
Montesquieu, Charles Secondat de, 19, 164
Mozart, Wolfgang Amadeus, 201, 202
music, 112, 116–17, 181, 201–2
Mussolini, Benito, 119, 240

naive realism, 49, 55, 153
Napoleon, 24, 132
nation state, 19, 78; *see also* state, the
National Socialism, 146, 163–4, 187–8, 242
national sovereignty, 18–19
nationalism, 175
nature, domination of, 76, 77–9, 117, 175, 217–18
Nietzsche, Friedrich, 36, 43, 61, 82, 121, 159, 161, 200, 216, 247
nominalism, 15, 41, 70, 72, 111, 125–8, 133, 140–2, 145–9, 152, 193, 204, 214–15, 239, 241

object, freedom towards, 27, 28, 150
objective idealism, 26
objectivity, 17, 26–7, 43, 65, 69–70, 92, 99, 103–18, 124, 128, 133, 144, 147–8, 150, 152–5, 160, 166, 195–6, 203, 205–6, 226, 238, 242, 248, 250
observation, concept of, 23, 25–8, 32, 41, 51–2, 56, 58, 66, 213, 217
Ogburn, William Fielding, 129

On Suicide (Durkheim), 70–1
'On the Social Situation of Literature' (Löwenthal), 181–4, 246
order, 14, 15, 17–22, 49, 50–1, 75

Panaetius of Rhodes, 232
Pareto, Vilfredo, 118–19, 120, 155, 219, 239, 240
Parsons, Talcott, 38
particularity, 9, 40, 63, 70–1, 77–9, 95–6, 137, 143, 157–8, 243
petit bourgeois mentality, 130, 168, 181–4
phenomenology, 4, 187, 195, 219
Phenomenology of Spirit (Hegel), 99–100
Philosophy of Right (Hegel), 86, 112
physical labour, 97–9
picture theory, of knowledge, 241
Plato, 17, 32, 85, 91, 104–5, 151–2, 161, 192–3, 200, 204–6, 230–2, 238, 251
Platonism, 17, 125–6, 140
Plessner, Helmuth, 44
positivism, 12, 14, 21–3, 25–8, 32, 36–47, 52–6, 58–63, 67, 102, 108–11, 114, 118–19, 126–7, 135–9, 142, 154, 187, 223, 238, 243
power, 41, 45, 112, 119, 144, 164–5, 167, 187–8, 239, 241, 243–4
powerlessness, 166–7, 244
pragmatism, 37, 135, 213
primitive societies, 42, 66, 72, 73, 75, 222
production, realm of, 17, 50, 79, 94, 98–102, 105–7, 112–13, 129, 132, 138, 142–4, 165–9, 171, 186, 218, 238, 245
progress, concept of, 11, 14, 17, 37, 41, 49–52, 60, 74–80, 130, 217–18
Prolegomena (Kant), 9, 10

proletariat, the, 130, 168–70, 180, 182
propaganda, 119, 153, 163–4
protocol sentences, 32, 59, 110
Proust, Marcel, 182
psychoanalysis, 12, 131–2
psychology, 7–12, 48, 64–5, 70–3, 78, 87–9, 109, 125, 131–2, 153–5, 174–5, 211, 220
psychology of interests, 154–5, 169–71, 174–5, 191, 242
public opinion, 86, 102, 111, 112–13, 238
purity, as an ideal, 5, 9–12, 210

rationality, 15, 17, 20, 31–2, 65–7, 73, 76–9, 89, 106, 117, 130, 133, 137–8, 142–5, 159, 160–1, 178, 205–6, 218–19, 225, 242–3, 248, 252
realism, 22, 49, 55, 125–6, 140, 152–3, 158, 168, 171, 174, 193, 215, 223, 239, 248
Reformation, the, 177
Règles de la méthode sociologique (Durkheim), 81
reification, 57, 67–8, 71–3, 89, 125, 147–50, 174–5, 177, 190, 197, 203, 241–2
reified consciousness, 112, 121, 123–5, 127, 147, 149, 175, 190–1, 200, 226
relativism, 104, 118–24, 149–50, 153, 191, 197, 203, 215, 219, 223, 239, 242, 247–8
religion, 15, 21, 42, 70–1, 72, 73, 84, 107, 135, 167, 177, 178, 204; see also theology
Republic (Plato), 85, 205
resistance, 34, 48, 55–6, 77–8
revolution, 14–15, 17–20, 125–7, 227, 239
Rickert, Heinrich, 135
Riehl, Wilhelm Heinrich, 68
romanticism, 79, 161
Rosenberg, Alfred, 164

Russell, Bertrand, 110
Russia, 164, 229, 241; *see also* Eastern bloc

Saint-Simon, Claude-Henri de Rouvoy, Comte de, 7, 14, 17–18, 50, 126
sceptical generation, the, 168–72, 173, 244
scepticism, 104, 118–19, 123, 128, 168–73, 204, 215, 225, 229, 239, 244
Scheler, Max, 94, 125–6, 140, 191–2, 219, 223, 249
Schelling, Friedrich Wilhelm Joseph von, 26
Schelsky, Helmut, 4, 33, 44, 133, 168, 210, 244
Schiller, Friedrich, 92
Das schwarze Korps, 163
Science of Logic (Hegel), 40–1
second nature, concept of, 24, 41–2, 68, 106, 115, 165, 166, 174–5, 178
secularization, 15, 36, 61, 74, 202
self-determination, 79–80, 218
self-preservation, 19–20, 38, 65, 97
Simmel, Georg, 78, 146
Smith, Adam, 143
social anthropology, 66, 222
social base, 129–32, 135, 160, 184, 245
social cohesion, 37–8
social compulsion, 34, 63, 64, 66, 72, 214, 221
social Darwinism, 25–6
social psychology, 72–3, 87–8
social systems, 22, 32–5, 38–9, 63, 79, 133, 136, 213
social totality, 102–4, 107, 115, 127, 133, 135, 173–80, 206–7, 237, 239, 244, 252
socialism, 19–20, 130, 168–9, 180
socialist realism, 241
socialization, 38, 83, 86, 112, 165, 242

socially necessary illusion, 93, 98, 100–2, 154, 165, 236
socially productive labour, 30–1, 44–5, 136
'Sociology and Empirical Research' (Adorno), 4, 44
sociology of knowledge, 5, 18, 93–7, 105, 108, 111, 118, 191–2, 197–8, 205, 236
Socrates, 91
Sophists, the, 85
Sorel, Georges, 161
space, in Kant and Durkheim, 94–7
Spencer, Herbert, 25, 26, 53
Spengler, Oswald, 52, 75, 129, 166
Spinoza, Baruch de, 159
Stalin, Joseph, 164
state, the, 18, 19, 32, 86, 158, 205, 230, 232
state of nature, the, 21
statistics, 45, 70–3, 86–7, 111, 112, 221, 238
Stein, Lorenz von, 68
Stoicism, 157, 205
Storm, Theodor, 181–3, 245
Strauss, Richard, 117
subjectivity, 24, 26–8, 42–3, 64, 103–17, 123, 131, 145–8, 152–5, 160, 165–6, 169–70, 173, 177, 195–6, 203–6, 211, 238, 241–2, 244, 247–8, 250
suicide, 70–1, 73
Sumner, William Graham, 55
surplus value, 101, 113, 138, 236
synthesis, concept of, 158, 159–60, 195, 197–8

technology, 50, 76, 78–9, 84, 105, 117, 166–7, 171, 218, 244
theology, 14, 15, 22–3, 36–42, 61, 74, 92; *see also* religion
Third Reich, 87, 116, 163–4
three stages, theory of (Comte), 14, 15, 41–2, 52–3, 217

Thus Spoke Zarathustra (Nietzsche), 43
time, concept of, 9, 94–7, 177–8, 201, 230
totalitarianism, 24, 87–8, 144, 164, 188, 224
transcendental philosophy, 9–10, 109, 194, 211, 220
Troeltsch, Ernst, 64
truth, 2, 8, 20, 28–31, 38, 42–5, 54, 72, 75, 79, 100–20, 123–4, 128, 134, 149, 151–6, 163, 188, 190–205, 210, 215–16, 223, 225, 227, 234–44, 247, 249, 250
Truth and Ideology (Barth), 151, 242
Twilight of the Idols (Nietzsche), 200
typologies, 176, 185–6; *see also* classification

unconscious, the, 131–2
understandability, of society, 42, 44–7, 64, 214
unintelligibility, of society, 66–7, 69, 89
United States, 2, 25, 37, 39–40, 55, 64, 66, 84, 86, 111, 129, 164, 202, 204
universality, 27, 40, 61, 73, 95–6, 107–8, 111, 134, 153, 157–8, 194, 205, 243
Der Untertan (Heinrich Mann), 184

validity, concept of, 83, 92, 95, 116, 124, 189–96, 197–203, 207, 210, 247–50, 252
Vienna Circle, the, 110

Wagner, Richard, 7, 117, 201
Wall Street Crash, 76
Weber, Max, 7, 51, 61, 64–6, 67, 69–70, 73, 88–9, 134–5, 185, 219, 221–2, 233
Whitehead, Alfred North, 110
Windelband, Wilhelm, 135
world view, concept of, 129, 134, 135, 147, 164, 198, 241